THREE KEYS TO
SELF-UNDERSTANDING

THREE KEYS TO SELF-UNDERSTANDING

An Innovative and Effective Combination of the Myers-Briggs Type Indicator® Assessment Tool, the Enneagram and Inner-Child Healing

Pat Wyman

CAPT

Gainesville, FL

Published by
Center for Applications of Psychological Type, Inc.
2815 NW 13th Street, Suite 401
Gainesville, FL 32609
(352) 375-0160

CAPT, the CAPT logo, and Center for Applications of Psychological Type
are trademarks of the Center for Applications of Psychological Type, Inc.,
Gainesville, FL.

Myers-Briggs Type Indicator and MBTI are registered trademarks of
Consulting Psychologists Press, Inc., Palo Alto, CA.

Printed in the United States of America.

Library of Congress Cataloging-in-Publication Data

Wyman, Pat, 1942-
Three keys to self-understanding: an innovative and effective
combination of the Myers-Briggs Type Indicator, the Enneagram, and
inner-child healing/Pat Wyman.
p. cm.
Includes bibliographical references.
ISBN 0-935652-57-4
1. Inner child. 2. Myers-Briggs Type Indicator. 3. Enneagram.
I. Title.
BF698.35.I55 W95 2001
158—dc21

2001047507

To Deborah and Michael:
Both Gift and Miracles

TABLE OF CONTENTS

ACKNOWLEDGMENTS

I owe many thanks to many people. I wish to express my immense and heartfelt gratitude and love particularly to:

My daughter, Debbie, who has lovingly embraced her beautiful soul and shown
me what could have been and what can be.

My charming, bodacious and simply wonderful son, Michael.
God used him to encourage my first big step toward home.

My brilliant sister, Bobbi, who shared both laughter and tears as only a sister can.

My parents, Mary and Ted; I am grateful for their love and for all they have done for me.

Mary Reinagel whose constancy, love and friendship have never ceased to sustain me.

Susan Edwards who moved me towards the light. I could not be where
I am without her help, tutoring and encouragement.

Peg Burdge who took my hand and kept me on the journey. She holds my head above water and my feet to the fire.

Rosemary Watts for her gifted guidance through the uncharted territory of my dreams.

Jack Labanauskas and Andrea Isaacs of the Enneagram Monthly *for their continued encouragement.*

Reilley with deep and heartfelt thanks for the privilege of working with her and for the extensive use of her story.

All my clients who have shared their souls and their journeys with me.
Each has been an enormous gift to me and has significantly contributed to my journey.

Helen Palmer and Rachel Naomi Remen who have both been an inspiration to me. Helen is gifted in knowledge of
the Enneagram, what lies behind it and in working with people. Rachel came all the way to St. Louis to talk to me
thinking she was simply making a speaking stop on her book tour. Many thanks to both.

All those at CAPT who worked so long and tirelessly on this project, especially Keven Ward,
Eleanor Sommer, Elayna Rexrode, Charles Martin and Christy Freeman.
All at CAPT have been exemplary in their professionalism, kindness and guidance.

AUTHOR'S NOTES

When addressing topics such as psychotherapy and spirituality, language becomes a problem. Many words have baggage that is difficult to set aside. Some words are strongly connected to a specific theory or religious tradition. I have tried to avoid such words when possible and to define my use of them when not possible. I would encourage the reader to look to the broader meaning of the text rather than to focus on the baggage of a specific word. This may be much easier for Intuitive types than Sensing types!

The use of personal pronouns is always problematic. I have chosen to use *she* for second person singular because I work almost entirely with women. We have become accustomed to using *he* to represent both genders. I take this opportunity to bring a small degree of balance back into the world by employing *she* exclusively. Perhaps seeing it in print will act as a mirror to some of the cultural customs we accept without question.

In this text as in my work, I use the word *incest* as a verb. I have chosen to sacrifice proper grammar in the interest of conveying the sense of perpetrator and innocent victim. To say a parent "committed incest with" or "engaged in incest with" suggests the parent or adult and child were partners. I use *incest* as an active verb to make it perfectly clear there is an initiator of the action and an unwilling, innocent recipient.

Throughout the book, I will refer to parents or to Mom and Dad. I am aware that many people were not raised in a traditional family. For simplicity sake, let such phrases represent whatever primary caregivers had the most influence in shaping the person you became.

I use the term *Core Self* as profiled by the MBTI to refer to the spirit or soul. *True Self, Wisdom Child, Inner Child,* and *Child* have been used in the same context. I have capitalized *Inner Child* and *Child* when using these terms as a metaphor for spirit or soul. When using these terms to refer to the wounded child within each of us, or to the little person that existed in your childhood, I have used the lower case.

I use the terms *Higher Power, Internal Wisdom, Higher Wisdom, Light* and *Wisdom Figure* interchangeably with the term *God Within.*

ILLUSTRATIONS

In the course of working with a client, I use my own form of art therapy. I ask clients to draw for a variety of reasons. First, in order to draw something, the client must visit that memory, feeling or impression in her mind thereby accessing a wider range of information. Since language resides in the left brain, to simply talk about an issue limits the information provided to that which is located in the left brain. Drawing also gives us a pictorial documentation of the client's story and helps to monitor her progress.

Occasionally, various items from clients' files have been used to illustrate points. The original artwork was done with crayon on newsprint. The samples of non-dominant handwriting were done in the same manner. You may notice misspellings and grammatical errors in the nondominant handwriting. I have intentionally left these in place to point out that the client is accessing the part of the brain where language is not a strength.

Some client artwork has been used to illustrate the beginning of chapters, and as you explore the text you will learn more about the context of these drawings.

RELIGION AND SPIRITUALITY

I repeatedly use the term *spirituality* and do not intend it to be interchangeable with *religion.* I use *spirituality* to mean connecting with the soul or God part within each of us, with others on a spiritual level and with an undefined Higher Power. Spirituality is a universal term implying living as an expression of who we were intended to be. Religion can aid in this process or it can impede it. Nothing in this work is intended to either support or detract from any religious practice or sect.

MEMORIES

There is a lot of controversy over the topic of repressed memories. Incest is one of the last heavily guarded societal secrets. Few people want to believe it is as rampant as it is and even fewer want to address the problem. We live in a culture that is largely left-brain oriented. If there is not conscious memory, the culture maintains it did not happen. That attitude completely discounts the right side of the brain where feelings reside, the subconscious where nonverbal memories and the impressions of experiences reside, and the body which holds memories in every cell. Conscious memories cannot exist pre-verbally and before cognition is operational. Conscious memories cannot exist if a child finds a way to leave her body so as not to experience the betrayal. To discount feelings, body memories, and the right brain is to assault and betray those who have already been victimized. Therefore, in my work and in this text, I completely honor the "repressed" memories of the women with whom I work.

PERSONAL CASE HISTORIES

The case histories and personal stories recounted here are those of real people. Kay, Paige, Ellen and Valerie are composites of several women. The others are true stories of clients who have been so generous as to allow me to share the actual events of their lives with you. In some cases, a few identifying facts have been changed to protect their anonymity. The epilogue contains updates on some of these women.

INTRODUCTION

She sat in my office sobbing, "I can't do it! I don't know the answers! I don't know who I am. . . ." Her hands were trembling and tears streamed down her face. Jeanne was attempting to complete the Myers-Briggs Type Indicator (MBTI) which is a personality-typing instrument.

Jeanne had seen a variety of psychotherapists and psychiatrists for one to three sessions a week for twenty-seven years. This was her first session with me. At this time, she was fifty years old, in deep depression, unable to work, taking antidepressants and very concerned about her future. She had never married and

lived alone. There was a part of her that was tired of the battle and no longer wanted to be alive.

When she was calm enough to participate in a dialogue, I told her she would not have to complete the MBTI on paper, that we would talk it through. She was able to participate in a discussion of the four dichotomies of the MBTI and the four temperament types which are covered in chapter 3. She answered my questions clearly and with certainty. However, she never stopped crying.

Today, seven years later, Jeanne is a hospital chaplain, recognized by her peers for her many gifts and for

When the significance and ramifications
of the MBTI type formula are truly understood,
the individual can begin to
accept and celebrate who she is designed to be.

her spiritual depth. She is extremely effective in dealing with terminal patients and their families. She is fully present to those she serves. She is happy, active, enjoys a wide range of activities and looks forward to the future with assurance and confidence. Her inner peace fills the room and her smile is infectious. She is strong, solid and very much in control of her life. Like all of us, Jeanne is occasionally triggered and has periods of doubts and fears. Yet she continues her own process of personal growth and empowerment.

Jeanne is who she is today because she fully participated in an interactive process of self-discovery and Inner-Child therapy. This process is an "interactive" approach because it combines knowing, understanding and accepting the self and the way an individual personality operates with the intense affective work of Inner-Child therapy. I use the word *process* because the course of therapy has a beginning, a middle and an end. It is noncognitive. The personal growth that follows is ongoing, but the therapy itself is limited. Jeanne's work took about a year and a half although she still comes to see me occasionally to touch base. Now, she continues her personal and spiritual journey primarily with the help of a spiritual director.

Each of us has a Core Self. Theorists use various names to identify this part of personality: True Self, Essential I, Soul, Spirit, Core and the like. Here is the essence of who a person is wired up to be. It is the home of the gifts, talents and qualities that define the individual. When living originates in this part of personality, the very best of the individual is being expressed and talents are being used effectively to the maximum benefit of the self and others. It is my belief that the Myers-Briggs Type Indicator, based on the work of the eminent psychologist Carl Jung and

developed by Katharine Briggs and Isabel Briggs Myers, profiles this part of personality. When the significance and ramifications of the MBTI type formula are truly understood, the individual can begin to accept and celebrate who she is designed to be.

Early in life, everyone experiences reasons to be emotionally defended. Therefore, the personal Defense System is activated very early. This Defense System is profiled and understood through the Enneagram system of personality typing. Obviously, some people have grown up in situations more emotionally damaging than others and it is apparent that those Enneagram Defense Systems are more fully engaged. When life is lived from a defended position, the locus of control rests in the Enneagram rather than within the Core Self. The Enneagram part of personality is designed for protection and is not useful in making decisions or living a full, rich life. When locked in a defended position, there is limited access to the most valuable part of the self, the essence or Core Self where solid, rational decisions can be made. Jung recognized the two parts of personality, not only in his patients, but also in his own life at a very young age. He called the part that was not the Core Self the "shadow." I feel this shadow part is best understood through the Enneagram.

Jeanne's childhood included a parent with mental illness; she was sexually abused and she was emotionally incested. As she grew, the assaults to her spirit mounted until she lived almost completely out of her Defense System with no conscious knowledge of who she really was. As she sat in my office that first day, she was operating almost exclusively from her defense of the Enneagram Four. She was in emotional agony, not wanting to be alive. She focused on the losses in her life. She was certain no one could understand her because she could not begin to understand herself.

When Jeanne felt safe and supported enough to look at her losses and grieve them, she no longer needed to be as defended. She could get acquainted with her Core Self described by the MBTI as Extravert, Intuitive, Feeling and Perceiving. As an ENFP, she had rich spiritual and creative qualities and the ability to understand and empathize with others. After her healing work, she could begin to understand and own who she really was and she started living out of her own bountiful gifts, talents and wisdom. Currently, at this point in her life, Jeanne has learned to use the traits of her Defense System, the Enneagram Four, to lend support to the ENFP part of her personality instead of controlling it. When she finds herself moving heavily into the Enneagram Four defense, she uses that as a signal that something has happened to upset her. With this awareness, she can process through her feelings to restore control to cognition and her Core Self.

A personality is like a castle with a wall around it. In the castle resides the little prince or princess, the delight and the hope of the kingdom. If the parent of this little person stays out at the wall to guard the castle and keep the heir safe, that parent never gets to really know, love and appreciate the child. At the same time, if the child is kept locked in the castle for safekeeping, the kingdom will never benefit from the contributions the child can make. It is important to create a safe

enough environment so that the child can leave the confines of the castle. With a safe environment, the walls do not have to be as big and heavily guarded. The same can be said of each individual. The castle and its grounds represent the self; the child represents the Core Self (MBTI type); the parent is the cognitive part; and the wall is the Defense System. Concentrating exclusively on the Defense System causes loss of awareness of the part of self being protected. Efforts must be directed at creating an environment safe enough for the Core Self to be free and accessible.

In the following pages, I will discuss the model and the process of an interactive approach to Inner-Child therapy that has helped Jeanne and others like her reclaim their lives. Of course, this book is not meant to be a substitute for therapy. Rather, it is to enhance personal work and to act as a guide and a support. I feel this and similar approaches are on the cutting edge of therapy today. It is an alternative to labeling and medicating. Twenty five years ago, the MBTI was first being introduced, the Enneagram was first being put in print and Inner-Child therapy was all but unknown. Putting these three keys together creates a dynamic and effective approach to therapy. Working with this approach has been an exciting journey for me and I hope it will be the same for you.

PART I

The Need for Healing Is Universal

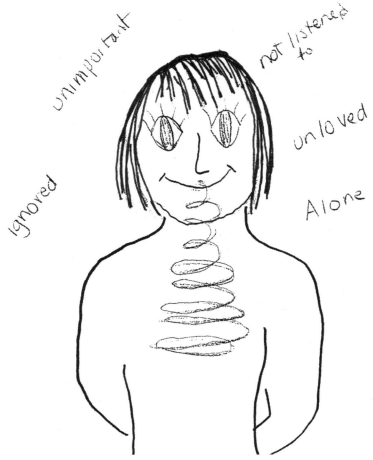

CHAPTER 1

WOUNDEDNESS:
THE HUMAN CONDITION

Wounded? Who? Me?

When the topic of emotional work or personal growth comes up, most people take the attitude that it's fine for others but "I'm OK." The position they take is following the old adage: "Everyone in the world is crazy except you and me—and I'm not always sure about you." We are just coming out of an era that associated therapy and the like with neurosis or worse. My purpose is not to convince anyone to enter therapy, but I hope I can make a case for the fact that being human means that emotional damage has taken place at some point in everyone's life. Examining that damage can result in a fuller, richer life through self-acceptance and understanding.

So, for whom does the bell toll? Engaging in a process of self-examination is for anyone who comes from a dysfunctional family.

FUNCTION AND DYSFUNCTION

The term *dysfunctional family* is bandied about so much that it is easy to become caught in the psychobabble around it. I personally dislike the term immensely because it implies that, somewhere in the world, there is a perfectly functional family. How many people have invested tons of energy into trying to live up to Ward and June Cleaver? There should be an exposé on prime time TV letting the world know the truth: They are fiction! They never existed! There is no such thing as a perfectly functional family because families are made up of human beings. Try as we might, we cannot give our children the happy childhood we did not have. Try as we might, children sometimes come out of childhood barely alive emotionally.

Actually, most people come from families that more closely resemble the Munsters than the Cleavers. The Munsters meant no harm and the family seemed to "work" in a strange sort of way. They had their share of weird ducks but they found a way for all to coexist in some kind of balance. This is how most families work. There are relatively caring parents, who may not always show their love in the most effective ways, and a few relatives who are "a little off."

Families all fall somewhere on a continuum with the fictionally perfect family at one end and the worst atrocity imaginable at the other.

credible job of parenting and are certain they are giving better than they received. These parents look at the child, knowing what they needed in their own childhoods and did not receive, and then proceed to try to provide it for their child. Generally, the problem is that the child needs something different. That child grows up, has children and tries to provide for them everything that was missing from her own childhood. And so the cycle repeats itself. It is more effective not to try to be a better parent but to be a better *you*. When John Bradshaw is asked what is the best thing a parent can do for a child, he replies: "Do your own healing work." When the pain from not having childhood emotional needs met is healed, there is no longer a need to try to have those needs met vicariously through a child. That frees the parent to look at the child a little more objectively and see the child for the unique little package God created.

Parent-bashing is a term often heard around the topic of Inner-Child work. I strongly disagree with that criticism because Inner-Child work is not about the

Totally Dysfunctional		Perfectly Functional
Hannibal Lecter marries Cruella De Vil	x	The Cleavers and the Waltons
	Average Family	

So whenever the term *dysfunctional family* is used, substitute *normal* or *average*.

When a child is born, few parents sit and plot out how they can emotionally mess up their precious child or send that child negative messages; yet inevitably, that is what happens. Generation after generation. I feel it is the real definition of "original sin." Parents pass the "woundedness" on to those they love the most, their children. Although it is generally not done purposefully, it can be devastating nonetheless. If I back the car out of the driveway and run over your foot, whether I did it on purpose or accidentally, your foot is just as squished.

Most parents are convinced they are doing a fairly

parent but about the child. The intent of Inner-Child work is not to bring us to hate Mom and Dad. Rather, it is to bring us to accept that they made mistakes, often unknowingly. From this understanding, the family dynamics are seen more objectively and we begin to accept ourselves and them without judgment. Without seeing and acknowledging the mistakes, we live with a distorted version of reality.

Adult or Child?

Sometimes we begin to look at the mistakes made by our parents and get stuck there, stuck in the anger, resentment and bitterness that can surface when these issues are addressed. We may begin to think about the high price we paid for their mistakes. Without some guidance, it is easy to get caught in a loop and identify so strongly with the wounded child that we become the child. When that happens, we feel victimized, powerless, hurt, angry and hopeless that anything can ever change. Even though we are adults, we react to our parents as if still a small child. You may have experienced walking into the house where you grew up and feeling yourself becoming smaller and younger. Although you may be a fairly competent and responsible adult in other settings, you find yourself reacting like a child to your parents who still seem to be so much larger than you.

Alyse's story. Alyse, twenty-nine, is a professional woman, self-supporting and living in her own home. Her parents divorced when she was five years old. Her father's visits were infrequent and often canceled at the last minute. When he did spend time with her, he made it clear she needed to be happy and behave in public in such a manner as to show she had good breeding and manners. Alyse grew up trying to win his love and approval. As an adult, she still looked forward to the times her father came to town, always hoping he would find time for her. When he was in town on business, she often canceled other engagements to wait at home in the event he would call and come to see her.

One evening when he was in town, he took her to dinner. Throughout the meal, he criticized her table manners and some of her life choices. Alyse reported to me that she felt ten years old and was certain that, as she sat at the table, her feet did not reach the floor. She felt shamed by his criticism and hopeless of ever winning his love and approval (figure 1-1).

Alyse had regressed into the child and had begun responding to her father in the same ways she had responded to him as a child. Just as a child cannot talk back to an adult, Alyse could not speak up to her father on her own behalf. She could not request that he treat her as an adult. She could not even tell him how much he hurt her when he treated her in such a manner. Alyse left this encounter with her father feeling frustrated and confused.

Figure 1-1

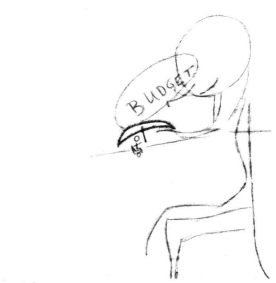

Figure 1-2

Rhonda had the same experience as Alyse.

Rhonda's story. Rhonda was a college student when her father visited her to discuss how she handled her finances. By the time the encounter was over, Rhonda felt very small, very young and very stupid (figure 1-2).

Most of us have had similar experiences. Sometimes a meeting with a parent will leave us feeling frustrated and confused like Alyse. How can Mom or Dad always get to me like that? Parents unwittingly know how to push all our buttons because they installed them. If you have a version of Windows installed on your computer, you know how you can take a program and store it on the bar at the bottom of your screen. Think of your body as the computer screen. On the bar, you have a program for the wounded child and a program for the cognitive, rational adult. You position your mouse on the adult, press it and start off acting out of your adult self. Before long, someone comes along who points the mouse on the wounded child program stored on the bar and with a whooshing sound and, just as fast, the child is up on the screen, occupying your body. You feel smaller, with less power, and begin acting out of a worldview that may not be the same as when the adult was "on the screen."

Family dynamics are like a mobile. Each of us contributes to the balance of the mobile. For the mobile to remain in balance, we each must continue to behave and react in the same ways we have always reacted. If we try to change, the mobile becomes out of balance and that sets all the pieces bouncing. When this happens in a family dynamic, all the other family members escalate in their behaviors to try and bring the offending member back into alignment, back into balance.

Being caught in this "dance" with family members leaves us with ambivalent feelings. We may be resentful, unhappy and frustrated but, at the same time, it feels comfortable and familiar. We are without a clue as to how to stop the same old patterns from repeating themselves.

THE POWER OF FEELINGS

Another frequent trap is trying to move straight to acceptance without looking at the pain left over from childhood. With this approach, there is an emphasis on "the value of forgiveness" and what a virtue it is. We try very hard to release all our feelings of anger, sadness and resentment with statements such as "That was then, this is now" or "That is all behind me now" or even "It's the Christian thing to do." Unfortunately, it simply does not work. Instead, the problem is usually compounded by intense guilt for not being able to get past the anger and forgive.

The external behaviors of showing anger can be modified, but remaining inside are the feelings and the emotional pain. These feelings will eventually insist on

being expressed and that usually happens when they are least welcome.

Sarah's story. Sarah, forty-two, is married with two young children. She was the third oldest child in a very large family. She was very badly abused emotionally, physically and sexually. She has always been aware of her anger towards her parents, particularly her mother, but she felt the noble and Christian thing to do was to just "let go of it and move on." However, she found that every time she had to return to her hometown for a family function, she was nearly debilitated by intense stomach upset and agonizing diarrhea. All her prayers and resolve to put it behind her and get on with life were over-ruled by her unresolved anger.

Here we can clearly see the concept of the wounded inner child at work. No matter the opinions and resolve of the adult, the wounded inner child wins out *every time*. In Romans 7:19–21, Paul asks why he keeps doing the things he does not want to do. He, too, had an inner child who occasionally acted out. Until the inner child is heard and attended to, that child will continually and determinedly work on getting some attention.

And so, Inner-Child work is about the child. It is about the effects of unresolved hurts and abuse on the child and the way the child incorporated those events into her worldview and understanding of self. It is further about how that child takes that information and moves into adulthood, still operating out of old information and out of the unresolved feelings that continually resurface.

When Sarah first came to me for therapy, her "burning question" was why she could not just let her anger, hatred and bitterness go. All of her resolve, all the self-help books she had read, all her prayers and all the advice she had received had not helped her to let it go. She was surprised when I told her I would be helping her access those feelings rather than bury them. It is similar to the advice given to a new driver going out on snow for the first time. If you skid, turn your wheels in the direction of the skid. What? That is not logical. Inner-Child work is not logical. It takes place on the right side of the brain where feelings reside. The right side of the brain does not understand or care about logic. That is in the realm of the left side, which is analytical and structured. It is the left side of the brain that continually tries to take a rational approach and talk us out of our feelings. However, if the desire is to not only change behaviors, but to resolve the internal pain and unrest, it will be necessary to "turn in the direction of the skid" and have some feelings.

THE BEGINNING OF DISTORTED THINKING

When a child is subjected to abuse, intentional or not, the child has to incorporate the incident into the child's understanding of her world. In order to feel a sense of safety and that all is right with the world, the child must know, first and foremost, that the parent is right. For a small child, parent and God are one and the same. To be safe, the child must conform her thinking and worldview to that of the parent. Therefore, when a parent acts irrationally, the child has to interpret that behavior as rational. In order to do that, she has to distort her own thinking.

It is rather like an emotional version of the children's game Twister, which results in the participants getting into a variety of grotesque physical contortions. Suppose you were required to stay in that position for the rest of your life while trying to carry on a normal, day-to-day existence. That is what actually happens emotionally when a person tries to get through life with distorted views of self, others and how the world works.

The more a child distorts her worldview to accommodate parental behaviors, the more prevalent the need for the Defense System. The purpose of the Defense System is to minimize emotional pain, make life more bearable and act as an insulator from further wounding. If Mommy says I made her bump the car into the side of the garage because I was talking too much, as a three-year-old, I believe her. My perception of myself, my power, my mother and what happens when I am "bad" becomes distorted. My understanding of bad and good becomes distorted. I adjust my under-

standing of myself and a part of me is put away. My Defense System swings into action and I use those behaviors to compensate for my shortcomings—my talkativeness. Inner-Child work is about re-examining some of those distorted conclusions and restoring lost parts. In so doing, there is less need for the Defense System because personal power, options and choices have been restored.

LIVING DEFENDED

Many people come from seriously disturbed families filled with violence and abuse. Children from these families have very distorted ideas of themselves and their worth. They have few choices in life because they live mainly out of their Defense Systems. A Defense System does not offer rational choices, only protection. Through emotional healing, these victims of childhood abuse can come to acceptance of themselves and their family members.

So, in reality, no one can get out of childhood unscathed. Small and defenseless children have few skills and fewer still resources for protecting themselves emotionally. They have no car, no job, no credit cards and cannot leave home because they are not allowed to cross the street. Therefore, when emotionally wounding messages come along, the Defense System is designed to self-activate and become an emotional shield (figure 1–3). It is not necessary to think about it, it just happens. In fact, it is operational at birth and probably before.

This Defense System is the Enneagram part of personality. It is not good or bad; it just is. It has a job to do and it does it. So, because all children were wounded and because all have Defense Systems, it's not possible to get out of childhood without problems. Because

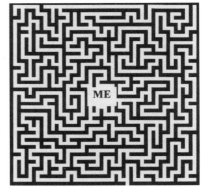

Figure 1-3

the Enneagram Defense System was not *willed* into action, it cannot be tuned down by will either. So coping skills that were necessary to survive childhood are brought, fully operational, into adulthood. Dangerous territory to say the least. As adults, these coping devices are outmoded and often contradictory to who we want to be. However, after many, many years of living defended it
is hard to realize there are alternatives. Even when psychologists and religious figures point out that there is a better way, more than likely we are without a clue as to how to access that part of ourselves.

MASLOW AND MIRRORING

Abraham Maslow proposed that we have certain basic needs that are hierarchical in importance. That is, we cannot concern ourselves with making a mark in this world and achieving recognition when homeless and hungry. Maslow represented the steps in the hierarchy as follows:

Self-actualization
Fulfilling potential
Unity and integration
Using gifts and talents
Spirituality

Esteem
Recognition
Prestige
Acceptance
Status

Love and Belonging
Safety
Structure
Order
Security
Predictability

Physiological/Survival
Food
Water
Sleep
Sex

We move *up* the hierarchy. We cannot concern ourselves with safety needs until basic survival needs of food and water are met. In an average family, survival needs are met. Therefore, the next step is getting the needs for love and belonging met. This

becomes the major stumbling block for most of us. If these needs are not well met, we cannot move on and attend to esteem and self-actualization needs.

Each child when born wants to look into welcoming eyes and have mirrored back that she is the most perfect miracle ever created. Each child wants to know that she is complete and totally acceptable in her parents' eyes. The child needs this unconditionally loving environment to grow emotionally. In such an environment, differences and individuality are celebrated and explored. It is essential the child know at the very core of her being that she is totally loveable just as she is. She rests assured in the knowledge that she does not need to do anything to be loved. She is loved for who she is.

Because parents are human, no child receives this kind of mirroring. Parents may do their best, but because children do not come with instruction manuals (the way they should), parents try to give children what seems, to the parents, to be the best of everything. Later, I will show more precisely why this does not work. That leaves the child still looking for that mirroring, that unconditional love and acceptance. When perfect mirroring is not received, the child goes through life trying to get that basic need met before moving up Maslow's hierarchy. Many try to earn love and acceptance by doing or working at being "better." Others just give up and accept being flawed and defective as fact, just making the best of life.

CONFLICT AND CONTAINMENT

Another reason it is difficult getting out of childhood without damage is because the average family does not deal well with conflict. Most of us have not had good conflict resolution modeled for us. We may have witnessed raging on the part of one parent or perhaps passive-aggressive behaviors on the part of another parent, with slamming doors and cold silence conveying the message.

Most children are not allowed to express their anger *and receive validation for it.* Generally, children are not given the right to be angry. Often children are punished for showing anger instead of being taught how to express it in an acceptable manner. Many religious traditions send the message that anger is sinful instead of just one of the four major emotions (anger, fear, sadness and happiness). Many times, a client will tell me she *was* angry as a child and *did* express her anger. However, what generally happened in those situations was punishment and shaming, not validation. We have all heard statements such as:

"Get that pout off your face!"

"Go to your room until you can act civil!"

"I'll give you something to cry about!"

"Don't be a scaredy-cat!"

"There's nothing to be afraid of."

Even a statement as benign as "cheer up!" denies the child the opportunity to sincerely express what is happening inside.

We learn as children how to contain our feelings of anger and any other feelings around conflict. We learn it is not good to express certain feelings, and another little part of us is put away. In response, the Defense System kicks into a higher gear and gives us alternative ways of coping. Each time this happens, access to our true self becomes more and more limited.

Rhonda's story. Rhonda is the youngest of four children. She was severely emotionally abused by two of her siblings. As we examined the abuse together, she reported that each incident caused a fragment of herself to be split off and inaccessible to her. She stated, "Each time, it was like a shard of light broke off" until she felt very fragmented, like "many fireflies" rather than one being.

The Enneagram personality type system that acts as a Defense System will be examined more closely in chapter 4. Each of the nine types of the Enneagram Defense System will react differently to stressors. Each type will be identified and you will be able to see how the behaviors of your Defense System can act as a flag signaling a movement into dangerous territory. Rhonda is an Enneagram Seven. She reacted to the abuse by making light of it and appearing outwardly happy. Her placement in the family encouraged her role to be that of family mascot whose job was to make everyone laugh. Her Defense System and her family role worked well together. It was not long before she was no longer aware of who she was.

Feelings will be examined more closely as well. The purpose of this approach is not to eradicate feelings. Rather the purpose is to identify the feelings, validate them, receive the information they are providing and then move through them. By doing so, control can be restored to the Core Self and, with it, clear thinking and wisdom. It will soon become clear how using the keys of the Enneagram, the Myers-Briggs Type Indicator and emotional healing work can expedite a journey of personal recovery.

REFERENCES AND SUGGESTED READING

Bass, E., and L. Davis. *The Courage to Heal.* New York: Harper Perennial, 1988. This is a classic on the effects of childhood sexual abuse. See pages 149–154 on forgiveness and pages 122–132 on anger.

Bradshaw, J. *Bradshaw On: The Family.* Deerfield Beach FL: Health Communications Inc., 1988. Bradshaw delves into the topic of early childhood wounding due to family dysfunction. He describes how a false self develops and explains the need to uncover the true self. Bradshaw examines the family as a system within the culture and contrasts functional and dysfunctional family systems with each other. Bradshaw is one of the few who call attention to religious and work addictions. He outlines how enhanced spirituality is an outcome of recovery.

Hergenhahn, B. R. *An Introduction to Theories of Personality.* 4th ed, 519–551 on Abraham Maslow. Englewood Cliffs NJ: Prentice Hall, 1994.

CHAPTER 2

FIVE LEVELS OF HEALING

Many people go through life and never embark on any healing work. An old Polish woman once told me, "You work. You peepee. You die." And that was her philosophy of life. It is safe to assume she left this world unhappy and unfulfilled. Others make efforts towards resolution of old wounds but get bogged down somewhere before reaching the desired results. Theologian Tony DeMello described it as finding a signpost to a city and thinking the signpost *was* the city. These people then climb the signpost and cling to it tenaciously, fervently hoping and believing they have the answer. A look at the five levels of healing will act as an overview as well as a road map: awareness, information gathering, behavioral modification, deep emotional healing and spirituality.

AWARENESS

Before anything can happen, there has to be an acknowledgment that a problem exists. To quote Tony DeMello again, "Awareness, awareness, awareness." Awareness moves us into the process of healing. Awareness can and will look different for different personality types. For some, raging may be a clue that something is amiss. Others may find themselves

Mary was aware that she was out of control but did not know why.
She only knew she was powerless to control her rages.
It was her awareness, the ability to recognize something was amiss,
that helped her move to the next level.

dissociating or not feeling they are fully present in their own bodies on a regular basis. Many people recognize depression and may have sought medication for it. Or perhaps there is an inability to control emotions and they are expressed at inappropriate times. Of course, addictions are always an indication of some unresolved issues. Remember, *addiction* does not have to mean chemicals. It can mean something as culturally acceptable as work or religion.

Most people are very aware of an empty feeling inside in addition to some of the problems mentioned above. Sometimes that empty feeling is described as a black hole. Many times we find that the black hole really controls much of life. We become aware of it because we find ourselves throwing things into it to try to fill it or to answer its incessant demands. The types of things that go into people's black holes are as varied as the people trying to fill them: alcohol, drugs, sex, food, sleep, religion, work, material things, TV, play, chocolate, etc., etc., etc. When we become aware that these things are happening and affecting our lives, we are ready to move on.

Mary's story. When Mary came into therapy she reported she was raging on a daily basis. When this happened, she was completely out of control. She raged at her husband and her children for major transgressions and minor infractions of her rules. When this happened, she hated herself but no matter how often she vowed never to repeat the behavior, it was only a matter of time before it happened again.

Mary was aware that she was out of control but did not know why. She only knew she was powerless to control her rages. It was her awareness, the ability to recognize something was amiss, that helped her move to the next level. Many people rage and blame everyone

around them for it. Mary took responsibility for her own behavior and was courageous enough to be willing to examine it.

Often relationship problems raise awareness. However, it is often easier to be aware that a partner has a problem than to use the opportunity to look within. Those who use marital or relationship problems to be aware that there is a problem within themselves are ready to move ahead. No matter how we may try, we cannot change the other person. Although this information is not new and we all subscribe to it in theory, we frequently act otherwise. Many times, people reach awareness when they move from one abusive relationship to another. The only thing that changes is the name of the offender. In these situations, the abuser definitely has a problem but we are unable to work with someone who is not present. If the victim is aware that *she* continually finds this type of person, then we can move forward and make some significant advances.

If we allow ourselves to see it, often one of our children will show us there is a problem. When a child acts out, either at home, school or in the community, it is very often the child who receives the focus of attention. The child is merely an indicator of a system that is not working. If we are open to the information, the seemingly errant child can be the messenger telling us to look at ourselves and the family system.

Alison's story. Alison came to see me very upset about her eight-year-old daughter who was lying, stealing, rage-filled and generally acting out. The girl was defiant and over-eating, which was rapidly leading to a weight problem. Alison and her husband were focused on their daughter, wanting help for her and suggestions on how to deal with her. They were concerned parents who had tried every trick in the book to motivate, compel, bribe, cajole or otherwise get the child to comply with family and societal values and standards. All this was to no avail. The harder they tried, the more the girl acted out.

Alison began her own healing work with me. Shortly thereafter, Alison saw the family dynamic that was causing her daughter to "misbehave." It was not long before Alison's husband entered therapy with another therapist. Eventually, they participated in couple and family therapy. The focus was taken off their daughter and the girl's conduct improved. After a while, Alison was able to see that her daughter was acting like a family barometer. When she began acting out, Alison knew the family system was "off balance" again and they would return for some family counseling.

The amount of therapy in which this family participated may seem like a lot to some people. However, Alison clearly sees that the alternative is a system so off balance that it caused her daughter, and ultimately all of the family members, to pay a very high price.

Without being aware that life is not all it could be, there would be no reason to move to the next level.

INFORMATION GATHERING

Talk shows and self-help books exist to fill the need to gather information about a personal problem without taking any risks. Talk show hosts such as Geraldo Rivera and Oprah Winfrey built very successful careers by supplying viewers with information in the safety and anonymity of their own homes. Often people will have entire personal libraries on the topic that causes them distress—managing anger, over-eating, co-dependence and the like. Some people are seminar and workshop junkies, going to hear the latest expert provide the missing piece to their personal puzzle. In fact, some people have even gone so far as to obtain a master's degree in counseling in order to try to fix themselves without benefit of therapy. None of these methods brings about any lasting changes nor can they effect emotional healing. But it does feel better to talk about a problem with someone or to read about someone who has dealt with the same issue. For a moment, it takes away the feeling of being alone, different or weird. In the end, however, all we are left with is a well-defined problem and we are no closer to a solution.

The reason information gathering cannot solve the problem is because the information is directed to a completely different part of personality than where the problem resides. The two never meet. The information enters the cognitive part of the self, the left brain. Many times the behaviors that we find distressing are located in the Defense System. That part of personality is automatic and does not stop to think or consult with cognition. It just acts. It is supposed to defend. It has no brain of its own and does not stop to consider consequences.

If a person is in emotional pain and finds that when she is triggered she goes directly to the donut shop, it will not help to join a weight-loss group or read about dieting. It will not help to listen to someone explain how to eat healthy and live longer. And it certainly will not help to have someone patiently give her all the reasons she should not eat donuts. All of this is directed towards cognition. Besides, does anyone think she did not know all of this and more? I am certain women like this can recite the calorie count and fat content of every known food. The part of personality that is compelling her towards the donut shop is only interested in one thing, numbing out the emotional pain.

Kim's story. Kim was considerably overweight. She had explored many methods of weight loss but found that when she became emotionally stressed, her eating was out of her control. On one occasion, she was attending a work-related seminar about 100 miles away from home. The speaker made an unkind comment about overweight people and looked in her direction. The shame and resulting emotional pain were nearly unbearable for Kim. She left the seminar as quickly as she could. It was not until she arrived home that she realized she had eaten continually during the drive home, stopping at numerous fast food restaurants. By the time she reached home, she was physically ill from the amount of food she had consumed.

Although Kim was unaware of how much she was

eating on her trip home and why she was eating it, I am certain that someone pointing it out to her would have made no difference whatsoever. When she was hurting that badly, her Defense System could only direct her towards something that would kill the pain, if only temporarily. There was no thinking this through and there was no negotiating. All of her vast knowledge of nutrition and healthy eating was totally unavailable to her until she found a way to look at the emotional pain, move into it and deal with it. Only then could control be restored to her Core Self and cognition so that she could make good, sound, healthy decisions for herself.

Julia's story. Julia arrived in my office very distressed. She had just come from the hairdresser's. It was her second trip back after a haircut earlier in the week. She was upset because she was certain that one side of her hair was a fraction longer than the other. I, of course, could see nothing wrong with the cut. Julia admitted that probably no one would notice it but her yet it continued to occupy much of her time, thoughts and energy. There was no amount of reassurance that could keep her from returning to see the hairdresser one more time to get it even.

There was nothing I could have said to Julia to bring her to see that her hair was just fine. She was not operating out of the rational part of her personality. She had even admitted that no one could see the problem yet she could not stop obsessing about it. I have had clients who would miss work because of a perceived "bad hair day." Of course this is not a rational decision. But the part that made the decision to stay home from work was the Defense System, which is not rational and cannot be reasoned with. So gathering information from me, her spouse, and all of her co-workers would never make Julia feel one bit better about her hair. The part that decided it was unacceptable was beyond our reach.

BEHAVIOR MODIFICATION

Close on the heels of information gathering comes behavior modification. Many people reach this level.

They train themselves or receive training to modify or eradicate unwanted behaviors. What actually happens is that they take a tool away from their Defense System. However, the Defense System is very dedicated and resourceful and quickly replaces it with another. We can continue to look at the problem of over-eating to illustrate. Occasionally, we hear of someone who has lost a tremendous amount of weight and has kept it off for years. Often this person will lecture, write a book or open a fitness center. What the resourceful Defense System has managed to do is replace a socially unacceptable strategy with one that garners praise and admiration. However, when the new behavior is used in the same manner as the old one, to numb out emotional pain, it is not any more emotionally healthy than over-eating. Many of us are willing to settle for this arrangement and that is called successful behavior modification. The unacceptable behaviors have been exchanged for behaviors that are more acceptable. The hope is that accomplishing this will cause an enhanced self-esteem, which is not always the case.

Twelve-step programs such as Alcoholics Anonymous (AA), Al-Anon and Adult Children of Alcoholics (ACA) employ behavior modification. These programs have made an important contribution to the well-being of countless people. Author M. Scott Peck has said that the twelve-step movement is the most important movement of the twentieth century. Every sober AA member will join me in underscoring the value of these programs. However, the majority of the work that happens through a twelve-step program is directed at changing damaging behaviors. Some gains in self-esteem take place due to facing and conquering behaviors that have been debilitating. But there is little attention given to the original pain that may have initiated the behaviors. Therefore, the Defense System goes to work looking for a substitute. If you ever attend an AA meeting, you will see a group of resourceful Defense Systems making a valiant attempt to replace alcohol with cigarettes and coffee.

Cognitive or "talk" therapy employs behavior modification. Various theories of cognitive therapy

When all the attempts at behavioral modification are done, what is left is a Defense System that is scrambling around for new and innovative ways to take care of the wounded Core Self by finding alternative methods to kill the emotional pain.

work by showing the left brain the distorted thinking behind the offending behaviors and offering more acceptable behaviors as replacement. Cognitive therapy works for many people to bring about the desired behavior changes. And because of having faced the problem and having conquered the offending behavior, there is greater self-esteem. However, cognitive therapy does not heal the pain caused by the wounding messages received early in life. It only deals with the way those messages manifest themselves.

When all the attempts at behavioral modification are done, what is left is a Defense System that is scrambling around for new and innovative ways to take care of the wounded Core Self by finding alternative methods to kill the emotional pain. All the attempts to talk the Defense System out of its job are fruitless because it is automatic, it does not have a logical component and it does not respond to threats, promises or reason. The Defense System will only relax if there is no threat to emotional safety or if it sees that an equally strong part of the personality is taking responsibility for protecting the Core Self. That cannot happen with a cognitive approach. It is time to move to the next level.

DEEP EMOTIONAL HEALING

When the words *emotions* or *feelings* are used, it is a signal that we are now talking about what happens on the right side of the brain rather than the left. This is an affective approach to healing rather than a cognitive approach. When talking about affective work, it is necessary to set logic aside and move into the realm of feelings, creativity and intuition. This is a major stumbling block in a culture that finds all those areas highly suspect. We live in a culture that values rational, concrete tools that work in a controlled, logical, step-by-step manner. When the nebulous right-brain

approach is suggested, there is immediate resistance. Going against the mainstream cultural approach is bound to raise suspicion. However, that is not cause to dismiss this approach. Christopher Columbus went against the cultural belief that the world was flat and those who were willing to risk a new approach benefited greatly.

It is no secret we live in a patriarchal society. The majority of men are left-brain oriented. Starting with Freud, the vast majority of psychological theorists have been men. Their approaches have been pointedly logical and rational. It is not that they did not deal with the topic of emotions; they did. However, emotions have been treated analytically. The goal is to control and dispatch emotions and not allow things to get too messy with feelings.

The majority of women are right-brain oriented, trying to fit into a culture that sees things differently. Most women find that in order to be accepted as credible and to be successful in this culture, they must work from a left-brain worldview that is not native or natural. Most women are at home in the right side of the brain. Women, then, have adjusted somewhat to navigating between the left and right hemispheres because the culture demands it. Scientists have found that the bridge between right and left brain, the *corpus callosum*, is larger in women. However, the same demands are not made of the majority of men who are left-brained. They feel completely at home in the culture and see few reasons to look at right-brained viewpoints. At best, the male-dominated culture finds anything with a feminine orientation perplexing; at worst, threatening.

Scientific studies and analytical research are in the domain of the left-brained. When a new, right-brained approach to therapy is offered, the scientific types want to know the research behind it. Right-brained people, by their very nature, do not do research. Therefore, affective therapy does not have the studies and statistics behind it that every cognitive theory has. University faculties are overwhelmingly left-brain populated. Very little affective therapy is taught in universities, which contributes to this approach being treated as suspect.

All these factors and more explain why affective therapy is not part of the mainstream approach to counseling. What is important to remember is that this does not take away from its effectiveness. This method of therapy is highly effective and it works equally well for the left-brained group as for the right-brained. What is different is that the left-brained group must set aside logic and allow themselves to be led into the unfamiliar territories of a more inexact, imprecise and ambiguous type of therapy. Most find it uncomfortable for a while, like wearing slippers on the wrong feet. However, those who are right-brained by nature will find it quite comfortable. Right-brained people live the majority of their lives in the left-brain world and move back and forth with more ease. It is important to note that the purpose of affective or right-brain therapy is not to keep the client locked into right-brain thinking but to work through the programming and feelings that are stored there in order to restore control to cognition and the Core Self.

Many of my clients are left-brained by nature. They are very logical, rational, concrete and want to be given practical tools to deal with very basic everyday problems. Perhaps they are unhappy with their jobs, are having marital problems or their children are out of control. When I explain that we will be working with imagery and examining their childhood, they look at me askance. To say they have misgivings is mild. My standard response is to suggest they give the process five or six months and then we can re-evaluate. One client agreed to five months or twenty sessions. She numbered her checks to keep track. I breathed easier when she admitted at check number eighteen that she could see her life changing. Another took out her calendar and counted out twenty weeks. She circled the

target date on her calendar, which happened to be April 15, and reminded me regularly how rapidly Income Tax Day was approaching. She, too, admitted to changes in her life but at first insisted they were coincidences. When she spoke up to her boss for the first time ever in a staff meeting and felt confident and sure of herself, she had to admit something was very different.

Another woman agreed to the trial period and noted five months on her calendar. Each time she came in, she spent the first ten minutes arguing that we were wasting time. Her marriage was dissolving before her eyes, her business was nearly bankrupt, her children were completely out of control and she was crying all the time. She was frustrated with me because all I wanted to do was talk about her childhood and cajole her into participating in imagery. Before reaching the twentieth week, she saw she was coping better and she was no longer raging at her family. However, she continued to argue for months that the process made no sense. Today, five years later, she says, "It has become a way of life" and she cannot imagine living any other way. Although an affective approach never met her logic needs, she was not one to argue with success.

All of this is to say that, when moving into a discussion of an affective approach to healing, logic and a left-brain orientation must be set aside.

The purpose of affective work is to deal with the emotional wounding received early in life and to reverse the resulting negative messages about ourselves and the world in general. If this can be accomplished, the Defense System will, in effect, "back off," seeing there is not as great a need for its services. However, it never leaves entirely. It simply takes a back seat and returns control to the Core Self. Then, the traits of the Defense System can be used to *support* the Core Self and its agenda rather than dominate it.

Inner-Child work is a form of affective therapy. It works by examining a trigger or behavior that interferes with living or causes distress, and traces it back to its origin. When we can look at the original context with a more adult, objective perspective, we can deal with the feelings and the resulting negative messages in a more rational manner. Notice the word *rational.* The left brain is employed but not until the right brain has done its job in accessing the origins of the problem and dispatching the leftover feelings.

We all have triggers or buttons that other people can push inadvertently or on purpose like the Windows computer program I referred to earlier. Once a button is pushed, the Defense System program is mobilized and we act out in some way. Inner-Child work takes a close look at the button, the associated feelings that were triggered and the conditions under which that button was originally installed (figure 2-1). Then a decision can be made as to how the program should be adjusted to bring about more desirable results.

Figure 2-1. Emotional triggers in the adult lead back to unresolved issues in childhood.

More than likely, when we are around family members the buttons get pushed more frequently. Of course! Those are the people who installed them. They know exactly where the buttons are and the effect of pushing them. They may not do it consciously or purposefully, but they do it and we respond like clockwork. I call this programming. As noted, we work very much like a computer. Mom and Dad are the master programmers. Some of the programs they installed on our hard drives were put there on purpose, such as table manners. Other programs were installed unintentionally, such as how to deal with conflict or which topics are off-limits.

A cardinal rule I employ is this: If there is a war between your head (left brain) and your programming, the programming wins, hands down, every time. That

is because the programming triggers original emotional pain that activates the Defense System—we all know what happens next. The Defense System bypasses the rational brain and takes control. It eliminates choices in most situations. Just like St. Paul, we find ourselves wondering why we continue to do the things we do not want to do. Inner-Child work is a method to make the unconscious programming conscious. Engaging the feelings associated with that programming allows us to change it. When the programming is disengaged, the Defense System can relax.

I invite you to participate in a little exercise that will demonstrate the early programming, the buttons involved and the associated feelings. Without reading ahead to the next paragraph, think of a person in your adult life who can really push all your buttons, someone who never fails to find a way to drive you up a wall. It can be someone with whom you work, your spouse or a friend. Take a piece of paper and list all the adjectives to describe that person. Try to note at least ten words or phrases to paint a verbal picture of this person. On the same page, make a list of all the feelings you experience when that person pushes your buttons. Remember, *feelings,* not thoughts. Feelings would be: angry, sad, alone, scared, stupid, etc. Feelings are not: "I feel like I shouldn't let him get me like that." If you can substitute the word "think" for "feel," it is a thought not a feeling. Make these lists now.

Next, read over the adjectives that describe the person in question. Does the description more closely resemble Mom or is it a better portrayal of Dad? When you have decided which parent this person represents to you, put a check mark in front of each adjective that describes the parent. Try to forget about how that trait looked in the original person because it may look different in your parent. If you are objective, you may see that the description may not be manifested in the same manner, but the word applies to both your challenging person and your parent.

For instance, if you have listed *controlling* among the words describing your boss, you may find that your mother was also controlling. It may look different in your boss than it did in your mother, but they both possess that trait. Now look at the feelings you listed. Do you feel the same way around your mother as you do around your boss? It can be rather disconcerting to find you work for your mother or you married your dad.

Judy's story. Judy came in very distressed with her situation at work. Her boss, Jennifer, made Judy very uncomfortable. She felt scared, stupid and intimidated in her presence. Judy made the following list describing Jennifer:

> Judgmental
> Uses
> Unreasonable
> Critical
> Threatened
> Gives away responsibility
> Does not accept input
> Uncommunicative
> Does not measure up to expectations

When I asked Judy which parent Jennifer reminded her of, she immediately answered "Mom." I asked her to check the words/phrases that described Mom. She checked them all and added "self-absorbed" to the list for both women.

Knowing she was, in effect, working for her mother brought a new perspective to the situation for Judy but it was not until we handled the matter of feeling scared, stupid and intimidated that any real change occurred. The emotional healing around this situation applied not only to her relationship with Jennifer but also to her relationship with her mother. She began feeling more adult and emotionally strong when she dealt with both women.

With a little detective work, it is not difficult to trace the buttons and see the patterns of behavior across the years. Providing a person with this information furnishes insight and gives what is called an "aha" experience. However, it does not accomplish the emotional healing that is necessary for the kind of transformation we desire. That is because the information is going to the left brain. It is necessary to use the information from a right-brained perspective to access the feelings

associated with the programming installed in childhood.

SPIRITUALITY

Spirituality is not usually the goal of therapy, however it is often a welcome by-product. When the Defense System relinquishes control to the Core Self, we become spirit-based instead of defense-based. Life and living look very different from this perspective. Decisions are based on a totally different set of criteria. We have a sense of being connected to a Higher Power and experience the ability to tap into the strength and peace that comes from that connection.

Kory's story. Kory was an unusual client because, despite having a fun-loving Core Self, she managed to find her way into affective therapy to begin with and then cooperated fully in looking at the pain of her childhood. Kory's childhood was a nightmare by anyone's standards. Her father was a violent alcoholic who incested her. He alternated between making a great deal of money and losing it all. Sometimes they lived in luxury, such as a house with a swimming pool and hired help; and other times they would live in inadequate housing in poor neighborhoods. At one point, they slept between mattresses to keep warm. Kory's father was a womanizer and was violent towards Kory's mother. He was also abusive towards the children although Kory did not receive the worst of it because she was his favorite.

Kory brought the intensity of her personality to our work in therapy. She was dedicated to recovery. Kory had always believed in God and accepted the concept of a God Within. However, she felt none of it applied to her. God was very external for her, watching from a distance. For everyone else, the principle of a God Within was very real. She was a counselor and encouraged her clients to believe in their own Internal Wisdom source. Yet, she was very certain that she was an exception.

The more personal healing Kory experienced, the more real God became to her. When she finally accepted, at a feeling level, that the horrendous things that happened to her in her childhood really were not her fault, she began to own a very real internal peace. With that, her sense of being connected with God and her sense of God working through her took root. At the end of therapy, Kory began talking about God and spirituality. She looked for spiritual direction and began exploring her own personal spirituality. She decided on the best ways she could connect to God as she understood God. She became more and more aware of God Within and God's presence in her daily life.

Recently, Kory experienced a crisis in which her nephew became seriously ill. She realized she was triggered with feelings of impending loss and felt the need to take care of everyone else in the family. Because of the healing work we had done together, she was able to gain some reaction time and distanced herself emotionally from the situation long enough to work through her feelings. After that, she was able to use the gifts of her Core Self, which functions well in crisis, to effectively deal with the crisis without over-reacting. She found she was calm and able to be present to others without moving into her Enneagram Defense System. She felt grounded in her Core Self. Kory listened well and provided a safe environment for herself and others to work through the fears and sadness attached to the situation.

While sitting in the hospital waiting room, Kory had a real sense of the presence of a Higher Power. She sensed that the family was being held and cared for. She was filled with peace and her personal faith was strengthened. Kory reports these types of encounters with a Higher Power are happening more and more frequently for her. (Kory's story was first reported in The *Enneagram Monthly,* February 1998.)

Kory did not enter therapy with the expressed purpose of becoming more spiritual in her daily living yet she has been delighted to find it happening without the need to consciously pursue it. She is just one example of countless clients who begin to bring up the topic of God as formal therapy draws to a close. My experience echoes Charles Whitfield who indicates in *Healing the*

Child Within that spirituality enters the picture as healing progresses. We cannot appreciate ourselves as spiritual beings until we feel safe enough to enter the realm of the Core Self.

REFERENCES AND SUGGESTED READING

Bradshaw, J. *Healing the Shame that Binds You.* Deerfield Beach FL: Health Communications Inc., 1988. One of the pioneers in Inner-Child work, Bradshaw explores the pain and effects of shame imposed early in life. Bradshaw sees shame as the underlying cause of undesirable behaviors such as addictions. A thorough discussion of the topic is presented as well as a variety of techniques and exercises to address the problem. Bradshaw points out that spirituality is an end product of the Inner-Child process.

De Mello, A. Speaker. *Wake Up to Life.* New York Conference. Cassettes 1–12. St. Louis MO: We and God Spirituality Center, 1989. De Mello brings a mixture of eastern and Christian theology to the topic of awareness and letting go. He urges the listener to stop doing and begin being. He makes a distinction between the *me* and the *I*; that is, the person we present to the world and the true self.

Edwards, S. "Those Hidden Wounds." Workshop. St. Louis MO. I am indebted to Susan Edwards for much of the information on family roles presented in this chapter.

Hoff, B. *The Tao of Pooh.* New York: Penguin Books, 1982. A charming and easy-to-understand little book explaining the need to suspend reliance on the left brain in order to learn to just be. Presented from an eastern, Taoist spiritual perspective.

Steinem, G. *Revolution from Within.* Boston: Little, Brown and Company, 1992. This book clearly shows that before we can change the world we need to address our own issues and make our own personal changes. Steinem explores the early effects of family and culture on self-esteem using her personal story and those of other women. I would have preferred a stronger emphasis on expressing emotions, especially anger but, nonetheless, an insightful and courageous book.

The 12 Steps for Adult Children. San Diego CA: Recovery Publications Inc., 1987. A simple, basic book explaining the twelve-step approach to recovery from the perspective of the Adult Children of Alcoholics (ACA) program.

Whitfield, C. *Healing the Child Within,* 120. Deerfield Beach FL: Health Communications Inc., 1987. A highly respected pioneer in the field of Inner-Child work, Whitfield presents a description of early wounding and addresses the recovery process

including the expression of feelings such as anger and grief. The role of spirituality as the final outcome of Inner-Child work is examined.

Wyman, P. "Trigger Points." *Enneagram Monthly* (February 1998)4:1. Kory's story first appeared in this article for the *Enneagram Monthly.* For a more detailed account of Kory's history, contact *Enneagram Monthly,* 748 Wayside Rd., Portola Valley, CA 94028; 877.428.9639, for a copy of that article and information about subscribing.

PART II

Three Keys to Self-Understanding

CHAPTER 3

WHO'S HOME?
UNDERSTANDING THE MYERS-BRIGGS TYPE INDICATOR

We all know the story of the Ugly Duckling—the poor, little baby swan raised to think he was a duck. Of course he did not look like a duck, sound like a duck or act like a duck. He did not fit in at all. The Ugly Duckling measured himself against the standards of his family, and he came up quite short. He simply made a very poor duck. His self-esteem was nonexistent. He felt so badly about himself, he was ready to die to escape the emotional pain. Eventually, he found out he was not a duck but a swan. With that knowledge, he found a place to fit in and be accepted. That is the end of the official version of the story. However, I wonder about "the rest of the story." How did he think and feel about himself from that point on? Did he revel and delight in being a swan? The story does not lead us to believe so. It appears he accepted his "swan-ness" tentatively and with uncertainty. It is not an altogether happy ending. It does not do the Ugly Duckling much good to find out he is a swan only to continue to think and feel like an ugly duck.

The reason we all know the story so well is that we can all identify with the little Ugly Duckling: growing up thinking we somehow do not measure up, do not quite fit in. Even if we grow into adulthood to become successful, accomplished and renowned, inside there is still a wounded inner child who feels like an ugly duckling. The first key to self-understanding and healing is to let the child know about being a swan, what that means, and just how wonderful it is.

THE MYERS-BRIGGS TYPE INDICATOR

Getting a clear understanding of the Core Self is the first key to reclaiming yourself. The Myers-Briggs Type Indicator (MBTI) can provide a good description of the person you were designed to be. It is a good profile of the Core Self. The Myers-Briggs Type Indicator is simplicity itself, measuring just four dimensions of personality. Yet, when these four are combined, they are more than the sum of their parts. Your four-letter MBTI type formula outlines how you take in information and make decisions; it identifies your energy source and your style of living. It is the interaction of the four aspects of your MBTI profile that determines your worldview, values, communication style, spirituality, career preferences and much more. Knowing your MBTI type provides information on your gifts and talents and how you relate to people. It can predict how you have fun, your leadership style and your learning style. In other words, knowing your MBTI type provides a fairly detailed portrait of the person you were wired to be.

Many people have taken the MBTI and consider it little more than a parlor game. They are surprised at the accuracy with which the MBTI describes them and then let it go at that. The MBTI can be used for much more. It can be used as a tool to help heal the wounded inner child and liberate that child to enjoy full self-expression. To participate fully in a journey of inner healing, that journey must begin with the wounded child. To start with the child, it is necessary to recognize that child when she is encountered and validate the child for the miracle that she is. The MBTI provides grounds on which to base validation of the child and gives direction in allowing the Core Self expression. Understanding MBTI type will help the Core Self begin to receive permission to be real.

At times, each of us has joined the enemy against ourselves. Each of us can relate to occasionally feeling defective, flawed or not good enough. For some, this happens on rare occasions. For others, it is a state of being. When this happens, further emotional damage is being done. In actuality, each of us is different from whoever has been designated as the current cultural standard. You may be old enough to remember when seemingly every woman was measuring herself against the body standards of the current top model, Twiggy. Emotional damage is inflicted when we are forced into a mold for which we were not designed. Understanding your MBTI profile can help stop the damage and break the mold.

It is not until self-understanding and acceptance is reached that we can begin to understand and accept others. When we each understand and value the unique way in which we have been designed, we can appreciate the uniqueness of those around us. Otherwise, there is a danger of expecting everyone to think and act alike. We must know the strengths we bring to any situation to appreciate the contributions other types can make.

There are many wonderful books on the market that thoroughly explain the MBTI and help with a self-assessment. Of course, the best method of getting a good grasp on your MBTI type is to do a one-on-one session with a trained professional who can administer the MBTI and, *most importantly,* confirm the results. A qualified counselor can provide an in-depth explanation showing what the results mean in the context of how you are currently living your life. Are you working in a career totally unsuited to your abilities? Are you self-critical of behaviors that are normal for you but may go against cultural demands, such as a tendency to be less than punctual? Perhaps, try as you might, your housekeeping abilities do not measure up to those of Mom, Martha Stewart and your next-door neighbor. Or you may have seemingly insurmountable communication problems with someone close to you. Using the MBTI to understand yourself and others can begin to lift some guilt and unrealistic expectations from your shoulders.

Going into an in-depth explanation of the MBTI is beyond the scope of this book. A brief overview is presented to afford you the possibility of typing yourself for the purposes of understanding this model of personality dynamics and healing work.

Four Dichotomies of Personality

(E) Extraversion	Introversion (I)
(S) Sensing	Intuition (N)
(T) Thinking	Feeling (F)
(J) Judging	Perceiving (P)

Figure 3-1

The MBTI is based on the work of Carl Jung. His theory of psychological type was further developed and made accessible to the world by a mother-daughter team, Katharine Briggs and Isabel Briggs Myers. The MBTI defines four dichotomies of personality. The instrument is a *sorter;* that is, in each of the four dichotomies of personality, you have a choice between two polar opposite positions. You have a natural, inborn inclination to one or the other. The line down the center of the table in figure 3-1 indicates that, in each dichotomy, there is no true continuum but polar opposite processes. You are one or the other; never a blend of both. However, in order to function in this world, you have to employ both processes. One will feel comfortable and familiar while the other will feel out of your comfort zone. For instance, the first dichotomy considers how you are energized: Are you an Introvert or an Extravert? Although at times you exhibit behaviors of both sides of each dichotomy, your personality is characterized by a preference for one or the other. The MBTI instrument presents you with a preference score that indicates the clarity of your preference for one side of the dichotomy. However, that only lets you know how much *permission* you have given yourself to exhibit this preference. It does not give you the degree or strength to which you have this preference. If you take the MBTI and, in the first dichotomy, you have a high Extraversion score, it *does not* mean you are more of an Extravert than someone with a low Extraversion score.

It means you are comfortable being an Extravert and that you indicated clearly on the instrument that you prefer Extraversion. On the other hand, if your score for Extraversion is low, it does not mean you are a blend of Extraversion and Introversion. It means that you did not clearly indicate which you prefer. There are several possible explanations for this. One may be that you are unclear because you were not supported in your natural preference. Another may be because you responded to how you thought you *should* be.

Beatrice's story. Beatrice, age forty-four, came to see me because of problems with her family of origin, depression and low self-esteem. She took the MBTI during our first session together and scored clearly Introverted. We spent the next hour and a half discussing the results during which time she expressed a very clear preference for Extraversion. In our discussion, I learned she was raised by immigrant parents in a very patriarchal cultural and religious subgroup that expects women and girls to be quiet and unassuming. Her MBTI type and her Enneagram type were both very susceptible to "shoulds." She had put a lot of energy into trying to keep a low profile, which was contrary to her Extraverted nature. Fortunately, Beatrice was able to integrate this information into her very orthodox religious orientation by accepting that, if God designed her that way, she was free to be an Extravert. She subsequently became more comfortable with that facet of her personality and removed the shame and guilt she had felt for her natural inclination to be outgoing and talkative.

In her own words, Beatrice says, "For years and years, I considered myself shy, reserved and a loner (an Introvert). But with the MBTI, it showed me to be an Extravert. Outgoing, social and so on. I could now understand why I had those feelings lying underneath my programmed ones."

Another influence on your score can be your Enneagram Defense System type. The Enneagram will be examined more closely later. However, if you are an Introvert and your Enneagram Defense is outgoing, you may answer more questions on the MBTI from an Extraverted standpoint than someone else. This does not make you "almost" an Extravert. It only explains why you answered the questions in that manner. I am personally an Introvert. My Enneagram designation is often called The Performer. An Introverted Performer seems to be a contradiction in terms, and there have been many times in my life when I would agree with that assessment. Each time I have taken the MBTI, I score right in the middle between Extraversion and Introversion. However, there is no question that I am an Introvert. I am not a blend of the two. I merely answer some of the questions on the instrument from my Enneagram performing perspective. That is why it is so important that you not take the results of the MBTI at face value but thoroughly examine those results to be certain that the information is accurate. Although that is best accomplished with a trained professional, careful study of some of the books listed at the end of the chapter may help facilitate your own discernment process.

As noted, when you examine each of the four dichotomies, you will find that frequently you can identify with behaviors on both sides of the spectrum. Often a client will express frustration saying, "But I can do both!" The operative word is always *can*. Try to keep in mind that it is not to determine what you *can* do, but which feels the most natural. There is no question that you *can* do whatever you have to do. But what feels right and natural? What feels like home? Be extremely cautious of the words *can* and *should*. With all these caveats in mind, let's take a look at the four dichotomies of the MBTI part of personality.

Extraversion and Introversion

The most important thing to keep in mind when examining this dichotomy is that it is about energy source and not about whether or not you like people. How are you energized? Would you enjoy sales? Is meeting new people fun and energizing? Do you like shopping with the crowds on Christmas Eve? Would you look forward to attending a large convention where you know no

one, seeing it as an opportunity to make new friends? After leaving a work or social environment that calls for a lot of social interaction, are you too wired to sleep? Do you think out loud, processing your thoughts externally? When a question is posed, do you find yourself talking immediately until you work your way through to the answer? Would you rather give a verbal report at a meeting than write it out for distribution? Are you likely to engage total strangers in conversation? If you answer a resounding YES! to most of these questions, you are probably an Extravert who receives your energy from outside sources. An Extravert enjoys working in an environment filled with people. Being around people from the start of the day to quitting time is comfortable and energizing. Careers in sales, hospital nursing, teaching, secretarial work and the like—which call for continual interaction with others—are attractive and stimulating for the Extravert. An Extravert (E) will probably embrace most of the following descriptors:

- Preference for socializing in groups
- Sociable
- External processor (needs to talk it through)
- Becomes lethargic when isolated
- Externally oriented
- Many casual friendships
- Talkative
- Outgoing and interactive
- Talk/think/talk some more

Remember, Introverts may enjoy people as much as Extraverts and be very relational. However, Introverts are not *energized* by outside sources. Instead, Introverts are energized from within. If an Introvert works in a very Extraverted environment such as a clerk in a department store, the Introvert will be searching, instinctively and constantly, for a quiet spot. Do you enter the restroom at work hoping no one else is there? Do you welcome an opportunity to go to an unpopulated area of the workplace in order to get away from the commotion? Would you enjoy eating a quiet lunch in your office alone or in your car rather than in the employee cafeteria? If you worked in an office setting, would you prefer a private office, no matter how small, to a desk in the middle of all the activity? When a question is posed, do you get annoyed when an Extravert begins talking immediately before you have the opportunity to think through your answer? When you speak, do you use spacers, such as *uhm, well, OK, ahh,* and the like? (Because Introverts process internally, they need the opportunity to go inside for a split second to find out what to say next.) Would you rather have a root canal than attend a New Year's Eve party where you know no one? Do you keep your fingers crossed that no one will sit next to you on an airplane? Do you feel more disconnected and alone in a large group than in a small one? Do you ever come home in the evening and feel relieved to find the house empty? Do you welcome environments that discourage interaction, such as church/synagogue, libraries, quiet retreats and other solitary environments? Do you dislike drop-in visitors? Is the phone often a nuisance and an interruption? If you respond positively to most of these questions, you are probably an Introvert. An Introvert finds external activities to be energy draining and internal activities such as reading, writing and working alone to be energy generating. Introverts (I) will recognize most of the following descriptors in themselves:

- Preference for socializing one-on-one
- Private
- Internal processor (needs to take thoughts inside)
- Becomes exhausted by lengthy interaction with many people, particularly strangers
- Internally oriented
- Usually one or two close friends
- Reflective; contemplative
- Quiet
- Think/talk/re-think

Once you have determined your preference in this dichotomy, you may want to examine some of the messages you received as a child for your natural, inborn energizing inclination. One important fact is that the cultures in the United States and many countries throughout the world favor Extraversion. Preference for Extraversion within these populations ranges from 50 to 65 percent. Therefore, Introverts receive messages all their lives that they are out of sync with the culture.

Watch movies, TV commercials and situation comedies to see what the media tells you about Introverts and Extraverts. As young children, Introverts are encouraged to be more outgoing and sociable. Terms such as shy, wallflower, withdrawn and the like are used to describe an Introvert in a negative manner. Introverted children are encouraged to leave their rooms and their singular activities to join the other children, implying there is something wrong with being by themselves. Schools provide another environment more suited to Extraverts, giving the Introvert more disapproving messages. Often the Introverted child is considered less intelligent because of being quieter. Although girls are expected to be quieter than boys, the school environment rewards Extraverted behaviors. Grades are often influenced by class participation and discussion, even at the college level; Introverts feel the burden of this requirement. The Introverted college student is expected to live in a very Extraverted dormitory environment or risk peer disapproval and nonacceptance. If you are an Introvert, whether you have been consciously aware of it or not, you have not felt at home in an Extraverted society.

Extraverts sometimes receive negative messages for this feature of their personalties. Terms such as *jabbermouth, mighty-mouth* or *motor-mouth* send disapproving messages. Extraverts may be accused of thinking with their mouths or "thinking too loud." They may frequently be reminded to think before they talk when in actuality they have a difficult time processing their thoughts without talking.

In our patriarchal culture, we have different standards for boys and girls. Often Extraverted little girls are chided for being too chatty, visiting with friends too much during school time, having a telephone permanently affixed to their ears and the like.

Ronnie's story. Growing up, Ronnie was constantly told to stop talking and be good. "Good" was equated with quiet. As an Extravert, Ronnie found it difficult to be quiet. She received low marks in conduct because she talked too much while her Introverted friend who seldom said a word received high marks in conduct. By the time she finished school, Ronnie was convinced she was inherently bad because of her inability to control her talking as well as for other qualities of her personality that went against cultural and family norms.

There have been countless jokes circulated about talkative women. You seldom hear the same criticism of an Extraverted male. The culture expects, even demands, that men be outgoing. Consequently, Extraversion in males is reinforced and Introverted males struggle to meet cultural expectations in their work and social lives. It may be living hell for an Introverted adolescent boy to approach girls in order to get acquainted. Later, trying to make small talk by telephone to keep friendships going is equally painful. Introverts may be accused of being shy or antisocial.

If you are trying to move ahead in your career choice, it pays to be an Extravert. The need to market oneself and network in order to advance career goals is extraordinarily taxing on an Introvert. An Introvert would rather chew ground glass than have to make twenty networking calls in one day. An Extravert relishes the idea of talking to new people and finds the experience fun and energizing. The culture expects Extraversion in the workplace. Introverts expend vast amounts of energy trying to meet cultural expectations in order to advance in their chosen careers, all the while feeling they are inadequate in some unexplained way.

Whether Extraverted or Introverted, if you grew up in a family in which the majority belonged to the other persuasion, you instinctively tried to modify yourself in order to fit in. Even though the culture is overwhelmingly Extraverted, if you were the only Extravert in your family of origin, you are certain to have received negative messages for your energy orientation. My son had the distinction of this experience in our family. Dealing with his uninhibited Extraversion was difficult for the rest of our Introverted family. His friends dropped in constantly at all times of the day or night and the phone never stopped ringing. I am certain we all, inadvertently, gave him a great deal of negative feedback on this aspect of his personality. Although none of us can

recall that it ever slowed him down, it was unfair to him to receive negative messages for an inherent trait of his personality.

In understanding your preference in this dichotomy, can you identify the ways you received negative messages about yourself in this area and from whom?

Thought Processes

The next two dichotomies (Sensing–Intuition and Thinking–Feeling) examine the two basic thought processes: Sensing and Intuition refer to the information-gathering dimensions of processing information. Thinking and Feeling govern the decision-making process. Together, these two dichotomies are strongly related to the interests you have and the field of work you choose.

None of us sees the world totally and objectively. We would be on sensory overload were we to see everything around us. These two dichotomies of personality, which govern our mental activity, help define the lens with which we view the world and come to conclusions about what we see. If others see the world from a totally different perspective, it stands to reason each will have trouble being heard, understood and valued by those whose methods of processing information are opposite. Each of us has had the experience of explaining something over and over only to be met with blank eyes and a lack of comprehension. But, remember, the reverse is also true. We may not hear or understand messages from people whose preferences are different from our own. There is no good and bad; it just is.

Sensing and Intuition

This dichotomy examines how you take in information. Sensing types take in information through the five senses. When they take information in through their senses, they receive it in small sensory bytes. Information is stored in their brains in the same way, in small sensory bytes of information, very much like a computer. When a Sensing type needs a piece of information, it can be accessed easily and most often accurately. Therefore, Sensing types are very good at facts and details. They speak in specifics and think in specifics. A Sensing type is the person you want doing your income taxes, keeping your investments straight and cleaning your house. Attention to detail is the name of the game.

So, do you enjoy keeping files and records in order? Does it come naturally to keep your house quite neat and tidy, with shoes lined up in the closet? Sensing types are concrete and reality-based. They abhor generalizing and talking about vague possibilities. Are you practical, realistic and down-to-earth? Do you need the specifics of a project before you can approve of its implementation? Do you live in the moment, referring to past experiences to guide your decisions? Do you look at a forest with an awareness of the varieties of trees composing it? When you enter a room for the first time, are you aware of the colors, placement of furniture and dimensions of the room? Sensing types learn and work sequentially. They work item by item through an agenda. They learn a concept step by step until they have assembled the whole concept. Does memorization of isolated facts such as dates and places come easily? Do you take most things you hear literally rather than metaphorically? Do you give accurate and detailed directions and instructions? Do you consider yourself practical and sensible? Do you get frustrated when some people jump to the bottom line before you are finished telling the whole story? If you respond positively to most of these questions, you are likely a Sensing (S) type. Sensing people will recognize most of the following descriptors in themselves:

- Detail oriented
- Practical
- Realistic
- Down to earth
- Concrete thinking
- Specific, precise, exact
- Generally neat and tidy
- Accurate
- Lives in the present
- Stays with the status quo
- Sensible
- Prefers routine
- Relies on experience
- Direct

Intuitive types do not rely on their senses to take in information. They are not quite certain how information comes in, but are pretty sure it is not through the senses. They are more likely to use a sixth sense or intuitive powers. They are more likely to simply absorb the general context of a given situation than see the specifics of it. They think in terms of the overall big picture rather than the details that comprise it. They will see the forest and have no idea what types of trees grow there. Intuitive types are future oriented and always thinking in terms of what could be, possibilities, and how things can be changed for the better. Sometimes change is preferred just for the sake of change; variety is desirable. These are imaginative, innovative and creative people, often unconcerned with practicality.

Do you talk metaphorically or figuratively? Do you need a lot of variety in your work? Would you rather design a project than carry out its myriad details? Would you rather restructure the organization of your entire company than balance its books? Did you have trouble memorizing the dates, names and places for the weekly history test? Did you ever really memorize *all* your multiplication tables, being able to recite them rapidly? Do you hate, loathe and despise filling out forms, reading insurance papers, deciphering contracts, trying to comprehend what the IRS wants? Do you find you are unable to spend longer than two hours memorizing for a test, or some other detail work, without screaming or pulling out your hair? Do you seem to collect piles of papers all over your house and office? Is your housekeeping less than stellar? Do you have trouble remembering how long ago certain events happened, such as changing the oil in your car or the death of someone significant? Do you find the world of imagination and possibilities far more fascinating than reality? Are you captivated by complex concepts and new ways of looking at old ideas? Does the prospect of brainstorming with a group of creative people excite you? Do you dislike repetitive tasks and routine? In conversation, do you find yourself going off on tangents easily? Do you give poor directions, often finding you do not know even the names of significant streets? If you answer in the affirmative to most of these questions, you are most likely an Intuitive (N) type. Intuitive types generally recognize the following descriptors in themselves:

- Big-picture overview
- Creative
- Innovative
- Entertains possibilities
- Talks in generalities
- Thinks in terms of concepts and theories
- Can get carried away with lofty ideas
- Future oriented
- Enjoys change for change sake
- Speaks in metaphor, symbolism and imagery
- Prefers variety to routine
- Idealistic
- Imaginative
- Insightful
- Engages in abstract or theoretical thinking

Again, there is an imbalance in the population as a whole. Approximately 70 to 75 percent of the population is Sensing and only 25 to 30 percent Intuitive. Generally, this favors the Sensing child growing up. A natural inclination to be detail oriented is accepted and reinforced by the culture. This can be difficult on the Intuitive child. An Intuitive child is likely to have at least one Sensing parent. The Sensing parent is usually impatient with the Intuitive's cluttered room and proclivity to daydream.

Jodie's story. Jodie, an Intuitive, grew up with two Sensing parents. Her room was never neat enough. When, as a small child, she was sent to clean it, Jodie saw that the room was messy but was unable to focus enough to know where to begin. Periodically, her parents lost patience and took matters into their own hands, throwing away much of the clutter. Some of these things were of great importance to Jodie. One item that was discarded was her favorite stuffed animal. Nearly fifty years later, Jodie can still remember the emotional pain associated with that incident.

School is another challenge for the Intuitive child. Elementary and high schools are typically designed by, administered by and taught by Sensing types. Adult Intuitive types who think they would like to teach

generally do not last long in the highly Sensing system and leave. The student Intuitive child does not have that option and so must adjust. In the beginning, the Intuitive child feels as if she is on a different planet. The learning style of Sensing and Intuitive types is totally different. If most elementary and high school teachers are Sensing, it is not difficult to figure out which style of teaching will prevail in the average classroom. The Sensing teacher gives information in small, sensory bytes that build the whole concept. The Sensing learning process is like building a structure. Start with a good foundation and add a floor only after the previous one is solid. If you continue in this manner, eventually the Sensing learner understands and owns the concept. The Intuitive type does not learn this way. The Intuitive needs to be given an over-all picture or framework before being given the details. This is like looking at the cover to the jigsaw puzzle before trying to assemble it. Without that picture or overall framework, the small pieces of information the teacher is delivering are only so many isolated, disjointed, meaningless pieces of a puzzle. Until the teacher reaches the end of the lesson and the concept is presented as a whole, the Intuitive has to store all these isolated facts. When the Intuitive child has problems juggling this system of learning, loses some of the details or gets some facts out of order, that child may be labeled learning disabled. Or, if the Intuitive child becomes bored and finds other things to do, that child may be labeled a behavior problem.

Memorizing isolated pieces of information is also a challenge for the Intuitive student. Many have a problem with spelling which is simply memorizing the order of letters in a word. Most will admit they never were able to hold on to all the isolated facts in the multiplication tables. To this day, don't ask me, "Quick, what is 9 x 7?" On the positive side for the school-age Intuitive types, they are generally very good at reading because they see the whole word and not the isolated letters in the word. Intuitive types instinctively look at the parts, see the relationship between those parts and are able to picture the whole. Sometimes they can

A Sensing type may begin giving a detailed account of a project to an Intuitive only to have the Intuitive jump immediately to the concluding concept. Sensing types find this habit of Intuitives very frustrating. Intuitives find that most Sensing types will want to go ahead and present the entire detailed explanation anyway . . .

accomplish this when very little information is presented. Intuitive types do not need a lot of information to get the big picture. In fact, they get bored with long, detailed stories and continually urge the speaker to get to the bottom line. A Sensing type may begin giving a detailed account of a project to an Intuitive only to have the Intuitive jump immediately to the concluding concept. Sensing types find this habit of Intuitives very frustrating. Intuitives find that most Sensing types will want to go ahead and present the entire detailed explanation anyway, even after the Intuitive has demonstrated a grasp of that concept. The Intuitive finds this Sensing need to proceed with a lengthy description equally frustrating.

In the classroom, creativity, the home base of the Intuitive child, is generally confined to art classes. Yet, even in that setting, there are parameters. There are generally specific directions, projects and holiday-related decorations to be completed. What happens if the child creates a black Valentine card? What happens if the Intuitive child would prefer to create an abstract drawing instead of making a Valentine card at all? Daydreaming, leaving a lesson to investigate something more interesting and asking "why" are generally not encouraged. Intuitive children are often at a disadvantage in the average classroom.

Intuitive children are bound to receive negative messages about themselves when they have problems comprehending in a Sensing environment. Without some understanding of this situation, these negative messages are reinforced throughout adulthood. I am constantly faced with forms to fill out for which I am only confident in the accuracy of my name, address and social security number (and sometimes I am not sure

about the social security number). The rest of the questions seem to be written in another language. I can recognize the individual words, but often they do not make sense when they are put together. If I did not understand that I am Intuitive, I could easily conclude that my brain is not operating properly, and I would not be alone in that conclusion. It is easy for details "in the fine print" to get overlooked by Intuitive types. They tend to quickly skim-read the text to get the big picture. There is no big picture when it comes to dealing with the IRS or an insurance company.

If Intuitive types have trouble in elementary and high school, the situation is reversed in college where the emphasis is on concepts, abstracts and theories. The Intuitive student begins to feel more comfortable while the Sensing student is often more challenged. The teaching style is quite different because college and university faculties generally are staffed with more Intuitive types than Sensing types. However, long before college age, the child has formed her views of herself and her abilities and therefore Intuitive types are more likely to receive wounding messages in the school environment than Sensing types.

Many sources, including Isabel Myers, suggest that the difference between Sensing and Intuitive types is the biggest barrier to communication. That is because Sensing and Intuitive types have different worldviews. The Sensing type sees the trees and the Intuitive sees the forest. Keeping accurate records and neatly filing receipts is important to the Sensing spouse. The Intuitive spouse throws these things in a drawer or shoe box and prays to God there will never be a need for them. The Intuitive sees the Sensing type as obsessive-compulsive and consumed with details. The Sensing type may wonder how the Intuitive type cannot see something that is "as clear as the nose on your face." The Sensing type sees the Intuitive as irresponsible, head-in-the-clouds and out of touch with the real world. Both responses to the opposite type are simply misperceptions and misunderstandings. The hope, in the best of all possible worlds, would be that these two types recognize the gifts of the opposite type and bring their differing gifts together to complement each other.

Mary's story. We met Mary in chapter 1. A forty-two-year-old Sensing type, Mary is married to an Intuitive. Mary and her husband are also in business together. He is a lawyer and she manages the financial records and files. Although Mary is extremely competent and comfortable in such a detail-saturated position, she came to me convinced she was totally off base in asking her husband for receipts and substantiating tax documents. As an Intuitive, those were the furthest things from his mind. Her constant demand for the data she needed to do her job came up against his disregard for details. At home, this difference in personality continued to cause stress. She tried to keep the house neat and orderly. He did not subscribe to her level of tidiness. Mary was totally frustrated. She saw her roles both at work and at home as very detail oriented and although she was capable of handling all those details, she felt her husband's lack of cooperation interfered with the completion of her duties. This presented a communication problem so large that it threatened the marriage. Because she was lacking self-confidence and had trouble believing in her own abilities, Mary readily accepted the blame for the impasse. She was convinced she was stupid. So, although as a Sensing type Mary was a member of the majority group of the population, in her environment she was convinced there was something wrong with her for her attention to detail.

Remember, this dichotomy is about how information is taken in. It says nothing about intelligence, competence or character. Intuitive types may be a puzzlement to Sensing types and vice-versa but there is no right or wrong here. Further, there is definitely no

way to convert someone—spouse, child or co-worker—to your method of gathering information, no matter how hard you try. Simply be very aware that when a Sensing type and an Intuitive type view the same situation, they are perceiving information from completely different perspectives.

Polly's story. Polly, an Intuitive type, was in charge of marketing for the organization for which she worked. She reported to a Sensing supervisor. Polly often presented him with innovative marketing concepts with the intention of brainstorming and expanding on her ideas. Her boss, being very concrete, specific and detail oriented, would refuse to even consider her ideas unless she came with a typed marketing proposal from which they could work, line-by-line, item-by-item. The very thought of such preparation for each of her many innovative ideas exhausted and frustrated Polly. She found herself less enthusiastic about her work and with feelings of resentment towards her boss. He felt he was being a responsible administrator and was teaching Polly the proper procedures for presenting a new concept.

It is no wonder that this dimension of personality is often pinpointed as causing the most problems in communication. With knowledge and understanding, however, both types can bring their differing perspectives to the situation to develop a comprehensive and effective method of problem solving.

Can you identify some specific negative messages you have received for how you take in information and the sources of those messages?

If you find yourself in the minority group in either of these first two dichotomies (Introvert or Intuitive), take special note of how that affected you and how it continues to affect you. If you find yourself in *both* minority groups, Introvert *and* Intuitive, be aware that that puts you in a very small segment of the population (11 percent). Growing up, you probably did not know many people like you. You may still have trouble feeling understood and finding people with whom to share your thoughts. You may have always felt you were different and you probably have not considered that difference a positive quality. Learning more about yourself can help to change that opinion.

Thinking and Feeling

This dichotomy of personality describes how you make a decision. Thinking types base decisions on logical analysis of the pertinent criteria. The correct decision will make sense and be justified by a preponderance of supporting data. Thinking types do not like to place value judgments on information and as a result are not inclined to take feedback personally. Thinking types can work in an environment where there is disharmony. They devote their energies to doing their work well for which they do not expect praise. Effusive appreciation makes them uncomfortable and they may wonder what they are "being set up for." Thinking types are truth-based and this can get them in trouble. If they are asked, "How do you like my new hair style?" they are likely to give an honest answer. Because Thinking types seek objectivity, they don't always understand how directness can hurt the feelings of others. Thinking types often have an objective standard of truth by which they live their lives. It might be The Golden Rule, The Ten Commandments, The Twelve Steps or something similarly specific. They use these guidelines to evaluate how they are living their lives and make any necessary adjustments accordingly.

Do you think people generally take things too personally? Can you stay in an unhappy work situation by staying emotionally detached and uninvolved? Have you been accused of being tough, heartless or cold? Do you often make a decision by drawing a line down the center of a sheet of paper and listing the pros and cons? Is clarity and precision important to you? Are facts more important than feelings? Do you feel compelled to point out the flaws in other people's illogical thinking? Do you enjoy discussing ethics and arguing a point as an intellectual exercise? Do you generally make difficult decisions logically and without personal judgment? Thinking (T) types will probably recognize the following descriptors in themselves:

- Objective
- Logical
- Rational
- Analytical
- Principled
- Firm
- Values fairness and justice
- Actions show love
- Critical
- Concise
- Task oriented

Feeling types are personal. They base their decisions on how that decision will affect them and the people they care about. They employ personal values in the decision-making process. These values can change and evolve with time and the situation. They are comfortable with the concept of situational ethics. Feeling types require harmony in the workplace. If harmony is lacking, it is only a matter of time before they have trouble going to work in the morning and begin thinking about changing jobs. At work, no matter how good a job looks to them, if it does not please the boss, client or customer, the Feeling type will change it. Pleasing is the more important consideration. Feeling types are easily subject to co-dependence and putting others' needs and comfort before their own. They willingly sacrifice for those they care about. Feeling types can empathize and understand how it would feel to be in the other person's position. Because of this, they are more concerned with tact than with truth. They never want to hurt someone's feelings. If the truth might hurt, they will modify it somewhat.

Do people accuse you of taking things too personally? Could you be satisfied with less pay in an harmonious work environment that was overwhelmingly appreciative of your services? Do you tell people they look good even when they do not so as to avoid hurt feelings? Have you been accused of not using your head or of thinking with your heart? Do you list the pros and cons only to disregard them and go with your feelings? Do you often defy logic and just go with your heart? Do people classify you as sensitive and easily hurt? Do you agree with others for the sake of harmony? In working through conflict, do you look for areas of agreement to build upon? Do you try hard not to offend people? Is emotional intimacy important to you? Those who are Feeling (F) types will accept most of the following descriptors:

* Subjective
* Embraces personal values rather than external values
* Sympathetic and empathetic
* Needs appreciation
* Values harmony
* Understanding and considerate
* Accommodating
* Outwardly affectionate
* Gentle
* Pleasing
* Complimentary
* Relational
* People oriented

Culture complicates this decision-making dichotomy even more than the others: more than half of Thinking types are male and three-fourths of Feeling types are female. From this, we derive our cultural stereotypes of what a male and a female "should" be like. A cursory examination of what is presented in the media will reveal how the culture expects a woman to look and act. She should be pretty, soft, thin, emotional, illogical and concerned with superficial things such as a blemish or the texture of her hair. The central focus of her life is attracting a male. There are literally countless other examples of gender stereotyping. There are corresponding expectations for a male. He needs to be consumed by sports, be physically strong, logical, hard driving without a show of emotions, prone to violence and take a no-nonsense approach to any situation. Again, there are countless examples of the cultural stereotyping in our patriarchal society. Schools, government, religions and social organizations all contribute to the care and feeding of these stereotypes. The women's movement has done a lot to free both women and men from being categorized in this manner but there is still a long way to go. A wider understanding of this dimension of personality and its contribution to stereotyping would help free people to be themselves.

What happens when you do not fit into the stereo-type? What about the one-fourth of Thinking types who are female? When they attend a movie, it is unlikely that the heroine is a Thinking type. If a Thinking female appears, she is usually the one to walk calmly into a room and shoot someone between the eyes—the dark female that defies understanding in our culture. When the Feeling types who are male attend the movies, they see *Rambo,* the *Terminator* and similar fare. What does that tell them about themselves when the behaviors attributed to men are so foreign to them? Many Feeling males are blessed with bodies suited to athletics and so they immerse themselves in sports at an early age in order to fit in and win acceptance. Over and over, these men have told me that they would have preferred other activities, particularly the Intuitive Feeling (NF) males. However, peer acceptance is paramount when you are a teenager. There is no question that Thinking females and Feeling males grow up wondering what is wrong with them because they measure themselves against a cultural stereotype that shows they are somehow lacking. In the extreme, this may lead to gender identity problems or, at the least, confusion about gender roles.

If you, like I, were the only Feeling type in your family of origin (or the only Thinking type), you can be sure that you incorporated some negative messages about your preference in this dichotomy. I am certain you can compose a credible list. If nothing else, Feeling types in a Thinking environment are inadvertently wounded because Thinking types are not aware of the sensitivity of the Feeling types. When a Feeling type expresses emotional pain, the follow-up message is, "You take things too personally!" which places the cause of her pain on the Feeling person.

When a Thinking type grows up in an environment that expects Feeling, it makes the Thinking type question her own thought processes. This is especially true of a Thinking girl being raised by a Feeling mom who puts unspoken expectations on the girl to think as mom does and as the culture expects. This was the case with my own daughter. It was not until she was college age that we determined her to be a Thinking type. This

It is important to be clear that both Thinking and Feeling types have feelings (emotions). The Feeling type is more likely to show these feelings. The Thinking type, particularly the Introverted Thinking type, is more likely to hold them inside.

knowledge profoundly changed her life, her career, the way she thought about herself and the way I treated and communicated with her.

In a patriarchal culture, schools encourage a Thinking orientation, as do most religions and businesses. Feeling women have a difficult time in these environments unless they learn to adjust their orientation and teach themselves to work from a perspective that does not come naturally for them.

Thinking women also have a challenge because they are presumed to be Feeling types by virtue of their gender and have to prove they can speak the same language as the Thinking males with whom they associate. But they still lose because they are then accused of being cold, controlling and ways that are even less pleasantly described. Think of women in our political history such as Hillary Clinton and Janet Reno who get more negative press for their personality types than for anything they do. In an attempt to treat these women in accordance with the stereotype, the press directs more coverage to these two women's hairstyles than their political contributions. Male political figures do not receive attention for hairstyle because attention to hairstyle does not fit the male stereotype.

It is important to be clear that both Thinking and Feeling types have feelings (emotions). The Feeling type is more likely to show these feelings. The Thinking type, particularly the Introverted Thinking type, is more likely to hold them inside. Our culture does not reward men who show their feelings. Remember Edmund Muskie and Tom Eagleton? Similarly, both Thinking and Feeling types "think" using their cognitive abilities. The definitive feature of this dichotomy of personality is that it is the basis of making a decision. Here is an example:

Consider a stereotypical married couple, Thinking male and Feeling female, as they try to decide which house to buy. The Thinking male will consider the best value for the money, the cost per square foot, the tax district, the school district, the re-sale potential, the investment potential and expected rate of appreciation, the physical placement in the neighborhood and the practicality of the layout of the rooms. The Feeling female may consider all of these factors, but will come to a decision on the basis of how she feels about the house. Is it warm, cozy and inviting? Can she picture having Christmas in the living room? Does it make her feel good to be in the house? What is the view out the kitchen window? It is for these Feeling types that realtors suggest baking cookies or bread when showing your house to prospective buyers. When the Feeling wife conveys her feelings to her logical Thinking husband, he puts those on the pros side of the page with no more weight than the tax rate. For the Feeling type, her feeling assessments outweigh all the logic in the universe. She maintains it does not matter if they have purchased the best possible real estate investment on the market if she is not happy living there. This is when the argument generally begins. She is accused of not using her head. He is accused of being thoughtless, uncaring and cold. Without an understanding of this part of personality, people can get hurt!

Values, judgments and prejudices are rampant around this dimension of personality. Having an awareness of it, particularly as it is associated with gender, enhances communication and interpersonal relationships.

Judging and Perceiving

The first thing to address with this dichotomy is that Judging does not mean judgmental. It means decisiveness: Looking at information, judging that information and making a decision based on your evaluation. Neither does Perceiving signify being perceptive. Perceiving merely refers to taking in information. This dichotomy points to whether you are oriented to taking in information (Perceiving) or whether you prefer to move quickly to making a decision (Judging).

Judging types are decisive, structured and goal oriented. They need an efficient plan, come to conclusions easily and need closure. Do you have a sense of urgency when there are things that need to be done? Does work come before play? Do you take deadlines very seriously and expect the same of others? Have you been accused of being rigid, inflexible or compulsive? Do you keep a to-do list and work from it? Have you ever added things to your to-do list that you have already done just to get the satisfaction of scratching them off? Do you attack your vacation with a complete itinerary that may include reservations, confirmation numbers and planned activities? Do you think of yourself as task oriented? Do you like to know in advance what the plans are for a social engagement? Are you punctual, perhaps to the point of arriving early? If this style of living sounds comfortable and familiar, you are probably a Judging (J) type. Judging types will accept most of the following descriptors:

- Decisive
- Orderly
- Structured
- Needs closure
- Timely
- Planned
- Sense of urgency
- Organized
- Needs control
- Goal oriented

Perceiving types like to play it by ear and put off decisions as long as possible. Do you hate schedules and structure? Does locking into social engagements that are more than a week away go against your natural inclination? Do you tend to wait until the last minute to complete reports and assignments? Are you one of the people driving to the post office at 11:59 p.m. April 15th? Is your idea of a great vacation throwing your

things in the back seat of the car and heading out with the intention to stop when you are tired, eat when you are hungry and see what you feel like seeing at the time? Do you habitually run late? Do you adapt to changes easily? Do you think the word *deadline* should be outlawed? Are you accused of procrastinating? Do you consider yourself flexible only to find other people call you indecisive? Do you like to include play with your work? Do you keep a daily to-do list and then forget to refer to it? If you see yourself in this description, you are probably a Perceiving (P) type. Perceiving types can identify with most of the following descriptors:

- Flexible
- Adaptable
- Open
- Wait and see
- Likes options
- Spontaneous
- Exploring
- Play it by ear

Although Judging types are about 55 percent of the population and Perceiving types are about 45 percent, the culture in the United States overwhelmingly values Judging. The culture demands timeliness, structure and decisiveness. Therefore, even though Perceiving types make up nearly half the population, they still receive negative messages because of being measured against cultural standards.

Even though Judging and Perceiving types have a tendency to annoy one another, the differences are not insurmountable. With an understanding of this part of personality, you will be less likely to take the behaviors that are associated with this trait as unacceptable or annoying. You will also be less likely to see those behaviors as indicative of a serious character flaw on the part of the other.

By choosing one designation from each of the four dichotomies (figure 3-1, page 31), you have a four-letter personality identifier, or type formula, such as ESTJ (Extraverted, Sensing, Thinking and Judging) or INFP (Introverted, Intuitive, Feeling and Perceiving). There are sixteen different possible combinations of letters that designate these preferences (figure 3-2).

Sixteen Personality Type Formulas

ISTJ	ISFJ	INFJ	INTJ
ISTP	ISFP	INFP	INTP
ESTP	ESFP	ENFP	ENTP
ESTJ	ESFJ	ENFJ	ENTJ

Figure 3-2

Sometimes people resist an MBTI designation feeling that it somehow boxes them in, or limits them. In actuality, the reverse is true. Knowing and understanding your MBTI type formula is very freeing. It gives you permission on an emotional level to be who you were designed to be without need to conform to any social or cultural standard which *does* box you in. Reading about your MBTI type can encourage you to explore aspects of yourself you have been denying or minimizing. This knowledge can help you to trust qualities such as Intuition and Feeling that do not receive the cultural stamp of approval.

Culturally, the ESTJ male and ESFJ female receive the most positive reinforcement for their innate personalities. The INFP male and INTP female probably receive the most negative cultural messages for who they are. A short description of each personality type is provided in figure 3-3 on pages 44 through 47. For a more in-depth understanding of who you are, consult any of the books listed at the end of the chapter. As you begin your study of type, *do not* feel compelled to read these books cover-to-cover. (This is a special danger to Judging types who need to complete what they start.) Read only the sections that pertain to your personality type. It is not necessary to try to learn sixteen different personalities and try to keep them straight. For now, the purpose is self-understanding. When you are comfortable with knowing, understanding and accepting yourself, you may want to read about someone close to you such as a spouse, parent or child.

TEMPERAMENT TYPES

Keirsey and Bates in their renowned work, *Please Understand Me,* divide the sixteen types into four categories, or temperament types. David Keirsey later expounded on this information in *Please Understand Me II.* These four temperament types (SP, SJ, NT and NF) act as four larger categories containing the sixteen personality types outlined in figure 3-3. The four temperaments display a pattern of descriptors that sets each temperament group apart from the other three groups. Keirsey and Bates point out how these four temperament types have been recognized throughout the ages, apart from the MBTI. You can double check your self-assessment process in determining your four-letter MBTI type formula by seeing if you relate to the descriptors associated with your temperament category.

Although you may have had no trouble typing yourself from the information provided above, it is usually difficult to type others by reading over the sixteen different types. It is far easier to discern the MBTI type of another by beginning with the basic two-letter temperament type because you have only a choice of four rather than a choice of sixteen. Understanding personality type is made easier by grouping the sixteen types into the four categories of temperaments because the four temperament types have very distinct profiles.

The SP Temperament (Sensing and Perceiving)

This group is comprised of those whose type formula contains Sensing and Perceiving.

Includes: ISTP, ISFP, ESTP, ESFP

These are fun-loving, resourceful people who enjoy life and would prefer to never entirely grow up and be serious. The ESFP and ESTP types are especially Peter Pan-like. SP types are charming and cheerful. They are optimistic free spirits and action oriented. They live in the moment and like their fun to have an element of risk attached to it, such as white-water rafting, sky-

Continued on page 48

Sixteen Myers-Briggs Personality Types

ISTJ

Analytical, critical, logical	Goal oriented	Cautious
Committed, loyal	Hierarchical	Practical, realistic
Concrete	Independent	Precise
Conservative	Strong opinions	Quiet, reserved, private
Consistent	Neat	Responsible
Decisive	Needs security and stability	Rules and regulations
Detail oriented, observant	Needs to feel useful	Serious
Dutiful, dependable, dedicated	Obedient	Strong work ethic
Efficient	Objective	Timely
Frugal, good investor	Organized, structured	Traditional

ISTP

Accurate	Enjoys sports	Opportunistic
Action oriented, adventuresome	Fearless, free spirit	Practical, pragmatic, realistic
Adaptable	Good in crisis	Quiet, reserved
Artisan, technical	Hands-on learning	Skilled with weapons, warrior
Concrete, factual	Highly observant	Sparse verbal communication
Dislikes structure, schedules, routine	Impulsive	Success driven
Easily bored	Independent	Troubleshooter
Efficient	Logical, analytical	

ESTP

Action oriented	Enjoys material possessions	Objective, open minded, tolerant
Adaptable	Enjoys crisis; troubleshooter	Persuasive, charming
Assertive	Entertaining	Realistic, pragmatic, resourceful
Athletic	Enthusiastic, energetic	Results oriented
Competitive	Fearless, risk taker	Short attention span, sometimes
Conciliator	Free spirit, independent	labeled learning disabled
Concrete	Good with tools	Social, friendly
Curious	Hates routine	Spontaneous
Efficient	Ignores authority, procedures, rules	

ESTJ

Able to take charge	Dutiful, responsible, fair	Objective
Administrator	Efficient, timely	Strong opinions
Analytical, critical	Goal oriented	Practical, realistic
Assertive	Gregarious	Respects authority, hierarchy
Common sense	Hardworking	Sacrificing, protective
Concrete, literal	Impersonal, tough, impatient	Scheduled, structured, rigid
Consistent	Logical	Tradition and ritual
Decisive	Loyal	
Detail oriented	Neat	

Figure 3-3

16 Myers-Briggs Personality Types

ISFJ

Accurate	Efficient	Patient
Cautious	Friendly, gentle, giving	Practical
Conforming, cooperative	Goal oriented	Quiet, introspective
Conservative, traditional	Loyal	Responsible, dutiful
Considerate, tactful	Meticulous	Sacrificing, protective
Consistent, dependable	Modest	Serious, stoic
Devoted to family	Needs stability/security	Sympathetic
Diligent	Obedient	Timely

ISFP

Accepting	Friendly	Needs excitement
Action oriented, impulsive	Gentle, sensitive	Optimistic
Adaptable	Good in crisis	Private, quiet
Artisan, creative, skilled	Harmonious	Protective
Caring, generous, sympathetic	Loyal, trusting	Relational
Concrete, practical	Modest	Sensual
Easygoing	Natural inclination towards music,	Service oriented
Enjoys leisure	dance, athletics	Strong values
Free spirit	Nature oriented	

ESFP

Accepting	Friendly, social	Needs harmony
Action oriented, adventurous	Fun loving, entertaining	Nonconforming
Charming, witty, performer	Generous	Often overextended
Concrete, factual	Good in crisis	Optimistic
Cooperative	Hates routine	Practical, realistic, common sense
Easygoing	Helpful, supportive, caring	Relational, sensitive, sympathetic
Energetic, enthusiastic	Impulsive	Sensual
Flexible	Joie de vivre	Trusting

ESFJ

Able to take charge	Gracious, hospitable, congenial	Outgoing
Active	Hardworking but fun loving	Patient, persevering
Concrete thinking	Harmonious	People oriented, relational
Controlling, strict, critical	Helpful, giving	Practical, realistic
Cooperative	Loyal	Responsible
Decisive	Most sympathetic	Scheduled, structured
Detail oriented, factual	Needs to belong, status	Sensitive, tactful
Frugal	Obedient	Traditional, conforming
Goal oriented	Organized, efficient, neat	

Figure 3-3

16 Myers-Briggs Personality Types

INFJ

Abhors violence, hostility
Accepting
Achiever
Affirming
Artistic, creative
Caring, compassionate, gentle
Complicated, complex
Devoted
Diligent

Eloquent
Empathic
Facilitator, motivator
Imagery, symbolism, imagination
Listener
Mystical, visionary
Organized
Perfectionist
Perseverance is intense

Premonitions, ESP, psychic phenomenon
Private, quiet
Rich inner life, ideals
Search for knowledge; intellectual
Sensitive and vulnerable
Understands people and how they work
Work must be meaningful and people
    oriented

INFP

Accepting, affirming
Adaptable
Calm, gentle
Dedicated idealist, passionate
Caring, compassionate
Compliant, cooperative
Creative
Devoted, loyal
Harmonious

Symbolism important
Empathetic, relational
Facilitator
Eloquent
Gracious, warm
Idealist
Independent
Inspirational, persuasive

Integrity
Intense, serious, determined
Perfectionist
Private, quiet, reserved
Rich inner life
Nonstructured
Service oriented
Visionary

ENFP

Able to improvise, brainstorm
Accepting, affirming
Charismatic, charming
Childlike, curious
Creative, artistic
Dramatic
Energetic, adventuresome
Enthusiastic, fun loving
Friendly, gregarious, helpful

Genuine, integrity
Good communicator
Harmonious
Idealist; values are important
Independent
Ingenious, innovative, imaginative
Insightful, perceptive, psychic
Inspiring, persuasive, passionate
Intensely relational

Multifaceted
Nonconformist
Nonstructured
Optimistic
Spontaneous, impulsive
Successful
Sympathetic

ENFJ

Affirming
Caring, compassionate
Charismatic, charming, social
Committed, persevering
Cooperative, helpful
Creative
Diplomatic, eloquent, motivational
Empathetic, sensitive
Entertaining

Enthusiastic
Facilitator
Harmonious
Idealist
Imaginative, visionary
Insightful
Inspiring, persuasive
Leader
Loyal

Organized, structured
Positive
Problem solver
Relational
Responsible
Serving
Value oriented

Figure 3-3

16 Myers-Briggs Personality Types

INTJ

Abstract thinking
Administrator
Analyzes, critical, logical
Avoids redundancy, terse
Capable, competent, values
   knowledge
Confronts easily
Conscientious, dedicated
Determined, disciplined

Dry humor, sarcastic
Enjoys playing with language
Fascinated by systems and theories
Firm
Frugal
High standards
Improves everything, visionary
Ingenious, inventive, creative
Insightful, introspective

Most independent
Not outwardly affectionate or emotional
Not very social, aloof
Orderly, organized
Pragmatic
Private, reserved
Self-reliant
Understands, controls and predicts
   realities

INTP

Abstract thinker; strategic thinker
Acquisition of knowledge
Adaptable
Analyzes; critical, logical, rational
Autonomous
Aware of contradictions,
   inconsistencies
Competent, competitive
Concerned with universal truth
Detached, impersonal

Difficulty with emotions
Easily engrossed
Enjoys problem solving, insightful
Enjoys theories, systems, models,
   research
Indifferent to authority
Ingenious, visionary, imaginative
Intellectually profound
Likes to understand and manipulate
   reality

Nonstructured
Open to new information
Private, quiet, reserved
Reluctant to state the obvious
Rich inner world
Sees connections
Terse
Unconventional

ENTP

Action oriented, adventurous
Adaptable, versatile
Administrative; entrepreneur
Alert to possibilities; theoretical
Analytical, logical
Devil's advocate
Autonomous
Competitive
Complex, conceptual thinking

Creative ideas, imaginative
Effervescent, enthusiastic, gregarious
Enjoys debate
Humorous
Impersonal
Improves the system
Improvises, ingenious
Impulsive
Loves learning, competency

Maximizes opportunities
Motivator
Nonconforming
Objective, open
Optimistic
Problem solver, strategist
Success driven, opportunist
Values change, variety

ENTJ

Administrator, leader
Analytical, critical, logical, rational
Assertive, enjoys debate
Competent, competitive
Confident
Decisive
Designs systems, innovative,
   strategic thinking
Efficient

Energetic
Fair
Good communicator
Gregarious
Hardworking
High standards, firm
Impatient
Impersonal, objective
Independent

Intellectual, values education
Needs variety
Organized, scheduled, disciplined
Problem solver
Success driven
Theoretical
Visionary

Figure 3-3

diving, hang-gliding or anything that increases the adrenaline flow. They often have trouble looking ahead to the consequences of their actions.

Sensing Perceiving types have a difficult time in the standard classroom setting. They learn hands-on; they dislike practice; they are action oriented; and they are impulsive. None of these qualities are welcome in the standard classroom. Unfortunately, most SP types barely survive formal education. Many drop out. Often, they are recommended to a technical school, which is good for them in one way because it allows them hands-on learning with reduced structure. However, the messages they receive are that they are not smart enough to make it in a "regular" school and that they are being sent to a technical school to provide them with a trade to keep them off welfare. Few SP children get through school without significant emotional damage. I have not met many who have not internalized their treatment by the educational system to mean there was something wrong with them. For a personal account, read about Lyla and Ray in chapter 6.

Members of this group are often musical or artistic. Many enjoy performing; however, they do not enjoy practicing. Precise handwork comes natural to an SP and it is particularly enjoyable if it is combined with action. Sensing Perceiving types are attracted to careers that are crisis oriented. Such careers provide action, hands-on work and allow the SP to move quickly on to the next adventure. They are often found in careers such as firefighting, emergency room nursing, ambulance driving and troubleshooting for a corporation.

Although this group is about 27 percent of the population, they have little impact on our culture. They are subject to many negative cultural messages, especially the SP women who find few career outlets for their temperament inclinations.

The SJ Temperament
(Sensing and Judging)

This group is comprised of those whose type formula contains Sensing and Judging.

Includes: ISTJ, ISFJ, ESTJ, ESFJ.

This group is about 47 percent of the population.

Unlike the SP group, this group has an enormous impact on our culture. It is the SJ types who design and run the government, schools, religions, most businesses and various social organizations. They trust and believe in these structured systems. Most cultural standards that society and individuals measure themselves against are SJ qualities. Sensing Judging types have a strong work ethic and a strong sense of duty and responsibility. They are hierarchical in their thinking and believe in working their way up the corporate ladder. They respect titles, credentials and social standing. They have high moral standards with many rules, regulations, procedures and "shoulds." Sensing Judging types uphold ceremony and tradition. We all eat turkey instead of lobster on Thanksgiving because of SJ traditions. We have the tradition-minded SJ people to thank that we even have Thanksgiving. The SJ types provide the structure of our communities on local, national and global levels. Sensing Judging types are rather black and white in their thinking, are thrifty and believe in saving for a rainy day. SJ types believe in traditional gender roles and see the family as the basic unit of society. There is a strong need to belong, to be useful and to feel safe and secure. Sensing Judging types find satisfying careers in structured, service-oriented areas such as schools, hospitals, businesses, government and other traditional institutions.

As little people, SJ children need a stable, safe environment. They feel most secure and comfortable in a traditional family environment and would prefer to spend their entire childhood in the same house with the same neighborhood friends. A sense of stability and security is increased if SJ children have routine and structure. If the family is broken, if there is employment instability and/or a lot of change and disruption, SJ children will sustain some degree of emotional damage.

When children go off to school for the first time, they move into an SJ environment. Elementary and high school teachers and administrators are overwhelmingly SJ. Many ESFJ types are particularly attracted to teaching and are very good at it. For SJ

Intuitive Thinking types are attracted to careers which utilize a systematic approach. They are often found in careers involving computers, science, architecture, advertising and other arenas where their considerable knowledge can be put to good use.

children, that is no problem; in fact, it is affirming and comfortable. For the other 53 percent of the population, there is an adjustment. Along with that adjustment comes an internalized message that there is something wrong with the non-SJ child. Educators and parents would be wise to be aware of type differences and celebrate those differences instead of trying to encourage conformation.

The NT Temperament (Intuition and Thinking)

This group is comprised of those whose type formula includes Intuition and Thinking.

Includes: INTJ, INTP, ENTP, ENTJ

The central theme of the NT temperament is smart, competent and capable. NT temperament types value these qualities above all else. You can think or say anything you like about NT types as long as you recognize their intelligence and competency. When meeting a person for the first time, the NT is liable to appear aloof. The NT feels it is most important to take a position of competency from the beginning so there will be no questions later. Furthermore, the NT evaluates each person encountered according to competency and therefore assumes everyone is evaluating the NT by the same criteria.

Intuitive Thinking types cannot accept an authority figure, such as boss, parent or teacher, who is not respected as intelligent and competent. When given the choice between a college instructor who is knowledgeable but tough and demanding or an instructor who is amiable and easy but less accomplished, the NT will go for the former. Intuitive Thinking types would rather work harder and risk a lower grade than study under someone who is less than brilliant.

Intuitive Thinking types are concerned with the

workings of the universe and are the biggest fans of *Star Trek*. They have a tendency to work at their play, practicing their recreational activities until they feel competent in them. You can find an NT hitting tennis balls against a wall, or practicing a golf swing, with the utmost seriousness. NT types are very competitive and can easily become hooked on computer games. They are interested in games of strategy where they can match their competence against man or machine. If you spend much time around NT types, you will notice a very dry sense of humor generously sprinkled with sarcasm.

Intuitive Thinking types are attracted to careers which utilize a systematic approach. They are often found in careers involving computers, science, architecture, advertising and other arenas where their considerable knowledge can be put to good use. The NT is on a life-long quest for knowledge. Colleges and universities have a large number of NT types on faculty because the NT enjoys working in an environment of continual learning and relishes being around other people with the same desire. Members of this group enjoy stretching their minds and playing mental gymnastics with complex concepts. They automatically question anything presented as a truth, wanting to know "why?" An NT can be in danger of studying life instead of living it.

Intuitive Thinking types are only about 10 percent of the population and can easily grow up feeling misunderstood, especially the female NT types. NT children are especially vulnerable to emotional wounding around their need to be seen as competent and smart. If they are subjected to verbal abuse such as being called stupid or retarded, they will have a lot of emotional work ahead of them to turn those messages around.

Danielle's story. Danielle, a forty-one-year-old ENTJ, was in therapy for more than two years before she would even entertain the idea that she possessed more than marginal intelligence. She assured me that in high school she was classified at the very lowest end of normal. She was not able to explain to my satisfaction how she managed to earn a master's degree in science and work in a scientific field with her limited intelligence. She had convinced herself that she had managed to fool a lot of people. With considerable emotional work on Danielle's part, she was able to see that her mother had installed a "stupid button" by continually questioning her intelligence. Some of the things she heard from her mother were:

- You're slow.
- You can't write.
- You're not competent.
- Are you college material??? We hope!
- You need help!!!!
- Are you normal?
- You're not like your sister.
- What's wrong with you?
- You procrastinate.

The rural school system she attended was unequipped to deal with her NT questioning mind and her Intuitive method of learning. Things were complicated even more by a vision problem and infected adenoids, which affected her hearing.

As an NT, the facet of self that was most important to Danielle was her need to feel intelligent and competent. Whether intentionally or unintentionally, influential people caused her to not only question her competency, but to completely accept that it did not exist. Consequently, Danielle reached adulthood with a complete lack of confidence in her own competency. Depending on her own abilities was "like stepping off into nothing."

The therapy that Danielle had received over the years addressed the fact that she was not an ugly duckling but it did not allow her to accept what it meant for her to be a swan. In order for Danielle to begin living her life fully, she had to accept her own intelligence and competency and begin to live out of it. That was one of the most difficult challenges of her recovery.

The NF Temperament (Intuition and Feeling)

This group is comprised of type formulas that are both Intuitive and Feeling.

Includes: INFJ, INFP, ENFP, ENFJ

The NF temperament types are just 16 percent of the population. Being in the minority is especially hard on the male NF types who would usually prefer writing poetry or music to the usual culturally acceptable male activities. Male NF temperament types often do their best to hide a very sensitive inner self from a society that is less than approving. By adulthood, most NF types, male and female alike, are convinced they have been dropped onto the wrong planet and the people around them are inclined to agree.

The theme of the NF life is: What's it all about? What is the meaning of life? The NF is on a life-long search for meaning all the while knowing and accepting that there is no answer. The search is what holds their interest. Intuitive Feeling types have a deep spirituality and they have trouble finding a church or religion through which to express it. Traditional religions often do not support their quest for meaning. They generally find that organized religions are too structured and SJ oriented to allow them full NF spiritual expression. Many of the hippies of the '60s were NF temperament types who felt confined by the culture and were looking for an alternative way of expressing their spirituality. At the time, John Lennon's music expressed that quest.

This group is the most empathetic. The Feeling function focuses them on people and the Intuition function allows them to truly understand and experience what another is experiencing. Often they are overwhelmed in a movie, identifying strongly with what is happening on screen. The impressions they take away from the movie are as strong as if they had experienced the events themselves.

Intuitive Feeling temperament types are highly relational. They have a deep need to connect with a

By knowing and understanding your MBTI type formula, you can begin to explore what it means to be a swan and prepare to move into expressing yourself to the full extent of your being.

significant other on a soul-to-soul level. Few people can meet them on such an intense level, much less sustain that intensity, and that leaves the NF searching for the romantic ideal.

The NF temperament is drawn to careers that can facilitate fulfilling human potential. They want to help others be all they can be. They are drawn to ministry, teaching and counseling. However, they encounter problems when they pursue these occupations in a structured environment such as a church, school or agency. They will often feel smothered and inhibited by rules, regulations, forms, structure and routine. Since this group is also extremely creative, they are drawn to careers that allow for artistic expression.

Because NF types are extremely sensitive, they are very vulnerable to emotional wounding as children. There need not be violence, verbal abuse or the like to wound an NF. Just the lack of the show of affection and affirmation can be wounding to the NF child. The NF is highly intuitive and can easily pick up all the covert messages and feelings in the family. This is heavy material for a small child who often takes responsibility for the family dynamic. In families where there is open conflict or severe abuse, the NF is emotionally devastated. The hypersensitive NF child is completely vulnerable to criticism, rejection and abandonment.

MBTI AND THE CORE SELF

By now, you probably have a good idea of your MBTI type formula or at least your temperament type. By reading about your type in some of the books listed at the end of this chapter, you can begin to become more comfortable with the person you were designed to be. You can let go of some unrealistic expectations and begin investigating gifts and talents you have not as yet fully explored. Many people follow this game plan: to discover who you are, first learn who everybody else is,

and you are what is left. Many people go through life with about that much understanding of themselves. By knowing and understanding your MBTI type formula, you can begin to explore what it means to be a swan and prepare to move into expressing yourself to the full extent of your being. Melody Beattie (author of *Codependent No More*), who made the term *co-dependent* a household word, joins many philosophers, theologians and psychologists in saying the key to life is knowing who we are.

Most importantly, when you read about your MBTI type, you will get a good picture of the Inner Child, that part of yourself that was put away very early in life. For whatever reason, the child you were could not develop to the full extent of her potential. For whatever reason, the child needed to live defended and not allow all of her Core Self to show to the outside world. In a review of her book, *An Affair to Remember*, Katharine Hepburn illustrated this concept when she wrote, "I'm going to put this piece of me in a little box and I'll never let anyone see it—not anyone" (*St. Louis Post Dispatch*, 11 July 1997, 5E). This intrinsic part of personality is so vital to our being yet so vulnerable that it must be protected at all costs.

Sometimes the idea of taking such a close look at yourself can be a bit daunting. Nelson Mandela, in his 1994 inaugural speech, said we don't fear our darkness, we fear our greatness. "It is our light, not our darkness that most frightens us." Perhaps you fear seeing what has been lost to you for many years. Perhaps there is a concern that you will be ridiculed or teased if you tried expressing gifts and talents not explored heretofore. If there is some hesitancy to learn more about your Core Self for any reason, make it your goal to keep working until you reach a place where you can accept and celebrate the miracle that is you.

EXERCISE

A PICTURE OF YOUR INNER CHILD

Nurture By Nature, an excellent book by Tieger and Barron-Tieger, provides descriptions of the sixteen MBTI personality types as children. *Please Understand Me* by Keirsey and Bates briefly describes the four temperament types as children. Other books on the MBTI make some reference to the MBTI types as children. Choose one of these references, prop up a picture of yourself as a child and read about that little person. Try to empathize with the child and how it felt to have that personality growing up in the environment of your childhood. What were that child's needs? To what extent were they met? Was the child validated for the person she was designed to be or did she need to learn to be someone different in order to receive acceptance and approval? What elements of the child's personality received the most negative messages? Finish this exercise by writing the child a letter, validating and affirming her for who she is.

REFERENCES AND SUGGESTED READING

Beattie, M. *Codependent No More.* New York: Harper/Hazelden, 1987. This is the first major work devoted to the recovery of the co-dependent. It is a highly acclaimed work and continues to be the handbook for recovering co-dependents. Melody Beattie has written other insightful books on recovery and spirituality. Many of her works are available on tape through any recovery bookstore.

Berens, L. V. *Understanding Yourself and Others: An Introduction to Temperament.* Huntington Beach CA: Telos Publications, 2000. An excellent guide to understanding temperament. Berens breaks down the worldview of each of the four temperaments into their components so comparisons can be made in order to better accept and understand differences and improve communication.

Card, C. *Discover the Power of Introversion.* Gladwyne PA: Type and Temperament Press, 1993. Comprising the minority of the population and without adequate recognition by the culture, Introverts are susceptible to early emotional wounding. This book is an exploration of the differences between Extra-version and Introversion written with the hope that the differences will be not only accepted but valued.

Cauley, L. B. *The Ugly Duckling: A Tale From Hans Christian Anderson.* San Diego CA: Harcourt Brace Jovanovich, 1979. A classic story retold by Cauley that is both delightful and insightful and one that is suitable for reflection by "children" of all ages. Spending a few minutes reading this Hans Christian Anderson story to your inner child might be both healing and affirming.

Hirsh, S. K. and J. Kummerow. *Life Types.* New York: Warner Books, 1989. A good description of the MBTI scales and the sixteen types; however there is no information on temperament.

Jung, C. G. *Modern Man In Search of a Soul.* San Diego, CA: Harcourt Brace Jovanovich, 1933. Jung explains that the distinction between body and mind is artificial. There is some discussion of his theory of personality type and some information on dream analysis.

Jung, C. G. *Psychological Types.* H. G. Baynes, trans. R. F. C. Hull, rev. trans. Princeton NJ: Princeton University Press, 1971. First published in 1923, this work presents Jung's assessment of psychological type, examining extraversion and introversion, sensation and intuition and thinking and feeling. Jung pays particular attention to the E–I dichotomy. It is this theory of type on which Isabel Myers and Katharine Briggs based their work in developing the

MBTI. You may not want to choose this as your first book by Jung. In his later works, his writing becomes more conversational and less scholarly in tone but not in content.

Keirsey, D. and M. Bates. *Please Understand Me.* Del Mar CA: Prometheus Nemesis Book Company, 1978.

Keirsey, D. *Please Understand Me II.* Del Mar CA: Prometheus Nemesis Book Company, 1998. *Please Understand Me* and *Please Understand Me II* are excellent in presenting clear, nonjudgmental descriptions of type and temperament. David Keirsey is brilliant, learned and unequaled in his understanding of the intricacies of each of the sixteen MBTI types and the four temperaments.

Kroeger, O. and. J. Thuesen. *Type Talk.* New York: Delta, 1988.

Kroeger, O. and J. Thuesen. *Type Talk at Work.* New York: Delta, 1992. Both knowledgeable and charming, *Type Talk* and *Type Talk at Work* are written with an excellent understanding of type. The temperament component is included. Otto Kroeger has worked with type for many years and is well respected in the field. He writes with a sense of humor that keeps the reader engaged.

Kroeger, O. and J. Thuesen. *16 Ways to Love Your Lover.* New York: Delacorte Press, 1994. This book addresses the problems and joys of relationship from the standpoint of MBTI type and temperament.

Lawrence, G. *People Types and Tiger Stripes.* Gainesville FL: Center for Applications of Psychological Type Inc., 1993. Uses Jungian type theory and the MBTI to understand individual differences to improve teaching and learning. Provides methods of applying the understanding of type and type development in the classroom.

Murphy, E. *The Developing Child.* Palo Alto CA: Davies-Black Publishing, 1992. A brilliant explanation of type development in children and how this information can be applied at home and in school.

Myers, I. B. with P. B. Myers. *Gifts Differing.* Palo Alto CA: Consulting Psychologists Press Inc., 1980. The pioneer book on the MBTI type system. Isabel Myers and her mother, Katharine Briggs, developed the MBTI based on the theories of Carl Jung.

Myers, I. B. and M. H. McCaulley. *Manual: A Guide to the Development and Use of the Myers-Briggs Type Indicator.* Palo Alto CA: Consulting Psychologists Press Inc., 1985. Presents the theory, use, and statistical data behind the MBTI instrument, including validity and reliability. On page 8, Myers and McCaulley refer to the MBTI type as "the True Self."

Myers, I. B, M. H. McCaulley, N. L. Quenk, and A. L. Hammer. *MBTI Manual: A Guide to the Development and Use of the Myers-Briggs Type Indicator.* 3rd ed. Palo Alto, CA: Consulting Psychologists Press, Inc, 1998.

Tieger, P. D. and B. Barron-Tieger. *Do What You Are.* Boston: Little, Brown and Company, 1992. This book presents an introduction to the aspects of personality measured by the MBTI and then devotes a chapter to each of the sixteen personality types. Each MBTI type is presented through case histories that focus on the career chosen by the person and why that particular career works for that personality type. The Tiegers outline the strengths of the type, the areas that can be challenging and the type of workplace which most suits that type. Several career options are suggested along with a strategy of job-hunting tailored to that particular personality type.

Tieger, P. D. and B. Barron-Tieger. *Nurture by Nature.* Boston: Little, Brown and Company, 1997. Describes each of the sixteen MBTI personality types from birth through childhood with many examples. This book assists the healing process by allowing you to read about yourself as a child and understand that your individual needs were probably not met. Helpful to parents for gaining insight into their children's behaviors, especially understanding why siblings can be so different. The examples presented in the book appear to portray "perfect," completely savvy parents who at times appear unrealistic.

Tieger, P. D. and B. Barron-Tieger. *The Art of Speed Reading People.* Boston: Little, Brown and Company, 1998. Explains how to determine the MBTI type of others through understanding the temperament types.

Tieger, P. D. and B. Barron-Tieger. *Just Your Type.* Boston: Little, Brown and Company, 2000. Encourages understanding, accepting and valuing differences in a relationship through the use of the MBTI types and temperament typing.

Wyman, P. "Integrating the MBTI and the Enneagram in Psychotherapy: The Core Self and the Defense System." *Journal of Psychological Type* 46 (1998):28.

Wagner, J. P. Speaker. *Two Windows on the Self: The Enneagram and the Myers-Briggs* [Cassettes 1–6]. Kansas City MO: Credence Cassettes, 1992. Wagner offers a discussion of the influences of the two typing systems, MBTI and Enneagram, upon each other. For instance, an Introverted Three will look different from an Extraverted Three. He also provides some statistical correlations of the Enneagram with the MBTI; for example, he notes that two-thirds of Threes are Extraverted. This tape set can be ordered from Credence Cassettes at 888.595.8273.

CHAPTER 4

WHO'S GUARDING THE HOUSE?
UNDERSTANDING THE ENNEAGRAM AS A DEFENSE SYSTEM

The Enneagram Defense System is dedicated to protecting us by providing a variety of coping skills and techniques. As such, some of the qualities manifested by this part of personality appear when we are at our worst, such as during periods of stress. Sometimes when discovering her Enneagram type, a person will feel uncomfortable because the descriptors are not always flattering. It would be a mistake to look for affirmation or identity in your Enneagram type. You are not your Defense System. You are much more.

The Enneagram is a system of personality typing with no documented origins. The word *Enneagram* is Greek, meaning a figure with nine points. The Enneagram system defines nine personality types identified by numbers one through nine. The system is generally illustrated with a circular diagram with the numbers displayed as on a clock face (figure 4-1). Each personality number has a distinct profile of traits which are described in this chapter and summarized on pages 76 through 78. Many people are familiar with the Myers-Briggs Type Indicator (MBTI) but the Enneagram is not as widely known and accepted. That is because the evidence that supports the Enneagram is mainly anecdotal and therefore not readily recognized by the

The Enneagram

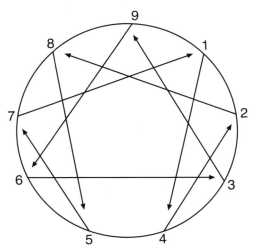

Figure 4-1

scientific and medical communities. Some people who require scientific evidence with substantiating data to support a new approach may have trouble with the Enneagram because of the lack of scientific research supporting it. I have worked with the Enneagram for many years and have found it completely reliable and a very powerful and effective tool for self-understanding. I am certain that it is only a matter of time before the Enneagram will meet the same high standards for reliability and validity as the MBTI has.

Whereas the Myers-Briggs types are designated by four-letter combinations, the nine Enneagram profiles are designated by numbers. And, just as the sixteen MBTI types are divided into four temperaments, the nine personality types of the Enneagram are divided into three centers (figure 4-2). The Eight, Nine, and One are in the Gut, or Instinctive, Center with a key issue of anger. The Two, Three and Four are in the Heart Center, with a key issue of identity. The Five, Six and Seven are in the Head Center with a key issue of fear. I will provide a brief description of each of the nine types. As you read over the descriptions, keep in mind that the Enneagram is best explored orally with a trained facilitator. In exploring the Enneagram by reading about it, it is important to look at the underlying motivations when trying to decide your type and not to check off and tally the number of behaviors with

which you can identify. Pretend you are trying on a pair of shoes in the dark; see if they feel like yours and if you have them on the proper feet. Trying on the various Enneagram types is pretty much the same. When you come across the right type, if you are honest, it will feel like an old, familiar pair of shoes. Just as there were no blends of MBTI preferences, there are no blends of Enneagram types. You are one and only one of the nine types. You may need to narrow down the field by process of elimination, but always keep the underlying motivation in mind when making your final choice.

REINFORCEMENTS

In the Enneagram diagram (figure 4-1), each of the nine types is connected to two other types by two lines. During times of stress, these lines indicate the direction of behavior changes that seem to manifest. With stress, many Enneagram experts explain that we slide in the direction of the arrows and incorporate some of the lesser qualities of the connecting position. In other words, the Enneagram One (the Perfectionist) displays certain defensive characteristics but during times of increased stress will incorporate some of the lesser qualities of the Four. In contrast, during times of personal growth, we have a tendency to move against the arrows and incorporate some of the better qualities of the other connecting number. In that case, the One will pick up some of the finer characteristics of the Seven. Some theorists believe that in times of stress, we will incorporate lesser traits from *both* connected numbers. In that case, the One would adopt some of the negative aspects of both the Four and the Seven. With growth, the One would adopt some of the better qualities of both these connected numbers. Although I will not be going into this at length, my experience with clients supports the latter viewpoint.

In reading about each Enneagram type, remember that these are defense strategies and by their nature can be negative. Look for affirmation and positive qualities in the descriptors of your MBTI Core Self. You may meet yourself when you are not at your best in reading about your Enneagram type.

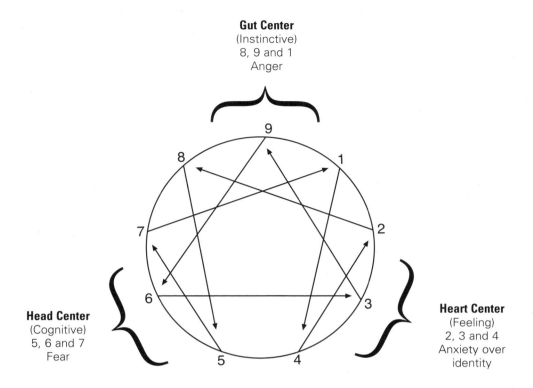

Figure 4-2

GUT CENTER

Eights. Eights are in the Gut or Instinctive Center with the key issue of anger. Eights take their anger and turn it out and against. An Eight can come on pretty strong. The words *aggressive* or *confrontational* would not be an exaggeration. For Eights, everything is about power. They fear feeling weak and being controlled. When entering a new situation, they immediately want to know where the power lies in a group and whether their power is strong enough to take over if the need should arise. However, an Eight does not always need to be the one in charge or the most powerful person in the group. If the Eight respects the leader, she is more than willing to allow that person to be in control. If the Eight does not respect the person in power, it is all out war.

An Eight will unconsciously and continually evaluate others for vulnerable spots so, if necessary, the Eight knows exactly where to go for the emotional kill. It is not always about injustice. Eights hate weakness and see it as a challenge or game. It is similar to a cat playing with a bug on the kitchen floor. The cat's intention is not to kill the bug but to bat it around for fun. It is something to do to keep from being bored. When an Eight finds the need to eat someone's face for lunch, there is an adrenaline rush with the surge of feeling powerful. Later, the Eight may regret doing damage but, at the moment, there is quite an adrenaline high.

People are quick to make judgments about Eights, but let me hasten to add that they are tremendous champions of the underdog. They will put their lives on the line for the power*less*. They are wonderful with babies, small children, the elderly and the handicapped. They are tender with animals, particularly if they are injured. They will risk life and limb for an animal in distress. They are our Robin Hoods, championing and protecting the powerless while defying those who are unworthy of their position of power. I believe many of the civil rights activists of the '60s were Eights.

Eights enjoy nothing more than a good debate. They will bait you and manipulate you into verbal battle. It is sport for them. They feel much more connected when they are doing verbal bantering and sparring than when the conversation is more low-keyed and amicable.

Eights are pretty much all-or-nothing people. They either love something or hate it. If they take up a new hobby or sport, they are into it during every waking moment. When they tire of it, it is history. If asked to evaluate something on a scale of one to ten, it will be either one or ten. They do not understand the need for gradation. It appears wishy-washy and indecisive.

It goes without saying that this Defense System is much more acceptable in males in our culture than in females. It is also more acceptable in adults than in children. The need to continually challenge the seat of power, or authority, is difficult when the Eight is still a child and the authority is the parent, teacher or police. It is particularly hard if the little Eight has determined that the authority person is not worthy of the position of power. In that case, it is one long continuous battle. I generally advise parents of an Eight to raise the white flag whenever possible because the child is younger, more energetic and better equipped to win. This is an instance when the understanding of personality type can bring acceptance to replace a dogged determination to treat all children alike regardless of type. So, if your young Eight answers "No" to every request, try not to take it personally. The only way an Eight can cope is to go *against* authority. Unfortunately, as the parent, you fall into that category. I usually advise parents of Eights to try to avoid putting themselves into a position of going head-to-head with the little Eight. Instead, find ways to provide choices, thereby restoring the Eight's personal power in making the decision. People often question this advice because our culture insists on a certain stereotype family dynamic and a little Eight does not fit into that stereotype.

In some ways, it is easy to see the Eight as a highly effective Defense System. Few people want to do battle with an Eight unless they enjoy pain. But the Eight is not as effective as a defense in children, particularly female children. The child defended as an Eight is likely to receive more emotional wounding because she is inconsistent with the cultural stereotype. But even as a child, when the Eight concentrates on anger turned outward and focuses on someone else, the Eight is protected from intense feelings of fright or sadness. When the Eight defense is not enough, the Eight slides to the Five where there can be a tendency to withdraw, the favorite tactic of the Five. When the Eight feels whole and integrated, there is often a move toward the Two with genuine caring for the other person without involving the power drug.

The following is a list of the key descriptors of an Eight. The words in italics are most important. The words in bold italics are essential.

Eights . . .
Are focused on ***power***
Instinctively ***know others' vulnerability***
Protect and *champion the powerless*
Abhor *injustice*
Enjoy ***mock anger*** and ***bantering***
Tend to be *all-or-nothing*
Fear being *controlled*
Associate *anger* with *power*
Need to "push the envelope" in ***bucking authority***
Must ***go against*** authority, rules, the system, etc.
Use *arguing* as a way to connect
Enjoy a good fight
Are very comfortable with *confrontation*

Nines. Being in the Gut or Instinctive Center, Nines also have anger as a key issue. Unlike the Eights, however, Nines bury their anger deep in the subconscious. When they do, they bury much of who they are as well. So on the outside, the world sees someone who is very "beige." Nines are not ambitious and do not draw attention to themselves. A Nine appears to have a very flat affect with little voice modulation. If you give a Nine a winning lottery ticket, you are lucky to get a very low-keyed "Wow." There will be no screaming and jumping up and down. There will rarely be a display of any other emotion either; no anger, no tears, no fright. Nines may experience all these feelings, but it is done at a very deep, internal level. Rather than an overt, outward display of anger, Nines are more likely to be passive-aggressive. If you force them into an argument, they are more likely to be angry that you made them angry than at the original issue.

Because most of their personality resides in the

The Nine will compare her own feelings to that of the
other person in order to see if those feelings are the
same or different, thereby coming to a determination of how she feels.

subconscious, the Nine goes down there often to visit it. Nines call this "spacing out" or "going to a parallel universe." The medical or scientific community may label it "dissociating." When they do this, it is easy to see they are gone. Often, their eyes become fixed and glazed, they are not hearing or seeing what is happening in the room and they are fairly nonresponsive. Elvis has truly left the building. Some Nines report they are up on the ceiling watching the proceedings. Others say they go "out the window." But most feel like they have just "gone away" for a bit. Sometimes, the Nine is not completely "gone." When performing a repetitive task which takes little active attention, the Nine will allocate the minimum amount of energy to get the job done while the rest of the Nine's attention is directed to the subconscious. In truth, the Nine is much happier in this "spaced-out" state. The internal world is where the action is for the Nine. It holds much more appeal than mundane, boring reality. Because the subconscious is without time, the Nine is usually unaware of the passage of time. When a Nine glances at the clock, it is always a surprise to see how late it is. The Nine is always wondering, "How did that happen? Where did the time go?" Nines are frequently MBTI Perceiving types for whom time is problematical as well. So when these two factors are combined in the same person, it seems like P to the ninth power. There is a complete lack of understanding of the very concept of time.

Nines have a great love for comfort. They shop for their clothes by feel. Clothing must first be soft and comfortable. Style, color and size are considered next. Flannel is their favorite fabric and they often have flannel sheets. It is most important that their beds be comfortably furnished. The Princess and the Pea story was undoubtedly about a Nine girl. Female Nines are not much into makeup and hair because of the discomfort involved. They particularly abhor hose,

heels and business attire, preferring sneakers and sweat suits.

A Nine will make decisions by process of elimination. The Nine never really knows what she wants. It is easier to decide what she does not want and go with what is left. In deciding what to wear in the morning, the Nine will eliminate everything that is not comfortable or appealing and wear what is left.

Since Nines bury so much of who they are in the subconscious, it leaves a lot of space in the conscious part of personality to do what they call "merge." A Nine will take on the agenda, personality characteristics and speech pattern of whomever she is with. This allows the Nine to connect with another person and be on the same wavelength as that person. The Nine feels a source of energy from the other person and feels an emotional high from making the connection. In accessing the other's feelings through merging, the Nine can discern her own. The Nine will compare her own feelings to that of the other person in order to see if those feelings are the same or different, thereby coming to a determination of how she feels.

The Nine does not allow herself an agenda of her own. This is because a Nine's key issue is "no conflict." Nines will do anything to keep the peace. So if you ask where the Nine wants to go for dinner the answer is inevitably, "I don't care." What movie do you want to see? "Whatever." To offer an opinion is to offer just the slightest amount of resistance. Resistance is potential for conflict and the Nine will have none of it. So Nines are great to be with because they always are willing to do whatever you want to do.

Nines use their ability to merge in order to settle conflict. If family members or co-workers are getting into a disagreement, the Nine acts as mediator/negotiator and takes one at a time aside to merge, makes each feel heard and, hopefully, settles the dispute. The Nine never cares who is right or wrong or what the issue is. The Nine's efforts are contributed simply to settle the conflict and restore peace. If that is not possible, the Nine is gone as fast as possible. Conflict is *very* distressing. The Nine cannot even tolerate it on a TV talk show. So it is clear that Nines have few enemies and everyone seems to be very comfortable in their presence.

Nines move at one slow, steady pace. There will be few bursts of energy and no sporadic movement. They are very much like the tortoise in the *Tortoise and the Hare* story; they are Steady Eddie. In the mornings, a Nine will have to build up a bit of a momentum in order to get into the activities of the day. Once moving, a body in motion tends to stay in motion. However, if the Nine relaxes, a body at rest tends to stay at rest and the process starts all over again. Some people have used the word *lazy* to describe Nines and that is simply not true. Nines will work long and hard once they are in motion. When they are very distressed, Nines become more and more lethargic and are drawn to sleeping a lot or to just sitting and staring.

It is easy to see how the Nine acts as a Defense System. If the Nine offers no resistance and works continually to maintain peace, there is a lot less chance of being emotionally hurt. When the Nine is "spaced out" while visiting a fascinating internal world, there is little chance of being hurt or feeling any emotional pain. When the traits of the Nine are not enough to protect against the situation, some of the fear and uncertainty of the Six will be incorporated as well. When the Nine is feeling strong and integrated, some of the traits of the Three will manifest themselves, such as becoming more goal directed and action oriented.

The following is a list of the key descriptors of a Nine. The words in italics are most important. The words in bold italics are essential.

Nines ...

Frequently **space out** or *dissociate*
Feel they **merge** with the other
Put a high value on *comfort*
Have a **flat affect** and do *not show feelings*
Do everything possible to **avoid conflict**

Are seen as *negotiators, arbitrators* and *mediators*
Love to *just "be"*
Can be overcome by *inertia* and *lethargy*
Often answer with *"I don't care"* and *"whatever"*
Make decisions by *process of elimination*
Get along with everyone
Escape into *sleep*
Appear extremely **low-keyed** and *laid-back*
Are outwardly *compliant* while inwardly *defiant*
Are *passive-aggressive*
Are challenged by the concept of *time*

Ones. Ones are in the Gut or Instinctive Center and so their key emotion is anger. The main focus of the One's anger is the self: anger turned inward. Ones beat up on themselves more than anyone else ever could. The result of anger turned inward is depression and Ones are often in the grip of depression. This anger at self is often manifested in systemic physical problems such as arthritis, fibromyalgia, lupus and the like.

Having anger as the key emotion presents a problem for the Ones because their main focus is trying to be *perfect*. In the mind of the One, perfect people are not angry and angry people cannot be perfect. So Ones will do everything they can to suppress their anger. They start very young forcing that anger down and out of sight. It is held down under pressure, rather like being trash-compacted, until the One just cannot hold down one more morsel of anger for one more minute. The anger erupts like a volcano as the One emotionally explodes in rage. The rage is totally out of control and out of proportion to the precipitating event. A child might spill a glass of milk or forget to turn off a light and that can be the piece the One has no more room to stuff in. Everything that has been shoved down comes flying out in one wild, explosive discharge. When it is over, the One is filled with shame and self-loathing because of the setback to the goal of perfection and because others have seen the imperfection.

Ones take their goal of perfection very seriously. They feel a biochemical payoff, or rush, when there is a momentary sense of doing something "perfectly." They know there is no such thing as a perfect person, but that does not stop them from trying to attain the

Ones have this voice going constantly.
It is relentless. It drives them to work harder,
do more, try again, do better and on and on and on,
all in the drive towards perfection.

distinction. Ones are acutely aware of their imperfections and faults and of how much personal work has to be done to get closer to perfection. This gives them a certain sense of urgency. So many faults, so little time!

Because of the drive towards perfection, Ones are acutely aware of the flaws in any situation. They are quick to focus on what is wrong or missing because it stands in the way of perfection. Because of this, they are very susceptible to what the medical profession has labeled obsessive-compulsive disorder.

Ones systematically attack the job of achieving perfection by dividing life and living into small, manageable chunks. They then determine the "perfect" way to do each of these things. There is a perfect way to make a bed, to load the dishwasher, to mow the lawn and to lace your shoes. Years ago, Ann Landers launched an extensive inquiry into the proper way to hang a roll of toilet paper. Ones know the answer to such dilemmas. Ones have given a lot of thought to these and other tasks as well as issues of greater importance. Ones feel that they have come up with the right approach in each instance; just ask them.

If the One really cares about someone, the One will be compelled to let that person know what she is doing wrong and the right way to do it. This is often perceived by the recipient as criticism, but the One would be very surprised to learn she is perceived as critical. The One is only trying to help the loved one reach perfection without having to go through all the many discernment processes to which the One has devoted so much time.

If the One is the parent and the recipient of the attention is the child, the One has an additional and ulterior motive. That is, in order to be a perfect parent, the One has to produce a perfect child. If the child makes the bed in the morning, the One is likely to

come along and adjust the pillow or straighten the last wrinkle. It is the focus on the flaw that draws her attention. The adjustment of the flaw in the bed making is only part of this scenario. The flaw in the child is also being adjusted, bringing the One that much closer to being a perfect parent.

Ones have an internal critical voice that is operational just about twenty-four hours a day. We all have an occasional internal voice with which we may dialogue or which may be critical now and then, but Ones have this voice going constantly. It is relentless. It drives them to work harder, do more, try again, do better and on and on and on, all in the drive towards perfection. Although the internal critical voice is unforgiving, relentless and sometimes screaming, Ones are not upset to learn they are the only ones to have this demanding internal taskmaster. They see this critical voice as helpful and as leading them in a positive direction for personal growth.

Ones also have an internal set of rules by which to live. These rules, if printed and bound, would fill a building the size of the Library of Congress. Ones have given much thought and consideration to these rules and they feel that all normal, rational people would come to the same conclusions if they took the time to consider these things. For example, the One is driving down the highway and comes upon a sign that says "Right Lane Ends 1500 ft." The One enters her internal library and consults the book of rules for highway driving. The One *knows* that as soon as the sign is spotted, the right thing to do is put on her turn signal and begin to move over. Unfortunately, along comes someone who thinks, "Why would they have paved these last 1500 feet if they did not mean it to be driven on?" When this driver goes breezing by the One, she could easily run the person off the road, believing that the unwritten rules are known and being ignored. This driver is clearly cheating. The anger is immediate and intense and can easily be turned into road rage by a One, who has more problems than this inconsiderate driver.

Ones, knowing the right way, feel compelled to tell anyone within range about it. It is nearly impossible for them to keep their opinions to themselves. In addition, Ones have a tendency to repeat for emphasis, often using the pointed, wagging index finger to underscore their position. Ones will tell you their thoughts on something only to start all over again from the beginning and tell you a second time (and perhaps a third and fourth). Ones feel that if you "don't get it" or agree with them, it is only because they have not said it enough. The result is that the recipient has the desire to respond with, "Give it a rest!" But if you are not convinced, the One will be urged by the internal voice to keep repeating because the situation is now saying something about the One being less than perfect in the act of convincing you.

Ones' focus on perfection results in black-and-white thinking and a liberal use of the word "should." They are devoted to fairness and justice and can be crusaders. Nothing makes them more angry than unfairness and they can be very vocal on the topic. They know the world is not a fair place to live, but it "should" be.

In Genesis, we are told that eating of the Tree of the Knowledge of Good and Evil is what caused "the fall." I think this particularly applies to Ones. Their quest for knowing with certainty what is good and what is bad, what is right and what is wrong, causes them untold stress, keeps them locked in their defense and keeps them from knowing their True Selves.

At this point, it is important to remember that what I am describing here is how this group of people defends itself from emotional wounding. Ones want to be loved and accepted like everyone else does. Their particular Defense System tells them that to avoid emotional pain and to be worthy of love, they must be perfect. While focused on perfection, the One is too occupied to feel any emotional pain associated with early issues of childhood. When striving for perfection does not seem to protect them enough, Ones will often take on many traits associated with the Four, such as "nobody understands me," become self-absorbed and melancholy, and may consider suicide. Ones, without exception, report a strong desire for peace, serenity and the cessation of the critical voice. When Ones have experienced emotional healing, they relate feeling happy and able to have fun, taking on some of the qualities of the Seven.

The following is a list of the key descriptors of a One. The words in italics are most important. The words in bold italics are essential.

> **Ones . . .**
> Try to be **_perfect_**
> Have an internal **_critical voice_** that is virtually nonstop
> Know the **_right_** way to do everything
> Use **_"should"_** liberally
> Feel **_anger is wrong_**
> Feel they stand for what is _right, **fair**_ and _just_
> Focus on the **_flaw_**
> Want to help you be perfect, too, which appears _critical_
> Have volumes of unwritten internal _rules_

HEART CENTER

Twos. The Two is in the Heart Center, which means the Two is interested in people in order to determine identity. The Two determines identity from the person she serves. Twos need to be needed and have no sense of self outside of a relationship. If you think of the stereotype of an overbearing, smothering mother, you can get an idea of Two behaviors. Remember that although I will describe the traits of the Two in feminine terms, a male is just as likely to be a Two as a female.

There are two reasons that the Defense System of a Two is the most difficult to determine by simply reading the description. First, the traits of the Two look very much like co-dependence. Virtually every woman on the planet has been raised to be co-dependent and so most women will identify with the traits of the Two as they are simply listed on paper. Second, the traits of the Two are highly valued in women in our patriarchal culture. A Two's primary focus is to gain identity through service. Who would not want to be on the receiving end of that? And so our patriarchal culture rewards Two-like behaviors in women. For these reasons, most women will identify with many of the behaviors listed under the Two description. Co-dependence has been learned and can be addressed and remedied quite readily in therapy, but a Two will always use these innate traits in a defended position. Because it is so easy for co-dependent women to identify with some of the traits of the Two, please keep an open mind and consider the Two only when you are certain no other Enneagram position really applies.

The Two does not know who she is outside of the people she serves. She is Bob's wife, Judy's mother, Betty's daughter, etc. She will introduce herself at the soccer game as Timmy's mom. She may have a personalized license plate that says "Mrs. Bob." Depending on who is making the assessment, a Two can be thought of as a saint or a martyr.

It is important for the Two to keep people needing her because without the other person the Two has no identity. So the Two sets out to learn what the needs, wants, and desires of the other are and to meet them. The goal is to become indispensable to the other person. In a new relationship, the Two is energized by the challenge of learning how this person likes his coffee, what his favorite music is, his favorite food and the like. The Two will repress her own needs, feelings and sense of self in the service of the other. There is no real sense of self. Instead, the Two molds herself into the person the other wants or needs. There is a biochemical high from figuring out a new acquaintance and attending to his needs. Eventually, the person becomes dependent on the Two and the Two has an identity. At this point, the Two then has to maintain the style of service that the other person has come to expect. The Two begins to feel some unexpressed resentment. Often feelings of being trapped, imprisoned and restricted begin to creep in. On one hand, the Two longs for freedom yet fears the loss of identity while out of relationship.

The Two will raise children to be dependent because, without their dependence, the Two's identity is no longer associated with being a parent. The Two will want her children to get married and move next door. It will suit the Two just fine if Suzy calls every morning to ask what to feed the baby or John stops by for coffee on his way to work. The Two is known for sacrifice and possessive smothering which she equates with love and a sensitivity to the needs of others.

Twos easily anticipate others' needs. Before you know you are thirsty, the Two has fixed you a cold drink. Twos do not understand that others are not able to or are not interested in anticipating people's needs in this manner. The Two becomes resentful when no one seems to anticipate her needs and serve her. A Two may be sitting on the sofa watching TV with her husband and decides she would enjoy a cup of coffee. There is an expectation that her husband will become aware of her needs without her making them known and then meet those needs. Eventually, when that does not happen, she will make some remark about getting some coffee for him, letting her resentment show through. The Two wonders why she always knows and meets his needs, yet the favor is never returned. This can precipitate short bursts of anger or some passive-aggressive behaviors.

In a sexual relationship, the Two can be alluring and seductive as the partner's needs require. The Two is not concerned with her own sexual needs but rather finds enjoyment and fulfillment in meeting the needs of her partner. A Two can be very sexual yet unable to be intimate because intimacy requires a sense of self to share with the other. The Two has no sense of self outside of her relationship to the other person.

As a Two ages and perhaps her spouse dies, her children move out of state and her friends are not as available, she moves into an identity crisis which can lead to depression. If she is no longer able to serve as she used to, and there are few people around to serve, the question of "Who am I?" becomes monumental.

Twos have no problem using guilt to control, coerce and manipulate people into staying close and dependent. The implication is often, "After all I've done for you. . . ." Twos can get caught in the Victim-Antagonist-Rescuer cycle, alternately playing all the roles. First, the Two is rescuing, fixing and meeting needs in order to get a sense of identity. Soon, a feeling of "poor me" sets in with the victimlike attitude that no one will ever take care of me. This may be followed by a short display of temper out of frustration and resentment. The anger, however, is short-lived and is quickly replaced by the caring, serving, "thoughtful" Two everyone depends upon.

The traits of the Two are used in a defended position to keep her focused outside of herself and, in that way, to avoid feeling any internal emotional pain. The Two further thinks that by keeping others happy with all their needs met, the Two will avoid getting hurt. When all this serving still does not protect the Two, she is likely to take on some of the aggressive behaviors of the Eight in a short outburst of anger. With emotional healing, the Two is able to incorporate the Four's ability to think of self and to get personal needs met.

The following is a list of the key descriptors of a Two. The words in italics are most important. The words in bold italics are essential.

Twos . . .
Control and manipulate through helpfulness
Identity is determined by those whom they **serve**
Are energized by learning the needs, wants and desires of another
Work to make others **dependent** on them
Use *guilt* to manipulate
Anticipate others' needs
Become the person the other needs
Feels **no identity outside relationship**

Threes. Being in the Heart Center, Threes are interested in other people in order to determine identity. Threes have a persona, false front or facade that they put out to the recipient. Threes carefully monitor how the persona is being received and then very subtly adjust it to gain the approval and acceptance of the other person. Threes sometimes call this adjusting "repackaging." They give you the version of the truth you want to hear, bending it as need be. Because of this trait, Threes

readily get into politics and sales. They can be charming, charismatic and persuasive in winning over the other person. Threes can compromise their own beliefs and values in their attempts to win another. In order to do that, Threes must first convince themselves of what they are trying to sell the other. The first deceit of the Three is self-deceit. Threes are often called chameleons because of their ability to package and repackage for different recipients. Threes generally feel they play a variety of roles depending on the situation and the people involved. They cannot be authentic because that may threaten the success of the interaction and, besides, what does authentic really mean?

The driving force of the Three is the need to succeed. Failure is not an option. The impossible just takes a little longer. Threes seem to succeed at everything they do. There are good reasons for their success. Threes are often high-energy workaholics and will keep working at a project until they pull it off. In addition, Threes are very careful of what they take on. If there is a chance of failure, the Three will take a pass. The Three would rather forgo an activity than take the chance of failing at it. When working with someone I suspect to be a Three, I will ask, "When was the last time you failed at something?" The Three is frozen on the spot because failure is anathema and yet not to answer the question is failure in itself! For a few moments, it is almost possible to see the internal mechanisms screaming, "Does not compute! Does not compute!"

Because of their high success rate, Threes can come across as extremely competent, which may intimidate others. The Three seldom intends to intimidate and is usually surprised to find others have had that reaction.

Image is very important to Threes. They believe in dressing for success and that first impressions count. Titles, credentials and the like are valued as indicators of the Three's success. A Three is delighted to be called a thorough professional. A chain of stores called Successories meets the image needs of Threes. Having an office and home that broadcast success would be valued by the Three. If a One and a Three jointly put on an event that went well, the One would say, "It went off perfectly" and the Three would say, "It was completely successful." Although these two types both have a high standard for their endeavors, their motivations are quite different.

Threes identify themselves by their work and cannot imagine not "doing." They are frequently doing more than one thing at a time and are able to think on more than one track at a time. They are experts at efficiency. Since Threes place a high value on doing, the more efficient and the more that gets done, the better the Three feels. There is a biochemical payoff of an adrenaline high in doing more and doing it successfully.

Threes are good at leadership and enjoy developing a team effort. They can win over team members by custom packaging the project for each member of the team and can keep them all motivated to reach the goal. The purpose of this style of leadership is to achieve success for the Three. The Three knows that the chain is only as strong as its weakest link and so has a personal investment in developing a highly effective team.

Because Threes live mainly in the facade of their performance, they are generally unaware of their feelings and have little notion of who they are outside of their doing. Threes have to be taught how to recognize feelings. They seldom experience fright, other than the fear of failing, because they have so carefully scoped out any situation to be certain of success. Threes are therefore quite literally "human-doings" unable to be in touch with what is going on within and unable to stop to smell the roses.

Threes have a particular challenge in recognizing their traits as defense mechanisms because of the value placed on those traits by the culture. Our society is very Three-oriented. Remember SJ types form the backbone of our culture. SJ types value status and credentials and so the Three is a natural fit. Often Threes fail (no pun intended) to recognize themselves in the Three description because it seems like normal behavior based on society's values. I referred to Threes as chameleons earlier because of their ability to "package." I see them as chameleons because they are camouflaged by a

culture that values their defense strategies. It is also difficult to see these strategies as critically as some other Enneagram types because they are so rewarded by the culture.

In living in the facade of the successful Three, the Three is protected from feeling any emotional pain, equating success with well-being. By keeping perpetually busy, the Three does not have to think, examine any issues or have a feeling. In addition, as long as Threes are successful and can intimidate others with their competency, they feel protected from the threat of being emotionally hurt again. Like other wounded people, Threes are certain they cannot be valued for themselves and so attempt to win approval in their doing. When doing and success are not enough to protect from emotional pain, the Three will sink into the lethargy and not caring attitude of the Nine. The normally energetic Three can become immobilized with fatigue and retreat to bed. With emotional healing, the Three takes on some of the better traits of the Six, feeling loyal to others rather than focused on the goal of success.

The following is a list of the key descriptors of a Three. The words in italics are most important. The words in bold italics are essential.

Threes . . .
　Must *succeed*
　Have a **facade** or *false front*
　Need to stay *busy*
　Easily do ***more than one thing at a time***
　Work at being *efficient*
　Must feel productive or feel worthless
　Continually *monitor* their impact and ***"repackage"*** until
　　they win you over
　Dress for success
　Can unintentionally *intimidate*
　Can ***deceive themselves*** into believing what they are
　　saying
　Feel they ***are what they do***
　Feel ***image*** is important

Fours. Fours are the last group in the Heart Center. They, too, are interested in other people. Fours continually measure themselves against everyone they come in contact with in order to assess whether they are more different, more special and more unique than anyone else. The underlying drive of the Four is to be different and unique. The worst thing imaginable is to be thought of as average and ordinary. As much as Fours enjoy their unique status, they lament that their very uniqueness makes it impossible for anyone to truly understand them, thus increasing their sense of being alone.

Fours have an attraction to symbolism, often keeping mementos and souvenirs that have significance and meaning for them. A rusty key found on the sidewalk can become the key to the future, taken home and kept as a symbol of good things to come. Fours may also find significance in numbers. A unique date such as 6/7/89 will be seen as a special day, and the place where the car odometer numbers line up may hold special significance.

One of the hallmark traits of Fours is the wide mood swings that cause them to be perceived as dramatic and intense. If you think of emotions on a long continuum with deep melancholy and sadness on one end and happiness and joy on the other, Fours can be found at either end of the spectrum. They avoid the middle ground because that is where average people live and Fours are unique, not average. So Fours may feel totally despondent one moment and, with a hopeful word, can move in a nanosecond to the happy end of the spectrum. Unfortunately, they can move back to deep sadness just as quickly. Fours can easily sit for hours in the dark listening to the blues, smoking cigarettes and sipping wine in a state of deep melancholy. They put a high value on the depth and intensity of their feelings. Because there is a biochemical payoff in the deep melancholy and the opposite manic high, the Four is reluctant to give it up. When evaluated through the medical model, Fours are often labeled manic-depressive or bipolar and put on medication to even out the mood swings. I often tell them I have good news and bad news. The good news is that they are not bipolar, they are just Fours. The bad news is that they are *just* Fours, implying that there are others just like them and they are not as unique as they may have thought.

Fours can be quite self-absorbed, feeling that the world should pay a great deal more attention to them than it does. When confronted on this position, they are confused, wondering where else the focus would be placed. They enjoy being the center of attention and expect it. The sense of being different and self-absorbed underlies a disdain for rules and authority whether it be family, work or societal rules or just social niceties. The Four will often dress distinctly in order to underscore her uniqueness and to draw attention.

Fours continually go after the unattainable and can focus on what is missing in their lives. They are most interested in people who have no interest in them and in jobs in which they have no training. Whatever they do have is not nearly as desirable as what they do not have. They will want to live in California to be close to the ocean and then wish they were back east where there is a change of seasons. The Four is not likely to act on these longings. It is more the idea of experiencing something that is currently unattainable that fascinates the Four. Wanting the unattainable and feeling deprived can often leave the Four consumed with envy. It seems others always have what the Four wants most.

In relationships, Fours are most interested in people who are totally unavailable. If they are able to attract the attention of the person, the Four quickly loses interest. Nothing is more attractive to the Four than a partner walking out the door. Nothing is less attractive than someone who is crazy about the Four. This push-pull phenomenon of the Four can be very confusing for the recipient. If the Four is in a committed relationship, she can easily lose interest. If there is an argument and the other person walks towards the door, the Four will become upset about the potential deprivation and begin longing for what was lost. It would not be unlike a Four to pull you close while walking you to the door.

Fours have a sense that when they were put together, an essential component was left out. They feel different from other people who received this missing ingredient and believe it will be restored to them when they are loved unconditionally.

Death holds a particular fascination for Fours. As

children, they may hold funerals for their dolls. Fours may fantasize about their own funeral, wondering for example who will attend, what music will be played, how they will look, or what people will say about them. Fours find the very concept of death interesting and seem less frightened of death than others, causing them sometimes to consider suicide as a serious and viable option.

Fours have a great deal of trouble with goodbyes and loss. They feel separation and the resultant loss deeply and intensely. The loss can be significant, such as the death of a loved one or the break-up of a relationship, or it can be as simple as the loss of a favorite pen. Both have strong emotions attached to them and are felt deeply. Fours have trouble with change as well since it is a type of loss. They are very particular about their surroundings and do not want anyone changing anything. A friend who is a Four has a sign saying, "As long as you don't change anything, I can be flexible."

Fours are usually surprised to be told they need to do emotional healing work. In the mind of the Four, all they are ever doing is feeling. However, what Fours are experiencing is not necessarily authentic feelings. Fours remind me of the little bird that feigns a broken wing to distract a potential predator from its nest. The intense feelings of the Four can often be what some call racket—feelings that distract the focus from what is really going on. The intense feelings of the Four seem to lack a drive shaft. There is a lot of activity but the feelings do not really lead anywhere. So Fours protect themselves by keeping distracted in order to mask the emotional pain that seems overwhelming. When the traits of the Four do not offer enough protection, they will become very solicitous of other people in taking on the co-dependent characteristics of the Two. When Fours have done some emotional healing, they incorporate some of the better traits of the One, abandoning their self-absorption in favor of justice for others.

The following is a list of the key descriptors of a Four. The words in italics are most important. The words in bold italics are essential.

Fours ...
Are *intense* and/or ***dramatic***
Feel they are ***unique*** and *different* from everyone else
Abhor the ordinary
Have instant and wide ***mood swings***
Desire the unattainable
Are fascinated by the topic of *death*
Have trouble with *goodbyes* and *loss*
Are attracted to *ritual, symbolism* and *deep meaning*
Get caught in *yearning, longing* and *"if only ..."*
Value ***depth of feeling***
May be filled with ***envy***
Are often *melancholy*
Are seen as ***self-absorbed***

HEAD CENTER

Fives. Fives are in the Head Center and the key issue of the Head Center is fear. Fives have a basic fear of emptiness. In addition, they want to keep their emotions, thoughts, knowledge and lives to themselves. There is a basic fear that another person will gain access to these hidden parts of themselves and then the Five will no longer possess them. Fives want to fill themselves up with information and so go through life basically observing rather than participating in life. Fives feel as though their eyes are windows and they are standing back from the windows looking out at the world, observing. Fives strongly relate to the word *observer* and readily admit that they feel detached and watchful. They are usually located at the edge of the group where they can observe without being observed, and from where they can leave unobtrusively if they feel the need to withdraw.

Fives are intent on gathering more and more information to keep themselves filled up. They will read just about anything, and usually carry a book everywhere. They will read the material in the seat pocket of the airplane; they will read a "help-wanted" sign in Burger King when they have a Ph.D. The point is to take in data. The Five experiences taking in data the way a gourmet cook experiences tasting food. The cook is not tasting because of hunger but simply to enjoy the taste. The Five is not taking in data for knowledge but just to enjoy the intake process. There is a biochemical reward for taking in more information, causing the Five to feel secure and protected.

Fives are pretty much walking heads. They consider their bodies nothing more than a mobility unit for their heads. It is difficult for a Five to be aware of a feeling because feelings take place lower in the body. If a Five is asked "How do you feel about this?" or "What are you feeling now?" she has a very difficult time. The standard answer to almost every question of this kind is, "I don't know." Moving out of the head and into the body where feelings are experienced is a challenging task in itself. Furthermore, answering the question means *giving out* information instead of taking it in. This feels invasive and the Five's immediate response is to resist. In order to even know what feeling is being experienced, the Five must withdraw into a private space where thoughts and feelings can be examined alone. If the Five is able to decide what feeling is present, it will be considered a piece of data. Do not make the mistake of thinking the Five will seek you out to give you the answer to your question. That would be data *out* and Fives fiercely guard against being put in such a position.

Fives can live very simply and minimally. They can do with a cot, a table, a chair and a naked light bulb if necessary as long as they have their data. Books, magazines, files, video tapes, cable TV and the like are important to fill the continual need for data. They usually keep their data bank in a particular room in the house to which they withdraw whenever given the opportunity. There is no need for aesthetics. The Five sees living with less as a challenge and can do very nicely with the bare minimum.

People are a source of data for the Five. Fives are extremely good listeners with intense eyes. They will ask questions to get the other person talking and then sit listening intently. The recipient of this attention feels flattered and concludes that the Five is taking real interest. The assumption is that the Five cares about the person. In actuality, the Five mainly cares about the *data* and the speaker is just the source of that data.

Fives have a difficult time relating to people and are often seen as loners with poor social skills. It is hard to connect with people while observing them. Intimacy requires mutual vulnerability and that is very threatening to Fives. The very thought of commitment causes the Five to pull even further back. There is a deep desire to connect, yet no understanding as to how to go about it. They feel their best shot at connection is through knowledge, using that as the common denominator. Fives find it easier to communicate by telephone or e-mail than face-to-face. They can become Internet junkies, talking to people anonymously and putting out very little of themselves. They are far more comfortable with computers, books and movies than with real, live people.

Fives have no interest in clothes and feel clothing is simply a cultural necessity that is required to cover one's nakedness. They give little thought to style, color or appropriate attire. Fives also have very soft voices and often have to be asked to repeat themselves or to speak louder. It is almost as if they do not want what they say to be heard since that, again, is data out.

Fives can be very frugal. Because they live so simply, they save and store things. There was a story several years ago about a woman in New York who retired from her teaching job and lived in a one-room flat with the barest minimum of furniture. She wore the same clothes every day for years, regardless of season. Every day she walked to the public library and spent the day there. She died at 105 years old and left twenty million dollars to a women's university. She had used the library daily to monitor her stock investments, thereby saving the cost of a newspaper. The news reporters, speaking through their own lenses, remarked that it was a shame she did not just spend her money and enjoy it. It is clear the reporters had no understanding of Fives. The enjoyment was in virtually no output, only input. If she had spent her money, she would have been extremely uncomfortable.

Fives compartmentalize their lives. People at work know little about the home life of the Five. People in an activity group will not know what the Five does for a living. The various sectors of the Five's life are kept distinctly separate from each other. This gives the Five a sense of secrecy that she equates with freedom from invasion.

It is easy to see how the Five is used as defense. It is unlikely a person will get emotionally wounded if that person is detached and unwilling to become vulnerable. Staying in the head also keeps Fives away from their feelings by keeping them out of their bodies. When the Five defense is not enough, the Five employs some of the techniques of the Seven and simply does not see the problems at hand, ignoring them in hopes they will go away. When the Five has done some emotional healing, there can be a movement to pick up some of the better qualities of the Eight and become more action oriented, moving forward rather than withdrawing.

The following is a list of the key descriptors of a Five. The words in italics are most important. The words in bold italics are essential.

Fives . . .

Observe rather than participate in life
Live entirely in their *heads*
Are *frugal*
Live very simply with a *minimum of possessions*
Have a **soft voice**
Have a strong need to **withdraw**
Are seen as *quiet* and as a **loner**
Are on a constant search for **information** and **data**
Prefer to remain *uninvolved* and **detached**
Desire to connect yet *hide from intimacy*
Can readily *listen* but **hate to share**
Are generally *unaware of their feelings*

Sixes. Sixes are in the middle of the Head Center with the key issue of fear. Sixes are born with little invisible antennae that help them detect "How can I be safe? Who is a threat? What can I do to be safe and secure?" Their first line of defense is to figure out who in the house is the authority figure. If it should happen to be the father, the Six will determine what his agenda is and give him whatever he wants to keep the heat off. Above all, the Six wants to stay out of trouble. When the little Six goes off to school, she determines what the rules are, what the teacher wants and basically what it means to be a student. Then the Six sets about giving those in

charge what they want in order to stay out of trouble. As an adult with a new job, the Six immediately wants a copy of the job description in order to be sure to meet it to the letter. Sixes are comfortable and feel safer with well-defined guidelines, rules and laws. They will gladly follow them and hope others will as well. Sixes align with an authority figure but never really trust that person.

Sixes are hyper-vigilant and more aware of threats and danger than others. Sixes report that it feels more comfortable to be on guard and vigilant than to relax their watchfulness. To be totally relaxed and trusting is to invite disaster. Sixes put a high value on the virtue of loyalty. Trust issues are central. If a person breaks the trust, the Six will have a very hard time trusting that person again. The Six feels that if that person can break the trust once, it could certainly happen again and the Six does not want to take any chances.

Sixes feel more comfortable around people who think as they do; it is safer that way. They are happiest being with people with similar backgrounds, socio-economic standing and/or religious and ethnic heritage. When Sixes are around people like themselves, they are more comfortable because they feel they know how these people think and what to expect. When around people of very different backgrounds, Sixes are more vigilant and suspicious because it is hard to know what to expect of people so very different from themselves. With this thinking, it is easy for Sixes to move into an "us and them" mind set. Anyone designated "them" is automatically suspect. Anyone on the "us" team can easily be banished to the other side by breaking the group rules or going against group norms. Such actions render that person less than completely trustworthy and unsafe to be included in the "us" team. Along these same lines, the Six is highly aware of contradictions. If you said one thing last week and something slightly different this week, the Six is sure to notice and wonder if you are trustworthy.

Making decisions is difficult for Sixes. They are very concerned with making a wrong decision and getting into trouble. Therefore, they research the decision as best as possible, talk with everyone they know and wait as long as they can in the hopes of obtaining any pertinent data. When the decision is finally made, the Six will again call every person imaginable to ask, "Did I do the right thing?" and wonder, "If I had it to do over again, would I make the same decision?" They are literally plagued and consumed by doubt.

Sixes readily agree that fear plays a large role in their lives. They feel that fear at all times. When they have cause to be especially alert, most Sixes report that the fear is felt in their stomachs either as butterflies or a stabbing, wrenching pain. Many Sixes are never far from their antacid tablets.

With Sixes, there is a high degree of family loyalty and often loyalty to government, church and employer as well. Sixes are the only ones who believe the greeting, "I'm from the government and I'm here to help you." Sixes are the ones getting the family together for special occasions. They are frequently with the same company for years and are often in a position of authority because of their loyalty and sense of responsibility and duty. The position of authority, however, is a mixed blessing because it usually requires a lot of decision-making and that is hard on the Six.

Careful, cautious, doubt-filled and prudent all describe the typical Six. Do not move too quickly or too radically because you never know what could happen: "What if . . . ?" Sixes are conservative, middle-of-the-road people who try hard to stay firmly perched on the fence.

There is a subgroup of Sixes called the Counter-phobic Sixes. This group is just as fear-based and hyper-vigilant, but takes an aggressive stance in order to ward off perceived threats. This coping device is often labeled paranoia because the reaction is generally out of proportion to the perceived threat. Because fear in the male is not accepted in our culture, many male Sixes take this approach particularly if they happen to have been in the scapegoat position in their family of origin. The Counter-phobic Six is blustery, aggressive and loud (often appearing to be Eightlike but Sixes are motivated by fear, not the Eight's need for power). The

Counter-phobic Six hopes to make a lot of noise and scare you off, sort of like the little guy behind the big voice of the Wizard of Oz.

Obviously, hyper-vigilance and being very aware of who may be a threat is a good protection device. Furthermore, being loyal and willing to submit to the authority person certainly lessens the chance of being hurt by that person. While caught up in the primary feeling of fear, the Six is unlikely to look at other feelings. The fear helps Sixes de-focus from other feelings that may be having considerable impact on their lives. When the Six's primary defense is not enough, there will be a move to incorporate some of the "busyness" of the Three, hiding in activity. When Sixes have done some emotional healing work, they generally welcome some of the better qualities of the Nine and become more peaceful, calm and unruffled.

The following is a list of the key descriptors of a Six. The words in italics are most important. The words in bold italics are essential.

Sixes . . .

Are ***fear-based***
Are ***hyper-vigilant***
Place an extremely high value on ***loyalty***
Tend to *align with authority*
Have *difficulty making a decision* for fear of doing the wrong thing
Tend to value *structure, guidance, rules* and *laws*
Have a heightened *sense of danger*
Are highly aware of *contradictions*
Cannot tolerate *broken trust*
Are more comfortable with *people of like minds*
Are very ***prudent, careful, cautious*** and ***suspicious***
Look for ***hidden meanings*** and ***ulterior motives***
Easily *feel threatened*
Find ***doubt*** is more comfortable than certainty
Worry more than most people

Sevens. The last group in the Head Center is the Sevens. Their fear is fear of pain. Sevens deal with pain by not dealing with it; indeed, not even seeing it. Sevens unconsciously avoid any cognitive knowledge of anything remotely painful. They pride themselves on having a positive attitude and optimism. When life seems to get rough, the Seven is the first to remark,

"With all this manure, there must be a pony around here someplace!" They will always make lemonade out of every lemon handed them. They can put a positive spin on any event. If you express your sympathy to a Seven on the death of her mother, she will respond with "Oh, it's OK! She's in heaven!" Sevens are often accused by others of living in La-La Land, of not being completely in touch with reality. They can have quite the Pollyanna attitude, which can be frustrating to a spouse trying to get cooperation on a serious issue.

Sevens are focused on having fun and turning every event into a fun-filled adventure. I once had a Seven describe to me how she was going to have fun the next day cleaning her bathroom with an old toothbrush. Some people wake up with a to-do list running in their heads but Sevens wake up with a list of all the fun things ahead of them for the day. Sevens will have trouble being realistic about how much fun can be squeezed into a given period of time, often over-scheduling in an attempt to get even more enjoyment out of life. They hate to limit their options. If you give them a list of five choices for the day's activity they will want to do them all. Everything sounds like so much fun!

People love to socialize with Sevens because they are effervescent, outgoing, enthusiastic and know how to have a good time. They are often the life of the party and their exuberance is contagious. At times they can be playful and childlike, which is refreshing to others who are naturally more serious. Those living with the Seven may have a different opinion, however, wishing there was a way to get attention to the negative side of life. The Seven will be the last to notice that there is a problem looming on the horizon. When adversity hits or tragedy is unavoidable, Sevens will find an optimistic way of dealing with it. Within hours or days, they will minimize the suffering surrounding the incident until they have completely lost sight of any emotional pain.

Upon entering therapy, Sevens are usually confused as to why they are even there because their lives seem to be so good. They always remember their childhood as happy, even magical. Many have compared their childhood favorably to the Cleavers. Yet little tears leak out

indicating that there must be pain buried in there somewhere. When asked if their siblings remember their childhood with the same fondness, Sevens are often perplexed, admitting that they do not. But the Seven can always come up with good reasons why the others in the family have less favorable memories.

Sevens can be narcissistic with an exaggerated idea of their own importance. They are usually surprised when others call them on this issue. They want nothing to interfere with their gilded perception of themselves and the world.

The Seven is emotionally protected by filtering any emotional pain out of conscious awareness. Focusing on fun keeps the Seven from the discomfort of more troublesome feelings. Furthermore, by keeping everyone happy around them, Sevens cut down the chances of being hurt. When the defense of the Seven does not offer enough protection, the Seven takes on some of the traits of the One with anger and indignation at having to face the pain. After emotional healing, the Seven incorporates some of the traits of the Five and takes in a broader spectrum of information that would include events and issues that may be distressing.

The following is a list of the key descriptors of a Seven. The words in italics are most important. The words in bold italics are essential.

Sevens…

Place a high value on *optimism*

Avoid pain at all costs

Do not see the problems

Focus on *fun*

Put a *positive* slant on everything that happens

Always had a ***happy childhood***

Hate to limit their *options*

Are seen as *self-centered* and/or ***narcissistic***

Use ***pleasure*** to ***escape pain***

DECISION TIME

In reading about these nine types, some of you may have found it easy to identity your own Defense System from the list. Others will find it harder. When you look at the Myers-Briggs types, your Enneagram Defense part does not go for a walk around the block. Similarly, when you try to choose your Enneagram type, the MBTI part is not off somewhere, not to be heard from. Each system may influence your evaluation of the types in the other system. If you feel some confusion, this is probably happening to you. In making your determination of type, be certain to focus on the underlying *motivation* and not simply the behaviors associated with an Enneagram type. Do not attempt to narrow the field by choosing a Center first and then a type from that Center. Your choice of Center can easily be influenced by your MBTI type or other factors. Of course, the best recourse is to consult a trained professional to get it all sorted out. Before doing that, though, you may want to check out some of the books listed at the end of this chapter that go into far more detail than space allows here.

THE ENNEAGRAM AS DEFENDER

The Enneagram part of personality is often engaged in fighting a war that is long over. Many years ago, Bill Cosby had a comedy routine about having his tonsils removed as a child. Those tonsils had been good and faithful guardians but their usefulness was over and, in effect, their continued activities were aiding and abetting the enemy. So, too, with the Enneagram portion of personality. As an infant or small child, each of us needs someone or something to protect us emotionally. The Enneagram Defense System is dedicated to protecting the child by providing a variety of techniques and skills to cope with a hostile world. As the child moves into adulthood, the Enneagram Defense is still going strong, taking its duties seriously. And just like an immune system that is in overdrive causing physical damage, the Enneagram Defense can interfere with living a full life when it continues its all-out efforts long after its services cease to be helpful. Mary, an ISTJ-1, explains it this way:

Mary's story. "When I am trying too hard to be 'perfect' (Enneagram One) and the anger shows itself, it is much like a fever would be for the flu. It indicates something is going on with me that is keeping me from feeling authentic. You always have a temperature—it

never goes away—and it lets you know your level of health. The anger (of the Enneagram One) does the same for me. . . . The rages are very unhealthy for me. They are very scary and indicate I'm out of touch with my feelings at the moment."

We are designed by nature to be survivors. With a crash diet, the metabolism slows down to conserve the meager groceries provided. It is the natural response to try to preserve the life of the organism. The metabolic regulator cannot be talked into relaxing; it has the body's best interest at heart. In the same way, the Enneagram Defense cannot be talked into relaxing its vigil. Even though the war may long be over, the Defense System is not taking any chances. Just like Japanese soldiers found still combat-ready thirty years after WWII, the Enneagram Defense has taken its orders in an earlier setting and is still operating as if nothing has changed. In truth, something *has* changed. An adult has developed. However, the Enneagram Defense is not gauging the vigor with which it carries on its activities by chronological age. Rather, it is monitoring the condition of the wounded inner Core Self as defined by the MBTI. The Defense System will only relax if it knows that the inner Core Self is being protected in a manner equal or better than what it, the Defense System, can provide. Trying to talk the Defense System out of its job is about as effective as trying to talk the immune system of someone suffering from an autoimmune disease out of its job.

There cannot be true self-acceptance as long as the Core Self is safely tucked away and the Enneagram is running the show. There cannot be self-acceptance because there is no real knowledge and understanding of the Core Self. There will always be a sense of emptiness as long as the Core Self is protected and hidden. By its very nature, the Enneagram Defense System cannot provide unconditional self-love. It provides a limited number of options by which to respond to a stimulus. It can help create a feeling of safety but it cannot develop self-worth.

With awareness, understanding and some emotional work, the Enneagram Defense System will relinquish its

When a person is so well defended and the Enneagram Defense portion of personality is running the show, the person feels out of control, small and empty.

control to the adult with cognitive abilities and coping skills far superior to the child. However, it is important to remember that the Enneagram Defense never goes away. Nor would we want it to. It is always standing at the ready, just in case the adult messes up or does not rise to the occasion.

When we are living defended, with the Enneagram at the helm and the Core Self safely tucked away, it is as if our Core Self has gone into a room and locked the Enneagram door for safety. If someone on the outside starts pounding on the door, we automatically look around for things to shore up the door. We may pick up some additional Enneagram support from neighboring numbers. For instance, an Enneagram One under extreme stress will pick up some of the coping skills of the Four. She will become self-absorbed, overly dramatic or intense and possibly suicidal. If that is not enough, our Core Self will lean up against the door. In that case, some of the traits of the MBTI part of personality will be used as defense. The NT might come on as tough or intellectualize and analyze everything. The NF may become very helpful and co-dependent. If that is still not enough and we fear the door will be broken down, we begin to move some furniture in front of the door. Those are additional coping techniques such as addictions, humor, denial, etc. The resourcefulness of the organism to try to survive emotionally is remarkable.

Reilley's story. Reilley, an INTJ-4 whose case history is described in chapter 11, was so very wounded as an infant and child, that she employed every defensive tactic imaginable. Her first line of defense was the Enneagram Four. She then borrowed some coping techniques from the Two and became very solicitous of everyone around her including those who had hurt her the most. She even borrowed some One traits and

became very self-critical, thinking of herself as "a loser." When all this was still not enough to stop the emotional pain, Reilley as an NT became a super intellectual, analyzing and challenging the logic in everything. She put on a tough facade that could intimidate most people when in actuality she was anything but tough inside. Her dry, sarcastic humor was always ready to do battle and keep her away from any real feelings. For good measure, Reilley tossed in control and denial that anything bad ever happened to her. Add to all this, a string of addictions, some socially acceptable, such as work and TV, and some which are not, and you have a very well-defended person.

When a person is so well defended and the Enneagram Defense portion of personality is running the show, the person feels out of control, small and empty. There is often a feeling of having a big, black hole inside that nothing seems to fill.

Doing some healing work can alter a lot of things. Emotional healing work will move the locus of control from the Enneagram Defense part of personality to the Core Self. When that happens, the Enneagram, as second in command, can supply support and bring an additional perspective to each situation. The traits of the Enneagram can then be employed to enhance and round out the gifts and talents of the Core Self. When the cognitive adult is in charge and the contributions of the Enneagram are used only in support, there is a sense of strength and empowerment associated with internal peace and serenity.

When the Core Self is understood as profiled by the MBTI, and the Enneagram is understood as a Defense System, it is quite possible to discern which position is being taken at any given time and techniques can be employed to move out of living defended and into expressing the Core Self.

Once you have identified your Enneagram Defense System type, you have an understanding of the traits you have used all your life to protect yourself from a seemingly emotionally hostile world. If you see that you have been and still are using those traits a lot, it is a clue that you have been living a very defended life. If you feel you live most of the time out of your Core Self (MBTI part of personality), there will still be times when you are sent into a defended position in a heartbeat. It is an automatic response. Just like you automatically blink if someone's finger comes too close to your eye, the Enneagram Defense is immediately in place if there is an emotional threat. This can act as a red flag or warning sign to you that you are in emotional trouble. It gives you the opportunity to examine what just happened—how you were triggered—and allows you to take steps to reverse the process.

Sarah's story. Sarah, whom we met in chapter 1, is an ISTJ-9. Normally, she is a very organized, efficient and task-oriented person. She feels best when she is working from her to-do list and getting things accomplished (ISTJ). She recently told me she had a heated encounter with her husband over the topic of finances. Before they were finished arguing, Sarah felt small and powerless. The next thing she knew, two days had gone by and she had spent them sitting on the couch basically doing nothing at all. She had moved out of her productive ISTJ Core Self and into her Nine Defense System. When she was barely in the room and virtually not in her body, she did not have to feel any emotional pain resulting from the argument with her husband. When she moved into the Nine's position of avoiding conflict at any price, she avoided any further emotional pain that voicing her opinions, and perhaps disagreeing with his, might cause. It was not until Sarah realized what had happened, and processed her feelings, that she understood she felt as though she were back living with her family of origin. After that, she could reverse what happened and return to her normally productive ISTJ Core Self.

It is important to realize that we are not our Defense Systems. The Enneagram provides a set of various coping skills and techniques, but it is only a Defense System. The person is defined by something far more exciting and spiritual. Furthermore, the Enneagram portion of personality is not a good tool to use in decision-making. It has no cognitive ability. If a person is under a lot of stress and living in a very defended position, that is not the time to be making any major decisions. The Enneagram part of personality, dedicated to protecting, will come to a very different decision than the rational, cognitive part. The standard for a decision by the Enneagram Defense System is emotional defense and protection, which was of paramount importance to the child, but the adult is now able to defend the self in other ways. When the cognitive adult is in charge, the standard may be such as to move the person in exactly the opposite direction than the Enneagram part is advocating. For instance, a person defended as an Enneagram Five will have withdrawal and silence as a first line of defense. If that person is stressed because of an argument with a spouse, perhaps the defense that helped when the Five was a child is no longer really in the best interest of the individual. Perhaps, just perhaps, moving towards the spouse and talking the problem through would be more helpful.

Decisions made by the Defense System may be shortsighted and, in actuality, may not be in the person's general best interest. Here is another example of how the Defense System may make decisions that would be very different from those made by the Core Self.

Paige's story. Paige, an ESTJ-3, is a lawyer who decided to open her own practice. Operating out of her Three defense, Paige would not allow herself to admit how fearful she was that she would not succeed. Her Three Defense System drove her to rent a high-priced office in a prestigious downtown building, to fill it with high-quality, expensive furniture and to decorate it with original art work. She hired a clerk/receptionist not because she needed that much help but because it looked good. She allocated a substantial amount of money for a new wardrobe so she would really look the part. In order to pull all this off financially, Paige borrowed against her life insurance and took out a second mortgage on her home. If the normally conservative ESTJ Core Self had been in charge, Paige would have made some very different decisions. When she first began considering going out on her own, Paige should have acknowledged and faced her fears. Working through her fear of failure would have put the Three to rest and allowed the ESTJ to make decisions that would ultimately have been more in her best interest. The Three's job was simply to keep Paige from being distressed by feeling her fears and anxiety. It had no business running her law practice and making financial decisions.

The stress of going out on her own triggered Paige and so her Defense System was there immediately to protect her. Unfortunately, Paige was not used to monitoring herself in this way and had spent so much time living out her Three Defense that it felt normal and natural. It caused her to become financially overextended, requiring some fancy footwork on her part to regain her financial security.

Paige reacted to the fear of opening her own practice by employing her Defense of the Three. Consider a lineup of eight other ESTJ lawyers ready to go out on their own, each with a different Enneagram Defense type than Paige's. There would be some very different behaviors and very different decisions. An ESTJ-6 operating out of the Six would be almost immobilized with indecisiveness and fear. This would look very different from the way Paige functioned while making decisions out of her Three. Depending on the Enneagram Defense System type, each of the nine types will act to defend that person from emotional pain in ways peculiar to the type. None of these is better or worse than the others, just different. Some may be more socially acceptable than others. Paige's Three defense looks good to others and presents well. The Six in the same career position may be the object of scorn by her colleagues because of her indecisiveness and paranoia.

Understanding of the Enneagram type can be used as a red flag calling attention to the fact that the Defense System is in control and not the Core Self. This is an enormously helpful piece of information. With this awareness, measures necessary to move into the Core Self, where true wisdom resides, can be taken. It was the awareness that she had been sitting on the couch for two days that caused Sarah to realize she was caught in her Nine Defense. When you have restored control to your Core Self, you can be assured that any decisions will be in your ultimate best interest because you have the ability to know what is best for you. Accessing that information and that wisdom is the trick.

Many people spend much of their life in pursuit of self-worth, self-acceptance and/or self-esteem. It is beneficial and desirable to look to ourselves for the unconditional love we never received from anyone else. However, it often seems to be an elusive dream. When control rests in the Enneagram Defense System, there cannot be self-acceptance or self-love. The True or Core Self is put away and not accessible so it is not possible to accept or love a Self that is not known or recognized. In understanding these two distinct parts of personality, it is possible to work with them and encourage the Defense part of personality to be at rest when it is not needed. When the Defense System is at rest, control is restored to the Core Self and self-worth/self-acceptance becomes a viable possibility.

Sometimes, a person's MBTI type and Enneagram type are very congenial. Other times, like Sarah, the ISTJ-9 mentioned previously, the MBTI type and the Enneagram type are very different and that can lead to a feeling of having two different people living in the same body. Sarah, normally active, busy and goal oriented, is rendered nearly motionless when she is triggered and the Enneagram Nine takes over the controls.

The next step is to take a look at how these two parts of personality cohabit the same body and have to come to some kind of working arrangement.

Descriptions of the Nine Enneagram Types

ONE

Anger is bad
Anger toward self
Compulsive
Controlling
Critical
Disciplined
Faultfinder
Feels inadequate
Inflexible
Internal critical voice going at all times
Intolerant
Irritable
Judging
Meticulous
Moral superiority
My way is the right way
Needs to be right
Nonadaptable
Nonspontaneous
Opinionated
Outspoken
Perfectionist
Preoccupied with rules, shoulds
Repeats for emphasis
Sense of urgency
Tendency to rage
The smallest flaw ruins the whole
Uncompromising
Work before play

TWO

Alters self to please others
Anticipates needs
Attracted to powerful people
Compelled to please
Complaining
Controls through giving, helping
Desires to become indispensable
Encourages others' dependence
Exaggerated idea of self-importance
Fears true intimacy
Feels used, controlled, victimized
Flatters
Gives to get
Hovering, intrusive
Manipulates to get needs met
Martyr, needy
Needs to be needed but desires
  freedom
Outwardly compliant
Patronizing
Possessive
Power behind the throne
Pride in service
Readily relinquishes personal power
Receives identity from others
Represses personal needs, feelings
Rescues
Seductive
Seeks protection
Trapped; controlled by others' needs
Uses sex to gain attention

THREE

Achievement oriented; ambitious
Action oriented
Adaptable
Appearance is important; image
  conscious
Assertive
Attention seeking
Can compromise values
Charming
Competitive
Disconnected from feelings
Do; busy; overactive
Efficient
End justifies the means
Energetic
Enthusiastic
Failure is not an option
Fears rejection
Future oriented, visionary
Goals
Good communicator
Hates criticism
Inspirational
Manipulates
Motivational
No private life
Organized
Positive
Professionalism
Self-confident
Self-deception
Talks
Team leader
The impossible just takes a little longer

Descriptions of the Nine Enneagram Types

FOUR

Abhors the ordinary
Competitive
Deep feelings
Desires the unattainable
Distinctive, intense
Drawn to symbolism
Elite
Envious
Feelings of being incomplete
Feelings of deprivation

Feels no one can understand me
Heightened sense of loss
Longing
Manic-depressive, bipolar, moody
Melancholy
Needs recognition
Pessimistic
Preoccupied with death
Preoccupied with what is missing
Prone to self-pity

Push-pull; long for and reject
Regret
Romantic
Search for depth and meaning
Searching
Self-absorbed
Sense of entitlement
Sense of tragedy
There is not enough
Unique

FIVE

Austere surroundings
Autonomous
Avarice, may hoard
Cannot ask to get needs met
Commitment is mental before
  emotional
Compartmentalizes
Connection through knowledge
Disdain for emotional display
Disembodied mind
Drained by interpersonal interactions
Feels in retrospect

Feels invisible
Frugal
Ignores rules, authority
Isolated, loner
Knowledge; information is central
Minimalist
Needs much personal space
Needs to know
Nonresponsive, evasive, delayed
  reactions
Nonsocial, nonverbal
Not present

Observes, listens
Passive
Preoccupied, reflective
Reclusive
Reserved, withholding, secretive
Sees needs and emotions as ideas
Sees world as invasive
Soft voice, gentle
Uncomfortable with emotional
  attachments
Withdrawn, detached, distant

SIX

Aligns with or challenges authority
Anxious, apprehensive, fearful,
  frightened
Associates with like-minded people
Avoids risks, timid
Careful, cautious, guarded, prudent
Conformational bias
Doubts others' intentions, sincerity
Dutiful, responsible, obedient
Fears anger
Feels powerless
Heightened sense of danger

Hyper-vigilant
Indecisive
Looks for contradictions
Looks for hidden agendas, intentions,
  meaning
Looks for underlying motivations
Loyal, especially to family
Moves into fight (counterphobic) or
  flight (phobic)
Needs certainty, consistency
Needs clear guidelines
Pessimistic, imagines the worst

Questioning, skeptical, doubt-filled
Respects laws, rules, power
Seeks safety and security
Self-doubting
Spots potential problems
Steadfast, reliable
Subscribes to group norms
Suspicious, unsure
Takes sides
Very conscious of power source
Watchful, wary; can be paranoid

Descriptions of the Nine Enneagram Types

SEVEN

Adventurous	Curious	Idealizes
Appears scattered	Dislikes routine	Impractical
Attracted to excitement, stimulation	Entertaining	Keeps options open
Avoids boredom	Enthusiastic, energetic	Narcissistic
Avoids responsibility	Escapist	Needs variety
Avoids the unpleasant	Excellent social skills	Not punctual
Busy	Excessive	Possibilities
Charming, engaging	Future oriented	Requires freedom
Childlike	Hates being defined, limited	Spontaneous, impulsive, uninhibited
Creative, imaginative	Highly optimistic and positive	

EIGHT

Action oriented, energy	Confrontational	Outspoken, provocative
Acts out when bored	Controlling, demanding	Power
Aggressive, dominating, intimidating	Defends the powerless	Protective, rescuer
All-or-nothing; excessive	Determined, persistent	Reluctant to be dependent
Anger equals power	Disregards consequences	Reluctant to trust
Arguing creates intimacy	Earthy; lusty	Respects a worthy opponent
Attention seeking	Enforces justice, crusader	Revengeful
Audacious, controversial	Fears being controlled	Strong, tough
Compromise equals weakness	Intrusive	Uninhibited, impulsive
Conflict reveals truth	Needs to be kept informed	Uses others' vulnerability

NINE

Accepting	Conserves energy	Keeps a low profile
Accommodating, adaptive	Controls through nonaction	Loses track of time
Agreeable	Difficulty setting and maintaining goals	Low energy
Ambivalent	Dissociates	Mediator
Avoids conflict	Easygoing	Needs harmony
Calm	Escapes into sleep	No self-awareness
Choices are difficult	Flat affect, monotone voice	Passive
Clothes must be comfortable	Holds onto unexpressed resentments	Passive aggressive
Complacent, compliant	Inertia, lethargic, phlegmatic	Stubborn
Compromising	Internally focused	Unpretentious

NOTE

Some theorists in the books listed here explain variations in people with the same Enneagram type by the concept of "wings." The wings theory suggests that a person's basic Enneagram type is affected by one of the two adjacent personality types. That is, the basic personality of type One is affected by either the traits of the Two or the traits of the Nine, producing many different variations in people who are identified as Enneagram Ones. Some others use the concept of "subtypes" to explain variations noted in people claiming the same type. Still others explain variations in Enneagram type by degree or level of mental health or spiritual state. If the Enneagram System is understood as the Defense System and *not* the defining personality type, it becomes clear that the differences seen in those possessing the same Enneagram type are differences due to the defining or Core Self and not "wings," "subtypes" or anything else.

So, if we look at two people, both having the Enneagram Defense of the One (perfectionist) but having different MBTI types, we will see vast differences between the two. If, for instance, we compare an INFP (quiet, relational, internally focused with wisdom and wanting to help people heal and grow) and an ESTJ (traditional, hardworking, structured, orderly and organized) who are both defended as Enneagram Ones, we will see two very different people. For one thing, the INFP will focus most of the perfectionism on herself while the ESTJ will try to reform those around her as much as she tries to reform herself. The INFP, with the NF's penchant for idealism, will have an idealistic sense of truth and justice. The ESTJ, being more practical and concrete, will simply know the right way to do everything and be ready to volunteer a whole list of *shoulds*.

To take this just a little further, if we had sixteen people, one of each MBTI type, yet each person was defended as an Enneagram One, they would all have the traits of the One in common, but each would look very different depending on the Core Self (MBTI) of the individual.

Professionals who work a lot with the MBTI are usually not very interested in the Enneagram. Those who work a lot with the Enneagram are often not terribly aware of the MBTI. Therefore, the experts in each system have always had a need to explain away the differences they see in individuals with the same type in their system. If we combine these two systems, there is no need to explain away variations in type. The two systems cover a vast area of discernable personality qualities. Using both systems and understanding the different roles each play takes nothing away from either system yet contributes a wealth of information that helps us to understand ourselves and others.

BIBLIOGRAPHY AND SUGGESTED READING

Beesing, M., R. Nogosek and P. O'Leary. *The Enneagram.* Denville NJ: Dimension Books, Inc., 1984. This is one of the first books written on the Enneagram. It contains some interesting and thought-provoking information written from a Catholic/Christian perspective with a chapter purporting that Jesus embodied all nine Enneagram types.

Palmer, H. *The Enneagram.* San Francisco: Harper, 1988. By far my favorite book and author on the Enneagram. Palmer writes clearly and elegantly without bias. She objectively conveys what she has seen in thousands of personal interviews. Besides providing in-depth descriptions of the nine Enneagram types, she offers background information on the system itself.

Palmer, H. *The Enneagram in Love and Work.* San Francisco: Harper, 1995. In this work, Palmer pairs each possible Enneagram combination in both a work and a personal relationship. She describes the dance or game that the pair is likely to engage in and some of the pitfalls to watch for. She also points out how each member of the combination can complement the other. Helen Palmer presents workshops around the world. She is gifted in her ability to work with people in drawing out Enneagram type.

Watching her work is like watching an artist and I highly recommend the experience. Contact her at Workshops in the Oral Tradition with Helen Palmer, 1442A Walnut Street PMB377, Berkeley CA 94709; 510.843.7621.

Riso, D. R. *Understanding the Enneagram.* Boston: Houghton Mifflin Company, 1990. Riso arbitrarily and arguably divides each Enneagram type into *healthy, average* and *unhealthy* and then further divides each of these into three levels of functioning. The best contribution of this work is that it points out how each Enneagram type, under extreme stress, will display a set of behaviors that may be diagnosed as specific mental illnesses. I do not know if Riso's assignment of the various psychological disorders to each Enneagram type is accurate but it does help raise consciousness about connections between Enneagram type and mental illness, and it helps in understanding the Enneagram as defense.

Wagner, J. P. Speaker. *Two Windows on the Self: The Enneagram and the Myers-Briggs* [Cassettes 1–6]. Kansas City MO: Credence Cassettes, 1992. Wagner offers a discussion of the influences of the two typing systems, MBTI and Enneagram, upon each other. For instance, an Introverted Three will look different from an Extraverted Three. He also provides some statistical correlations of the Enneagram with the MBTI; for example, he notes that two-thirds of Threes are Extraverted. This tape set can be ordered from Credence Cassettes at 888.595.8273.

CHAPTER 5

UNDERSTANDING INTERNAL CONFLICT
COMPATIBLE AND OPPOSITIONAL PARTS OF PERSONALITY

My first step with a new client is to administer the Myers-Briggs Type Indicator to determine the Core or True Self. I could tell by looking at Paula that her Core Self was far, far from her consciousness. I wanted to know her Core Self so that, when we went looking for her, we would recognize her when we found her.

Paula's story. It seemed to take all the energy Paula had just to walk into my office. I did not need her to tell me she was depressed. Paula, fifty-five, explained the circumstances that brought her to see me. She had been recently hospitalized for depression, was on a variety of medications and felt worse with every passing day. She

felt a great deal of self-hatred and internal conflict. Suicidal thoughts frequently plagued her. She had seen a variety of doctors and psychiatrists and felt she had exhausted conventional treatment. She was ready to try an alternative approach.

CORE SELF AND DEFENSE SYSTEM: IN BATTLE
Paula's MBTI results indicated her type formula to be ENFP (figure 5-1, page 82) and we spent about two hours discussing and verifying the results. I described each of the four dichotomies to Paula: Extravert, Intuitive, Feeling and Perceiving. She readily recognized her preference for each of these. When I described the

resultant ENFP, Paula looked at me in amazement. She stated that it sounded like someone she met a long time ago. She admitted that her life was anything but a reflection of the ENFP.

Figure 5-1

ENFP

Accepting	Idealistic
Attracted to adventure	Insightful, perceptive
Brainstorms	Intensely relational
Brings people together	Difficulty with follow-through
Charismatic, charming	Needs freedom
Childlike, fun loving	Needs harmony
Conceptualizes	Nonlinear thinking
Creative, artistic	Nontraditional
Curious	No need for neatness
Difficulty getting focused	No need to be realistic or
Dislikes structure, routine	practical
Easygoing	Optimistic
Energetic, tireless	People centered, sociable
Enthusiastic	Search for self, meaning
Flexible, versatile	Spontaneous, impulsive
Future oriented	

When Paula came in for her second visit, we discussed the Enneagram Defense System. It did not take long to determine that her Enneagram Defense was a One (figure 5-2). It was not difficult to see that there was an immense internal conflict going on within Paula and it was clear that her One Defense was winning hands down.

Figure 5-2

ONE

Anger toward self	Moral superiority
Anger is bad	My way is the right way
Compulsive	Needs to be right
Controlling	Nonadaptable
Critical	Opinionated
Disciplined	Outspoken
Fault-finder	Perfectionist
Feels inadequate	Preoccupied with rules, shoulds
Inflexible	Repeats for emphasis
Internal critical voice going	Sense of urgency
at all times	Tendency to rage
Intolerant	The smallest flaw ruins the
Irritable	whole
Judging	Uncompromising
Meticulous	Work before play

During Paula's third visit, I took her case history. We started with her birth and went straight through to the present. I could see from the events of her life that she had good cause to live very defended. Furthermore, her current circumstances were not any improvement.

In addition to the emotional healing work ahead of us, a large part of Paula's therapy would consist of bringing her to an understanding of the internal conflict she was experiencing between her Core Self and her Defense System, and learning how to manage and work with the two warring factions.

Sometimes the Core Self and the Defense System are friendly, cooperative neighbors. Sometimes, such as Paula's case, the Core Self and the Defense System are as opposite as an ultra-liberal Democrat is from an arch-conservative Republican. To take that a step further, they are living in one body like the liberal and the conservative sharing tight living quarters such as a dorm room or a small office, or like Felix and Oscar of *The Odd Couple*. Sometimes, the conflict is unbearable. More than one client in such a situation has told me they have considered shock treatment. Many are on medication. If the warring factions are numbed out on drugs, they are less likely to do battle, but that is not a good long-term solution.

THE FOUR MBTI DICHOTOMIES AND THE ENNEAGRAM

Extraversion and Introversion with the Enneagram

Looking at each of the four MBTI dichotomies of personality individually with regard to a possible Enneagram Defense, it is not difficult to see potential for conflict. Extraversion and Introversion determine energy source and there are several instances in which an Enneagram type can be in conflict. For instance, I am an Introvert yet my Defense is that of the Three. The Three is often called The Performer. An Introverted Performer shows me God has a sense of humor and I am a walking example (figure 5-3). When I schedule a speaking gig, the Three says, "Oh what fun!" When I arrive to give my presentation, the Introvert says, "Please NO. Whose idea was this anyway?" Public

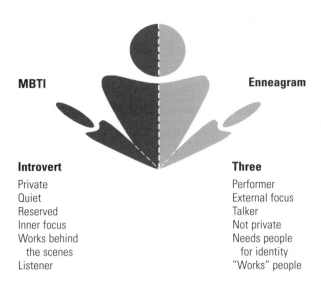

MBTI	Enneagram
Introvert	**Three**
Private	Performer
Quiet	External focus
Reserved	Talker
Inner focus	Not private
Works behind	Needs people
the scenes	for identity
Listener	"Works" people

Figure 5-3

speaking takes an enormous amount of energy for an Introvert. The Introvert would much prefer working one-on-one with a client, or a weekend alone in a cabin in the woods sounds delightful.

The conflict can happen in the other direction as well. Every so often, I will encounter an Extravert who is defended as a Nine or a Five, both of which are very internally focused. It is difficult for the Extravert to look outward for energy and at the same time defend herself by being internally focused (figure 5-4).

SENSING AND INTUITION AND THE ENNEAGRAM

The second dichotomy, Sensing or Intuition, describes how information is collected. In Paula's case, she is an Intuitive who prefers to take in information as a big picture, without much attention to facts and details. Her defense of the One has her focused on flaws and on every little detail of every situation in order to attain perfection (figure 5-5, page 84). The Intuitive is not equipped to do this easily. It takes a tremendous amount of energy for the Intuitive to look deeper into the big picture and focus on the details to fine tune them to perfection.

Those preferring Sensing are concrete, practical, realistic, literal and live in the present. If such a person should be defended as an Enneagram Four, there is definitely trouble ahead. The Four is fond of symbols

and drama and is future-oriented with longing and "if only. . . ." The Four is anything but practical and realistic in going after the unobtainable. I have never met a Sensing person defended as a Four who was not experiencing an immense amount of internal conflict (figure 5-6, page 84).

Ellen's story. Ellen, an ESFJ-4, would be anyone's idea of the All-American Girl. She is a teacher in special education. She desired nothing more than a traditional marriage and family in the proverbial cottage with a white picket fence complete with the requisite number of standard pets. However, she found herself unable to stay in a relationship and being inappropriately emotional at work. She was on medication because she had been told her brain chemistry was abnormal. She reported that she often felt like she had multiple personalities. As she approached her thirtieth birthday, she could not see things changing in the near future and saw her dreams rapidly slipping away.

Valerie's story. Valerie, an ISTJ-4, was in an even more untenable position. She is a CPA and head of her department. Besides the conflict between the sensible, practical, grounded Sensing preference and the dramatic, emotional Four, Valerie's Thinking preference made her logical and her Introvert preference wanted

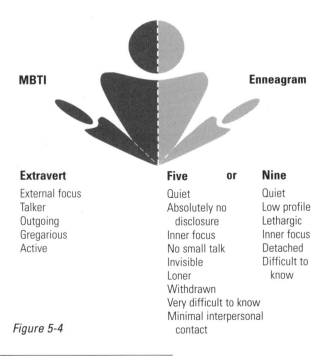

MBTI	Enneagram	
Extravert	**Five** or	**Nine**
External focus	Quiet	Quiet
Talker	Absolutely no	Low profile
Outgoing	disclosure	Lethargic
Gregarious	Inner focus	Inner focus
Active	No small talk	Detached
	Invisible	Difficult to
	Loner	know
	Withdrawn	
	Very difficult to know	
	Minimal interpersonal	
	contact	

Figure 5-4

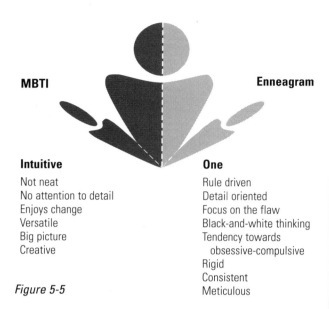

MBTI

Intuitive
Not neat
No attention to detail
Enjoys change
Versatile
Big picture
Creative

Enneagram

One
Rule driven
Detail oriented
Focus on the flaw
Black-and-white thinking
Tendency towards
  obsessive-compulsive
Rigid
Consistent
Meticulous

Figure 5-5

her emotions kept internal. Both these preferences were opposed by the outwardly intense Four.

THINKING AND FEELING AND THE ENNEAGRAM

In the decision-making dichotomy, Thinking types base their decisions on logic while Feeling types base their decisions on how their actions affect themselves and others. If a Feeling type is defended as a Three, there is a definite potential for trouble (figure 5-7). The Feeling type wants to do what is best for the people around her. The Three takes the position that no one should stand between her and success. People can be manipulated and used in pursuit of the goal.

Kay's story. Kay, an INFP-3, is in real estate sales. She works solely on commission, but that is not all that drives her. Her company offers exciting incentives to top salespeople. Kay finds herself working, manipulating and influencing her clients more often than she wants to admit. She begins to see each client as a potential sale that will get her closer to her goal of being top salesperson for that month. When we talked about it, she knew that sometimes she influenced people to buy a home they were hesitant about, and she found that disconcerting because the NF part of her Core Self is very relational and empathetic, wanting the very best for everyone with whom she comes into contact.

Kory's story. Kory, an ESFP-8, is another interesting example. By her true nature, Kory is warm and empathetic. Although she and her husband were struggling in their relationship, with considerable therapy on both their parts, they were doing very well. However, Kory often found herself acting out of her Defense System Eight and being very harsh and even cruel to her husband, although she maintained she really cared about him and wanted the marriage to last.

The same kind of conflict can occur with a Thinking type who is defended with an Enneagram type Four that defies logic (figure 5-8).

Reilley's story. Reilley, an INTJ-4 whose case study you will read in chapter 11, has the opposite problem from Kory. As a Thinking type who is logical, rational and very much left-brain-oriented, Reilley often felt crazy when the drama and intense emotions of her Four Defense took over. It was especially disconcerting at work where she very much wanted to maintain a professional demeanor. Before we met, Reilley had been taking Prozac in order to manage the Four mood swings that presented themselves at inopportune times at work. The out-of-control emotions of the Four were completely unacceptable to the rational Thinker Reilley. She was certain her brain chemistry was defective and was concerned there were even more troubling problems in her psychic make-up.

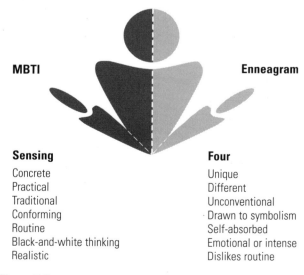

MBTI

Sensing
Concrete
Practical
Traditional
Conforming
Routine
Black-and-white thinking
Realistic

Enneagram

Four
Unique
Different
Unconventional
Drawn to symbolism
Self-absorbed
Emotional or intense
Dislikes routine

Figure 5-6

The drama and mood swings of the Four Defense often had Reilley questioning her own sanity. She would try to evaluate her own behaviors with her logical Thinking abilities and nothing ever made sense. She did not know what to make of her reactions or how to control them. She concluded there was something radically wrong with her. It was the only logical explanation that satisfied her rational mind. When the Four Defense was explained to her, it offered her logical side an acceptable alternative. When she began to see it operating in her life as a defense that immediately sprung into action when she was triggered, the logical left brain accepted the substantiating evidence and was satisfied.

JUDGING AND PERCEIVING AND THE ENNEAGRAM

Finally, in the Judging–Perceiving dichotomy, there are a variety of potential conflicts. Perceiving types like to keep their options open, taking in as much information as possible and putting off a decision until the last possible moment. They are not terribly concerned with the passage of time. When a Perceiving type is defended as a One, such as in Paula's case, there is considerable internal conflict (figure 5-9, page 86). So much to do

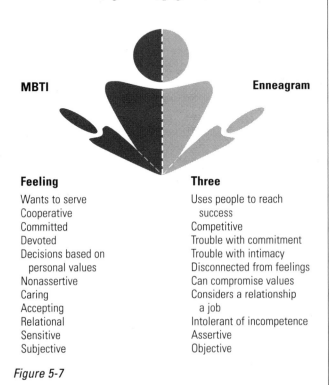

MBTI **Enneagram**

Feeling

Wants to serve
Cooperative
Committed
Devoted
Decisions based on
    personal values
Nonassertive
Caring
Accepting
Relational
Sensitive
Subjective

Three

Uses people to reach
    success
Competitive
Trouble with commitment
Trouble with intimacy
Disconnected from feelings
Can compromise values
Considers a relationship
    a job
Intolerant of incompetence
Assertive
Objective

Figure 5-7

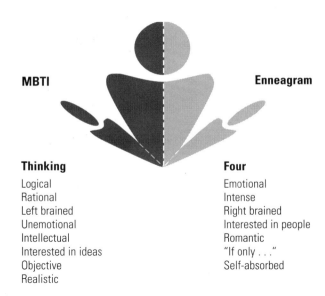

MBTI **Enneagram**

Thinking

Logical
Rational
Left brained
Unemotional
Intellectual
Interested in ideas
Objective
Realistic

Four

Emotional
Intense
Right brained
Interested in people
Romantic
"If only . . ."
Self-absorbed

Figure 5-8

perfectly and so little time in which to do it gives the One an impending sense of urgency.

Paula's story. Paula, the ENFP-1, drove herself physically and mentally every day trying to do everything in her life perfectly, as she was told she was supposed to, as she "should." Her One's internal critical voice urged her on, to do more and do it better, so she would be worthy. Paula hit the ground running as soon as the sun was up. She kept her house immaculate. The garage floor was as clean as the kitchen floor. Everything in her house shone. Everything had a place and everything was in its place. Her lawn was 100 percent weed-free. The flower beds were changed with the seasons. Household decorations were changed with the seasons. Hundreds of pounds of produce from her garden were harvested and canned. At the end of summer, the lawn mower, rototiller, porch furniture and lawn decorations were all washed, waxed and stored for the winter. All these things were dictated by the demanding One in pursuit of being the perfect suburban housewife. The Perceiving part of Paula's personality would have thought about doing those things, perhaps even made a to-do list which would get lost, but somehow the day would have just gotten away from her before those things could be accomplished. Paula's Perceiving part never got that chance. Her One Defense was far too

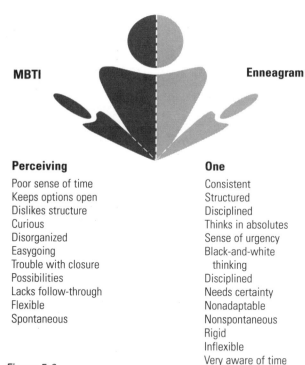

MBTI　　　　　　　　**Enneagram**

Perceiving	**One**
Poor sense of time	Consistent
Keeps options open	Structured
Dislikes structure	Disciplined
Curious	Thinks in absolutes
Disorganized	Sense of urgency
Easygoing	Black-and-white
Trouble with closure	thinking
Possibilities	Disciplined
Lacks follow-through	Needs certainty
Flexible	Nonadaptable
Spontaneous	Nonspontaneous
	Rigid
	Inflexible
	Very aware of time

Figure 5-9

demanding and relentless to let a day get away without working hard toward perfection.

In her own words, Paula describes her internal conflict: "I was always putting myself down as 'not good enough' and 'needing to try harder.' I think these have been my mantras for my life. I always was hard-working and felt guilty for mistakes, even if I did not make the mistake. I was willing to own it. I now know why I am excessive about cleaning and all the work I do. I would feel guilty if I ever tried to cut corners on a project or housework. If I did try to do a less than perfect job, the One Defense System would eat on me until I would re-do it the 'right' way. My faithful companion was a super-critical internal voice that never, never took a sabbatical. I believed there was a right way to handle a task and no other way to tackle it. I was great at seeing all the "shoulds" and being critical of anyone who did not. I worried constantly with ulcers and migraines. Finally, I am now having days that are not filled with excruciating migraines and stomach problems."

Kay's story. Kay, the INFP-3, faced a similar problem. Her Perceiving part would have liked to face each month with a sense of "What's the rush?" There's

plenty of time to make her quota. Besides, all she had to do was beat Jim's sales in order to be top salesperson and that was certainly do-able. But Kay's Perceiving part was cut off at the pass by her Three Defense which could not take the chance that things would not go as well as hoped. The Three had her out working fast and furious from the very beginning of each month to insure that failure was never a consideration (figure 5-10).

Although for both Paula and Kay, the Enneagram Defense won out, there were still parts of their Core Selves that were disappointed and hurt to be overlooked and not allowed expression.

Let's look as well at Judging types who are goal oriented, structured, organized and desire closure. How can an Enneagram Defense type interfere with that?

Danielle's story. Danielle, the ENTJ referred to in chapter 3, is defended as an Enneagram Seven. The Seven hates to limit options. Plans, schedules and structure threaten the fun possibilities the Seven covets so much. While the decisive Judging part is focused and goal-oriented, the Seven is scattered and always entertaining new options that would bring more

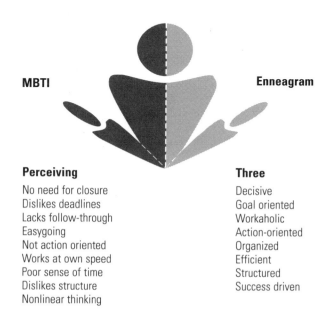

MBTI　　　　　　　　**Enneagram**

Perceiving	**Three**
No need for closure	Decisive
Dislikes deadlines	Goal oriented
Lacks follow-through	Workaholic
Easygoing	Action-oriented
Not action oriented	Organized
Works at own speed	Efficient
Poor sense of time	Structured
Dislikes structure	Success driven
Nonlinear thinking	

Figure 5-10

enjoyment, pleasure and fun (figure 5-11). The Seven so influenced Danielle's life that she often became frustrated with herself for what she saw as a lack of accomplishment. The Seven could not stay focused long enough to get everything that Danielle's J wanted done. The Seven was so influential that four years after she took the MBTI and we began working together, Danielle was still asking me regularly, "Are you sure I'm not a P?"

Brenda's story. I first wrote about Brenda, an ISFJ-6, for the *Enneagram Monthly*. When she first came to see me, Brenda had been married to an abusive alcoholic for more than twenty years. Because of childhood abuse and subsequent abuse in her marriage, Brenda was well entrenched in her Six Defense. She was very fearful and unable to take any risks. Even though her Judging part called for decisiveness and follow-through, she was unable to make any decisions for herself, for her children or about her marriage (figure 5-12). She was caught in the sometimes misguided loyalty of the Six, feeling she had to keep the family together for the sake of the children even though they were showing all the signs of being children of an alcoholic. She told me she did not want to stay with her husband permanently but could not decide when a good time to leave would

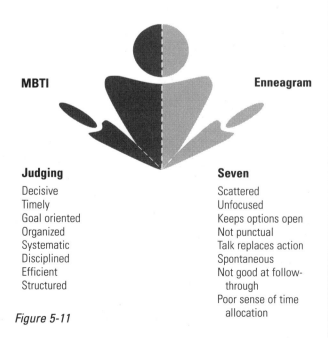

MBTI   **Enneagram**

Judging   **Seven**

Decisive   Scattered
Timely   Unfocused
Goal oriented   Keeps options open
Organized   Not punctual
Systematic   Talk replaces action
Disciplined   Spontaneous
Efficient   Not good at follow-
Structured   through
                            Poor sense of time
                               allocation

Figure 5-11

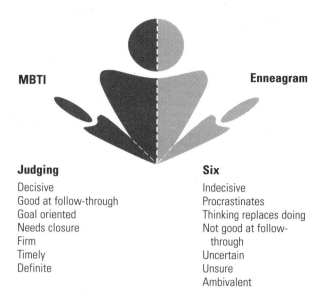

MBTI   **Enneagram**

Judging   **Six**

Decisive   Indecisive
Good at follow-through   Procrastinates
Goal oriented   Thinking replaces doing
Needs closure   Not good at follow-
Firm   through
Timely   Uncertain
Definite   Unsure
                            Ambivalent

Figure 5-12

be. From the first day of the marriage, she had known it was a terrible mistake but had not been able to make the decision to leave. Even though her husband was drunk most of the time, verbally abusive and even violent on occasion, Brenda was still unable to determine if and when to leave.

After the intake process, including personality typing, Brenda and I began her healing work together. At the beginning of each session, I habitually ask each client what has happened since we last met. At the beginning of Brenda's third session, she replied that she had rented an apartment and moved out over the weekend. To say I was shocked and surprised puts it mildly. I was confident Brenda would make the decision to leave eventually but felt it would take a bit longer than three weeks. A year after moving out, Brenda purchased a condo without any need to agonize over the decision. There she established a warm, welcoming environment for her children to visit.

The Judging part of Brenda's personality would have loved to have made this decision a lot earlier. However, Brenda's Core Self, where the Judging part resides, was not in charge; her Six Defense was. As soon as we did enough healing work so that Brenda could access her Core Self, she had no trouble making the decision. The J part was very much in operation. However, for twenty

Two possible scores of Introverted Threes

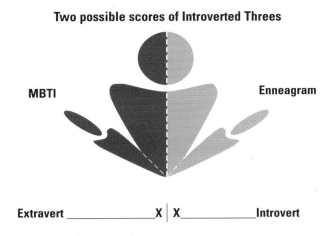

MBTI

Enneagram

Extravert _____ X | X_____ Introvert

Score of an Extraverted Three

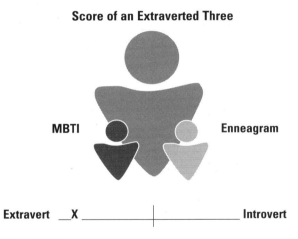

MBTI

Enneagram

Extravert __X_____ | _____ Introvert

Figure 5-13

plus years, there was a continual war within her. The Judging part wanted to make definite plans to leave and the Six was unable to come to terms with the decision.

As you can see, it is conceivable that an Enneagram Defense trait could argue with a Core Self quality in each of the MBTI dichotomies of personality. Often, the Enneagram traits are all that appear visible, causing the person to wonder if the opposite MBTI quality even exists. The response may be just like Danielle's, who asked, "Are you sure I'm not a P?" or like Paula who barely recognized her MBTI traits. So, if you have such a conflict in one of your MBTI dichotomies, how can you figure out which is which? In order to understand that, let's see about answering Danielle's question.

If you refer back to figure 3-1, page 31, you will

remember that the MBTI chart has a line down the center. I stressed that the line indicated that the MBTI was a sorter and that the distance between the two poles of each dichotomy of personality was not a true continuum. If your score falls close to the center of the Extravert–Introvert line, you would not be a happy blend of both. That type of score would indicate some internal tension or conflict suggesting that you are not certain. Often, the reason for such a score and the resulting internal conflict is that the Enneagram part of personality has answered some of the questions. I have described my own situation of being an Introverted Performer. I will always score close to the center line on Extraversion–Introversion. The Introvert part answers half the questions and the Performer Three answers the other half. Once, I even scored on the Extravert side on a day when the Three was particularly active. So how do I know I am truly an Introvert and not the Extravert the instrument indicated that day? There are basically two reasons. First, when I looked at what that dichotomy really measured, I knew without a doubt that I am energized internally, even though I like and work with people. I need down time and personal space in order to recover my energy. But the second point is the one I want to look at more closely here. If I were truly an Extravert, that part would have answered its half of the E–I questions on the Extravert side and the Three would have answered from its Performing standpoint on the Extravert side. The vote would be close to unanimous. There would be no conflict. I would have scored as clearly an Extravert (figure 5-13).

For Danielle, the same would have been true. If she were truly a Perceiving type, the P part of her personality would have answered some of the questions from a Perceiving perspective. The Seven would have influenced the remaining J–P questions from its desire to keep options open. There would have been no internal conflict. The score would have been clearly on the Perceiving side. Furthermore, Danielle would be living her life happily content to be spontaneous, perhaps even flighty, without much focus. As it was, Danielle agonized over the J–P questions, reporting she could have gone either way on most of them. Her score was very close to the centerline (figure 5-14). She further reported that she is very distressed when her life seems disorganized and without structure. In her job, she could be structured and organized yet she resented the prolonged restrictions that required.

So, if you are having trouble making a determination in any of the four dichotomies of your MBTI profile, take a closer look. With the knowledge of your Enneagram Defense type and a little detective work, you can probably come to an understanding of what is causing the conflict.

CORE SELF AND DEFENSE SYSTEM: ALL-OUT WAR

When we put together all four preferences of the MBTI Core Self, we find they are more than just the sum of their parts. Your MBTI four-letter type formula supplies more than just four pieces of information about you. Knowing your MBTI type formula provides a wealth of information about your Core Being. We have looked at the small battles that take place when one preference of your MBTI type formula is opposed by your Enneagram Defense System. Sometimes the conflict is on an even grander scale, and there is all-out war. That is the case with Paula. Let's return to her story.

Paula's story. Paula's Core Self is an ENFP. I call these people "puppy dogs in a field." There is so much to see, do and experience that it is hard to know in which direction to turn first. Life is so full of exciting possibilities just waiting to be explored. ENFPs want to experience it all. For them, life supplies a rich and unending source of fun, excitement and adventure. These charming people are enthusiastic and childlike with a great need for freedom and absolutely no desire to conform.

Unfortunately, Paula's Defense System is exactly the opposite. The disciplined and structured One insists on doing things the right way. Ones are serious, with rules boxing them in at every turn. A One will avoid risk and play it safe by doing things according to accepted cultural standards. The One has trouble relaxing, with a sense of urgency that insists on work before play.

To make a bad situation even worse for Paula, her father was a One as well. He was an extreme perfectionist setting unbelievably high standards for her and demanding nothing short of perfection. Paula's dad never asked any more of her than he demanded of himself. Each Saturday, after the entire house was cleaned to perfection, he would go out in the yard and meticulously remove every offending weed in the lawn. Paula was required to do every homework paper over and over until it met the standards of perfection imposed by her father. Needless to say, the little ENFP puppy-dog child was badly wounded and put away for safe keeping.

Adding to Paula's problems were the nuns who taught her, also imposing rigid guidelines that Paula's

Two possible scores of Judging Sevens

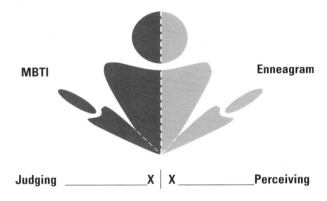

Score of a Perceiving Seven

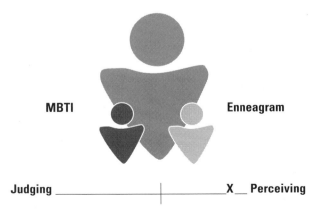

Figure 5-14

MBTI-Enneagram Qualities Correlation

ENFP-1

Corresponding Compatible Qualities

ENFP

1. Can get involved in causes
2. Can make mistakes in judgment
3. Can succeed at anything
4. Conformational bias
5. Hypersensitive to criticism
6. Works towards perfection
7. Self-critical
8. Values are important
9. Expressive
10. Idealistic
11. Integrity
12. Self-critical
13. Self-critical
14. Conformational bias
15. Trouble relaxing

Corresponding Oppositional Qualities

ENFP

A. Can be inconsistent
B. Affirming, sympathetic
C. Dislikes structure
D. Accepting
E. Curious
F. Desires harmony
G. Ignores the flaws in others
H. Disorganized
I. Fun loving, creative, imaginative
J. Easygoing
K. Trouble bringing closure
L. Optimistic, positive
M. Trouble with rules and regulations
N. Trouble with details
O. Attracted to adventure
P. Sees possibilities
Q. Lacks follow-through
R. Agreeable, easygoing
S. Hates routine; easily bored
T. Not neat
U. Sees the good in others
V. Hates routine; easily bored
W. Flexible, versatile, dynamic
X. Easygoing
Y. Fun loving
Z. Easygoing
AA. Not interested in financial matters
BB. Flexible, versatile
CC. Difficulty prioritizing
DD. Spontaneous, impulsive
EE. Work and play merge
FF. Initiates change; can improvise
GG. Likes variety, diversity
HH. Excellent people skills
II. Difficulty focusing
JJ. Poor concept of time

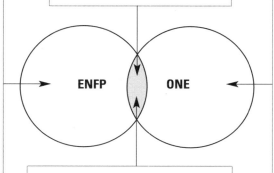

Corresponding Compatible Qualities

ONE

1. Crusader for justice
2. Judging
3. Hardworking
4. Conformational bias
5. Hyper-vigilant for criticism
6. Focus on flaws and personal faults
7. Extremely self-critical
8. High moral standards, ethical
9. Opinionated, outspoken
10. Focus on the ideal
11. Integrity
12. If people really knew me, they wouldn't like me
13. Constant internal critical voice
14. Carries grudges
15. Trouble relaxing

Corresponding Oppositional Qualities

ONE

A. Consistent
B. Intolerant
C. Structured, disciplined
D. Dissatisfied
E. Deals in absolutes
F. Fault finder
G. Everything can improved
H. Needs to control environment
I. Serious
J. Perfectionist
K. Sense of urgency
L. Focus on flaws and on personal faults
M. Preoccupied with rules, shoulds
N. The smallest flaw ruins the whole thing
O. Avoids risk
P. Black-and-white thinking
Q. Conscientious
R. Controlling
S. Disciplined
T. Meticulous
U. Moral superiority
V. Needs certainty
W. Nonadaptable, nonspontaneous, uncompromising
X. Easily irritated
Y. Prone to depression
Z. Tendency to rage
AA. Thrifty
BB. Rigid
CC. Disciplined
DD. Structured
EE. Work before play
FF. Inflexible
GG. Needs consistency
HH. Critical
II. Focus on the ideal; what's missing
JJ. Very aware of time

Figure 5-15

perfectionist One tried to meet. By fourth grade, Paula was vomiting every day before school and deeply depressed.

After high school, Paula's situation further deteriorated as she entered the convent, a decision made by the One Defense System to try to make her more acceptable and to attempt to "earn her way to heaven." After ten years, Paula was suicidal, on tranquilizers and had been hospitalized for depression. Happily, she decided to leave the convent.

As so many do, Paula married a clone of her father two years after leaving the convent. It goes without saying that the marriage was a mistake from the beginning and only deteriorated over the next twenty years. So it is no surprise that the woman I described at the opening of this chapter was at the end of her rope.

Figure 5-15 diagrams the all-out war between Paula's ENFP Core Self and her One Defense System. Paula explains, "My Enneagram One held a lot of my fun-loving ENFP in control. When I was in a position to let loose of the One, I was an entirely different person. I could relax instead of being on hyper-alert all the time. I now realize why I had trouble concentrating; with my mind thinking ahead to one hundred other things to do, I could not think of just one thing and do it. I was running in one hundred directions. When I was on trips, I could let go—a little—of my perfectionism. I could just put things out of order and not get upset for the duration of the trip. I could relax and just be easygoing. I never understood why this happened, and I wished I could be this person all the time."

In these personality diagrams, the Core Self MBTI qualities are listed on the left of the diagram and the qualities of the Enneagram Defense that conflict or oppose the MBTI qualities are on the right. Paula's list of opposing qualities is considerable. Please consider the seriousness of the conflicts even more than the length of the lists. For instance, the impulsive ENFP's love of spontaneity is obliterated by the One's insistence on structure and consistency. The seriousness of this particular conflict permeates every waking hour of an ENFP-1's life. It is not necessarily balanced off by a pair of qualities that are compatible (listed at the top and bottom of the diagram) such as the ENFP being drawn to causes and the One being willing to fight for justice. These two compatible qualities do not affect every moment of the ENFP-1's life. Not included in these diagrams are qualities I call neutral. They neither support nor oppose each other. For instance, in Paula's case, a One has a penchant to repeat things for emphasis. This trait is neither in support nor in opposition to any of her ENFP qualities. Likewise, the ENFP likes to talk in metaphor. There is nothing about the One that supports or opposes this trait. So these personality diagrams are not complete in themselves. The diagrams do, however, give us a good picture of the degree of internal conflict or harmony felt between the Core Self and the Defense System.

In order to get another perspective on Paula's personality, let's look at how different things would have been had Paula been defended as an Enneagram Seven instead of the One.

Figure 5-16

SEVEN

Adventurous	Excellent social skills
Appears scattered	Excessive
Attracted to excitement, stimulation	Future oriented
	Hates being defined, limited
Avoids the unpleasant	Idealizes
Avoids responsibility	Impractical
Avoids boredom	Keeps options open
Busy	Narcissistic
Charming, engaging	Needs variety
Childlike	Not punctual
Creative, imaginative	Highly optimistic and positive
Curious	Possibilities
Dislikes routine	Requires freedom
Enjoys brainstorming	Spontaneous, impulsive, uninhibited
Entertaining	
Enthusiastic, energetic	
Escapist	

Like the ENFP, the Seven is fun loving, adventuresome, energetic, spontaneous and positive (figure 5-16). There is a great deal of harmony between the ENFP and the Seven Defense (figure 5-17). If Paula had

MBTI-Enneagram Qualities Correlation

ENFP-7

Corresponding Compatible Qualities

ENFP

1. Attracted to adventure
2. Brainstorms
3. Charismatic, charming
4. Childlike
5. Curious
6. Creative, artistic
7. Needs affirmation
8. Dislikes decisions
9. Dislikes structure, repetition, routine
10. Dynamic, energetic
11. Easily bored
12. Engaging
13. Future oriented
14. Enthusiastic
15. Fantasizes
16. Lively; trouble relaxing
17. Externally energized
18. May be inconsistent
19. May overindulge
20. Optimistic, positive
21. Idealistic
22. Ideaphoria
23. Imaginative
24. Not realistic
25. Fun loving
26. Many interests
27. Multifaceted
28. Often overextended
29. Poor concept of time
30. Accepting
31. Lacks follow-through
32. Friendly
33. Needs freedom
34. Sees others' good
35. Nonconformist; nontraditional
36. Needs harmony
37. May be fickle
38. Plans, possibilities
39. Needs options
40. Sociable, excellent people skills
41. Gregarious
42. Expressive, good communicator
43. Spontaneous, impulsive
44. Difficulty getting focused; disorganized
45. Flexible, versatile
46. Likes variety and diversity
47. Sees possibilities
48. Needs approval

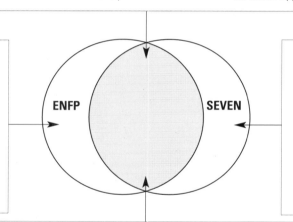

Corresponding Oppositional Qualities

ENFP

A. Anticipates others' needs
B. Needs meaning
C. Conformational bias, hyper-alert
D. Search for self
E. Service oriented
F. Service oriented, sympathetic
G. Self-critical

Corresponding Oppositional Qualities

SEVEN

A. Self-absorbed
B. Superficial
C. Too trusting
D. Idealized self-image
E. Narcissistic
F. Feels superior
G. Idealized self-image

Corresponding Compatible Qualities

SEVEN

1. Adventurous
2. Enjoys brainstorming
3. Charming
4. Childlike
5. Curious
6. Creative
7. Desires positive mirroring
8. Hates being defined/limited
9. Dislikes routine
10. Energetic
11. Avoids boredom
12. Engaging, entertaining
13. Future oriented
14. Enthusiastic
15. Escapist, fantasizes
16. Active, busy, lively, vivacious
17. External orientation
18. Appears scattered, flighty
19. Excessive
20. Positive
21. Idealizes
22. Ideaphoria
23. Imaginative
24. Impractical
25. Pleasure oriented
26. Many varied interests
27. Multitalented
28. Over scheduled
29. Not punctual
30. Not suspicious
31. Not good at follow-through
32. Pleasant
33. Requires freedom
34. Sees everyone/everybody as "nice"
35. Uninhibited
36. Avoids conflict
37. Avoids commitment
38. Loves to plan
39. Keeps options open
40. Excellent social skills
41. Gregarious
42. Talkative
43. Spontaneous, impulsive
44. Trouble focusing
45. Versatile
46. Needs variety
47. Possibilities
48. Desires adulation

Figure 5-17

been defended as a Seven, her life would have looked a lot different. That does not mean she would have been happier because even though the Seven looks very lighthearted on the outside, it is a Defense System nonetheless and acts to protect the Core Self from the awareness of emotional pain. However, if Paula had been defended as a Seven, at least the horrendous internal conflict between her Core Self and her Defense System would not have taken place, causing untold emotional, physical and spiritual damage over the years.

Paula's personality combines an ENFP Core Self, who is a free spirit, with a Defense System One that is rigid and demanding. Sarah, the ISTJ-9 we met in chapters 1 and 4, presents the opposite problem.

Sarah's story. Sarah, an ISTJ-9, first came to see me because she felt there was something radically wrong with her. She could not let go of her anger towards her parents for an abusive childhood. Sarah, forty-two, is the third oldest in a large family. She was raised in a rural area and was badly abused emotionally, physically and sexually. As an ISTJ (figure 5-18), Sarah was very well suited to be in the hero role in her family. Unfortunately, that role was already taken by her older brother, and the family system assigned Sarah the role of scapegoat. By definition, the scapegoat in the family is on the outside, is labeled as a problem and can never earn acceptance. The normal dysfunctional family needs a scapegoat to explain why the family has problems. If everyone's attention is focused on the problems of the scapegoat, then no one has to look at what is really going on in the family.

Sarah tried hard to please her family, being obedient, helpful, getting good grades and working outside the home. Nothing she did resulted in praise, affection or acceptance, much less the expression of love she so wanted. After years of fighting her fate as a teenager, Sarah finally gave in and began acting out for real. She used too much alcohol and became promiscuous. It was a lifestyle that did not suit her and did not last long. Sarah is a bright and capable woman. She finished college, went on for a Master's degree, eventually married and had two children.

Figure 5-18

ISTJ

Analytical, logical, critical	Neat, precise
Committed, loyal	Needs security and stability
Common sense	Needs to feel useful
Concrete	Objective
Conservative, simple lifestyle	Organized, structured, likes routine
Decisive	Pessimistic, cautious
Detail oriented, observant	Practical, realistic
Dutiful, dependable, dedicated, obedient	Quiet, reserved, very private
Efficient	Responsible
Frugal, good investor	Rules and regulations
Goal oriented, persevering	Serious
Honest	Sincere
Independent	Stable
Inflexible, not spontaneous	Strong work ethic
Judging, opinionated	Timely
Lives in the moment	Traditional
Maintains the status quo	Trustworthy

One fine quality of all scapegoats is that they are truth tellers. They are already on the outside and have nothing to lose. Therefore, often the scapegoat in the family is the one to seek counseling, and so it was with Sarah. She was the only one in her family to want answers and the only one willing to honestly speak out about what was happening in the family. The scapegoat is so used to being blamed for everything that, when entering therapy, she is fully prepared to face the music and be told, yet again, that the problem is all hers. Sarah, a practicing Christian, entered therapy wanting to know what was wrong with her because she could not practice the Christian philosophy of forgiveness and just move on. She blamed herself unmercifully because she could not let go of her anger.

When I took Sarah's case history, I certainly could not blame her for being angry. Growing up in her house was like living in a prison camp in a third world country. There were too many children and not enough money. Add that to emotionally unhealthy parents and it is a clear formula for disaster. The living conditions and basic hygiene in the family were such that, if discovered in a home today, they would make headlines with graphic pictures underscoring abuse and neglect. Sarah's childhood was nothing short of a nightmare. Each day was drudgery, desolate and dark. For Sarah to expect herself to be able to simply forgive and move on was asking more of herself than anyone could do.

Adding to Sarah's problems growing up was her Nine Defense System (figure 5-19). All she wanted to do was sleep and escape into her own inner world. The more pressure and stress Sarah experienced, the less she wanted to move. Yet she had to be up before dawn, working before she went to school, only to return home to work again. The lethargic, unfocused Nine did not cooperate well with the hard-working, efficient ISTJ. Having two such disparate parts operational within her was disconcerting to Sarah, to say the least, and continues to be so today. Anytime Sarah is triggered by being discounted or rejected, she finds the Nine takes over and she feels unable to move or be productive in any way. Figure 5-20 shows how Sarah's Core Self, the ISTJ, and her Nine Defense are at odds.

Figure 5-19

NINE

Accepting	Escapes into sleep
Accommodating, adaptive	Flat affect, monotone voice
Agreeable	Holds onto unexpressed
Ambivalent	resentments
Avoids conflict	Inertia, lethargic, phlegmatic
Calm	Internally focused
Choices are difficult	Keeps a low profile
Clothes must be comfortable	Loses track of time
Complacent, compliant	Low energy
Compromising	Mediator
Conserves energy	Needs harmony
Controls through nonaction	No self-awareness
Difficulty setting and	Passive aggressive
maintaining goals	Passive
Dissociates	Stubborn
Easygoing	Unpretentious

It is clear that the low-energy, lethargic Nine and the productive, goal-oriented ISTJ sharing a common body in Sarah contributed to some of her *dis*-ease. Mary is another ISTJ (refer to figure 5-18) and she and Sarah have a lot in common. Both were forty-two when they entered therapy at about the same time. Both were married to NF (Intuitive Feeling) men and both had two children. Both were scapegoats in their family of origin and each childhood was dismal. As ISTJs, both women fall into the SJ temperament, which readily accepts the stereotypical cultural definition of a woman. As the minority and untypical Thinking women, both Sarah and Mary had always felt they did not fit in. They both found this very wounding, as SJs want nothing so much as to belong. Both felt very different from the way they thought a woman should be, leaving each to conclude that something was wrong with her. So Sarah and Mary had a great deal in common. One major difference between them, however, is that Sarah is defended as a Nine and Mary as a One (refer to figure 5-2, page 82).

Mary's story. When Mary first came to see me she was in depression and had been having suicidal thoughts. She had been taking anti-depressants for quite a while and reported that her eight-year-old son was taking them as well. Her marriage and her husband's business were both in trouble and she found herself raging frequently although she hated herself for doing so. Rage is a common problem for Ones who try to contain their anger only to have it come out in an out-of-control rush when triggered, followed immediately by intense self-loathing. Mary found her rage directed at those she loved most, her family, and she hated herself for this. Neither ISTJs nor Ones are comfortable with tears, but Mary was so broken that she cried easily and often.

Mary, one of three girls, was raised in a household where her father ruled supreme. He was emotionally, verbally and physically abusive. Mary was his main target. Her mother developed cancer when Mary was a teen but that information was not shared with the children. When her mother died, her death was totally unexpected and Mary was completely unprepared. Grieving was not an option her father would consider, and so Mary tried to be stoic and contain her feelings.

Like Sarah, Mary was well equipped to be the hero of her family but she fell heir to the scapegoat role. Her

MBTI-Enneagram Qualities Correlation

ISTJ-9

Corresponding Compatible Qualities

ISTJ

1. Quiet, serious
2. Patient with rules and procedures
3. Never ostentatious
4. Prefers routine
5. Hardworking
6. Values harmony
7. Deep feelings rarely expressed
8. Relies on past experiences
9. Inner values give direction
10. Efficient
11. Underestimates self, modest
12. Not easily discouraged
13. Refers to past experiences
14. Persevering
15. Calm exterior covering internal stress
16. Reserved
17. Needs privacy
18. Detail oriented
19. Simple lifestyle; down to earth

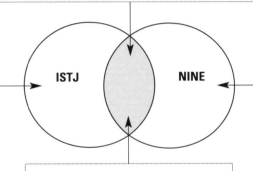

Corresponding Oppositional Qualities

ISTJ

A. Decisive
B. Dependable, aware of time schedules
C. Status is important
D. Understands and accepts societal institutions
E. Strict parent
F. Decisive
G. Practical, sensible, realistic
H. Needs closure
I. Black-and-white thinking
J. Systematic and painstaking
K. Hardworking
L. Scheduled
M. Wants to make a contribution to society
N. Clothes are serviceable and traditional
O. Able to prioritize
P. Inflexible
Q. Black-and-white thinking
R. Prompt with assignments
S. Concrete
T. Hierarchy, status
U. Able to concentrate
V. Can be driven
W. Lives in the moment
X. Needs to be productive
Y. Results oriented
Z. Task oriented

Corresponding Compatible Qualities

NINE

1. Quiet, flat affect, internal
2. Can merge with work
3. Comfort above appearance
4. Routine relieves stress
5. Can merge with job
6. Values harmony above all
7. Feelings contained in the inner world
8. When a plan works, use it again
9. Inner world most important
10. Conserves energy
11. Feels unimportant
12. Stubborn
13. Nostalgic about the past
14. Stubborn
15. Calm exterior
16. Detached
17. Keeps low profile
18. Long, detailed stories
19. Unpretentious

Corresponding Oppositional Qualities

NINE

A. Procrastinates, ambivalent
B. Loses track of time
C. Not ambitious
D. Lives in an inner world
E. Easygoing, no conflict
F. Trouble making decisions; inertia
G. Trouble distinguishing between essentials and nonessentials
H. Postpones goal setting
I. Nonjudgmental
J. Appears indifferent
K. Not ambitious, not self-motivated
L. Loses track of time
M. Does not expect to be valued or recognized
N. Clothes are comfortable
O. Cannot recognize differences between essentials and nonessentials
P. Adaptable, compromising
Q. Can see all sides
R. Hates deadlines
S. Global goals
T. Nonachiever
U. Spaces out
V. Easygoing
W. Trouble staying present
X. Loves to sleep
Y. Desires to just "be"
Z. Low energy

Figure 5-20

MBTI-Enneagram Qualities Correlation

ISTJ-1

Corresponding Compatible Qualities

ISTJ

1. Accurate
2. Sense of what is appropriate
3. Assumes others have same worldview, values
4. Applies past experiences to present situation
5. Avoids risks
6. Calm exterior covering internal crisis, strife
7. Can be inflexible
8. Can be compulsive
9. Dedicated, driven
10. Conservation of materials and personnel
11. Concrete
12. Consistent
13. Strong opinions
14. Demanding
15. Hardworking
16. Honorable
17. Honest, straightforward
18. Strong opinions
19. Justice
20. Painstakingly neat
21. Trouble seeing others' viewpoints
22. Not impulsive or spontaneous
23. Orderly
24. Systematic
25. Rules, regulations, procedures, shoulds
26. Serious
27. Strong work ethic
28. Timely
29. Details obscure big picture
30. Responsible
31. Frugal
32. Knows what's right
33. Structured
34. Work before play

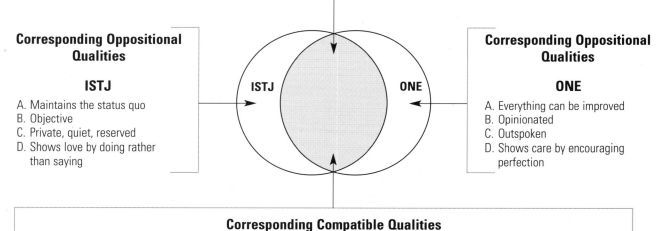

Corresponding Oppositional Qualities

ISTJ

A. Maintains the status quo
B. Objective
C. Private, quiet, reserved
D. Shows love by doing rather than saying

Corresponding Oppositional Qualities

ONE

A. Everything can be improved
B. Opinionated
C. Outspoken
D. Shows care by encouraging perfection

Corresponding Compatible Qualities

ONE

1. Perfectionist
2. There is a right way to do everything
3. Expects everyone to have same internal rules
4. Refers to past grievances, carries grudges
5. Avoids risk
6. Avoids expression of anger
7. Inflexible
8. Compulsive
9. Crusader
10. Thrifty
11. Deals in absolutes
12. Consistent
13. Critical
14. Impatient
15. Hardworking
16. High moral standards, ethical
17. Honest, integrity
18. Judging
19. Justice
20. Meticulous
21. Moral superiority
22. Nonspontaneous
23. Needs order
24. Disciplined
25. Preoccupied with rules, shoulds
26. Serious
27. Trouble relaxing
28. Very aware of time
29. Focus on ideal, on flaws and on faults
30. Conscientious, very responsible
31. Thrifty
32. Self-righteous
33. Structured
34. Work before play

Figure 5-21

father was relentless. Mary tried very hard to live up to all his expectations in order to win his approval and affection but there was nothing she could do. As she learned how to meet a demand or rule, it would change, so she did not have a chance. Like Sarah, Mary's family had some basic hygiene problems that left Mary with feelings in adulthood of being unclean and untouchable. Mary's One Defense System worked overtime throughout her childhood trying to meet the ever-changing, ever-unattainable standards her father set.

Her current situation was equally distressing. Her failing marriage to an INFP contributed to a great deal of her pain. Her husband's inability to be specific was stressing her unbearably. (An INFP often does not recognize a detail even when it appears and announces its presence.) Their basic differences in communication styles caused chaos and left Mary continually feeling as she did in childhood: "I'm trying to do my very best; the rules keep changing and no one hears me when I speak. It must be my fault." Mary's thinking is very linear and focused. Her husband's thinking is global with little ability to focus. She needed structure in her life very badly in order to meet one of her basic ISTJ needs of feeling safe and secure. To say her life lacked structure, safety and security was an understatement.

Mary's One Defense System kicked into high gear to try to help, only it simply made things worse. The One's approach is that if Mary does things perfectly right, the chaos will stop and harmony will prevail. However, it was not possible for Mary to do things perfectly when she did not have control of everything. The majority of the control of the business was in her husband's hands. She could not control their poor communication nor could she control a myriad of other aspects of their family life. The standard reply of the One Defense is, "Try harder! Do more! It's all your fault!" Her internal critical voice was continually screaming at her and condemning every move she made because nothing she did resulted in transforming chaos into order. Mary was stressed to the max.

Mary's already driven, demanding and hardworking

ISTJ was joined by the equally driven, demanding and hardworking One. The results are exponential. Mary was breaking down under the strain. She looked physically constricted and felt awful. Although there was no internal war between her Core Self and her Defense System (figure 5-21), Mary clearly needed to restrain her overactive One Defense System and come to terms with the aspects of her life that were out of her control.

It is clear to see that although Mary's Core Self and Defense System are not warring, the results are not necessarily a harmonious life. Whenever the Defense System is in control of the individual, that person is operating out of a wounded, defended position and access to the Core Self is limited, leaving a sense of emptiness and desolation, as Mary readily testified.

Some personality combinations have a preponderance of what I call neutral qualities. That is, qualities in the two systems that neither support nor oppose each other. In these cases, the Core Self and the Defense System are like neighbors in an apartment building who recognize each other but rarely communicate. An example of this configuration is an ENFJ-4 (figure 5-22, page 98). You can see from the list of qualities of the ENFJ and the Four (figure 5-23, page 99) that the two systems have little in common yet they do not seem to oppose each other either. Compare that to Kay's combination of INFP and Three (figure 5-24, page 99) in which seemingly every trait of one system is either supported or opposed by the other system (figure 5-25, page 100).

REFERENCES AND SUGGESTED READING

Wagner, J. P. Speaker. *Two Windows on the Self: The Enneagram and the Myers-Briggs* [Cassettes 1–6]. Kansas City MO: Credence Cassettes, 1992. Wagner offers a discussion of the influences of the two typing systems, MBTI and Enneagram, upon each other. For instance, an Introverted Three will look different from an Extraverted Three. He also provides some statistical correlations of the Enneagram with the MBTI; for example, he notes that two-thirds of Threes are Extraverted. This tape set can be ordered from Credence Cassettes at 888.595.8273.

MBTI-Enneagram Qualities Correlation

ENFJ-4

Corresponding Compatible Qualities

ENFJ

1. Needs order
2. Romantic ideals
3. Values variety
4. Expressive
5. Longs for the ideal relationship
6. Vulnerable to rejection

Corresponding Oppositional Qualities

ENFJ

A. Even tempered
B. Exuberant, lively
C. Future oriented, visionary
D. Noncompetitive, cooperative
E. Facilitator
F. Charismatic, charming, social, congenial
G. Positive
H. Concerned, sensitive, serving
I. Relational
J. Affirming, appreciative
K. Committed
L. Entertaining
M. Enthusiastic
N. Personable, popular; warm
O. Drawn to saving the world
P. Focuses on others

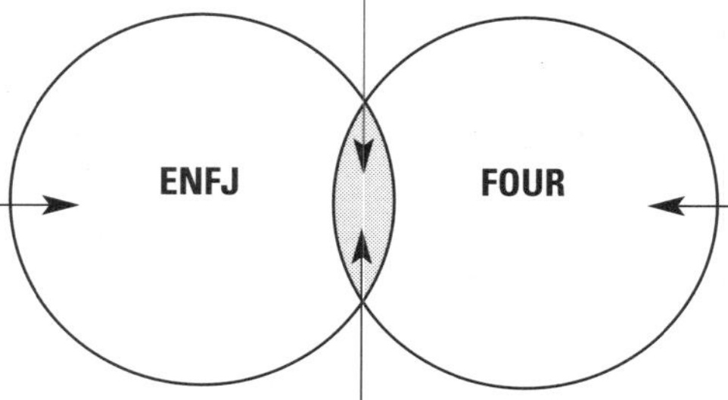

Corresponding Oppositional Qualities

FOUR

A. Manic-depressive, bipolar, moody
B. Melancholy
C. Nostalgic
D. Competitive
E. Not good team player
F. Aloof
G. Pessimistic
H. Self-absorbed
I. Feels no one can understand me
J. Envious
K. Push-pull; long for and reject
L. Serious
M. Sense of tragedy
N. Not easy to get to know
O. Self-absorbed
P. Self-absorbed

ENFJ   FOUR

Corresponding Compatible Qualities

FOUR

1. Nonspontaneous
2. Romantic
3. Dislikes routine
4. Dramatic
5. Longing
6. Reject rather than chance rejection

Figure 5-22

ENFJ

Affirming
Appreciative
Articulate, eloquent
Charismatic
Committed
Compassionate, empathetic
Conscientious
Cooperative
Creative
Enthusiastic
Even tempered
Facilitator
Idealist
Insightful, intuitive
Inspires, motivates
Needs harmony
Not competitive
Nurturing
Opinionated
Organized
People are the priority
Persevering
Pleaser
Positive
Problem solver
Relational
Responsible
Talkative
Values variety
Visionary
Vulnerable to rejection

Figure 5-23

FOUR

Abhors the ordinary
Competitive
Deep feelings
Desires the unattainable
Distinctive dress
Dramatic, intense
Drawn to symbolism
Elite
Envious
Feelings of deprivation
Feelings of being incomplete
Feels no one can understand
  me
Heightened sense of loss
Longing
Manic-depressive, bipolar,
  moody
Melancholy
Needs recognition
Pessimistic
Preoccupied with death
Preoccupied with what is
  missing
Prone to self-pity
Push-pull; long for and reject
Regret
Romantic
Searching
Search for depth and meaning
Self-absorbed
Sense of tragedy
Sense of entitlement
There is not enough
Unique

INFP

Adaptable, flexible
Affirming
Caring, compassionate
Congenial, cooperative
Contemplative
Creative
Deep sense of commitment;
  devoted
Deeply held beliefs, values
Difficulty expressing feelings
Difficulty with criticism
Dislikes rules and regulations
Dislikes conflict; needs
  harmony
Empathetic
Facilitator
Good communicator
Idealistic
Independent
Insightful; visionary
Inspirational
Integrity
Internally focused
Leads reluctantly
Loyal
No facade, self-effacing
Not assertive; aggressive
Not competitive
Not action oriented
Nurturer
Passionate, intense
Private, quiet
Search for identity
Seems disorganized
Sensitive
Service oriented
Tolerant
Very relational

Figure 5-24

THREE

Achievement oriented;
  ambitious
Action oriented
Adaptable
Appearance is important;
  image conscious
Assertive
Attention seeking
Can compromise values
Charming
Competitive
Disconnected from feelings
Do; busy; overactive
Efficient
End justifies the means
Energetic
Enthusiastic
Failure is not an option
Future oriented; visionary
Goals
Good communicator
Hates criticism
Inspirational
Manipulates
Motivational
No private life
Organized
Positive
Professionalism
Self-confident
Self-deception
Talks
Team leader
The impossible just takes
  a little longer

MBTI-Enneagram Qualities Correlation
INFP-3

Corresponding Compatible Qualities
INFP

1. Adaptable, flexible
2. Compliant
3. Congenial
4. Good communicator
5. Encouraging; inspirational
6. Difficulty with criticism
7. Difficulty expressing feelings
8. Doesn't want to reveal mistakes
9. Draws people together
10. Facilitator
11. Frustrated by trivialities
12. Hard to get to know
13. Intense
14. Future oriented; internal vision of perfection
15. Keeps emotionally distant
16. May loosely interpret assignments, directives
17. Persuasive
18. Search for identity
19. Passionate
20. Encouraging
21. People pleasing
22. Gracious
23. May seem to agree outwardly while disagreeing inwardly
24. Can get caught up in the needs of the other

Corresponding Oppositional Qualities
INFP

A. Prefer getting more information than closure
B. Wants to serve humanity
C. Conciliatory except where personal values are concerned
D. Not competitive, cooperative
E. Contemplative
F. Needs privacy
G. Does not readily speak out; quiet
H. Deep sense of commitment; devoted
I. Dislikes deadlines; trouble completing projects
J. Does not enjoy limelight; reserved
K. Easygoing
L. Not action oriented; enjoys time for reflection
M. Extremely protective of ideals, values
N. Hard on self
O. Ideals are paramount
P. Internally focused
Q. Not attracted to business careers
R. Idealistic
S. May have trouble seeing another's perspective
T. Nonlinear thinking
U. No façade
V. Not aggressive/assertive
W. Dedicated to helping humanity
X. Self-challenging
Y. Self-effacing
Z. Strong values, ideals, convictions
AA. Works at own speed
BB. Reflective
CC. Subjective
DD. Work must have meaning
EE. Enjoys helping others grow
FF. Integrity
GG. Leads reluctantly
HH. Visualizing completed project replaces completion
II. Writer
JJ. Inner focused and service oriented
KK. Devoted to family; faithful
LL. Forms loyal relationships
MM. Caring, compassionate, empathetic
NN. Needs quiet recognition
OO. Self-effacing
PP. Gentle

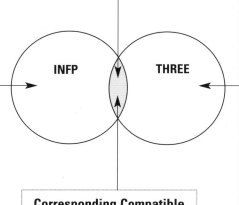

Corresponding Compatible Qualities
THREE

1. Adaptable
2. Chameleon
3. Charming
4. Good communicator
5. Compelling; persuasive
6. Hates criticism
7. Puts aside feelings
8. Failure is not an option
9. Team leader
10. Socially skilled; leader
11. Details are ignored
12. Self-deceptive
13. The impossible just takes a little longer
14. Future oriented, visionary
15. Disconnected with feelings
16. Can package and re-package to suit the need
17. Manipulates
18. Heart centered; identity
19. Enthusiastic
20. Motivator
21. Approval seeking
22. Socially skilled
23. Will tell you what you want to hear
24. Other directed

Corresponding Oppositional Qualities
THREE

A. Decisive
B. Considers a relationship a job
C. Can compromise values
D. Competitive
E. Not interested in depth, just image
F. No private life
G. Talks
H. Problems with commitment
I. Goal oriented
J. Attention is necessary
K. Workaholic
L. Action oriented
M. Can compromise values
N. Self-assured
O. Prestige is important
P. Disconnected from the inner world
Q. Achievement important
R. Prefers measurable goals
S. Approval seeking; other directed
T. Organized
U. Image conscious; appearance important
V. Assertive
W. Use others to achieve success
X. Self-confident
Y. Ambitious
Z. The ends justify the means
AA. Efficient
BB. Energetic
CC. Objective
DD. Work must bring recognition
EE. Uses others to achieve success
FF. Can compromise personal values
GG. Team leader
HH. Goal oriented; needs closure
II. Talker
JJ. Money, possessions, material worth
KK. Problems with intimacy
LL. Social connections important
MM. Considers relationship a job
NN. Attention seeking
OO. Self-assured; self-confident
PP. Can be aggressive

Figure 5-25

Wyman, P. "MBTI & Enneagram," Part 1. *Enneagram Monthly* 33 (November 1997): 1.

Wyman, P. "MBTI & Enneagram," Part 2. *Enneagram Monthly* 34 (December 1997): 11. These articles describe my model using some of the case histories presented in this chapter. For a copy of this article, contact the *Enneagram Monthly,* 748 Wayside Rd., Portola Valley, CA 94028; 877.428.9639.

Wyman, P. "The Enneagram and the MBTI: Scoring." *Bulletin of Psychological Type* 24, (Summer 2001): 26–27.

Wyman, P. "The Enneagram and MBTI in Affective Therapy." *Enneagram Monthly* 54 (April 1999): 1. This article uses Brenda's personality combination (ISFJ-6) to discuss MBTI and Enneagram types that are compatible. For a copy of this article, contact the *Enneagram Monthly,* 748 Wayside Rd., Portola Valley, CA 94028; 877.428.9639.

EXERCISE
MBTI/ENNEAGRAM COMPATIBILITY

In order to determine the degree of compatibility or incompatibility of your own Core Self and Defense System, refer to the list of qualities of each in chapters 3 and 4. Number the corresponding supporting or compatible qualities in each list. Then go through the two lists again using the alphabet to identify corresponding oppositional qualities. Take note of how many neutral qualities are in each list. Keep in mind that these lists are quite abbreviated. You can compose more complete lists by referring to the books at the end of chapters 3 and 4.

Can you see both the MBTI and the Enneagram qualities operational in your life? Can you see that when you are stressed, triggered or otherwise in a defended position, the Enneagram qualities dominate? To what degree do you feel the Enneagram Defense System runs your life? If the Defense System exercises a little more influence than you would like, perhaps it is time to examine how you came to be in such a defended position.

CHAPTER 6

HOW DID I GET INTO THIS MESS?
UNDERSTANDING YOUR EMOTIONAL BAGGAGE

In doing your self-assessment so far, you have looked at two of the keys to self-understanding: Your Core Self as profiled by the Myers-Briggs Type Indicator (MBTI) and your Defense System as profiled by the Enneagram. You probably have a good idea how compatible or incompatible these two systems are as they operate within you. The third major component to understanding what "makes you tick" is your emotional baggage. Baggage is the inaccurate and damaging views about yourself, your world and your Higher Power that you bring into adulthood from childhood. These were installed in the course of being emotionally wounded, often inadvertently, by those whom you loved and believed. Before jumping to the defense of your family of origin, remember that the wounding is rarely done on purpose. As the topic of wounding is examined more closely, it will become apparent that no parent in the world can possibly avoid inflicting emotional wounding. I call this "original sin." It is part of the human condition and is passed on generation after generation. As adults, we may take a long, hard look at our parents and say to ourselves, "I will *never* do that to a child of mine!" And we may not, but we do something else that is just as emotionally damaging as that which was visited upon us.

As an infant, the child must take on the values, worldview and reality of the parent. The child has no choice. At the risk of sounding dramatic, it is a matter of life and death to the child. The child's parents are the only people standing between her and death. If the child is to survive, she must accept without question everything about the people who feed, clothe and protect her. If some of the parents' views are distorted, the child must adjust her own views and accommodate theirs in order to be accepted by the people she needs in order to stay alive.

Sometimes it is hard to recognize your own woundedness and the resulting baggage because you have lived with it all your life. It is often hard to see the forest for the trees. Clients will sometimes say to me, "I thought I had a happy childhood until I met you." I try to make the invisible visible. It is difficult to see what you live with on a daily basis. It is like the little fish swimming around asking everyone directions to the ocean. But if you are open and honest with yourself, I am sure you will identify with some of the problematical situations described in this chapter. Rather than seeing the resulting woundedness as a flaw or imperfection, try to see it as an opportunity for personal growth and spiritual expansion. Remember, awareness is always the first step.

And so it is not whether you were wounded in childhood, it is to what degree. There are a myriad of ways to be wounded as a child. I will present an overview of some of the major ones with examples to demonstrate. The examples provided here may seem extreme, and I have chosen them purposely in order to clearly illustrate the point. Your situation may not be as severe. Please do not minimize your own history by making comparisons to the cases described here. What happened to you affected you just as surely as the events outlined here affected those involved.

This examination is by no means exhaustive. You may easily come up with other ways in which you received some very damaging messages as a child. Do not discount your own history just because your type of wounding is not delineated here.

WOUNDING FROM FAMILY ROLES

In the standard, garden-variety dysfunctional family, each child is given a role determined by the needs of the system. The system requires balance and each role serves to provide balance to the system. The child does not have a voice or vote in her role assignment. Remember, the child is just doing what is required to survive. The child has to learn the family game and how to play. The role is simply determined by the needs of the system and is not a conscious decision by anyone. Often, the child's personality type is not suited to the role assignment and this makes it doubly hard on the child. However, the role assigned is the role the child is stuck with, usually for life, unless the system, not the child, undergoes some major alterations. Even with that, the saying is, "What we learn first, we learn best." In crisis, the child will ordinarily revert back to the original role. Although the roles are presented here with examples that may appear extreme, the damage imposed by having to carry out the duties of a family role is undeniable even in families with less "dysfunction."

The Hero

Usually, the first need of the system is for a family Hero. The Hero makes the family look good and covers for all the blemishes and imperfections inherent in the system. The Hero is a high achiever who goes on automatic pilot. In school, the child will get good grades, lead and participate in school activities, receive awards and generally make the folks proud. This model child learns early to put away her own needs, wants and feelings and just do what will earn her the approval of the system. She is a performer, an achiever, over-responsible, successful, dependable and hardworking (to name a few) and learns early how to live and work under pressure. In figure 6-1, Vanessa depicts herself as the busy Hero, resplendent with crown. She describes herself as achieving, leader, nonstop, busy, optimistic and ambitious.

Susan's story. Therapist Susan Edwards describes her Hero role in her workshops on family systems in words that leave no doubt about her Hero status and make the

Figure 6-1

reader tired: "When I was in high school, I was desperate to fit in but mostly I wanted to show the world that there was nothing wrong with my family and NOTHING wrong with me even though I secretly believed that the world would be a better place if I wasn't in it taking up food, space, air and water. In order to fulfill my mission, I created a very accomplished person:

- Vice-president of my senior class
- Basketball Queen in my junior year (It was unheard of for that honor not to go to a senior.)
- Coronation Maid in my freshman year
- Cheerleader for four years (made varsity squad as a freshman)
- Captain of the cheerleaders
- Straight *A* student
- Class Salutatorian
- Student Council member for two years
- President of the National Honor Society (There was no chapter of the National Honor Society, so I joined the National Honor Society Committee to found one.)
- President of the Future Homemakers of America (completed two years of course work in one year)
- President of the Future Teachers of America (member for three years)
- Captain of the volleyball team (member for four years)
- Member of the basketball team for four years
- Played French horn in the Band for four years

- Twirled baton and flags
- Starred in the senior play as Kitty in Charley's Aunt
- Member of the school orchestra
- Member of Girls' Athletic Association for three years
- Member of Secretary's Club
- Member of Science Club
- Member of Pep Club
- Chosen as representative for annual Sophomore Pilgrimage to State Capitol
- Won an academic Curators' Scholarship to a university
- Maintained a very active social life with friends and boyfriends (part of the 'in' clique)

"To illustrate how compulsive I was, I recall a typical boys' basketball game. I was cheerleader captain so I wore my saddle shoes, green Bermuda shorts and letter sweater to cheer the first half. Then I changed to my white boots, satin short circular skirt and braided jacket with majorette hat to twirl my baton for one musical number with the band and then twirled my flag for another number. I quickly changed into my band uniform, trousers and jacket, and played another song with the band. Fast as lightening, I was back in my cheerleading outfit to lead the audience in cheers for the last half of the game.

"It wasn't until I had two daughters who were not cheerleaders, presidents of anything and certainly didn't make straight *A*s that it ever dawned on me that any of this was unusual and maybe even excessive. All this activity was to mask the internal pain."

The role of the Hero is often envied by other siblings because they see the approval and adulation that role provides. However, what they do not see is the price the Hero pays. The Hero is indentured to serve the best interests of the family, not herself, for life. The Hero's own wants, needs, feelings, dreams, truth and the like must be put away in order to best serve the system. The Hero is not allowed to speak her own mind. She must always support and enhance the system she serves.

Those defended as Enneagram Ones, Twos, Threes and Sixes are well equipped for this role and, if assigned the Hero role, their Defense Systems will become highly

*Sometimes, those assigned the Hero role do not have
a Defense System well equipped for the task. Unfortunately, there is no
appeals court for the role assignment and so the child must shore up her
inadequate Defense System as best she can.*

developed and serve them well. In each of these cases, the Enneagram Defense System soon will be running the show and the reward will be the approval of the family and cultural system being served. If the Core Self is not particularly Hero material, it does not matter. The family role comes out of the survival mode and that is in the realm of the Enneagram Defense System. If you will recall Paula, a first-and-only child, whose story opened the last chapter, you can see that the playful ENFP would have much rather done other things than be family Hero. She would have opted for such activities as daydreaming, playing, creating, exploring, being silly and simply experiencing life. Her One Defense System, however, was well suited to the demands of an only-child Hero and she did her best to perform perfectly.

Sometimes, those assigned the Hero role do not have a Defense System well equipped for the task. Unfortunately, there is no appeals court for the role assignment and so the child must shore up her inadequate Defense System as best she can. Often, the child resorts to some secondary traits supplied by the Enneagram points connected to her own point by the lines in the diagram of the Enneagram System (figure 4-1, page 56). In cases of extreme and intense pressure, the Core Self will even supply some key traits to use *in defense,* not self-expression. In any event, the psyche is very resourceful and, somehow, each child finds what is needed in order to fulfill the role assignment. Susan, who described her well-developed Hero role so eloquently, is defended as an Enneagram Four, which is not particularly suited to the duties and responsibilities of the Hero. The Four is self-absorbed, internally focused and prone to searching for what is missing in her life rather than fixing the family. However, Susan, an ENFJ-4, used her connecting points of One and Two

to meet the needs of the family and to do it as perfectly as she could. She also employed the outgoing, charismatic qualities of the ENFJ to achieve Hero status.

When the Hero is male, he often becomes the standard-bearer of the family. When the Hero is female, she often fulfills her Hero status by taking care of younger siblings and generally being Mom's right hand. Sometimes, the Hero role goes far beyond the achievement-oriented style described by Susan. The Hero child can be forced to take on the responsibilities of a parent who is nonfunctioning.

Jessica's story. Jessica's mother was divorced and chemically dependent. She was a poor provider and often not home. When she was home, she was not in any shape to care for Jessica (ENTP-4). To make matters worse, there was another child. Jessica has a brother just eleven months younger than she. As the older child, Jessica found herself caring for herself and her brother as well as her mother who was often incapacitated by the effects of drugs and alcohol. Jessica cannot remember a time when she did not feel responsible for her brother and her mother.

At one point, the children were separated and sent to separate relatives in different states for a year. Not knowing how her brother was faring was extremely hard on Jessica. "That was the worst part. I failed him." She felt responsible for him even though she was powerless to change the circumstances. As an adult, seeing her brother's pain left over from childhood, she felt guilty for not taking better care of him. Even as an adult, Jessica could not see that it was too much responsibility for one little girl.

As a teen, Jessica was using drugs herself, yet she maintained a job. When her mother had the family living with an abusive man, Jessica found an apartment, loaded the car and moved her mother and brother out, all before she was old enough to drive.

Jessica entered therapy at age thirty-one and often asked how she could help her brother. She continually encouraged him to get help himself and continued to feel a degree of responsibility for him even though they were both adults.

In this situation, the family system called for more than a Hero; it called for an adult, a parent. Jessica can remember trying to fill the role of parent to *both* her brother and her mother as early as age two. Her Enneagram Defense System of a Four was not well designed for the Hero role, but Jessica called on the traits of the connected One and Two to assist the Four. Her Core Self is an ENTP so she was able to use the rational, competent NT traits to aid her in caring for her family. Interestingly, Jessica is a perfect example of how the Core Self can lend some traits to the Defense System while, at the same time, not owning those traits as really defining the Self. With her history showing such a high degree of responsibility and coping skills and with the NT kicking in to help defend her, Jessica still entered therapy convinced she was stupid. She is a clear example of how a person can sometimes exhibit a trait from the Core Self but be using it in defense rather than in self-expression. Jessica now teaches concert violin and is using the NT traits of competency and smartness as a true expression of who she is rather than in defense.

Beth's story. Beth found herself in a similar position to Jessica. As an INTJ, Beth was very suited to her first-born Hero role. However, Beth's Defense System of the Four put her in the same position as Jessica. Beth's mother was not at all interested in raising children although that did not deter her from having six. As a toddler, Beth can remember trying to care for her little sister, eighteen months younger. Once she dropped the baby and thought she had killed her. She recalls feeding herself and her sister by spooning peanut butter straight from the jar as her mother secluded herself in her room watching TV endlessly. As a preschool child,

she tried her best to keep the house neat because the disorder only heightened her sense of chaos. Beth felt her responsibilities did not end with her siblings. She felt she had to take care of Mom and Dad as well. She has always felt like a parent to both of them. Whenever something went wrong, Beth felt it was her fault.

Of course, Susan, Jessica and Beth are examples of the Hero role taken to the extreme. Perhaps your Hero role is not as intense or dramatic as these nor as frenetic as Susan's. But if you are a first-born child, never gave your parents any cause for concern and made good grades, the chances are good you may be the family Hero. If you know that the motivation under your performance was to keep approval and to please Mom and Dad, the chances are even greater.

The Scapegoat

Often the second born falls into the role of Scapegoat. Few Scapegoats would have opted for this role, but when the Hero position has already been filled, the system assigns them the next most important role. It is the duty of the Scapegoat to keep the eyes of the world off the family system and focused on the Scapegoat. It is a very effective method for the system to protect itself and its dysfunction. The family and the community point to the Scapegoat and shake their heads in sadness. "Such a fine family. Goodness, just look at the Hero! How could two such opposite children come from the same family?" If the child does not elicit that response, the poor little Scapegoat has to act out all the more to fulfill the duties of her role. If one of the Scapegoat's parents happens to be an Enneagram Seven who has trouble seeing trouble, or an Enneagram Nine who does not show much reaction, the Scapegoat will have to work all the harder to pull the negative attention to herself.

Most Scapegoats will readily admit they hate the role they have been assigned. They want nothing but to be loved, approved of and accepted. When those things are not supplied by the family, the Scapegoat generally turns to a peer group to meet those needs. The more the love, approval and acceptance needs are met by the peer group, the more strongly the bond to the peers becomes. Therefore, telling a Scapegoat not to bow to peer pressure and "just say no" is futile.

Sometimes the Scapegoat is well suited to the role with an Enneagram Defense of Eight such as Kory, the ESFP-8 mentioned in chapter 2. As an Eight, her Defense System equipped her to go against the system. As an SP, Kory was not opposed to risk.

Kory's story. Kory stated, "I had to be a failure to fit in the family." She remembers being beaten with a belt by her father to the extent that she bled. She reports that she often felt it was worth it because she drew his attention and later he would feel guilty and try to make it up to her. She interpreted his attention as love. She said she felt "like the runt of the litter who is not accepted by the pack, yet they let it live." In imagery, Kory saw a wall separating herself from the rest of her family.

By junior high, Kory was a high-performing Scapegoat. She was well into drugs and alcohol and driving drunk at age thirteen. As a teenager, she became quite promiscuous. By her early twenties, Kory was doing things that threatened her very life. Kory tells about walking down one of the most dangerous streets in the city at 2:00 am one night, stoned, and screaming "Come and get me, you mother f—rs." She was pretty much at the end of her rope.

Kory's father died when she was fourteen. Her mother, an Enneagram Seven, denied there ever were any problems in the family at all. A few of the problems she overlooked were incest by Kory's father, alcoholism, periodic poverty, sexual abuse by a family friend, physical abuse, verbal abuse, emotional abuse, being evicted and losing all their possessions in front of the children's eyes. Even Kory's obvious suicidal tendencies did not give her mother a wake-up call. Kory, as the Scapegoat, felt that the family's problems were her fault, including her father's death.

In therapy, Kory expressed concern around her identity. "If I don't have my anger, who will I be?" In imagery, Kory saw her anger as a large rock that she hid behind. Her Eight Defense, expressed through her

Scapegoat role, had served her well. Kory said she was most proud of her trait of compassion, which she visualized as daisies. In her imagery, Kory watched as the daisies' root systems crumbled the rock of anger and aerated the soil supporting the daisies. For the first time, she could see her inner child peaceful, not angry, in a field of daisies.

Extraverted SP types seem to take to the role of Scapegoat with gusto. When drafted into being part of the Defense System, the SP contributes a live-in-the-moment attitude that leaves no room in the SP's mind for thoughts of consequences for her actions. I have a theory that if the personality types and family system roles of our prison population were investigated, there would be a preponderance of SP Scapegoats. One exception may be the area of white-collar crime where a Hero tries to surreptitiously pull a fast one.

One characteristic that Kory shares with most other Scapegoats is thinking that everything that went wrong in the family was her fault. Lori, an ENTJ-3 and a Scapegoat, was running away from home at age eight. She "knew" she caused all the problems in the family. She was found by her sister who told her it would "kill" Dad if she ran away. The little girl was in a no-win situation. If she stayed, she caused the family untold grief. If she left, her father's imminent death would be her fault. Imagine struggling with this choice at age eight.

Sometimes the Scapegoat is not at all designed for the role. Often these types don't have to do much in the way of acting out to fulfill the function of the Scapegoat because the family system is bound and determined that this is the role they will play. The system will keep the Scapegoat on the outside no matter how hard she tries to win acceptance. Danielle, the ENTJ-7 described in chapters 3 and 5, is such an example.

Danielle's story. Danielle's mom made it clear the only reason she had Danielle was to keep her older sister company. So, Hero material though she may be, Danielle was destined to take the Scapegoat role before she was ever born. Danielle's earliest memories are around seeing her mother and sister tightly bonded, with Danielle on the outside and literally across the room from them. There was no way that Danielle was going to be able to break into that enmeshed twosome. "I was expendable. My sister was protected."

Danielle tried to do well and earn the love, acceptance and approval she so desired, but for her efforts, she was labeled borderline retarded, angry and defiant. Danielle explains, "I was diseased, contagious, untouchable. I was to be ignored at all costs. I was excluded and undesired. I had no merit or worth and no value compared to my sister. It didn't matter what I did, I was going to get whacked anyway." Danielle was frequently punished physically; her sister was infrequently punished in a gentler manner.

Like most Scapegoats, Danielle grew up feeling the family problems were all due to her. In the course of therapy, Danielle was able to see that her parents de-focused from their own problems and the dismal state of their marriage by making her behavior a reason for their anger. The secondary purpose of her Scapegoat role was to make her Hero sister look even better in comparison.

Another reluctant Scapegoat is Sarah, the ISTJ-9, whose history is detailed in chapter 5.

Sarah's story. Sarah would have done anything to earn her parents' love and approval, but all her hard work was met with a long litany of derogatory comments. The school validated the self-image her family had already designed for Sarah. In first grade, "the nun slapped me hard for reading incorrectly. Now I was bad at school too." She hoped that if she kept "a low profile and was good maybe no one would notice how bad I was." But even Sarah admits, "I had a hard time coming up with the right strategy when I was six." In seventh grade, her teacher outlined "the seven criminal tendencies" and Sarah thought, "I have them all."

Even as valedictorian of her eighth grade class, she could receive no recognition from her family. She watched her oldest brother and saw he was not the

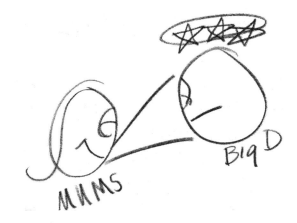

Figure 6-2

Figure 6-3

virtuous paragon her mother perceived him to be. Trying to point out that inaccuracy earned her even more condemnation. In figure 6-2, she depicts the way her mother responded to her brother as compared to her mother's response to her. In figure 6-3, she reflects the way most scapegoats feel about themselves.

After trying to displace the family Hero for a number of years, Sarah finally settled into her Scapegoat role as a teen and began using alcohol and became promiscuous. She hated it. With all that acting out, she still managed to graduate from high school with honors, to get through college and to earn a master's degree in business. None of her achievements were recognized by her parents. She married well and lives quite the middle-class, conservative lifestyle. But, in her family, she will

Figure 6-4

always be the Scapegoat. Sarah must constantly fight her anger at the injustice of this assignment.

Dianna's story. Dianna, an ENFP-3, who was totally unsuited for the role, provides a compelling portrait of herself as a Scapegoat in figure 6-4. The outside world saw her as angry, defiant and brooding. Inside, she knew she felt small, invisible, lost, scared, hurt, lonely and hopeless.

One of my most difficult tasks is to convince reluctant Scapegoats of the futility of fighting the system. They want to know what they did wrong and what they need to do to gain love and acceptance. The Scapegoat has a hard time understanding that it is out of her power. It is not about *her,* it is about the needs of the system. Look at Jesus, probably the most famous Scapegoat. He is an example of a Scapegoat who could not change his role. The needs of the system are what govern role assignments.

I try to console reluctant Scapegoats with the good news: They are the truth-tellers. Because the Scapegoat is already on the outside, the Scapegoat will tell it like it is. She has nothing to lose. If anyone will listen, the Scapegoat will tell the truth about the family.

Kory's story. As a truth-telling Scapegoat, Kory took a chance and told her fourth grade teacher what was happening at home, alluding to her father's alcoholism and sexual abuse. The teacher called Kory's mother and discussed it with her. Mom told the teacher that Kory "lied a lot," and in fact had "a real problem with lying." The teacher was satisfied with Mom's explanation and Kory received a beating, along with a lot of shame, for airing the family secrets. It was never spoken of again.

The majority of my clients are Scapegoats. The gift is that they can enter therapy and look honestly at the flaws and foibles of the family. They are not disturbed to upset the balance in the family by becoming emotionally healthy. They are used to taking the heat. Kory now prides herself on being the only one in the family with the courage to tell the truth about the family that had to look good for Mom and the outside world. But it is hard for all Scapegoats to realize that no matter how much therapy they undergo, no matter how many degrees they earn, no matter how much money and fame they accumulate, they will always be Scapegoats in their families of origin.

Sarah's story. Sarah now lives a considerable distance from her family of origin, yet when she returns home, she is met with the same derogatory comments. Meanwhile her Hero brother has earned a police record and two divorces, yet he cannot be budged from his Hero position because the system demands that he remain in that role, undisputed.

If, growing up, you found you could not do anything right, began acting out early and found the only attention you received was negative attention, you may be able to see that you are in the Scapegoat role. If you have no problems airing the family laundry in the name of truth, the chances increase. Acceptance of this knowledge may be hard, but fighting it is impossible.

The Lost Child

When the Hero and Scapegoat roles have been filled, the next child looks around and says, "Color me GONE!" This child keeps the lowest possible profile, often staying in her room and living in a fantasy world that is much more appealing than the real one provided by her family. The Lost Child feels nearly invisible.

Family members often do not notice whether the Lost Child is present or not. The Lost Child may make good grades in school like the Hero, but the reason is to keep from drawing attention with bad grades. The Lost Child is often an Introvert. The Enneagram Defenses of Five and Nine are well suited for the role of Lost Child although other Enneagram types can find themselves in that role as well.

Therese's story. Therese, an ISTJ-9, grew up trying to keep the lowest possible profile in order to protect her mother and not "be a burden." In school, she felt she did not fit in and had few friends. When her older brother went off to college, she could not understand how he could follow his heart. She said, "I didn't know how to follow my heart."

Therese was sexually abused by a family member as a small child and later raped in college. She did not feel she could tell her family about either of these situations because of the trouble it would cause. She never wanted to make a scene. As an adult, Therese became involved with a man who was physically and verbally abusive. Her family encouraged her to get married. She tried to tell them "No" but no one seemed to hear her protests. At the rehearsal dinner, she wondered, "Why won't anyone listen to me? I don't want to marry him." Before walking down the aisle, she tried to tell her father but he told her everything would be OK. Later, when her husband inflicted a concussion, she did not even try to tell her family.

In therapy, Therese imaged standing in front of her mother as an adult, holding herself as a child in her arms. The child was air and invisible. When Therese began speaking up to her mother as the adult, the child

Figure 6-5

began to take form. First her head filled in. The more assertive Therese became, the more the child's body began filling in from the head down until she was fully present. The child was impressed with Therese as an adult. From this point forward, Therese was better able to speak up for herself to family, boss and spouse.

Therese provides an eloquent and moving illustration of a faceless, voiceless Lost Child in figure 6-5.

As an Enneagram Nine, Therese was very equipped for the Lost Child role. But even personality types more suited to Hero roles can find themselves in the Lost Child position.

Sondra's story. Sondra, an INTP-3, felt lost in the middle of her large family of seven children. As a small child, she hid in the closet one day, hoping someone would notice she was missing, find her, and make a fuss over her. She heard her mother preparing dinner and people moving around the house. Eventually, the table was set and the family was sitting down to dinner. Sondra realized no one noticed she was not present. She came out of the closet pretending it was all a game, acting as if the incident meant nothing. However, that experience brought home her role assignment of Lost Child very poignantly to Sondra.

By definition, the Lost Child is off alone, playing with her toys, reading, talking softly to imaginary friends or doing little art projects. The Lost Child keeps her special possessions and pets close to her because they are all she feels really connected to. Quiet, withdrawn, passive, solitary, distant and invisible are words often used to describe the Lost Child.

Mascot

By this time, the family is in need of some fun and so along comes the Mascot. By providing an element of fun to the family, the Mascot takes the focus off any problems, tension or dysfunction. The Mascot must put aside her own feelings, dreams, wants and needs in order to keep the family happy and entertained. The Mascot learns early how each family member needs her to act in order to keep that person amused and cheerful. Everyone is glad to see the Mascot. Life will be better for a few minutes while the Mascot charms away the dark clouds.

Mascots can be effervescent, hyperactive, cheerful, witty, cute, entertaining and act the light-hearted clown. They are normally shielded from the family's trials and tribulations by other family members because they are seen as unable to cope with the stress. Mascots are seldom taken seriously, and it is hard for them to receive attention for anything other than the "happy element" they provide. Things do not change for Mascots when they reach adulthood. Their chronological age does not convince the family it is time to take them seriously. They will always be the babies of their families. If the Mascot happens to be defended as an Enneagram Seven, the fit is excellent and the Seven does not mind the role in the least. However, the Core Self may object at not being allowed to be real.

Figure 6-6

Rhonda's story. Rhonda, an ENFJ-7, was the fourth-born child and her Seven Defense was helpful in her Mascot role. She remembers being a high performer at a very early age. She put on plays to entertain the family and played fantasy games that required her to be her older sister's servant. She knew from the beginning she could not compete with her siblings any other way. She saw her job as that of keeping everyone happy, especially her mother. "I needed to keep smiling and keep everyone happy." Her mother let Rhonda know she was not supposed to be happy unless Mom was. That message was strong and persisted into adulthood when she entered therapy feeling she could not be happy until her husband was. She found one of the duties of her Mascot role was to act as go-between for Mom and Dad to smooth the bumps in their rocky marriage. "I felt like a caged bird with a string tied to my leg."

As a very young child, she became interested in music, dance and acting. Neither she nor her interests were ever taken seriously. Her interests were seen as proof of her immaturity. As she grew older, she continued to be treated as a perpetual child. When it came time for college, the entire family got together to vote on which school she would attend. She was not allowed to attend the school of her choice. She was not given the opportunity to manage her own life. She was treated as a child with regard to finances and given the message that she was completely incompetent in that area.

Rhonda was so entrenched in her Mascot role that, in therapy, it was a major struggle for her to access any of her anger for the wounding she experienced. She felt that it would somehow threaten the happiness of her family members. All of her feelings had been neatly stored away save the one that defines the Mascot: HAPPY.

Rhonda illustrates her Mascot role in figure 6-6 in which she portrays her child-self as a puppet with strings performing for the crowd.

Remember that each of the roles in the system exists to serve the system and to maintain balance in the family. If one person tries to change behaviors, move out of the role, or in any way upset the balance of the system, other members have to compensate. The major way that other members compensate is by escalating their own behaviors in an attempt to bring the errant party back into line. When one member of the family enters therapy, that action strongly threatens the balance in the family system. It is not at all unusual for other family members to begin acting out more blatantly.

Each child in the system is doing her best to make the system work as it has been defined for her. The way to find out if the system is working is to watch the parents. Every child wants to know that Mom and Dad are OK. If they are OK, then the child knows she will be OK. So each child monitors her parents and performs the duties of her role to the extent the balance of the system demands. When that happens, the child must put other parts of herself away, parts that may conflict with her role assignment or parts that may upset the balance of the system in other ways. When this happens, emotional wounding occurs.

Wounding for Personal Identity

It is common to receive wounding messages simply for personal identity. Sometimes these messages are subtle and covert and sometimes they are obvious. When a family is expecting a baby, *expecting* is the operative word. They may be expecting a specific gender, a child that resembles them and/or a child that is like them in personality. The parents may not even be aware of their own expectations. When I was waiting for my first child, I imagined a baby with a head of dark curly hair. I was so surprised to see a very bald-headed child that, if I had not been present at the birth, I would not have recognized her to be mine! Certainly, something as innocuous as hair is easily dispatched, but other traits may be more subtle and more important to the parents.

Physical Appearance

Peggy's story. Peggy's mother was the all-American girl, ESFJ. She was feminine in the traditional sense, and she expected her daughter would be the same. Peggy, an ENTJ-1, learned early that it was very, very important to be pretty. As an Enneagram One, the emphasis on "pretty" caused Peggy to equate the word with perfect. She found she evaluated not only herself but also everything in her life on the terms of pretty or ugly.

As Peggy grew and developed as a child, her mother fussed over her appearance. Peggy felt her mom was thoroughly absorbed in her looks. Because Peggy's One completely associated being perfect with being pretty, she became as obsessed with her appearance as her mother seemed to be. Unfortunately, when she was in junior high, it was discovered that Peggy was developing scoliosis. She was required to wear a back brace for several years, which affected her appearance and her own body image. To add to the challenge, Peggy was the tallest girl in her class and continued to grow to be six feet tall.

To complicate matters more, Peggy's Core Self, ENTJ, does not resemble the traditional feminine female. She was anything but soft, gentle, demure and dainty. Peggy would naturally rely more on her brain than on her feminine wiles. That would have been all right with her had she not had her mother's eyes to act as a mirror of her acceptability. Long before Peggy even knew she had a brain, she had completely accepted her mother's values, which centered around appearance.

When she learned the gauge for pretty or not pretty was male attention, the scene was set for disaster. Peggy recalled going to bed every night for seven years fervently praying, begging for a boyfriend to prove she was pretty (perfect) and therefore acceptable and loveable. As she struggled through high school, her prayers became more desperate. It is not surprising that the first male who looked her way was gratefully accepted, no questions asked and no demands made.

From her late teens until she entered therapy at age thirty-one, Peggy went through a series of men who were less than desirable. Any male was preferable to no male. No male meant she was not pretty and therefore not perfect. Peggy quickly became sexually addicted because she needed male sexual attention to know she was OK. She eventually married a man for whom she really cared but had to face her problems when her addiction threatened her marriage and cost her a job.

I think it is safe to say that Peggy's mom did not intend to put this dreadful set of events into motion. Seldom does a parent intend to bring pain into a child's life. Yet it happens. Messages that may not be intended are nonetheless received. Messages intended one way are sometimes interpreted another way. Peggy's life is well under control at this point. She has not had an episode of acting out sexually in more than three years, yet this is something she will have to work with all her life because "what we learn first, we learn best."

Reilley's story. Reilley's mother is an Enneagram Three to whom appearances and image are most important. From birth she began dressing Reilley as though she were a doll. Up until Reilley was old enough to have

Most families have difficulty coming to terms with the knowledge that their child is gay or lesbian. The wounding caused by that lack of acceptance is immeasurable and causes untold pain to the child.

some influence on what she wore, she was dressed in frills and frocks as though off to a fashion show. As a lesbian, Reilley found dressing in such a manner uncomfortable. Although she was not aware of her lesbian orientation that early, she did know she hated the way she had to dress. She fantasized about boys' clothing. Her favorite was a cowgirl outfit that, although it had a skirt, had fringe and a front-button shirt. She dreamed of growing up and getting to wear a tuxedo.

Although Reilley's mother had no way of knowing her daughter's sexual orientation, she did impose her own style of dressing on a very unwilling participant. Reilley, of course, became more and more confused, especially since she wanted to please her mother and win her love more than anything else in her life.

Gender

The issue of gender is a breeding ground for wounding. We live in a patriarchal society and many theologians have noted that if God is male then male is god. It is not news to many that women in our culture, and in most cultures around the globe, are marginalized and devalued. Although many have pointed it out, it is harder to see that this arrangement is as detrimental to the males in the culture as well. I will leave an in-depth discussion of this topic to those more versed in anthropology and sociology, but I will spotlight the effects that patriarchy and gender inequality have on the individual.

We are all familiar with the family who is hoping for a baby of a specific gender, generally a boy. Sometimes the little girl who arrives on this scene is named a version of the boy's name that had been chosen. Many times, the girl finds herself excelling in sports and other male-dominated arenas in order to win the approval she lost at birth.

Another way to be wounded in the area of gender is by having behaviors compared to the behaviors of the

female and/or male stereotypes, just as Peggy was compared to stereotypical female appearance standards. The culture forces boys to be macho and achieving whether they want to be or not and it forces girls to be compliant and demure no matter their nature. Sometimes problems around gender result from circumstances beyond anyone's control.

Brenda's story. Brenda, described in chapter 5, found herself the only female in the middle of seven brothers. As an ISFJ-6, she was, and is, the traditional feminine female. Growing up on a farm with seven brothers made it difficult for her to get a real sense of what it meant to be a woman. Her only role model was her mother who was totally co-dependent and lived a joyless life. Being a Lost Child in this family, along with other life-changing issues, brought Brenda to adulthood without any sense of self or ability to claim control of her life as a woman.

Sexual Orientation

Most families have difficulty coming to terms with the knowledge that their child is gay or lesbian. The wounding caused by that lack of acceptance is immeasurable and causes untold pain to the child. It is important to realize that sexual orientation is not about sex. It is about identity. Living a gay/lesbian lifestyle in a culture that is strongly heterosexual and condemns a person's very identity is difficult at best. When family disapproval and alienation are added to that, it can be devastating. Most gays and lesbians report trying to protect the feelings of the family at the expense of keeping the secret and denying their own identity.

It will not be long before it will be clear that sexual orientation is genetically connected to personality type. I have noticed that there are certain combinations of MBTI and Enneagram that are more likely (not positively) to result in a person being gay/lesbian. The most obvious to me is the Thinking female defended as a Four and the Feeling male defended as a Four. When adequate statistics are gathered by researchers, I am certain the evidence will prove that there is a higher percentage of gays/lesbians with these and certain other personality combinations. This issue needs to be fully explored so that the morality angle can be dispatched and the shame can be lifted from a random genetic combination. To suffer the condemnation of one's culture, religion, community and family for a genetic coincidence of birth is more than just unfortunate. It is tragic and completely avoidable.

Reilley's story. Reilley sat with her mother in the office of Reilley's therapist. She had invited her mother in for the purpose of telling her mother that she was a lesbian. She had fought the knowledge as long as she could. When she put the information out to her mother, the response was, "Those are the words I never wanted to hear." Reilley spent the rest of the session consoling her mother as she cried. Her mother never asked Reilley how she was dealing with the issue, never assured Reilley of her love and support and never made an effort to understand her daughter's struggle. Five years later, the topic is never so much as alluded to. It is as if the discussion never took place. When Reilley participates in gay and lesbian activities that could include family members, she attends alone. A whole part of her identity is sectioned off from her family.

Joan's story. Joan came to terms with her sexual orientation in her fifties. When she finally allowed herself to explore her own sexuality, all the errant pieces of her life fell into place. At the moment of realization and acceptance in a therapy session, her entire body relaxed and she smiled, "It must be right because I feel at peace." Joan's family, religion and community would never accept her as a lesbian. Coming to terms with her sexuality meant a great deal of loss and new beginnings for her as it does for most other gays and lesbians who brave coming out. For Joan, self-acceptance was worth the price.

Neither Reilley nor Joan has engaged in a lesbian sexual relationship. Yet it was of utmost importance to both of them to claim, understand and explore their own sexual identity as part of integrating all the parts of self that were put away to please others and earn love.

Personality

It should be clear by now that a child is going to have a different personality configuration from one or both parents. When parents insist the child conform to their values, worldview and generally see life through their lenses, it is very detrimental to the child's emotional development and emerging personality.

Paula's story. In the last chapter, Paula, an ENFP-1, was introduced. Besides the internal war between the ENFP and the One already examined, Paula had to deal with being very different from her family. Paula is an only child. Her father was an ISTJ-1. His insistence on perfection has already been documented. Her mother was an extremely co-dependent, compliant ISFJ-6. So both Paula's parents fell into the SJ temperament category. They espoused the traditional values of our culture. Paula, in an all-out effort for love and acceptance, tried to learn what those values were and subscribe to them. Her perfectionist One worked overtime to learn the rules. Her ENFP Core Self could never understand the rules or why they were important. But love and acceptance in that household were dependent on her embracing her parents' values and worldview.

Paula was raised Roman Catholic, another highly SJ organization. She did her best to learn all those rules, too. Even though they did not really make sense to her as an ENFP, she believed if she learned all the rules and lived by them perfectly, she would be assured of going to heaven when she died. Feeling she was losing the race, she entered the convent where the rules became tougher and more demanding. Paula tried with everything she had to make the best of the situation, believing she was assuring eternal peace for herself.

When Paula left the convent after ten years, she met and married a man who, as an ESTJ-6, was very similar to her father. During their twenty-three-year marriage, he helped reinforce her need to conform to the cultural and religious SJ rules with which she had been raised. They bought a house in a neighborhood in which the community was highly SJ. House and yard had to conform to certain acceptable SJ neighborhood standards. Personal values had to conform to community values. This need to conform was no problem to Paula's SJ husband but it took a tremendous toll on Paula because it forced her to continue to completely disregard and deny her Core Self and subscribe to a set of values she did not even understand. The results were a significant loss of health with permanent damage that will affect her quality of living for the rest of her life. Since finishing therapy, one of Paula's challenges is to relax into *being* herself instead of *doing* what was expected of her.

When family, community, religion, school and culture are strongly SJ, it makes for a very comfortable environment for SJ types. But since they comprise 47 percent of the population, it makes it a little tricky for the other 53 percent. It is not necessary to consider changing the culture or any of the institutions that comprise it. It would, however, be helpful to the SP, NT and NF types if they were acknowledged, thereby alleviating some of the wounding children receive for the personality with which they were born.

Lara's story. On the first day of second grade, Lara, an ENFP, walked around the classroom with the other children, playing a type of musical chairs, looking for her name on a desk. Before long, everyone was seated but Lara. The teacher explained to her in front of everyone else in the classroom that she would be repeating first grade and walked her down the hall to the first grade classroom. Lara remembers being completely devastated. The school had not notified her family and she had no way of getting in touch with them. She was humiliated and embarrassed. She felt alone and convinced she was stupid.

Lara's parents transferred her to another school where she did repeat the first grade. Her mother frequently worked with her on her homework, explaining to Lara that she had a mental block. Sometimes her mom would simply do the homework for her. That was easier and faster. Lara finished high school convinced she was incompetent and stupid. Although at age thirty she owns and runs her own business, she still questions her own mental abilities.

Of course, no one knew Lara to be an Intuitive type who learned differently from most of the other children. Further, as an ENFP, she would have been slower than others in maturing, which could be interpreted in a variety of ways. A simple understanding of Lara's personality type would have saved this young woman from a lifetime of self-doubt and low self-esteem.

Since children spend a lot of time in school, it is inevitable that the school situation has the potential for inflicting serious wounding. Another group that does not get out of school unscathed is the SP temperament. These light-hearted, talented people feel they are serving a prison sentence throughout their school experience and are just marking time until they can escape (drop out) or be paroled (graduate). Schools generally teach to one temperament group, the SJ types, who learn well and easily in the standard classroom setting. SP children need to learn hands-on. Reading can sometimes feel like torture to them. Because of poor performance, often the SP child is sent off to a technical/trade school where hands-on learning is the norm. Generally, they do very well there. However, it is usually too late for their self-esteem. I have not talked to any SP types who were not convinced by the school system that they were of marginal intelligence.

Ray's story. Ray, an ESFP-7, enjoyed grammar school for the socializing and play, but certainly not the academics. He reported feeling dumb in grammar school and even dumber in high school, but only blames himself. He classifies himself as lazy as a child and feels he just did not apply himself. He was much more interested in airplanes and building models. He observed that if the school had somehow incorporated airplanes into his studies, he would have had more interest.

*Men with a preference for Feeling, on the other hand,
have to be very careful in a culture
that insists men be macho, strong and without feelings.*

Following what was expected of him, he started junior college after high school only to find he had absolutely no interest. It was no fun. He dropped out and then really felt dumb. He again insisted that he was simply "too lazy to apply myself." He confesses to never reading a book completely through until well into adulthood.

Ray is a paramedic and firefighter. He has put two additions on his house and built his own airplane, which he flies. He repairs anything and everything around the house including the family cars. It is clear that Ray is neither dumb nor lazy, but those were the early messages he received and he accepted them.

Interestingly, Ray's daughter, Lyla, is also an ESFP-7. She hated grammar school and felt she was an average student because the good grades she received in art and music balanced the bad grades she received in her other classes. If grammar school was difficult for her, "high school sucked." She states unequivocally, "I hated everything but music, art and photography. I'm so glad I'm not in school anymore! I only went because I had to." She found the entire academic experience frustrating, stating that she does not remember anything she was taught. She is convinced that she learned more from life experience than from school and she knows her school experience left her with low self-esteem. Like her father, she claims that much of it was her own fault because she was lazy and did not apply herself.

Lyla has good things to say about trade schools, the venue that is made for SP types. "Trade schools are good, the way to go." Trade schools give the SP an opportunity to learn hands-on using tools. This is where these talented people excel and where their special gifts can be encouraged. Today Lyla is a performing musician and runs her own small business.

The third group that often does not fare well in school is the NT types. You may recall that this temperament group needs to feel smart, competent and capable above all things. If they are made to feel otherwise by the school system, such as was described in Danielle's story in chapter 3, they will be affected for a lifetime just as Danielle has been. Sometimes, the opposite can happen to NT types. They skate through grammar school and high school with a minimum of studying. They may not make tremendous grades, but they know they could if they put some effort into it so they do not feel particularly stupid. When they enter college, the stakes get higher. College faculties are highly NT and the little NT college freshman gets a wake-up call. This young person now has to scramble for study skills and discipline heretofore unneeded.

I have made several references to another aspect of personality that can precipitate negative messages and that is the plight of Thinking females and Feeling males. Upon questioning, all women with a preference for Thinking report feeling "unfeminine" and secretly wonder what is wrong with them. Their thought processes are more associated with male thinking, and they often feel more comfortable in conversations with men than with women. Men with a preference for Feeling, on the other hand, have to be very careful in a culture that insists men be macho, strong and without feelings. Gay Feeling men don't even try to fight the culture, but straight Feeling men generally do their best to cover with sports. Many Feeling men have compensated for something they have felt is an innate weakness by excelling in football or basketball.

When the Thinking female is also an SJ such as an ESTJ or ISTJ, she is even more confused because, as an SJ, she accepts the traditional cultural standards of what a female should be like and she knows, as a T she does not match up. You may remember Sarah and Mary, both ISTJ, in the last chapter. Both wondered what was wrong with them because their thought processes were different from most other women. Mary reports that in grammar school she "just existed." She always felt on the edge and never quite fit in. At home, no one in the family connected with her.

When the Feeling male is also an SJ such as an ESFJ or ISFJ, there is equal confusion. As an SJ, he accepts the traditional cultural stereotype of a male and he knows that, as an F, he does not match. Since about a third of our population falls into the category of Thinking female or Feeling male, many people are growing up feeling defective because the culture provides no positive mirroring.

Some personality types are such a small percentage of the population that they cannot help growing up feeling very different or weird. INTJ and INTP females and INFJ and INFP males fall into this lost group. Each of these types comprises less than 1 percent of the population of their gender. They are often the only person of their type in their grammar school classroom and most likely will not have a teacher or parent of their type. They are generally convinced there is something wrong with them and do their best to hide that information from the rest of the world.

Olivia's story. Olivia, an INTJ-1, reports she would have done anything rather than go to school where she felt weird and like she did not fit in. She states she always felt "out of sync," a loner and isolated. Absolutely no one understood her. She observed, "It was good to be Introverted so I could have a conversation in my head." Olivia describes her school experience as feeling like "a salmon swimming upstream. I wished the current would lighten up." By high school, Olivia was contemplating suicide. She could find no way to be accepted at home or at school for who she was. Fortunately, she survived her high school experience and found college to be a little more comfortable. She completed a master's degree and holds an administrative position in which she is responsible for 300 employees. She will quickly concede that she carries the emotional scars from her grammar and high school experiences with her to this day.

WOUNDING FROM ABUSE

Physical Abuse

The concept of physical abuse needs no explanation. How can a child believe she is innately good and has value while being hurt by the person who matters the most to her? Physical abuse is even more damaging when it feels unfair or unjust to the child. It does not matter how deserving of punishment the parent may think the child is, the degree of emotional wounding is increased if the child feels she is being hurt unjustly by someone she trusts who is much larger than she is. Another, often overlooked, aspect of physical abuse is the effect it has on the siblings who may be watching or hearing it happen.

Jessica's story. Jessica (INTJ-4), described above, felt totally responsible for her brother, only eleven months younger. Her brother was the Scapegoat in the little family and their mother took out all her anger, unhappiness and frustrations on him. There was nothing Jessica could do to protect her brother from the extreme physical abuse inflicted on him by their mother. Jessica would rather have received the abuse herself. She remembers one time that was particularly bad when her mother completely lost control, beating her brother until "he was a bloody mess." Some of the guilt she brought forward into adulthood was the fact she could not protect him adequately.

Another example of physical abuse is Beatrice, an ESFJ-1, mentioned in chapter 3. She was raised in an extremely abusive environment. She and her siblings were often badly beaten. Frequently, a broomstick was used. Being the eldest, Beatrice felt responsible for the safety of her siblings.

A form of physical abuse that is rarely addressed is inadequate hygiene. Both Sarah and Mary, referred to in the previous chapter, suffered emotionally from the effects of poor hygiene in childhood. Sarah was raised in a rural area of a southern state. She was one of the older children in a family of fifteen. There was one bathroom and the toilet was not adequate for the number of people. A large bucket was used in lieu of

Two decades after leaving that house, Sarah felt she could still smell the residual effects on her skin, hair and clothing. By high school, Sarah knew without any doubt she was ugly and smelly. She would have happily died.

plumbing when necessary. The children bathed once a week. One tub of water was used to bathe them all, starting with the youngest. Sarah, as an ISTJ, was naturally fastidious about her personal grooming. "My clothes smelled, the bed smelled, urine was everywhere, the bathroom smelled." Two decades after leaving that house, Sarah felt she could still smell the residual effects on her skin, hair and clothing. By high school, Sarah knew without any doubt she was ugly and smelly. She would have happily died. In therapy, we were able to dispatch the phantom odors and to restore her sense
of personal cleanliness.

Although Mary's family was smaller with just three girls, she experienced the same type of abuse around hygiene. The girls were only allowed to bathe and wash their hair once a week and had to use the same bath water. Her mother insisted on an open-door policy, denying her any privacy. Mary entered adulthood convinced she was dirty.

Many families have an "open-door" policy on bathrooms and bedrooms. Denying a child privacy in the bathroom or denying the physical safety of her own room is abusive. The child grows up without a healthy sense of boundaries. This is especially true for Introverted children who need more space and alone time than their Extraverted siblings.

Sexual Abuse

I am quite convinced that the extent of sexual abuse in our society is woefully underestimated. Various studies estimate that anywhere from 20 to 60 percent of women and about 10 percent of men were sexually abused as children. Certainly, the upper number is closer to the truth for women and even that might be conservative. Surely, the actual numbers are higher for

men as well, but much sexual abuse is not reported and often memories are repressed.

When a new client reports no childhood sexual abuse, it is unusual. If a group of women begin talking honestly about the topic of childhood sexual abuse, they are generally surprised to find how many of them have had some such devastating experience.

Sexual abuse often conjures up images of a father physically violating his daughter. Sexual abuse is a great deal more than that. Sexual abuse can be emotional incest with flirting and nonspecific inappropriate behaviors such as tickling and backrubs. In the perpetrator's fantasies, these seemingly harmless acts are put into another context. Often, the child will be left with feelings best described as "yuk."

Mothers sexually abuse their children as well. In my opinion, sexual abuse by a mother is the most damaging. During gestation, as a child develops within her mother, she becomes intimately familiar with the person who provides safety and nurture. Upon birth, the child instinctively turns to her mother for those same needs. How completely devastating when this mother violates that inborn trust. Maslow, Erickson, Piaget and others point out that the first task of the infant is to develop trust. When sexually violated by a mother, the child cannot develop trust and therefore cannot move on to other developmental tasks. The child views the world as a very scary place indeed when the one person she should be able to trust unconditionally has betrayed her.

Sometimes a client will present with every possible indication of childhood sexual abuse and all but tell me that it happened. However, in answer to the direct question: "Were you ever sexually abused?" the response will be negative. Most of the time, it is because the perpetrator is the icon, a person highly important to the victim, and it is necessary that she see that person in a positive light.

In most dysfunctional families, one parent is the identified villain. This parent is blamed for all the troubles the person and the family experienced. Often it is the alcoholic or mentally ill parent or the parent who left due to divorce. The remaining parent is all the child has left before utter and complete aloneness. A child is a dependent being and relies on a parent to provide the essentials for survival. If one parent is emotionally unavailable, the remaining parent becomes all-important. It becomes a matter of physical and emotional survival to align with that parent. The child makes that parent the icon. No matter the quality of the icon's parenting skills, the child projects upon the icon the parent that is needed:

- Poor Mom. She was a saint to put up with Dad's drinking and cheating all those years. She was so quiet and gentle. He was such a loser. I don't know what I would have done without her. She was my friend.

- I always felt sorry for Dad. Mom was in and out of institutions my whole childhood. Even when she was home, she stayed in her darkened room and took tranquilizers day and night. Dad never left her, though. He was faithful till the end. I was his favorite. I helped him with the younger kids. He was always very good to me. I was his Princess.

When the icon sexually abuses the child, the child cannot admit the abuse to herself because it contradicts the definition of the icon. It is easier and safer for the child to believe something is wrong with herself than with her icon. The need of the child to protect, in her own mind, the illusion of the loving icon compounds the effects of the abuse because the child then accepts complete blame subconsciously, if not consciously. To see the icon as a perpetrator means that she is entirely alone without either parent. It is better not to see. It is better to continue to project the perfect parent onto the icon. As an adult, this person may then enter therapy reporting any or all of the following behaviors:

- Sexually active at an early age
- Co-dependence
- Promiscuity
- Alcohol and/or drug abuse (or other addictions)
- Eating disorders
- Victimized physically, emotionally, mentally
- Inability to say no
- Prostitution
- Self-mutilation
- Suicide attempts
- Rape(s)
- Sexual dysfunction
- Distrust of the opposite sex
- Rage/anger
- Low self-esteem
- Equates self-worth with sex
- Shame
- Equates sex with power

In describing their childhood histories, these clients will often give blatant hints of inappropriateness on the part of the icon, but completely deny there was sexual abuse when asked directly. Many people will warn me in the telling of their case histories not to go near the icon. They will often tell about seeing previous therapists who indicated there *must* have been sexual abuse and so they left therapy. Or other therapists have told them they would have to look at their icon's behaviors honestly if they wanted to get well and so they left therapy. What such clients are saying to me is: Don't take my icon, my only hope, away from me. Then I will have no one.

A standard rule of therapy is not to take something away until there is something else with which to replace it. The client cannot give up the icon until the client has *herself* to replace it. Therefore, the therapist needs to join the client in her worldview and accept the icon as perceived until the client is strong enough and ready to dismantle the icon herself. The first thing necessary in order to begin emotional healing is a safe environment. Confrontation on such a crucial issue and a safe environment are mutually exclusive. Kory, an ESFP-8, is an excellent example.

Kory's story. Kory had tried cognitive therapy with disastrous results. One of the problems was that the counselor had tried to get her to face issues around her father. Kory put me on notice at the very beginning that she would not entertain any negative talk about her deceased father. Of course, I agreed completely. Later, Kory went on to describe her father's behaviors vividly and with clarity. Despite the honesty that she brought to any discussion of her father, I was careful to respect her warning and tread lightly. She reported having fond memories of caring for him when he was intoxicated. She readily admitted that he physically abused the children and often threatened to kill them all, chasing them around the house with a knife or calling for a gun. She also willingly disclosed that he was sexually inappropriate with her sisters. In Kory's mind, her mother was the main problem in the household. So I followed her lead and began approaching some of her issues around her mother in our first working session.

In the very next session, Kory brought up the physical abuse by her father. Although I continued to be cautious around the topic of her father, I knew we would eventually work through it. Soon, she admitted her fears around "de-mythologizing" her father. Just talking about those fears elicited a panic attack during the session. She did not want to face losing the dad she had been trying desperately to believe she really had. She imaged the enormous sadness around the loss of that fictional father as so large that it had to be contained with a chain-link fence. Allowing full expression of her feelings relieved her panic attack. It was not long before Kory was able to bring the memories of sexual abuse by her father into her conscious awareness.

Many times sexual abuse is not perpetrated by a parent but by a sibling. That usually happens because the sibling was violated in some way and is acting out of buried anger and aggression.

Denise's story. Denise, an ENFP-4, entered therapy profoundly depressed, bulimic and suicidal. She was trying to end another of a string of abusive relationships. She presented with all the classic symptoms of childhood sexual abuse. She was active in AA, recovering from both alcohol and drug abuse. She had been raped at age eleven. She was promiscuous throughout high school and prostituted on occasion to get basic survival needs met. She was victimized in every way possible by every man she ever knew. She had been hospitalized for severe depression and had at least one serious suicide attempt. She was currently taking large doses of anti-depressants.

She described a childhood rampant with neglect, mistreatment and every type of abuse imaginable. Her parents were divorced very early in her life. She and her older brother were raised by their mother who was an alcoholic and seriously mentally ill. Her mother had many abusive lovers. Her mother attempted suicide several times during Denise's childhood and finally succeeded when Denise was a young adult.

The mainstay for Denise was her older brother. "He was my god," she reported. He was the only one who really stood between her and all the forces at work against her. Without him, she was certain she would not have survived. At the same time, Denise willingly described her brother's sexual acting out with neighborhood girls, his abuse of alcohol and drugs and his raging. In answer to the question: Did he sexually abuse you? She replied in the negative. She went on to tell me about an earlier therapist who insisted he had molested her and so she discontinued therapy. I was warned. I joined her in her worldview and left her brother alone. I worked with the wounded little girl within her with whom Denise immediately bonded. Denise grew to love and delight in how special her inner child was and became very protective of the child.

As an adult, Denise knew her brother to be a violent alcoholic. As therapy progressed, she was distressed by unexpected memories, feelings and flashbacks that seemed to implicate her brother. As she became more stable and began to feel emotionally strong enough, she was able to face the sexual abuse she endured by her brother. In imagery, Denise entered the black hole she felt inside herself. Look at figure 6-7, Denise's representation of the black hole, which is a clear indication that there was sexual abuse. She moved deep into that black hole until she came upon something disgusting and repulsive. She recognized it to be her brother and saw the abuse. She reported she felt very young, possibly eight years old. She was filled with sadness, anger and hatred.

Figure 6-7. Originally drawn in red and black.

As a child, she could not allow herself to have conscious knowledge of the abuse because of the importance of her brother in her life. Even without that factor, whom would she have told? Who would have cared? The sense of betrayal Denise sustained was crushing. Watching Denise come to terms with his betrayal was heart wrenching. However, as long as she was not acknowledging the abuse, a part of her Core Self had to be kept locked away with the secret.

After expressing the emotions around the abuse, Denise could visualize herself as an adult validating the eight-year-old child and telling her, that she believed her. When the imagery ended, Denise reported she felt relieved and much lighter than she ever felt. She was smiling, happy and guilt-free. The sense of peace and well-being that filled her with the acceptance of her own history was worth the pain of the knowledge. Figure 6-8a shows how Denise depicted herself at the beginning of therapy and figure 6-8b represents how she saw herself after she had processed the sexual abuse by her brother.

Figure 6-8a

Figure 6-8b

If the child is able to tell a parent about being sexually abused, and feel validated and vindicated, the wounding will be minimized. However, that is almost never the case. Generally, the child knows not to upset the system by saying anything to the parent. The child has learned to protect the parent's feelings at the expense of her own. If the child (perhaps an outspoken Scapegoat) does report the abuse, it is not likely to be addressed. The parent may deny it happened or tell the child to keep the secret. She has been betrayed twice.

Bernadette's story. When Bernadette, an ESFJ-6, was eight years old, her father raped her one night while her mother was at work. Despite the blood, her siblings' accounts and the obvious trauma to Bernadette, her mother did not believe her. Her father continued to rape and sodomize her until age twelve. Her mother continued to ignore it. Bernadette knew her mom could not face leaving her father and needed to see herself as a good mother. Since her father was the designated villain, she only allowed herself to feel love and sympathy for her mother. However, as soon as Bernadette looked honestly at the sexual abuse, the first thought she had was, "Where was my mother?" Under light hypnosis, Bernadette wrote the following letter to her mother from the wounded child within her:

> *Dear Mom*
>
> *Hate you*
> *Mean alone*
> *Help me — hurting*
> *Scared please don't leave me*
> *don't leave us.*
> *Dad hurt me awful.*
> *I don't like him*
> *don't go away anymore*
> *he does things to us.*
> *Why do you go at night*
>
> *don't go*
> *Mad at you*
> *You didn't help us*
> *Why did you have us if you don't want us*
> *give us away*
> *How could you leave us he was bad to us.*
> *He hurt us*
> *he was nasty*
> ***HE WAS MEAN***
> ***HE DID THINGS TO ME THAT HURT ME.***

Bernadette finally faced the fact that her mother was equally to blame for what happened to her. She then had to accept how profoundly alone she really had been as a child—truly parentless.

Bernadette's story illustrates another aspect of sexual abuse which is the effects it has on siblings who were not themselves sexually abused.

The first time her father raped her at age eight, Bernadette's brother, age nine, was outside the door, trying to get in to help her. All he could do was listen to her screams and pound on the door. What happened to her brother that night was immensely traumatizing. Without a doubt, the emotional pain caused by their father that night contributed to his suicide eighteen years later.

In recent years, the topic of repressed memories has received a lot of attention. Some people even deny that there is such a thing. We live in a patriarchal culture that is based on a male worldview. Part of the male worldview is a Thinking perspective since more than half of Thinking types are male (see chapter 3). A Thinking perspective means that decision making is based on rational, logical thinking. A Thinking perspective does not allow for conclusions that defy logic. Therefore, our Thinking-based culture cannot understand how something could happen to a person and that person not have a cognitive memory of the event. It is even more mystifying to those with a Thinking perspective that the person could *know* something happened and yet not *know* it cognitively. Thinking types cannot trust any other way of knowing than knowing with cognition. When the entire culture is based on this perspective, it is difficult for a person with no cognitive memories to be understood, believed or validated. Anyone not taking this approach is taught to question herself. Without cognitive memories, a person is led to give the benefit of the doubt to the perpetrator. The culture will certainly not accept, "I just *know*!" and the victim is very aware of that.

In order to have a cognitive memory, it would make sense that the person would have to be present at the event. Many victims of sexual abuse are aware that they were not present in their bodies when the abuse occurred. Often, they report that they left their bodies completely, watching what happened from the ceiling or from a corner of the room. Some say they know they went out the window or so deep inside themselves as to not be present. In any event, the split from the body was great enough that the information was not transmitted from the spirit and the body to the brain. But the spirit and the body remember. Our Thinking-based culture does not trust the memories of the spirit or the body. Cognitive memories are the only "authentic" memories. Here is another example of the victim being betrayed twice. To have one's safety destroyed and entire life devastated through sexual abuse is beyond description. To be questioned, doubted and dismissed due to lack of cognitive memories is to be assaulted again.

A victim of childhood sexual abuse must come to trust her body memories and her emotional memories as completely as she trusts her mental memories regardless of what the culture, family, friends or anyone else says. Body and emotional memories are accurate and provide considerable information that, unlike cognitive memories, cannot be manipulated or twisted. Victims of childhood sexual abuse who distrust their own body and emotional memories, insisting on cognitive memories before condemning the perpetrator, subject themselves to endless internal torment. This insistence is at war with the messages from their bodies and spirits.

Darlene's story. Darlene, an INFP-5, came to see me after recently spending some time in a locked unit of a hospital due to suicidal tendencies and severe depression. This was not her first hospital stay. Six months earlier, she had been hospitalized and received shock treatments. Three months after the shock treatments her symptoms returned, eventually resulting in her recent hospital stay. She was advised to receive another round of shock treatments but elected instead to try affective therapy and so she came to see me. When she arrived, she was taking so many different medications she was unable to drive. Her hands shook so badly from the medications that she needed two hands to hold a cup of water. Her ability to do simple mental functions was impaired by the medications. She still wanted to kill herself.

We began work on areas unrelated to sexual abuse but eventually approached the topic. She reported being very close to her dad and, although both parents were now dead, she missed her dad much more than her mother. She acknowledged that her father was an alcoholic and that she knew he was inappropriate on at least one or two occasions. Darlene felt unloved by her mother from the very beginning. Her father was her main caregiver and her icon. She did not want to know he hurt her and voiced that many times. Yet there was a war within her. Her body and spirit were trying to get her to cognitively acknowledge what happened to cause her much emotional distress.

Acknowledging her father's sexual abuse would mean Darlene would have had to accept the fact that neither of her parents were there for her. That is too frightening for any child and so she did not remain in her body when the abuse happened. She simply "went away." As an adult, she still did not want to know that she did not have either a mom or a dad and so each time we approached the topic, Darlene just "went away" by dissociating. For some of our sessions, she was gone much more than she was present. It became my job to keep calling her back and to keep her safe enough to look at what she had to face. Although Darlene hated the work, she was devoted to her recovery and completely cooperative. As odious as the topic of her father's sexual abuse was, the more we brought it to the forefront of her mind, the less medication she needed until she was eventually off all of it, even before therapy was completed.

Darlene, like everyone else, wanted cognitive memories before giving up her icon and labeling her father as a child molester. Although she had the benefit of some cognitive memories of touching, she felt there was more. Her body and her spirit were giving her indications of oral and vaginal penetration. Together, we drew up the chart below of what her body, mind and spirit were telling her.

In a court of law, Darlene's case would be considered circumstantial and she would most likely not be vindicated. However, to the court deep within Darlene, the

Incident	Mind	Body	Spirit
In the car with Dad	He slobbered on me He was drunk	He touched me Nausea Rapid breathing Sensations in my hands	Terrified Alone Betrayed Dissociated
Being bathed by Dad	None	Nausea He touched me Vaginal sensations Rapid breathing	Alone Betrayed Scared Dissociated
Bedroom	He was in my room naked He touched me vaginally I said, "Leave me alone"	Touch Vaginal sensations Nausea Rapid breathing	Alone Betrayed Scared
Being raped	None	Feeling pinned down Nausea Hard to breathe Vaginal sensations Feelings in breasts Feeling crushed Feelings in arms/legs	Alone Betrayed Terrified Rage

evidence was overwhelming and when her mind did not want to accept what her body and spirit knew to be true, the war was intense and heated.

Looking at the incident of being bathed by her father is a good example. Until I asked Darlene who bathed her, Darlene never considered that this may have been an opportunity for sexual abuse. She reported she knew her father had always bathed her as a child, but she had absolutely no memories of those times, much less of sexual abuse during those times. I told her it may not have happened but she could try taking a bath by candle light and just pay special attention to her body and her feelings while doing so. She came to our next session saying she could not even get past thinking about bathing in a bathroom lit only by a candle. She felt terror and had body sensations of fingers in her vagina just at the thought of it. These feelings were accompanied by an overwhelming sense of betrayal. Darlene realized that, as an adult, she always showered and would never take baths.

It is not necessary to her recovery that Darlene ever have cognitive memories of the abuse. It is only necessary that she accepts that it happened and places the guilt on the guilty party instead of on herself. Darlene now understands why she has been filled with feelings of intense rage all her life. With no place to direct that rage, it was turned on herself. As healing continued with greater and greater acceptance, Darlene began to have hope for her future and could visualize the peace that should have always been hers.

Many of the Thinking persuasion are right now maintaining there is not enough evidence to determine Darlene was abused during bathing or to determine she was actually raped by her father. It is the discounting of body and emotional memories that has led so many victims of sexual abuse to despair. Discounting another way of "knowing" other than cognition discredits much of who we are as humans. As an Intuitive Feeling type, Darlene believed her body and her emotional memories, which brought her to acceptance of her history a lot sooner than if she had needed cognitive memories. In fact, Thinking types with only body and spirit

memories take a lot longer in therapy because they are hard-core holdouts for cognitive "proof." Reilley, whose story is presented in chapter 11, is a good example. She is a Thinking type and insisted on cognitive memories that her mother sexually abused her before she would accept that it happened. As fate would have it, her abuse occurred while she was an infant and before cognition was operational. Therefore, it was not a matter of *repressed* memories, it was a matter of having no memories at all. However, although she was too young to have developed cognition, her body and spirit were present enough to take note of the abuse and have it register. Because of her Thinking orientation, it took Reilley longer to accept the evidence provided by noncognitive sources than it did Darlene, a Feeling type.

Due to our culture, a great deal of weight has been placed on an objective, scientific approach. There is a place for this type of orientation. Yet if it is applied in all circumstances, it can be limiting and a broader understanding is denied. Rachel Naomi Remen in her tape series, *Final Wisdom,* tells a story of a man she saw while she was an intern. He was a terminal cancer patient whose entire body was affected by the disease, including his bones and lungs. Surprisingly, the cancer spontaneously and completely disappeared in a very short period of time. A group of 500 physicians all agreed that the chemotherapy that had been discontinued a full year earlier must have finally kicked in. Rachel admits that as a young intern, she accepted what the others accepted but that she now knows there are other things that come into play that defy cognitive understanding. If we could come to that broader understanding culturally, what an exciting and interesting world it would be.

Emotional Abuse

Whenever emotions are denied expression, discounted or refuted, it is emotional abuse. Telling a child she has nothing to cry about or that what is upsetting her really does not hurt is denying her reality and shaming her. That child begins to distrust her own feelings and begins to look to others to determine how she feels, or should feel, in any given situation. This arrangement contributes to a child relinquishing her own worldview for that of her parents'.

In every family, there are some emotions that are distinctly unwelcome. Sometimes, it is different feelings that are not welcomed by different people. A child may grow up knowing she has to be happy around Mom but she cannot show any other feeling. At the same time, she may know that she can show sadness to Dad who will comfort her, but that he does not want to see her angry. The child learns very early who accepts which of her emotions and puts away the offending feelings to please her parents. In some families, no feelings are acceptable at all. Some clients report that they were never allowed to show any emotion, not even happiness.

The culture, as well as the family, sets standards around the display of emotions. As already noted, boys are allowed to be angry but not scared or sad. Girls can be sad and scared but not angry. Certain situations allow tears, such as funerals, weddings and sad movies. But tears are not acceptable over dinner at a restaurant. At a party, it is mandated that everyone be happy and bubbly or blamed for being a party pooper and ruining the party. The culture definitely dictates which emotions are displayed, where and to what degree.

When a child has an emotional reaction to a situation and that feeling is shut down midway, the remains of that feeling stay stuck within her. There is an old joke that says, "What is worse than finding a worm in your apple? Half of a worm." It is the same with an emotion. Feeling scared is not pleasant but feeling scared and being told you are not scared, and to stop it, is even worse. The residual feeling is left within the child and, every time she encounters a similar situation, that half of a feeling will do its best to express itself and reach some resolution.

Many people have phobias of one type or another. A common phobia is the fear of flying. Often, the fear of flying can be traced to a feeling of being out of control. By simply tracing that fear back to where it was first shut down in its original context, full expression can be

provided to the original scare and that feeling of being out of control can be addressed and resolved. When that happens, a sense of well-being and of being in control can be restored, thereby eradicating the phobia.

Simone's story. Although a competent administrator with a master's degree, Simone, an ENFJ-4, was plagued by a phobia about bridges. She became extremely fearful about driving over bridges and, since rivers surrounded the city in which she lived, she was fairly well confined. She wanted to visit her parents more frequently but was unable to do so because they lived on the other side of a river bridge. Simone devised a variety of rituals to try to calm herself enough to get across a bridge, but she knew it was dangerous to herself and others to continue in this manner.

In a therapy session, we traced her fears to their origins in her childhood and the resulting feelings of being out of control. When we were able to address and resolve that child's fears, the bridge phobia was over. That was five years ago and Simone is still happily traversing bridges at will.

It is not only issues around fright that can be resolved in this manner. The same is true of other emotions. If an emotion is denied expression, it will find its way out later.

Bernadette's story. Bernadette, ESFJ-6, found herself becoming terribly angry with her supervisor at work who repeatedly failed to stand up for her. Although she had every reason to be angry in these situations, Bernadette realized her anger was out of proportion to the offense. We easily traced the feelings of abandonment to her mother ignoring her father's sexual abuse. When we could deal with the feelings that were left over from that original situation, Bernadette felt more in control and able to speak up to her supervisor. She was also able to address her own expectations of her supervisor and make them more realistic.

The main purpose of an emotion is to draw attention to the fact that something is amiss. A feeling is like a red flag or alarm system. Using the information the feeling provides can help resolve the troubling situation. When a child is trained to suppress her feelings and to question their validity, she is shutting down a vital part of herself. Later, when she gets a warning feeling in an uncomfortable situation, she is very likely to ignore it and suffer the consequences.

Verbal Abuse

It is safe to say we have all experienced verbal abuse. The childhood verse of "Sticks and stones can break my bones but names can never hurt me," is categorically untrue. In reality, it is much easier to heal a broken bone than a broken spirit. Being called stupid or being described as defective in any way is terribly abusive. The child looks to her parents for a mirror to reflect who she is. When the parent mirrors back that the child is defective or a mistake, the child has no choice but to accept that information. Remember, she needs these people in order to stay alive and so their view becomes her view. If there is a conflict between her worldview and her parents', she will quickly adjust hers to correspond with theirs. In no instance is that easier than in her view of herself. Criticism, constructive or otherwise, will bring a child down in a hurry. It is just as easy to validate as to criticize yet validation does not seem to happen with the same frequency as criticism.

Passive Abuse and Neglect

I routinely ask a client to give me a list of adjectives to describe each parent. When the client looks at me blankly and searches for an appropriate word, I am seldom surprised when the word that comes out is *gone*. When a parent is unavailable to the child to the extent that the child cannot even describe that parent, the message to the child is very clear. The child knows that she is not worth the time or effort. She does not matter to that parent. Beth, Jessica and Reilley had mothers who neglected them and fathers who were either physically absent or might just as well have been. All three did their best to raise themselves and their younger sibling(s). All came to adulthood wondering why their mothers had them, why they were not given up for adoption and/or what was so wrong with them

that their mothers turned away. Having a nonpresent father can be just as devastating.

Danielle's story. Danielle's mother was very present, very abusive and very arbitrary. Her father dealt with the problem by being gone as much as possible. When home, Dad would punish harshly, too, to placate Mom, without even knowing what was going on. Mom supported Danielle's father's absence so she would not have to deal with the sad state of the marriage. Danielle reports forever being told: "He does so much for us by working long hours and traveling. Don't bother him. What he does is so important compared to anything you are dealing with." Danielle had no problems reading between the lines. She interpreted her father's absence to mean the following:

* I don't care about you
* I don't love you
* I'm not available
* I'm not there for you
* I don't have time for you or your mother
* I may leave permanently
* My work/career is my priority
* My life and activities are important; yours aren't

These unspoken messages left Danielle feeling:

Forgotten	Sad
Lost	Uninteresting
Like trash	Powerless
Not valuable	Tired
Insignificant	Overwhelmed
Voiceless	Anxious
Scared/terrified	

In a drawing, Danielle depicted a nearly invisible dad with an X over his ears and his eyes indicating he never heard nor saw her. It occurred to Danielle that she went to her pet dog for all the things she wanted from a father:

Protection	Availability
Affection	Patience
Friendship	Gentleness
Love	Support
Fairness	Health
Play	Happiness

Each of these women admits that she is equally angry with the parent who was not there as she is with the abusive parent.

Chemically Dependent Parent

When a parent is chemically dependent, the addictive substance takes priority in that person's life. Everything else, including that person's children, takes a far distant second place.

Jessica's story. Jessica's mother neglected her children because her total focus in life was where her next high would come from. Jessica was smoking pot and partying with her mother when she was in junior high. Her mother's dependence on chemicals resulted in a lot of undesirable men being around, setting the stage for Jessica to be raped at age eleven.

Reilley's story. Reilley's mother was at work all day. When her father was home, he kept company with his alcohol. By the time Mom came home, he was drunk and the fighting began. To this day, Reilley will not speak with him on the phone after 3:00 p.m. because she knows she will be talking to a drunk.

Therese's story. Therese's father chose alcohol not only above his wife and children but above his very life. He died early of acute alcoholism. Therese wonders why he did not love himself and his family enough to stop drinking and be a father.

Children learn very early to monitor the addicted parent in order to know how to adjust their behavior.

Bernadette's story. Bernadette and her siblings devised a code to put each other on alert. If their father had not been drinking, they would make a happy face when a sibling entered the house to let that child know things were not so bad. If he had been drinking, they would make a sad face and the newly arriving child was warned.

Clearly, growing up under such circumstances is deeply wounding.

Cultural, Ethnic and Religious Traditions

I have made many references to cultural messages that can be wounding. The cultural standards for males and females, against which we are all measured, are blatant and pervasive. A male is expected to be an ESTJ-3 and a female an ESFJ-2 or ESFJ-6. Anyone looking or acting different from the stereotype is adjusted by family, school, religion and the culture at large.

The culture's most prominent agent is the media. If anyone is unsure of how to "be," just check out the magazines, movies, TV, advertisements, novels, fairy tales and newspapers. There is certain to be an article or authority ready to proclaim the exact shade of lipstick to wear and the exact length and shape to keep fingernails so as to be acceptable. And so, if the family of origin has caused the Core Self to be put away for safekeeping due to wounding, the culture offers a socially acceptable substitute. For girls, the negative feelings they have about themselves are often compensated for by "positive" reactions they receive for their bodies. If the body is "perfect," that is, meeting the current cultural prototype, then the girl is accepted and made to feel she has value. It is no wonder that the diet industry is so large when most females receive their sense of value for their bodies and for their servitude.

The media provides us with a variety of methods to kill the emotional pain of not having access to the Core Self: alcohol, money, fame, achievement, sex, "beauty" as defined by the culture, work and socializing are some examples. If only the Core Self were recognized, acknowledged, valued, celebrated and loved in the family of origin, the attempts by the culture to provide a false self would be largely ignored.

Various ethnic and religious traditions provide us with wounding messages about ourselves. In many orthodox religions, the female is treated as a lesser being than the male and marginalized. Religions can package these messages in any of a variety of sugarcoated ways, but the message to young girls is unmistakable: "You are not good enough. You are less than. . . ."

Some religious and ethnic groups raise their daughters to submit to abuse, and parents will take the side of the abusive male over the suffering of their own daughters.

Beatrice's story. Beatrice's parents were both born in a southern, strongly patriarchal European country. Their religion parallels the values and standards of their ethnic origins. Beatrice's husband raped her before they were married. She felt she had no choice but to go on with the marriage. When he became abusive, she mentioned it to her parents. They immediately sided with Beatrice's husband, telling him to beat her if she got out of line. When Beatrice's sister announced she was considering divorcing her alcoholic husband, these parents descended upon her, beating her with a stick and verbally attacking her for not submitting to her husband. Beatrice's parents were imposing their very strict ethnic and religious rules on their daughters to the point of extreme abuse.

Maureen's story. Maureen, an ISTJ-3, was raised in a very strict, fundamentalist religion. When she was eight years old, her father decided to become a missionary in the Far East. Maureen and her siblings were placed in a boarding school so that her parents could minister to the poor children of the poverty-ridden country to which they dedicated themselves. The boarding school was in the same country as her parents' work but many miles away. Maureen only saw her parents twice a year. She cried and her heart broke each time she had to say goodbye to her mother. The poor children may have benefited from her parents' labors, but Maureen and her siblings paid a very dear price. Imagine finding yourself in a foreign country and strange culture at age eight and seeing your parents only twice a year. Maureen knew in her heart that those unknown children were much more important to her father than she was. She felt abandoned and unloved. Yet she could not allow herself to feel any anger because her father was dedicated to doing God's will. Any unhappy feelings were quickly followed by feelings of guilt for her selfishness. She tried hard to submit herself to the will of God as her father explained it.

When she was a teenager, her class went on a kind of pilgrimage. During the trip, Maureen became extremely ill. She was taken to a local "hospital," which had no doctor, and the trip leader had to return to the group. Maureen was left alone, very sick, with primitive care and not speaking the local dialect. In figure 6-9, Maureen describes how small and alone she felt. Yet she never complained or allowed herself to think that she deserved more because her parents

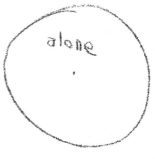

Figure 6-9

were fulfilling a higher calling than caring for her.

Maureen spent the next ten years in the boarding school and considered her classmates her extended family. Returning to the United States for visits and then later as an adult was a very difficult cultural adjustment for her. She did not know how to do such simple things as operate a soda machine or a pay telephone, things we take for granted. Of course, feeling so lacking in value to her family, Maureen willingly settled for a very abusive marriage and felt powerless to leave.

Virginia's story. Virginia's mother was a strict Catholic. When Virginia was born, she was christened Virginia Marie in honor of the Virgin Mary and dressed only in blue and white for the first seven years of her life. No one questioned the extreme nature of her mother's behavior. Her father suffered from depression and was in no shape to question Virginia's mother. Virginia had trouble establishing her own identity. In order to please her mother, she had to be a little replica of her mother's conception of the Virgin Mary.

Both Maureen and Virginia had parents who were religiously addicted. Religion is used as a method to numb emotional pain. It has nothing to do with God or spirituality any more than any other addiction does. But the small child growing up has no way of knowing that. And certainly, the child knows how powerful God is. God is someone you do not want to mess with so the child becomes very compliant. As an ISTJ-3, Maureen easily accepted her parents' religious viewpoints. As a Three, she tried hard to live up to them. Virginia, as an

ENTJ-4, was more questioning and, as an adult, more easily let go of her mother's extreme religious views.

Parenting Styles

Each MBTI type has a different parenting style, not to mention the twist put on each of these sixteen styles by the nine different Enneagram types. It is a given that, more likely than not, a child is going to be parented in a style that is very different from the needs of that child. David Keirsey in *Please Understand Me* and *Please Understand Me II,* clearly explains different parenting styles. Tieger and Barron-Tieger describe the parenting needs of each MBTI type in *Nurture by Nature.* A child of a very different temperament than her parents will require a very different parenting style than her mom and dad may be equipped to provide.

Reilley's story. Reilley, as an NT, needed a parent who was able to guide and direct, fostering independence and encouraging critical thinking. Her mother, as an ESFP, could not provide that nor even understand Reilley's needs. Her frequent comment to Reilley was, "Geniuses have no common sense." When her mother chose partying over being home with her children, Reilley felt rejected, abandoned, unloved and unvalued.

Beth's story. As an INTJ, Beth had a strong need for order. She described the family as "trailer trash." The house was always a mess and the children neglected. Beth tried to keep the house clean, but it was more than she could manage. Her mother's unconcern regarding homemaking skills conflicted with Beth's need for order. Beth interpreted her mother's lack of homemaking as a lack of care. Her mother's neglect profoundly affected Beth and removed her sense of self-worth.

Paula's story. Paula's father's strict parenting style has already been documented as has its effect on a very sensitive, playful ENFP spirit. Her father may have been trying to show his love for her by molding her into a "perfect" child, but all it did was destroy any sense of identity and self-worth she may have had.

Family Secrets

Many children grow up with the strong message that, above all things, the family must look good to neighbors, friends and extended family. Abuse, addictions, mental illness, financial problems and the like are kept a deep, dark secret. Acting out by a sibling, scholastic problems, sexual orientation and other sensitive issues are all kept very quiet.

* The fact that Reilley is a lesbian is never alluded to or mentioned by her family.
* Sondra has a mentally retarded uncle who lives in an institution and whom she has never met. The family never speaks of him.
* Beth was sexually abused by her grandfather's friend. When she told her mother, her mother said to keep it a secret because it would hurt her grandfather.
* At twenty-one, Brenda had a child out of wedlock. Her parents dropped her off at the hospital to have the baby, which was put up for adoption, and they never alluded to the incident again.
* It was clear that Danielle's parents' marriage was in bad shape, but they had to all pretend that Dad just worked long hours to take care of the family.
* Mary's mother was dying of cancer yet no one acknowledged she was even sick. After her death, her father would not allow her name to be mentioned.

These are only a few examples of having to keep family secrets, forcing the child to put away her own truth and worldview in order to be in alignment with the family's. It is easy to see how a child can grow up with a distorted idea of reality.

EVENTS OUT OF THE CHILD'S CONTROL

Children have magical thinking. They are very egocentric and interpret events around them through their egocentric lens. This may cause them to come to some inaccurate conclusions regarding the degree of their involvement in certain events. Children have a greatly inflated idea of their own power in causing things to happen or in preventing things from happening. By virtue of their magical thinking, they take a lot more responsibility than what is appropriate. In truth, children are, without doubt or exception, never responsible for the events in which they find themselves since they do not have the ability to predict the consequences of their actions nor the power to stop the actions of others.

Women who have been raped as young as age three can convince themselves (with a little help from their perpetrators) that they somehow caused it to happen and could have stopped it once it started. Other people grow up feeling that God placed them in an abusive family because they were inherently bad, defective, ugly and/or unlovable.

When a child assumes responsibility for events that are truly out of her control, the resulting guilt is enormous. Innocent and not-so-innocent comments by family, friends, church and school can add to the burden of guilt the child carries. The guilt from these situations is carried into adulthood and is rarely examined for validity. Some examples of these kinds of events are presented here. There are many more situations for which a child can mistakenly take responsibility. If you have such an event in your childhood, try to bring adult eyes and an adult's evaluation to the situation, as if it had happened to another child. To get a really compassionate perspective, have the "someone else" be a daughter/son, niece/nephew or other child with whom you feel close. If these cases seem dramatic or extreme, try to make a less severe or more moderate application to your own life.

Chronic Physical Illness

Sometimes a child is faced with a chronic physical illness or condition that may cause the child to wonder "why me?" Casual comments by family members or in a religious context may cause the child to feel she is being punished for something unknown. The child may spend a lot of energy trying to rationalize these events so they make sense. The rational abilities of a child are limited and so the conclusions are generally not valid.

Almost always, the conclusion is: "Something must be wrong with me. If I didn't *do* something bad, then I must just be bad."

Peggy's story. When scoliosis was discovered in Peggy's back, she was miserable. Not only did she have to deal with the discomfort of a back brace, but she was failing her mother's mandate to "be pretty." She could only think she had done something wrong or that something was wrong with her to warrant such a punishment.

Sometimes the child feels, or is made to feel, that the illness is a burden to the parent, adding to the degree of responsibility the child assumes and increasing the amount of guilt and shame.

Parent's Mental Illness

When a parent is mentally ill, the burden on a child is enormous. The child can easily assume that she is in some way responsible. The child can make this assumption on her own or have some help coming to that conclusion with comments such as, "You'll be the death of me!" or "No wonder I have to take all those pills!" The child easily assumes that she is in some way simply unlovable and that her badness has caused the parent's problems.

Kyla's story. Kyla's mother had never intended to get pregnant with Kyla (INFP-3) and cried for the first six months of her pregnancy. She imposed an extra burden on herself by feeling she had to have another child "to keep Kyla company." She already had four older children.

Just before her fifth birthday, Kyla watched as her mother's things were being packed. Her mom was suffering from depression and was going away for a while. Kyla's heart was breaking. She felt abandoned and in some way responsible. In her heart, she cried, "Please forgive me! Don't leave me! I'll do anything!" She was very confused and did not know what she could have done to change things or make them better for her mother.

Dorothy's story. Dorothy, an ENFP-1, had an alcoholic father and a mentally ill mother. To the outside world, each parent pretended there were no problems. The clear message was, "Don't talk or you'll pay." Dorothy's mother had a breakdown when Dorothy was two years old and "went away" for a week. That was followed by regular suicide attempts. She cut herself with razors, took overdoses of pills and once put a gun to her head in front of the children. She over-used prescription drugs, went into withdrawal and slept all day. By the time Dorothy was seven years old, she was getting herself and her five-year-old sister off to school each morning. When Dorothy came home from school each day, her mother was so drugged, Dorothy often could not wake her. She was never sure if she were alive or dead. Once, she found her mother passed out on the bathroom floor.

Her mother became pregnant again and considered walking into the ocean to drown herself and her unborn child. Dorothy was seven when her younger sister was born. It was hard to go to school and leave the baby alone with Mom, who slept all day. Dorothy's mother often said she would kill herself because the kids were so bad. As the oldest, Dorothy felt an immense degree of responsibility to care for her siblings and her mother. She knew she had to "be good in order to keep my mother alive."

Meanwhile, Dorothy's father was nowhere to be seen. He refused to see the problems and escaped into work and alcohol. As a child, Dorothy had no such options. She had two little sisters to care for and a mother to keep alive. Her only line of defense was her Enneagram One and so she set about trying to perform an impossible task perfectly. The pressures on this child are beyond description. A small child was being asked to handle what a grown man could not.

It seems inconceivable that extended family, friends, neighbors, school and/or church would not notice or intervene in situations such as Dorothy's but intervention seems to be more the exception than the norm. People seem to look the other way and avoid "becoming involved."

Divorce and Separation

Divorce will always be a difficult situation for a child to navigate. To have a fighting chance, the child will need to know that the divorce was not her fault. Secondly, she will need to know that both her parents love her without question. The word *know* must be examined more closely. The child needs to *know* that the divorce was not her fault not only on a cognitive level but also on an emotional level. The child must not only *know* intellectually that her parents love her because they provide for her and keep her, but she must also feel that love to the very core of her being. These two qualifications are very difficult to attain, particularly when the parents are immersed in their own emotional trauma. It is difficult for a parent to be present to a child when that parent's own thinking is clouded by unresolved emotions. Yet, this is exactly the time when a child needs to be parented and cannot be expected to be the parent to her parent.

Reilley's story. When Reilley was twelve, her mother woke her in the night and took her out on the front porch where she told Reilley that she and her father were probably divorcing. She cried and Reilley did her best to console her. When her mother felt better, they went back to bed. The topic was not brought up again until four months later when her father moved out.

Separation, whether it be a parent or other family member, is very hard on children.

Kory's story. The same year Kory's father died, when she was fourteen, her two older sisters left home. The loss of her father and both her sisters was almost more than she could bear. She had to emotionally care for her mother and younger brother. There was no one to meet her emotional needs or to comfort her in her confused grief.

Therese's story. Therese, an ISTJ-9, watched her favorite brother go off to college to "follow his heart" and could not even understand the concept. Her father was an abusive alcoholic. She could not imagine leaving her mother alone with him. She missed her brother terribly

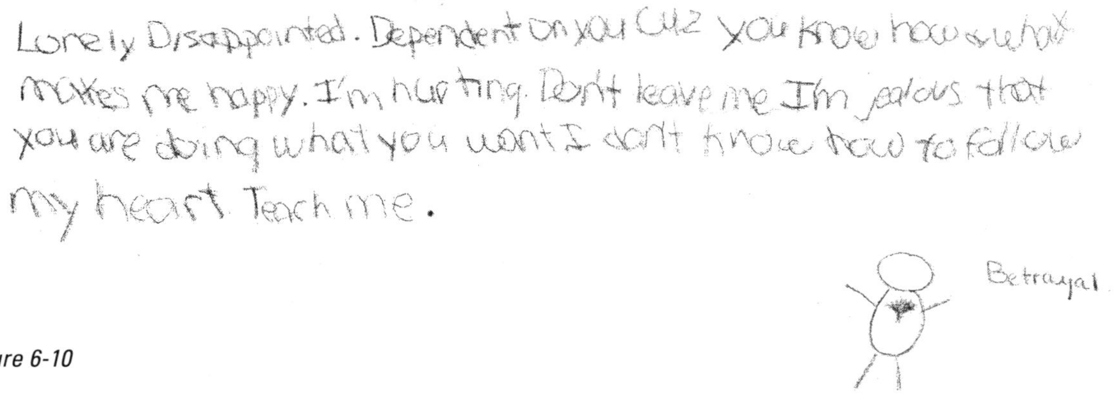

Lonely Disappointed. Dependent on you cuz you know how & what makes me happy. I'm hurting. Don't leave me I'm jealous that you are doing what you want I don't know how to follow my heart Teach me.

Betrayal.

Figure 6-10

and yet she was also angry with him for leaving her to handle the family situation alone. In therapy, her inner child wrote a letter to her brother, Tom (figure 6-10).

Therese was already in deep depression when Tom left. His departure only heightened her pain. She had no one to turn to in order to express her feelings and grieve her losses. She felt completely invisible and unimportant to everyone.

It is not unusual for separation and divorce to cause children to either withdraw into depression or begin acting out. Therese, because of her Enneagram Nine defense and her family role of Lost Child, became more and more withdrawn and depressed. Reilley and Kory began by withdrawing and sinking into depression but then moved into acting out with alcohol, drugs and promiscuity. Both are family Scapegoats and Kory, as an Enneagram Eight, is well equipped to act out in order to kill emotional pain.

Finances

Sometimes children who do not yet even understand the concept of money are faced with the consequences of not having enough or worrying that there will not be enough. Less frequently, there is residual damage from having too much and feeling that the amount of money the family accumulated is what took Dad away or, at least, removed his focus from his family.

Beth's story. Beth, INTJ-4, was embarrassed by the way her family lived and referred to herself and her family as "trailer trash." It was not only the lack of money but the lack of care, hygiene and basic cleanliness.

Kory's story. While he was alive, Kory's father made several fortunes and lost them. One week, they could be living in a mansion with a swimming pool and hired help and the next week be sleeping between two mattresses trying to keep warm. It was always feast or famine. Once, Kory stood on the sidewalk and watched as the family's belongs were repossessed. She stood helpless as their furniture and the children's toys were carried out of the house.

Jessica's story. Generally, the type of lifestyle led by Jessica, her brother and mother was dependent on the financial situation of her mother's current boyfriend. They could be living well with one man and not well at all with another. One long-time live-in had a gambling problem that affected the financial well-being of the family.

At one point, Jessica's mother pulled up stakes and moved them to the southwest. When she ran out of money, she put their possessions in storage and they lived in the car for a while. Then Jessica and her brother were sent off to live with different relatives for a year while Jessica's mother virtually lived on the streets.

In circumstances such as these, parents are too caught up in their own emotional pain to even recognize that the child witnessing these events is even more traumatized. Such events destroy the child's sense of safety and trust, leaving feelings of being out of control, helpless and powerless. There is unexpressed anger, sadness and scare, with no way to process and reconcile these feelings.

Comparisons

Often, it is part of the role of the Scapegoat to be compared to the Hero in the family with predictable results.

Danielle's story. Danielle's comparison to her older sister has already been described. Danielle was well into her forties and nearly finished with therapy before she realized that her abilities were every bit as good as those of her sister and, in some ways, superior. Never before had she been able to see her sister as a peer and equal.

Kyla's story. Kyla, INFP-3, was compared to her older sister for as long as she can remember. As an Enneagram Three, Kyla tried as hard as she could to measure up to the standards set by her Hero older sister but consistently fell short. Without her sister as the standard, Kyla's performance would have been more than just fine. But it was never close to being as grand as the achievements racked up by her sister. She was not chosen as homecoming queen as her sister had been and did not get the lead in the school play as her sister had. When her father died, Kyla "knew" that if her sister had been present, the outcome would have been different.

It is not always a sibling to whom a child is compared, as described in these examples.

Anita's story. Anita, an ENTP-1, was always compared to a cousin in another country by her mother, also an Enneagram One, who set the cousin up to equal perfection. Neither Anita nor her mother really had any way of knowing the truth about the cousin but that never stopped Anita from trying to live up to the standards of perfection her mother implied in the comparisons.

Natalie's story. Natalie, an INTJ-1, was compared by her mother to a neighbor girl of the same age. Natalie's mother, also an Enneagram One, had no way of really knowing the truth about the neighbor but kept the fantasy comparison going. Natalie, trying to reach perfection and win the love and acceptance of her mother, kept striving for the unattainable goal of a fictitious model of perfection.

Comparisons are always bad news. Comparisons are as difficult for the standard bearer as they are for the one being compared. If the child who is the standard bearer, such as the family Hero, is aware of her position, she has little choice but to keep the standard as high as possible and not let her parents down.

Conflict and Chaos

Living in constant chaos or conflict destroys any sense of safety, security and stability a child needs. Maslow, in his hierarchy of needs, makes it clear that nothing else can be accomplished in one's life if a sense of safety is not established. When there is no safety or trust, control becomes a viable alternative. Control becomes a method of obtaining some semblance of security. Abby, an ESFJ-1, described herself as "a control freak" during our first session.

Abby's story. Abby's mother was enmeshed with her parents, especially her own mother. When she married, she had a difficult time adjusting her loyalties to her new husband and baby. It is not surprising that the marriage did not last long. By the time Abby was two years old, her parents were divorced. Her grandmother never liked or accepted Abby's father and so when Abby and her mother returned to the family home, he was persona non grata. To Abby, he was portrayed as a monster. She became terrified of him yet he had visitation rights and so she had to go off with him on a regular basis. These visits were extremely terrifying for Abby. Her grandmother and mother impressed upon her what an awful person he was and, in her mind, he became a monster twenty feet tall. Besides arguing with her grandmother, Abby's father did nothing unusual to warrant her extreme fear. By the time she was four, her father could see that his attempts to have a relationship with his daughter were going nowhere. In fact, just the opposite was happening. His visits were causing her a great deal of stress and extreme fearfulness. Reluctantly, he discontinued seeing her yet continued sending support checks and cards. Abby reached adulthood not knowing why he stopped seeing her and assuming it was lack of love. She felt very much in between the

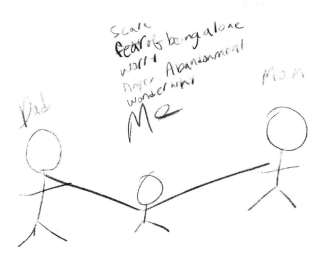

Figure 6-11

warring factions (figure 6-11) and any questions about her father were met with anger.

In the course of therapy, Abby was able to see how she was used as a pawn in the war between her mother's family and her father. She saw how unfair it had been to her and the price she had paid. Under light hypnosis, she wrote the following letter to her mother with her nondominant hand:

> *I don't like being alone*
> *You're scaring me.*
> *I don't like being scare*
> *A mom is suppose to love & take care of her*
> *   baby.*
> *Your not doing your job.*
>
> *Abby*

The grammatical mistakes show that she had truly accessed her inner child. Abby has a master's degree and is a high school teacher.

Without question, Abby needed to contact her father to find out for herself why he left and whether or not he loved her. She very fearfully sent off a letter to him asking if he would be willing to meet with us. His response to me was heart-warming:

I was overjoyed to hear from Abby. I have waited eighteen very long years for this to happen. . . . The damage being done to Abby made me decide to withdraw from further attempts to be with her. However, she continues to be in my thoughts and be loved as my daughter.

Her father arrived at their first meeting with flowers for Abby and she arrived terrified. Five years later, they have a tentative relationship but it is safe to say that there is nothing that will erase the effects of the conflict to which she was subjected and restore the father-daughter bond that should have been.

Parents have no idea the long-lasting effects of this kind of abusive conduct. The day Abby was reunited with her father, she was just as terrified of him as she was when she was three years old despite all the work we had done around this issue in therapy.

Death

Death of a parent, sibling, friend or family member is difficult for a child to understand. When the permanence of it registers, the child may feel some responsibility and guilt, even though it is illogical and ill-founded. If it is a sibling, the child will have guilt for being jealous of the attention that child received or for wishing the sibling was not around. Or, the child may feel guilty for having survived, convinced that the child who died was more loved and favored. If it is a parent, the child may wonder why the parent did not love her enough to stay or wonder what she could have done wrong that caused the parent to leave permanently. Sometimes the child feels directly responsible for the death as was the case with Kyla.

Kyla's story. One day, at age eleven, Kyla, the INFP-3 who was always compared unfavorably to her sister, had tried out for cheerleading and was not accepted. She complained all through dinner and felt very much a failure. Again, she was not good enough. Again, she was less than her sister.

Later, while watching TV with her father, he had a fatal heart attack. She called for help, but it seemed forever before someone came. She felt totally helpless. Later, the paramedics said it did not matter, that he had died instantly. Kyla knew in her heart that she had caused her father's death by not responding properly and/or not getting help fast enough. She never allowed herself to grieve her father's death because it was only a reminder of her greatest failure in life and would tap into the enormous guilt she carried. She would not allow the topic of his death to be discussed.

Kyla was consumed by guilt that was heightened because her mother, without any job skills, had to take a minimum-wage job to support the family. Life changed dramatically for them that day and Kyla knew she was to blame. To make matters even worse in her mind, her father's death benefits provided for a college education for her that would not have been possible otherwise. She felt responsible for his death and then profited from it.

When Kyla sat in my office and told me about her father's death, tears streamed down her face. I could have talked to her forever to try to convince her it was not her fault. It would have done no good because I was talking to the left side of her brain and the wounding was in another part of her to which her logical, rational head had no access. Through Inner-Child work, we were able to access that part and do the healing work necessary. Finally, the guilt was taken off of the eleven-year-old child.

Ungrieved Losses

When we suffer a loss, whether through death or any other separation, there is an innate need to grieve. Grieving is a natural expression of sadness, fright and anger. Elizabeth Kubler-Ross has written extensively on the stages of grief and how to navigate personal grief work. When a child experiences a loss, that loss needs to be grieved. It may be the loss of friends due to a geographical move or the loss of a pet through death. It can be an even greater loss; it can be the realization that a parent cannot meet the physical, emotional and spiritual needs of the child or, even worse, that the parent is a perpetrator.

Often a child's grieving will touch ungrieved losses in the parent, causing the parent to shut the child's feelings down. When a parent is uncomfortable with a child's grief, the child may be told there is nothing to be sad about since "Grandma is in heaven," or "It is just a goldfish and we can buy another one." Responding with anger is even more damaging, such as "If you don't stop it, I'll give you something to cry about!"

Jung remarked that neurosis is the avoidance of legitimate grieving. When parents do not provide a safe, warm, loving environment for a child to grieve, the child will go through life using any number of methods to avoid grieving because of a lack of an environment conducive to completing original grief work. In order to avoid the feelings around grief, the adult child will employ the Enneagram Defense System, addictions, control, intellectualizing, denial, a tough or helpless facade, co-dependence, achievement, sleep, physical illness, power plays, blaming, withdrawal and/or anything else available. Some people are very resourceful and creative in avoiding the pain associated with grieving. Yet when a child is stopped from grieving, there is a part that is put away with the grief until the child has very little sense of her Core Self. For this reason, as a person grows to adulthood, there is a compulsion to find similar circumstances to complete the original grief work that was aborted in childhood. The feelings may come out inappropriately. For instance, the anger can materialize as intense self-hatred or self-criticism, rage at others or in passive-aggressive behaviors. Often an adult child will marry someone just like the parent whose early abandonment was never grieved. Freud said all traumas come in chains of similar events. As a therapist, I regularly see patterns repeated throughout a client's life. Generally, these simply result in more wounding. In therapy, a safe, warm, caring environment is provided where the client feels secure enough to complete the grieving process.

In each of the cases cited heretofore, there were ungrieved losses. Kory had to grieve the father she wanted but never had. Mary needed to grieve the mother whose illness and death were never spoken about. Kyla needed to grieve her father's death, apart from her guilt. Brenda had to relive and grieve the giving up of her daughter for adoption. Every client I have had who has had an abortion needed to grieve the loss of that potential child and the fact that no one was there for the girl undergoing the procedure. Therese had to grieve the dad she lost to alcoholism. Denise had to see that her brother was not her god but her perpetrator and grieve that loss. Sarah, as family Scapegoat, had to grieve the fact that she would never be accepted by a family who, by virtue of its dysfunction, could not really see her and never will.

In order to reclaim the Core Self that was put away during wounding, such as described in this chapter, it is necessary to take a close look at the original pain suffered, grieve the losses and champion the little child who did all she could to simply survive both physically and emotionally. It is time to meet the Child Within.

REFERENCES AND SUGGESTED READING

Arterburn, S. and J. Felton, *Toxic Faith.* Nashville TN: Thomas Nelson Publishing, 1991. This is one of the few books written on the topic of religious addiction. It is presented from a Christian perspective with a twelve-step approach to overcoming the addiction. The authors include a checklist to help identify the addiction and, there is liberal use of examples and much supportive data. The book is stronger in helping identify a religious addiction than in helping to overcome it since the treatment is purely cognitive. Nonetheless, it is a good book for someone raised in a family with a religiously addicted parent because there is an additional burden of guilt carried by the child who is angry because a parent is too busy with "God's work" to effectively parent the child.

Bass, E. and L. Davis. *The Courage to Heal.* New York: Harper Perennial, 1988. This is a classic on the effects of childhood sexual abuse. The authors address the need to have a voice, break the secret, own your feelings and accept that it was not your fault. The personal stories are both compelling and difficult for survivors to read because they will trigger feelings and memories, which can be so useful in the healing process. Although this book is excellent, it does not offer follow-up interviews with those who shared their stories, and it almost exclusively addresses male upon female sexual abuse. Very little attention is directed to female perpetrators and male victims.

Bass, E., and L. Thornton, eds. *I Never Told Anyone.* New York: Harper Perennial, 1991. First published in 1983 before *The Courage to Heal,* this book is a collection of writings by women who have survived and recovered from childhood sexual abuse. Some of the contributors are well known such as Maya Angelou, Kate Millett and Billie Holiday; others are unknown and some are anonymous. The stories are deeply moving and eloquently describe the devastation of childhood sexual abuse. As in *The Courage to Heal,* the focus is on male perpetrators of female children.

Black, C. *Double Duty.* New York: Ballantine Books, 1990. Although Black describes the effects of growing up in an alcoholic family, she also addresses issues faced by those who come from families that were abusive but without alcoholism. This book emphasizes the problems of children facing other challenges, such as physical disabilities or belonging to an ethnic minority, as well as the problems encountered in a highly dysfunctional family.

Drews, T. R. *Getting Them Sober.* South Plainfield NJ: Bridge Publishing Inc., 1980. One of the first and best books addressing the co-dependent spouse of an addict. Although this book specifies alcohol addiction, the main principles of letting go and taking care of yourself apply to being in a relationship with any type of addict.

Edwards, S. "Those Hidden Wounds." Workshop. St. Louis MO. I am indebted to Susan Edwards for much of the information on family roles presented in this chapter.

Eisler, R. *The Chalice and the Blade.* San Francisco:

Harper and Row, 1987. A highly acclaimed study of the effects of patriarchy on our culture presented both from an historical perspective and with a look to the future.

Evert, K. and I. Bijkerk. *When You're Ready*. Rockville MD: Launch Press, 1987. Writing under a pseudonym, Bobbie Rosencrans tells her own story of recovery from sexual abuse by her mother.

Forward, S., and C. Buck. *Betrayal of Innocence*. New York: Penguin Books, 1978. Susan Forward delves into one of the last great secrets of our society: incest. She describes a variety of incestuous relationships including mother/daughter incest, which is rare and even more rarely addressed. An incest survivor herself, she presents many personal stories from case histories and describes her methods of working with other survivors.

Ginn, C. W. *Voices of Loss*. Gainesville FL: Center for Applications of Psychological Type, Inc. 1994. Provides a brief description of the four MBTI scales and summaries of how the sixteen MBTI types approach the grieving process differently. *Voices of Loss* gives an individual permission to grieve in her own way and provides understanding for those who want to assist in the grieving process.

Jung, C. G. *The Development of Personality*. Trans. by R. F. C. Hull. New York: Pantheon Books, 1954. In this collection of essays, Jung outlines the importance of early influences on the emerging personality. He addresses the significant impact of parents and teachers on the developing child. He links childhood problems with problems associated with individuation in the adult. The chapter after which the book is named, "Development of Personality" is a particularly eloquent discussion of the spiritual aspects of personality where Jung equates personality development with the meaning of life.

Kroeger, O. *Specific Type and Gender Issues in the SJ and SP Treatment* [Cassettes 1–2]. Garden Grove CA: InfoMedix. Tape set available from Otto Kroeger Associates, 3605-A Chain Bridge Road, Fairfax VA 22030-3245; 703.591.6284. Kroeger presents insights into the internal type conflicts of STJ females and SFJ males in a thorough and knowledgeable manner yet in his own inimitable style.

Kubler-Ross, E. *On Death and Dying*. New York: MacMillan Publishing Co., 1969. This is the classic book that sets the standard for other books on this topic. Kubler-Ross shows the stages of dying/grieving, which can be applied not only to the dying process but also to any great physical or emotional loss.

Kubler-Ross, E. *Living With Death and Dying*. New York: MacMillan Publishing Co., 1981. Kubler-Ross and others delve into the topic of the emotional effects of death and dying on children. She addresses the needs of a child facing her own death or that of a loved one. Many personal stories and samples of children's art created during therapy are included.

Leman, K. *The Birth Order Book*. Grand Rapids MI: Spire Books, 1985. As a lighthearted approach to understanding family systems, this book meshes scapegoat and lost child. Not a scholarly treatment, but easy to read and food for thought.

Love, P. *The Emotional Incest Syndrome*. New York: Bantam Books, 1990. The topic of parental enmeshment with children is examined. Because the culture highly approves of families that are close and supportive, enmeshed families often go undetected with this camouflage. Love describes the problem and provides guidance for recovery. Personal stories provide examples and helpful exercises are furnished.

Morgan, R., ed. *Sisterhood is Global*. Garden City NY: Anchor Press, 1984. Although the statistics and data in this book are dated, it is still an eye-opening and powerful account of the effects on women of more than fifty different patriarchal cultures, including our own. By taking an objective look at the emotional wounding of women in cultures foreign to us, we are more likely to recognize the impact of our own. This book does not address the effect of a patriarchal culture on males, whose wounds are even more invisible but nonetheless very present.

Penley, J., and D. Stephens. *The M.O.M.S. Handbook.* Wilmette IL: Penley and Associates, Inc., 1995. Describes the strengths and struggles of the sixteen MBTI types as mothers. Provides tips to improve parenting skills for each type. To order, contact Penley and Associates Inc., 604 Maple Avenue, Wilmette IL, 60091 or call 847.251.4936.

Pipher, M. *Reviving Ophelia.* New York: Ballantine Books, 1994. An excellent discussion of the effects of culture on young girls. Mary Pipher throws a light on many previously unexamined sources of wounding to little girls. She presents a compelling case for a thorough scrutiny of the culture from a feminist perspective. She gives little attention, however, to the primary source of wounding to young children: the family.

Remen, R. N. *Final Wisdom* [Cassette]. Boulder CO: Sounds True, 1998. In each of these selections, Rachel Naomi Remen brings stories of her personal history of dealing with a serious medical condition and of her professional work with those facing cancer and other life-threatening diseases. She brings an incredible wisdom and understanding of the healing process. Remen provides a rich description of her Jewish heritage. She writes and speaks simply, from her heart, and conveys uncommon depth, sagacity and spirituality. To order the tape, Final Wisdom, contact: Sounds True, Boulder CO 80302, 800.333.9185.

Rosencrans, B. *The Last Secret.* Brandon VT: Safer Society Press, 1997. A study and report on the topic of childhood sexual abuse of women by their mothers giving data and case studies of nearly one hundred women. (See Evert listed on page 138.)

Rush, F. *The Best Kept Secret.* New York: McGraw-Hill Book Company, 1980. There are many excellent books on the topic of incest and childhood sexual abuse. This one is interesting because Rush traces the treatment of children as sexual objects through various cultures, religions and the ages. She presents a particularly interesting discussion of Freud, and

her assessment of the impact his approach to childhood sexual abuse has had on the culture. She wisely points out that Freud's theories may tell us more about his childhood experiences than about universal early human sexuality.

Walker, B. *The Crone.* San Francisco: Harper, 1985. A compelling and masterful chronicle of the loss of feminine wisdom over the ages.

Wegscheider, S. *Another Chance.* Palo Alto CA: Science and Behavior Books, Inc., 1981. An examination of family dynamics in the face of alcoholism, including the various roles family members are assigned hero, scapegoat, etc. Heavy emphasis is placed on the twelve-step approach. Even if the topic of alcoholism does not pertain to you, this book explains the roles that are operational in all families. Although this book is twenty years old, the basic information is applicable today.

Wood, W. and L. Hatton. *Triumph Over Darkness.* Hillsboro OR: Beyond Words Publishing, Inc., 1989. A collection of personal stories, poetry and drawings of survivors of childhood sexual abuse. This powerful book is exceptionally encouraging because it provides follow-up interviews with the contributors later in their recoveries. This is a difficult book for those who have experienced incest or other sexual abuse because it evokes memories and feelings, which are the very things necessary for healing to take place. In addition, the opportunity to read about others who have had similar experiences and triumphed over their abuse alleviates a sense of aloneness.

Wyman, P. "Gender Identity." *Enneagram Monthly* 51 (January 1999): 5. This article explores the possible higher incidence of gays and lesbians with the combination of MBTI T–F and the Enneagram Four. For a copy of this article, contact the *Enneagram Monthly,* 748 Wayside Rd., Portola Valley, CA 94028; 877.428.9639.

PART III

Using the Keys to Clean House

CHAPTER 7

UNDERSTANDING THE KID WITHIN

Where did all these kids come from?

In order to understand how the child within works, it is helpful to remember that there are two types of approaches to dealing with emotional distress: cognitive and affective. In other words, we can look at the problems in life from a left-brained, rational, logical and objective viewpoint or we can examine those same problems from a right-brained, feeling perspective. Since the two sides of the brain take in different information from the same event and process information differently, there will be considerable differences between the left-brained and right-brained approach.

Cognitive therapy, sometimes called talk therapy, discusses the problems being encountered, suggests new viewpoints, brings insights and possibly changes in behaviors. This all takes place on the left, or rational, side of the brain. To our patriarchal, left-brained, thinking-based culture, it is the only approach that makes sense (pardon the pun). This approach will result in a well-defined problem and, at best, some changed behaviors; but it will not restore integration, well-being and internal peace. The intent of the cognitive approach is that, once behaviors are changed, there will be better self-acceptance and raised self-esteem.

So simply put, the major difference between a cognitive and affective approach is that the cognitive approach works on changing the outside and assumes the inside will then change, while an affective approach changes the inside and assumes the outside will follow suit.

An affective approach works with the underlying feelings associated with the problem and with the early messages instilled about the self, other people, the world in general and a Higher Power. The intent of using this right-brained approach is to bring about emotional healing by changing those early messages. When there is a new understanding of the self, other people, the world and a Higher Power, behavior changes naturally happen. So simply put, the major difference between a cognitive and affective approach is that the cognitive approach works on changing the outside and assumes the inside will then change, while an affective approach changes the inside and assumes the outside will follow suit. The cognitive approach is more scientifically based whereas the affective approach is more of an art form. Taking an affective approach does not mean that cognition is ignored. It means the actual *work* is done on the affective side. The goal is to facilitate a cooperative arrangement between both parts of the personality, utilizing both as effectively and fully as possible.

Inner-Child therapy implements the affective approach. Very early in life, possibly before birth, each person receives the early wounding messages described in the last chapter. These messages control how that person thinks of herself, the people around her and her concept of a Higher Power. It is helpful to think of these views as "programming." The programming is not kept on the logical, left side of the brain. It is stored on the feeling, right side of the brain. With a cognitive approach, the only part of the brain that can be accessed is the rational, left side. That part of the brain may even agree logically that the convictions that are being held are not accurate. But as the old saying goes, that and a dime will get you a cup of coffee. Talking

logically to the left side of the brain will not and cannot change the programming that does not reside there. Accessing an emotion attached to the early messages will shift the person to the right side of the brain where feelings originate and make access to the programming available. Emotions can be thought of as wires that lead to the programming. Talking to the left side of the brain in order to change the programming is like typing on your computer keyboard without having it plugged into the computer itself.

Danielle, ENTJ-7, whose self-concept included thinking she was stupid (chapter 3), was programmed to think that way about herself by her family and school. Many people besides me tried to talk her out of her conviction that she was stupid, but it was pointless because the discussions were directed to the logical side of Danielle's brain, which had no control over her programming. By accessing the feelings around believing herself to be stupid, we could access the programming and change it.

The same situation happens in cases of extreme abuse. I have worked with many women who were sexually abused as preschoolers. Every one of them believed she was in some way to blame. Logically, each woman knew better, but that fact did not help; feelings of guilt and shame and a state of depression were still present. Only through experiencing the feelings around being sexually abused as a very small child can the programming be changed and the guilt and shame be eradicated.

More than one type of programming can be operational in any given individual. Each traumatizing event, and each adult in a position to have a major impact on the child, programs that child. The child then grows up having these programs running her life and not understanding why she operates as she does. Remember, if there is a conflict between how an adult *thinks* cognitively with the left brain and the programming on the right side of the brain, the programming will win 100 percent of the time. It is stronger by far than logic and reason.

Each major programming event creates an ego state that consists of unexpressed feelings, defense strategies and coping skills, as well as distorted views of self, others and the world in general. An ego state can easily be triggered in the adult's life in the normal course of events. A person may find herself working with a boss or co-worker who reminds her of a parent. Any triggering situation, then, has the power to access the programming associated with that parent, sending her headlong into old responses and patterns of behavior that came into being when the ego state was established. These behaviors were used by the young child to deal with her parent but may be other than desirable in a work context. Working with such programming is made easier if form can be given to the ego state that is accessed through the triggering event. So, during Inner-Child therapy, the person determines the age she was and the situation that caused the programming and then the concept of that child is attached to that particular programming. Kyla, the INFP-3 described in chapter 6, is a good example.

Kyla has three main ego states, or sets of programming, that can completely mess up her life, especially if they are all operational at one time. First, Kyla felt unwanted and abandoned by her mother very early in her life. Secondly, she always felt "not good enough" as compared to her sister who excelled at everything. Finally, she felt guilty and horribly responsible for her father's death when she was eleven years old. In order to work with each program, we embodied each of them in a childhood age commensurate with the program. So the program that made her feel profoundly alone and unwanted by her mother was represented by Kyla at age five. The program or ego state that left her feeling "not good enough" as compared to her sister was symbolized by Kyla as a grammar school child who was in awe of

her big sister. The all-consuming guilt she felt around her father's death was represented by Kyla as an eleven-year-old.

Darlene, an INFP-5, whose history is given in chapter 6, is another person with three primary ego states. The youngest is age two and she is sad, alone/lonely, quiet, scared and confused. As with most people, this youngest child would eventually develop into an Internal Wisdom source, representing her spiritual Core Self, after emotional healing has taken place. Darlene's middle child was the most problematical in the therapy setting. This child is the one who developed the coping skill of dissociating. When all other ways of dealing with her pain were insufficient, she simply left. Darlene describes this child as quiet, in her own world, lost, zoned-out and alone. By the time the coping mechanisms represented by this child were operational, Darlene had been emotionally rejected by her mother, had experienced the death of her older sister and was being sexually abused by her father. It was too much for a young child to handle so she took the withdrawing techniques of the Enneagram Five to the furthest extreme and simply left her body. Darlene's third child is a teenager who felt betrayed and was filled with an anger and rage that had no way of being expressed.

Whenever feelings of sadness were accessed around the sexual abuse by her father, Darlene would involuntarily begin to dissociate. That was our clue that the middle child had control. The challenge was to convince the child that Darlene, as an adult, had better methods of coping, and that it was actually in the best interest of all concerned to examine the topic and express the feelings. Keeping her from checking out while we accomplished all this was quite the trick.

Darlene was in a more effective place when the teenager was present and in charge because that was the only ego state that could access the anger about what had happened, and the price she had paid. It was the expression of the anger embodied by the teenager that allowed Darlene to grow emotionally stronger and to regain a voice.

The ages of the various ego states are not so much

assigned as *given* by the person's own history. The ego state will present itself at a particular age in imagery and art, providing information and direction on how to work with the programming this child embodies. Whenever Kyla feels she is not good enough, she can readily identify that she feels grammar school age. Each time she feels vulnerable or unsafe, Reilley (chapter 11) feels very, very small—an infant—the age when she was sexually abused. Whenever Kory (chapter 6) feels abandoned, she literally feels age fourteen, the age when her father died and her sisters left home. In each case, whatever has happened has engaged the programming that was installed at that particular age. Attaching an age and form to the programming provides something concrete to work with and a method for allowing the person to engage those parts of personality that are so powerful and compelling.

In Kyla's case, the terrifying sense of being totally alone due to feeling unwanted and abandoned by her mother has often compelled her to get into relationships that were unhealthy and destructive. Even when she knew logically that she was moving in a direction that could not be good, she felt powerless to stop the progression. When she is triggered into feeling alone, Kyla reports she is consumed by the following feelings as well:

- Lost
- Lonely
- Rejected
- Sad
- Pain
- Empty
- Unloved
- Undesirable
- Panic
- Vulnerable
- Foolish
- Embarrassed
- Stupid
- Idiot
- Fool
- Naive
- Used
- Out of control
- Desperate
- Angry
- Disappointed
- Scared
- Hopeless

With all those feelings being triggered, it is no wonder Kyla's defenses kick in to try to cope, even though her coping methods may be less than desirable. When Kyla is so triggered, control is grabbed by the wounded-child program and *all* the coping skills she

has developed go into operation (figures 7-1 and 7-2). Kyla first utilizes her Enneagram Three defense and tries to always look good, achieve more and out-shine the competition. If that fails, she will call up the supporting skills of the Enneagram Nine (see explanation in chapter 4) and become lethargic and totally nonproductive, preferring to spend as much time sleeping as possible. Kyla also becomes very co-dependent and finds herself taking care of everyone else at her own expense. Finally, Kyla's relationship addiction will be activated, causing her to feel "elated, happy, high, desirable, Number One, fun!" just as any drug would. It is easy to see why this condition seems so preferable to the wounded-child part. Yet, just like any drug, coming down off the high can be simply dreadful. Kyla reports the after-effects are feeling "sad, let down, abandoned, despairing, disappointed, frustrated, angry, vindictive and revengeful." She readily agrees it is not worth it but often finds herself acting out of the programming before she knows it is even happening. Giving Kyla a way to work with this powerful programming by embodying it in her five-year-old inner child allows her to restore control to her INFP rational adult side where she can make good choices and decisions for herself. When Kyla slips and the child is left to fend for herself, she lets Kyla know she is not happy, as illustrated in this nondominant hand exercise (explained in chapter 10):

CHILD:

I'm scared. I worry about where we're going. What are you gonna do with me? Please don't forget me. Please don't forget what you promised me.

ADULT:

I remember what I promised you. It's just harder to stay on tract 100% of the time than I thought. I haven't forgotten you. As much as I hate it, keep bugging me!

At times, the overwhelming fear of being alone compelled Kyla to grab someone, anyone, to assuage her troubling feelings, even if only temporarily. I could not talk Kyla out of destructive relationships, nor could friends, nor could a twelve-step program, nor could Kyla herself. All of us would be talking to her logical left brain which was in total agreement but powerless to control the programming on the right side of the brain. As a mother herself, when Kyla looks at pictures of herself at age five, feeling motherless and unwanted, her heart aches for the child that she was. In eliciting these emotions, Kyla shifts to the right side of her brain where the programming can be accessed. Once accessed, the programming that contains her self-concept and her views about other people can be altered, if not permanently changed.

At times when Kyla feels compelled to work harder, do more, achieve more due to feelings of inadequacy and a sense of being lesser-than, she looks to the grammar school child who tried so hard to earn her family's love but was always overshadowed by her sister. As an INFP, Kyla's sense of empathy and compassion allows her to easily move into an emotion surrounding that child. Knowing she is defended as an Enneagram Three who needs success (chapter 4), Kyla realizes how her inability to compete with her sister robbed her of her primary Defense System that caused her to develop the additional coping devices shown in figures 7-1 and 7-2.

Often, the rational adult self and the inner child have conflicting ideas about what needs to happen. Without accessing and working with the inner child, there is great potential for unknown, unconscious inner conflict. After doing a great deal of work around her father's sexual abuse of her, I asked Darlene if she felt it would be helpful to visit her father's grave and express some of the anger she felt so strongly. She really felt no need to do so. I asked her to use her nondominant hand (chapter 10) in order to correspond with her inner child and get her opinion. Here are the results:

QUESTION:

How would you feel about beating on Dad's grave?

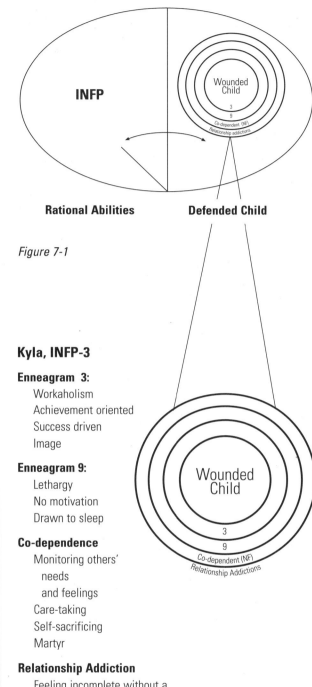

Rational Abilities   **Defended Child**

Figure 7-1

Kyla, INFP-3

Enneagram 3:
Workaholism
Achievement oriented
Success driven
Image

Enneagram 9:
Lethargy
No motivation
Drawn to sleep

Co-dependence
Monitoring others'
    needs
    and feelings
Care-taking
Self-sacrificing
Martyr

Relationship Addiction
Feeling incomplete without a
    partner
Needing romance to numb
    emotional pain
Unable to control the need
    to be in a romantic
    relationship
Risking everything for the
    relationship

Figure 7-2

ADULT:

> *I don't really think that jumping up and
> down on his grave would make a difference.*

CHILD:

> *I want to beat the crap out of his grave. I
> could stomp on it for a long time. It would be
> great!*

ADULT:

> *I don't think it will make us feel better.*

CHILD:

> *But I want to do it. I think it will help!*

At this point, we came up with a trial compromise involving creating a dummy Dad and destroying it.

ADULT:

> *Would the compromise be all right?*

CHILD:

> *I will have to see. I will try it.*

ADULT:

> *OK. I will help you with this. I will make
> a Dad dummy and we will destroy it.*

To ignore that we all have a subconscious part with opinions that conflict with the rational part is to ignore a very powerful part of the self. When these subconscious parts are not acknowledged, and the feelings stored there are not given proper attention, these parts will take control and operate out of the old programming and defenses. In Darlene's case, when her feelings were not brought out into the daylight and given the required attention, all her defense strategies took over. The defense strategies are headed by her Enneagram Five defense, but she has assembled several other tools (figure 7-3). In order to work with these defense strategies, Darlene embodied them and the feelings associated with them in her three ego states described above.

Like Kyla and Darlene, I find that most clients generally have three main ego states or "kids." The youngest is usually the one who, in the beginning of therapy, presents herself as wounded, abandoned and

Darlene, INFP-5

Enneagram 5:
Withdrawn, physically and emotionally
Out of touch with body and feelings
Looking at the world from the back of a cave or tunnel
Observing life, not living
Unable to disclose personal information

Enneagram 7:
Denial
Not willing to face emotional pain
Not willing to see the problems
Humor defense

Co-dependence
Monitoring others' needs and feelings
Care-taking
Self-sacrificing
Martyr

Dissociating
Moving into an altered state
Leaving the body
Spirit leaves the room
Moving into the subconscious

Suicidal Ideation
Coping with emotional pain with the knowledge that there is a way out
Considering methods of dying in order to relieve emotional pain

Figure 7-3

in great emotional pain. As Inner-Child work progresses and healing takes place, this young one is transformed into the Wisdom Child who embodies all the gifts of the Myers-Briggs Type Indicator type. It is the metaphor for the spirit part which now is open to communication with cognition and which feels loved, accepted and protected. This Wisdom Child embodies a sage wisdom that is spiritual in nature and can be totally trusted. The second child is usually a bit older; perhaps grammar school age. This child represents the earliest coping skills the individual developed. These methods may be dissociation, co-dependence, over-achieving, humor or other such defense strategies. The third child is usually a teenager or college age. This child possesses a well-developed Enneagram Defense. If necessary, the Enneagram Defense may be supplemented by addictions. Each child will have a distinct set of programming, feelings and descriptors. When triggered, it is helpful to figure out which child has taken over and to begin to work with that child just as an adult would work with any child who is out of control. By working with the child, it forces the adult to reclaim control and lessens the hold of the child.

THREE LEVELS OF INNER-CHILD WORK

In working with the inner child, we are working simultaneously at three different levels: historical, metaphorical and spiritual. Just like any art form such as poetry, music, plays or dream work, Inner-Child work can be utilized at more than one level.

Historical

At the historical level, Kyla looked at the events that actually happened in her life that led her to conclude she was not wanted by her mother, and that her mother's rejection was Kyla's own fault.

Kyla's story. Kyla knew that her mother was surprised and overwhelmed upon learning she was pregnant with Kyla and that her mother "cried for the first six months of her pregnancy." As a small child, Kyla watched her mom struggle with the responsibilities of raising six children. When Kyla was five, her mother had a

nervous breakdown (chapter 6) and went away for a hospital stay. Kyla was certain it was because she was too much trouble or had done something wrong.

Again, talking to Kyla logically about these conclusions is pointless. She knows the beliefs she held about herself, her worth and her relationship to her mother were inaccurate conclusions reached by a child less than five years old. Nonetheless, it is impossible to talk her out of these viewpoints because they cannot be accessed through logic.

There are many techniques used to heal wounding and they will be detailed in chapter 10. With Kyla, I employed a variety of techniques including imagery. In imagery, Kyla revisited the incident of her father dying in her presence. *By accessing the feelings,* we could re-examine Kyla's perceptions from the right side of her brain, where the programming is housed. By moving through imagery to the right side of her brain, Kyla could readily identify the errors in her conviction that she was the cause of her father's death. Her heart broke for the young girl who felt so helpless and guilty as her father died before her eyes.

Although imagery was effective with Darlene, because she dissociated so much, it was challenging. Consequently, we used various writing and drawing exercises to access her feelings. Here is an example of a letter she wrote to her father from her inner child using her nondominant hand:

> *Daddy,*
>
> *I don't like you. You make me feel guilty and it is wrong. You are bad not me. It was not my fault. How could you do it? I don't understand. Go away!!*

Acting out of her strong adult self, Kory (chapters 2, 5, 6 and 7), who was sexually abused by her violent father and used as a scapegoat by her mother, wrote a letter to both her parents about the abuse she suffered and how she had to keep it a secret:

Dear Mom and Dad,

I am not going to take this shit anymore. You dumped a whole lot of shit on this little kid. It is killing me and you can't get away with it. I am telling on you. No More Secrets. You will not lie anymore because I know the truth. What you did to each other is between you. But what you did to me was wrong. No more excuses! No More Protection from Me! I will not cover any more truth up. You both stink as Parents. So I'm giving you both up for adoption if anyone wants you. You can't hurt me anymore!

Liberated ex-Daughter

Kory followed that with a letter to her inner child:

Dear Kory,

I will never allow them to hurt you any more. I know you don't know this yet but you didn't deserve the shit those crazy people dumped on you. I will be there for you to protect you from them. You didn't deserve to feel shame. You did nothing wrong.

Each time an exercise examining childhood events is used to activate feelings, it affords access to the programming and lasting changes take place.

Metaphorical

At the same time we are looking at what actually happened in childhood, on another level we are looking at the condition of the spirit or soul. Archetypally, the child is the symbol for the spirit part of being. Therefore, when Kyla envisions her five-year-old self as being profoundly alone and feeling utterly abandoned, she is looking at the state of her inner being at that moment as well.

The very first imagery I do with a client is to take that person back to the house in which she was raised to meet the little girl she was. In doing Inner-Child work, the child is the metaphor for the spirit or soul.

The adult is the metaphor or symbol for cognition and rational abilities. The goal is to have these two parts of the self work as a team to increase communication between the two sides of the brain, which house these two parts of the person. So in this introductory imagery, we are uniting them and introducing dialogue between these two parts. Every person finds the child alone in the house, even if there were many siblings or extended family members living there. This is because the imagery reflects the state of the spirit, which feels profoundly alone in the "house" or body. The adult is never surprised to find the child alone, even at a very early age, until I point it out. That is because each person has become accustomed to feeling alone and isolated spiritually, even in the midst of many people.

In subsequent imagery, the symbols provided by the subconscious are crystal clear and riveting. Paula (chapters 5 and 6) looked at her inner child in an early imagery and found her totally encased and frozen in granite without a millimeter of room to move. It was a poignant and accurate representation of how she felt living encased in the rules imposed by her family and culture, and reinforced by the perfectionism of her Enneagram One Defense System. Mary (chapters 2, 3, 5 and 6) imaged her child in a large Plexiglas cylinder. She had her hands and face pressed up to the glass, screaming, but her family, outside the cylinder, could not hear her. This imagery accurately depicted how Mary has never felt heard or understood and how no one ever seemed to want to take the time to listen to her.

Anita, an ENTP-1 (chapter 6), tried to convince herself she was doing OK. In her imagery, she would see that she could come to the border of "Happyland" but could not quite seem to cross over and get there. Kory, ESFP-8, and Lori, ENTJ-3, both Scapegoats in their families, imaged and later drew their inner children behind bars (figures 7-4 and 7-5).

Dorothy, whose history was described in the last chapter, had to live in the chaos of a mentally ill mother and alcoholic, sexually abusive father. Dorothy still kept the whole family looking good to the outside world.

The internal war she felt over wanting the truth to surface and the programmed need to keep the family secrets was incredibly immense. To Dorothy, it felt as if she were reliving the chaos of childhood within herself. She imaged a bedroom that was a total mess—unmade bed, clothes on the floor, total disarray. Things such as encyclopedias and plates were flying around. When she cleaned one corner, the rest of the room became chaotic again. It was an impossible task, just as it was an impossible task for a small child to hold the family secrets and keep the family functioning.

After emotional healing work, there is a decided shift in the metaphor of the child. In imagery and dreams, the child becomes a wisdom source. Inner-Child work is a process with a beginning, a middle and an end. In the beginning, there is a dismantling of the early coping skills, fantasies and delusions assembled in childhood as protection. In the middle, there is an honest examination of the early programming. In the end, there is an awesome recognition of the beauty and wonder of the Child or spirit part. At this point, the child is represented in imagery as wonderful, magical and unbelievably wise. This is the basis of the mythical wonder child that permeates all cultures across time.

Spiritual

Finally, if the Child Within is a metaphor for the spirit or soul, then it stands to reason that accessing that part of personality will aid in the development of spirituality. And, in fact, this is found to be true. After a degree of healing work has been completed and the child is not feeling nearly as wounded as she had been, the child opens the door to an increased sense of and interest in spirituality. Pioneers in the field of Inner-Child work such as Charles Whitfield and John Bradshaw have recognized this draw to spirituality. The child evolves from the wounded little person to the Guiding Light, a source of sound, dependable Internal Wisdom. Just as in many religious traditions and in mythology, a child will lead the way.

As Paula continued her healing work, her inner child was liberated from her confinement in granite.

Figure 7-4

Figure 7-5

Whenever Paula would weaken, she would receive an image of her inner child pulling a little red wagon carrying her wounded parts. The child would write to her, using her nondominant hand, to encourage her to be steadfast:

> *Look at how sick I was a year ago and embedded in the granite—unable to move. I am not willing to go back to that condition. It was awful and there was no reason to live. I had a bad time last week but look at all the decent days I have had this year. I know it is hard for you but once you break free you do not want to go back to being so miserable and not in charge of your own life. We have to stay together and move through so you can see what life that you have tasted can be in HUGE doses. It's a lot better than how you feel now. Please fight for us to be free. We deserve to have a life for a change. We deserve people who see our value instead of those who are harmful to us. Fight for us.*

When the spirit feels a need to pull the adult into line, she is sometimes not as gentle as Paula's inner child. Lorna, an ESFJ-3, had a little dialogue with her inner child during a crisis in her life. Her inner child is the no-nonsense type:

CHILD:

This bites. *I don't know what to tell you. I'm angry too. F—k them. We've been down this road before and look where you are now. You can fix this. Screw the rest of them. Nobody was there before and they're still not there. Get over it but get healthy!*

ADULT:

I hear ya! I know you're in there and I've been talking to you a lot lately. I'm just unsure because the unknown is scary!

CHILD:

You're talking to me but you're not listening. The unknown is scary for me too but where I go, I go! So deal with it.

Notice how Lorna's inner child takes her to task for not listening. Higher Wisdom resides in the spirit. If Lorna does not consult with her spirit, she is using only cognition to make decisions. The spirit has a much greater understanding and can readily determine what is in the person's best interest. After consulting with her inner child on her dilemma, Lorna was able to deal with her situation in a more objective and rational manner and make the decisions that were for her higher good.

Peggy, the ENTJ-1 referred to in the last chapter, provides another example of the inner child leading the way and taking the adult to task:

CHILD:

Peggy, I don't like it when you don't talk to me. I need you! I feel tired and it may be because you have ignored me. It's your fault. I don't like feeling this way. Make it stop. Please talk to me more.

Reilley, INTJ-4 (chapter 11), is often taken to task by her inner child who, in this passage, not only chides her for not listening but provides some guidance and direction as well:

CHILD:

Hey, Reilley, I'm supposed to feel connected to you. Where the hell are you? If I knew you were there, I might not feel so alone. Why won't you take better care of me? I know you say you don't like me and just heard you think it. I haven't done anything to hurt you, that was your parents, not me. If you would love me more, you would feel more gentle about yourself and we could help each other feel better on days like today.

It is interesting to take note of how the different personality types will have very different tones and language in the dialogue between adult and child. The NF temperament types have a softer, gentler tone while the SJ and NT types seem to lay it on the line. Compare Paula's dialogue as an ENFP with Reilley's, an INTJ, and Lorna's, the ESFJ.

Personality type is connected to spirituality in another way as well. In Hebrew scripture and in Judeo-Christian tradition, the Deity is asked what name is to be used to refer to God and the reply is "I Am." Each of us, in understanding who we are, connects our individual "I Am" with the greater "I Am" of a Higher Power.

Often, a person nearing the end of therapy will begin to have a new concept of a Higher Power. This concept often includes the sense of a God Within and is often expressed as light. Notice the similarities between Reilley's rendition of a God Light (figure 11-22, page 254) and Darlene's (figure 7-6). Although Denise represented her spirituality as a dove in her artwork (figure 7-7), in imagery she saw her inner child walking in a green light with a lion, representing the strength she felt when in the presence of her Higher Power.

When this greater interest in spirituality appears near the end of therapy, it will be manifested in

heart good peace calming

Figure 7-6

Figure 7-7

accordance with the person's personality type. It does not necessarily mean an increase in religious activities. In actuality, some people may leave the religious tradition in which they were raised the way Sue Monk Kidd describes in *Dance of the Dissident Daughter*. Other people who have not been associated with a religious tradition may seek one out. NFs tend to leave an organized religious setting in favor of a spirituality more in tune with the Native American approach. NTs are drawn to alternative types of churches that focus on a universal cosmology. SPs and SJs generally feel

that the traditional religious settings best help them express their spirituality. Trigger Cycles, which will be introduced in chapter 9, give another view of when increased spirituality begins to blossom. We will examine the topic of spirituality in greater detail in chapter 12.

REFERENCES AND SUGGESTED READING

Kidd, S. M. *Dance of the Dissident Daughter*. San Francisco: Harper, 1992. A popular Christian writer tells her personal story of spiritual healing which lead her from conventional religion to the Sacred Feminine. Her approach has strong appeal to NF women because it is rich with non-traditional, feminine ritual.

Miller, A. *Drama of the Gifted Child*. Trans. R. Ward. NY: Basic Books, 1981. One of the earliest and most respected books on Inner-Child work describing early wounding by the narcissism of parents.

Whitfield, C. *Healing the Child Within*. Deerfield Beach, FL: Health Communications, Inc., 1987. This classic book on Inner-Child work contains a final chapter on spirituality that is insightful and thought-provoking. Dr. Whitfield graphically illustrates the Inner-Child process on p.120 showing how spirituality enters near the end of healing work and continues to grow.

CHAPTER 8

I You Love

IT WAS EASY TO GET HURT:
WOUNDEDNESS AND YOUR DEFENSE SYSTEM

When we are conceived, we are conceived as integrated beings. That is, a functional and interactive blend of body, mind and spirit (figure 8-1, page 156). But, as described in chapter 1, in every case, it is only moments before we begin to get wounding messages due to the family role assigned to us, for personal identity, abuse or because of events that are out of the control of a child (figure 8-2, page 156). When wounding messages are received, the spirit, or Core Self, is put away for safe keeping. A person generally does not put the Core Self away consciously because it is done so early. But instinctively, the Defense System snaps into action to encapsulate and protect the spirit.

When Danielle, ENTJ-7 (chapters 3, 5, 6 and 7), was in first grade, she drew a picture of herself. In going through some old papers, Danielle came upon that drawing (figure 8-3, page 156). As an Enneagram Seven, she drew a pretty picture of a smiling blonde child with hearts all over the page. The truth is that Danielle was a wounded child in a great deal of emotional pain. She would often bang her head in order to take the focus off her internal turmoil. Apparently, blonde was valued in her family and so Danielle, who had nearly black hair, drew herself that way. In the

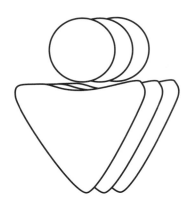

Figure 8-1. **Integration**

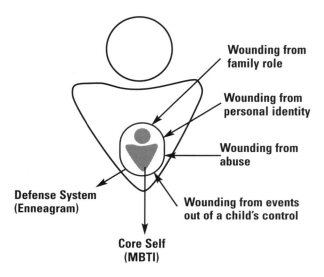

Wounding from family role

Wounding from personal identity

Wounding from abuse

Defense System (Enneagram)

Wounding from events out of a child's control

Core Self (MBTI)

Figure 8-2

lower left corner, she drew a small figure very similar to the encapsulated Core Self in figure 8-2. Next to that, the little six-year-old girl wrote, "I love you." Danielle knows that at that point she had put her spirit away and lost touch with her feelings, her identity, her Internal Wisdom and any connection to a Higher Power. Danielle, and others in therapy (figure 8-4), know at a young age and at a deep level that their souls have been put away; they depict that state of being "disintegrated" in a similar manner.

In his childhood, Carl Jung cut out a small, wooden mannequin, wrapped it carefully in wool, put it in a small box and then stole secretly up to the attic where he placed it on a high beam out of sight. He instinc-

tively knew he was putting a part of himself away for safekeeping and that, in some way, his very survival depended on the little person being hidden away.

When wounding happens and the Defense System springs into action by "secreting away" the Core Self, the Core Self receives some degree of protection from wounding messages. But just as the Defense System tries to keep wounding messages out, it effectively blocks the good messages as well. How often when someone says, "You did that well" or "You look nice today" or any other positive message, are we unable to take it all the way in?

In the same way that the Defense System keeps the bad stuff *out,* it also keeps the good stuff *in.* Access to the Internal Wisdom located within the Core Self is limited. Therefore, there is a need to seek an external authority or Wisdom Figure to find out what is best for us. There is often a sense of "unsureness," indecisiveness and a lack of confidence in our own decision-making abilities. It feels as though almost anybody knows what is best for us better than we could know for ourselves.

When a person is living defended with the Core Self put away, choice or free will, is removed. When living out of the Defense System, in a state of emotional survival, decisions are not made cognitively but by the elaborately constructed Defense System and the various wounded parts living in the unconscious world. The Defense System has no brain. It makes decisions based on the drive of emotional survival. So when someone says to me, "It is my own fault. I *chose* to marry him," or "I *chose* to give my baby up," I whole-heartedly

Figure 8-3

disagree. There is no choice. There is no access to Internal Wisdom. There is not even access to rational abilities. A person will do whatever the Defense System dictates for emotional survival. Most of the time, the unsuspecting person does not recognize that decisions were made by parts out of conscious awareness and that these parts are stronger than the conscious, rational part. Whether a person acknowledges those subconscious parts or not, it does not limit their power. Awareness allows that person to become conscious of what part is in the driver's seat and allows the person to open negotiations with those parts. Feelings that are out of proportion or inappropriate are a red flag that cognition is no longer in control, and that there has been an unconscious shift of control to the Defense System. Decisions made after that are not made consciously out of cognition. I am not saying we are not responsible for our actions. Responsibility rests with doing whatever is necessary to restore integration and to discontinue living defended, thereby restoring choice.

THE "BLACK HOLE" AND ADDICTIONS

When the Core Self is put away, it leaves a large hole in the psyche and a great feeling of emptiness. People often refer to a "black hole" within or a sense of profound emptiness. There is an instinctive drive to fill that hole by reclaiming the Core Self and restoring integration. When that does not happen, the black hole is relentless in demanding to be filled. We then begin to throw things into the black hole to try to satisfy it, something like feeding young virgins to a volcano to appease it. We can throw in alcohol, drugs, sex, shopping, sleep, work, religion, chocolate chip cookies or anything else that seems to briefly satisfy the demands of the black hole (figure 8-5, page 158). During the very moment something is being dumped into the black hole, it seems to calm the craving. As long as I am eating the donut, I feel OK. When I finish the donut, the empty feeling returns and is probably accompanied by guilt for eating the donut. This is the nature of addictions.

In our culture, certain addictions are condemned and others are quite acceptable. Chemical dependency, such

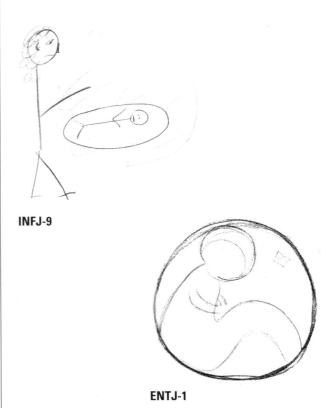

INFJ-9

ENTJ-1

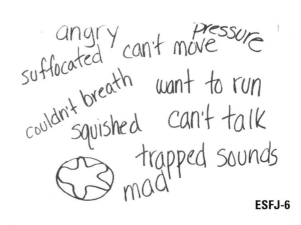

ESFJ-6

ENTJ-3

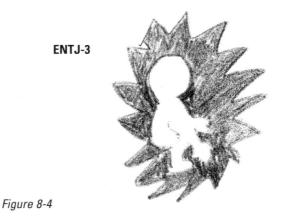

Figure 8-4

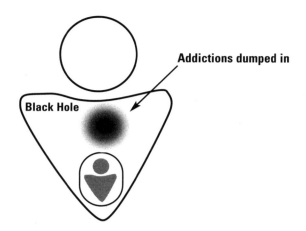

Addictions dumped in

Black Hole

Figure 8-5

as on drugs and alcohol, is flatly condemned and considered a character flaw or, at best, a genetic weakness. Other addictions, such as work and religion, are quite socially acceptable. When healing occurs and the spirit is liberated, the black hole disappears. There is no further call to fill the emptiness and no need for addictions. As long as the person continues to protect and care for her own Core Self, the Defense System will not need to put it away again.

Twelve-step programs, such as Alcoholics Anonymous, are wonderful, supportive organizations that go a long way in helping people conquer addictions. I frequently recommend a twelve-step program to a client because of the support and the nonjudgmental approach. However, twelve-step programs stop at the third level of healing (chapter 2) which is behavior modification. These programs create an environment for healing and encourage and support the healing process, but the strength of the program is in controlling the addiction, not fostering healing. In many cases, the offending addiction is simply replaced by one that is more socially acceptable.

The subject of the "black hole" is in itself very interesting. There appears to be some correlation between the concept of the black hole and Enneagram type. As an Enneagram Nine, Alyse (chapter 1) drew the black hole much like a spider web holding her immobilized. Sarah, also a Nine, depicted the black hole as a disorganized scribble, much the way she feels when she

is caught in it (figure 8-6). Those who are Enneagram Ones invariably draw the black hole in some type of funnel shape representing the ever-tightening self-imposed rules of the One (figure 8-7).

EXTERNAL FOCUS AND CO-DEPENDENCE

Living in the state of dis-integration, depicted in figure 8-2, in which a person is separated from her Core Self, causes her to become externally focused, becoming a human doing instead of a human being. It is as if the Core Self is the little princess I described in the Introduction who is locked in the castle for safekeeping. The princess's parent stations herself at the castle wall in order to watch for enemies and to protect the princess. As time goes by, they see less and less of each other, but the princess is protected. The parent misses out on the joys of knowing and loving the princess. The princess misses out on the guidance and love of the parent. Sondra, an INTP-3 (chapter 6), drew what it felt like to live behind the castle wall of the Enneagram Three defense (figure 8-8). She is smiling to the audience on the outside and crying on the inside. The wall of the Enneagram Three is protecting her breaking heart.

Being so externally focused is part of co-dependence. Co-dependence, simply put, is being other-oriented at the expense of self. It is trying to fill the black hole with the love/regard of others by earning it. It is trying to win the unconditional love and approval from others that did not seem to come from one's

INFJ-9　　　　　　　　　　　　　　**ISTJ-9**

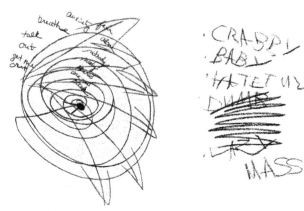

Figure 8-6

parents. Each child expects to be raised looking into her parents' eyes to see mirrored back to her that she is the most miraculous creature ever created, that God finally stopped practicing and got it right. Of course, that never happens and so each person goes through life still searching for the mirroring of unconditional love. Most often, a person will find a parent look-alike and try to win that person's love and approval, generally with less than favorable results. (See Parental Messages exercise, page 160.)

DEALING WITH FEELINGS

Part of the wounded condition is due to the fact that feelings cannot be expressed. When a child is frightened and is told to buck up and be brave, a feeling is buried and wounding occurs. When a child is angry and is shamed for the anger by being sent to her room to "get over it," a feeling is buried and wounding occurs. Even when someone tries to be nice, taking away a child's sadness by fixing the situation, a feeling is buried and wounding occurs. When a child is given the message that she must take care of someone else's feelings by suppressing her own, feelings are buried and wounding occurs. Feelings have a beginning, a middle and an end. When a child enters into expressing a feeling and that feeling is cut off before it can be fully experienced and validated, the unexpressed feeling is stored where it will surely be triggered sometime in the future.

As has been pointed out, the presence of these feelings shifts the young child to the feeling side of the brain where programming is stored. This is where messages associated with the feelings are then incorporated. Helen Palmer, who has done brilliant work in the areas of the Enneagram and accessing the Core Self protected by the Enneagram, says in *The Enneagram in Love and Work,* "It takes emotion to imprint an event and make it significant." Gary Zukav points out as well in *Soul Stories* that "the only way to get to know about the parts of yourself that you don't know is through your feelings." When an emotion stored in childhood is triggered later in life, it accesses and then activates the programming associated with the feeling, effectively

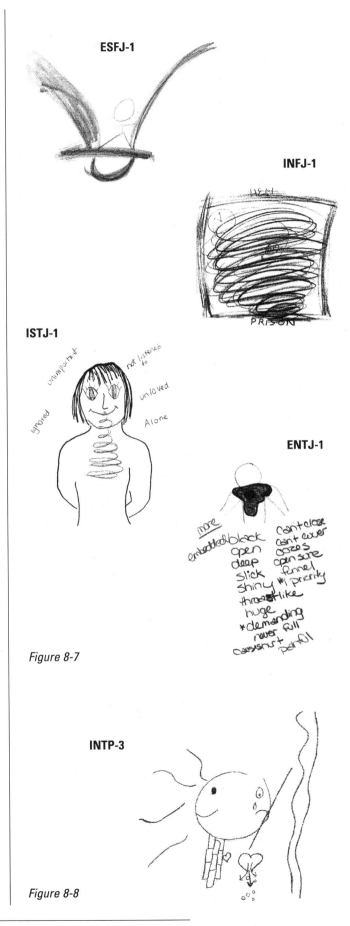

Figure 8-7

Figure 8-8

PARENTAL MESSAGES

If you find yourself discounting the wounding you received as a child, consoling yourself with the knowledge that your parents did the best they could, you might want to try an exercise that will hopefully give you a little more objectivity. Few parents intentionally do emotional damage to their children, but it happens nonetheless. As soon as a child enters a family, certain rules are set and certain assignments are imposed, whether overtly or covertly. You might take a look at the rules of your family of origin and the assignments that were given to you. Here is a limited list. Check off the ones that apply to you and add any others that do not appear.

____ Be quiet

____ Be good (as defined in that family)

____ Succeed

____ Keep the secrets

____ Take care of Mom's/Dad's feelings

____ Always be happy

____ Accept abuse (physical, verbal, emotional, mental, sexual) without comment/feelings

____ Be strong

____ Be Mom's/Dad's confidant

____ Achieve

____ Care for siblings

____ Care for an impaired parent

____ Be helpful

____ Don't fight

____ Be smart

____ Don't make waves

____ Keep Mom/Dad well/alive/sober/happy

____ Be perfect

____ Comfort a needy parent

____ Parent your parent

____ Parent your siblings

____ Have no needs

____ Endure sarcasm, criticism, judgment and stupid messages silently

____ Live in fear

____ Keep all the rules, no matter how difficult

____ Don't expect affection/nurturing

____ Put everyone in the family ahead of yourself

____ Accept rejection and/or abandonment through separation, divorce or emotional distance

____ Ignore inappropriate behaviors and addictions

____ Be a surrogate spouse

____ Accept all the guilt and shame that is imposed

____ Be or don't be feminine/masculine

____ Be invisible

____ Fulfill Mom's/Dad's dreams

____ Sort through mixed messages; know the difference between what is said and what is really meant

____ Be subjected to a parent's moodiness, rages or need for total control/domination

____ Make the family look good; keep up appearances

____ Don't be angry

____ Monitor your parents' moods so as to adjust your behaviors accordingly

____ Don't be a financial burden

____ Be independent

____ Be a big girl/boy; don't cry

_____

_____

_____

_____

Next, make a drawing of yourself as a very small child on the very bottom of a large piece of paper. Above the child, draw a rock for each of the rules or assignments on your list. Make your rocks proportionate to how heavy each particular issue was for you. If you are brutally honest, you will see that no one gets out of childhood alive emotionally.

sending that person back in time to relive the wounding event in order to release the feeling, work through it and bring closure (figure 2-1, page 23). Just as Therese, ISTJ-9, (chapter 6) imaged her inner child "filling in" with each expression of a feeling, we begin to recapture the essence of our Core Self by expressing the feelings that remain trapped deep within. With each expression of a buried emotion that is validated, we regain that part of the Core Self that was put away so much earlier. The symbolism of Therese's imagery is exquisite. She demonstrates how imagery accurately represents what is happening internally. Since it takes an emotion to imprint the wounding message, it takes an emotion to reverse the process as well. Through imagery, the subconscious sends a symbolic representa-

tion, in its own language, to cognition, showing what is taking place on a deep level.

Feelings are stored in the body as well as in the spirit and account for much of the physical distress we all experience daily. When feelings are allowed expression and are validated, many physical problems begin to be alleviated. Using the signals the body supplies in order to alert us to the presence of a feeling can be very helpful. We have all been trained so well to suppress our feelings that often we are unaware that we are even experiencing one. Therefore, it is useful, when first beginning to work with feelings, to identify each feeling somatically by applying terms such as heavy, sharp, hot, tight or other descriptive words. (See exercise below.)

The earlier you recognize you are having a feeling

Figure 8-9

FEELING CHART

One aid in identifying feelings is to make a personal chart of your own feelings. Draw several stick figures and label them angry, sad, scared, alone and any other feelings that are relevant and play a prominent role in your life. Take a moment to close your eyes and remember a time when you felt very angry. Review the situation completely in your mind, doing your best to enter into the anger and injustice of it all. After a few minutes, you will notice some changes in your body such as an increased heart rate, more rapid breathing, tightness in your jaw, heaviness in your chest, pain in your stomach, clenched fists or other somatic symptoms.

Another approach to accessing how your body responds during a feeling is to ask yourself, "How do I know when I am angry?" There is a definite combination of physical signals. The configuration will be different for each person, but often people of the same Enneagram type will identify similar feelings in a similar fashion. For instance, Enneagram Sixes will generally feel fright in their stomachs. Enneagram Ones will generally feel anger in their abdomens.

Next, take a colored pencil or crayon and mark all the places you can feel the anger on your anger stick figure. Repeat the exercise for each feeling and keep the chart in your journal. Figure 8-9 shows Darlene's chart. Yours can be as limited or extensive as you wish.

by paying attention to your body, the earlier you can work through it, thereby saving a lot of unnecessary physical distress as your body tries to get your attention. Body messages must be trusted. The body knows what the head has forgotten and what the Defense System does not want the Core Self to have to endure. The body stands firm in what it knows even if the head says that it does not make rational sense or is unimportant. Your body cannot make up a feeling.

Once it has been determined from body signals that a feeling is occurring, it is always helpful to identify and name that feeling. To some, that may seem like a simple enough directive. But many people have not a clue that a feeling is occurring, much less the ability to recognize what that feeling is. A bodily sensation of a knot in the stomach could be associated with many different feelings. Sometimes it is helpful to go through a short checklist of the four major feelings of mad, sad, glad and scared. Usually glad can be eliminated pretty quickly. Often, there can be a combination of feelings. For example, alone is generally a combination of sad and scare. Grief is usually a combination of sad, scare and anger. It is not unusual for a person to be so out of touch with her feelings as to have difficulty identifying and naming one when it appears.

Many times people use the term *depressed* interchangeably with *sad.* They are not the same. Depression is generally anger turned inward associated with hopelessness. This is different from sadness, which is usually associated with loss. Sadness is a genuine feeling, so it has a beginning, middle and end. When expressed, sadness can be brought to closure. Depression is a state of living without access to the Core Self.

Feelings are layered. Depending on personality type, certain feelings are easier to access than others. It is easier for an SP or an Enneagram Seven to feel happiness more than any other feeling. It is easier for an Enneagram Six to feel scare and sadness than anger. It is easier for an Enneagram Three to feel either sadness or anger than scare. So the main feelings needing attention in healing work—mad, sad and scare—will be addressed in the order each personality type presents them.

In our culture, it is understood that emotions are to be controlled at all costs. By the time we reach adulthood, we are so afraid of having a feeling that we will do almost anything to avoid it. It is important to regularly reassure yourself that whatever incident or issue being examined you have already *lived through, as a small child,* and have survived. Re-examining these issues and their resultant feelings as an adult can be survived also, and will restore Life.

Without dealing with feelings, we have a well-defined problem. And so it becomes necessary to take a deep breath and declare, "It's been lovely, but now I have to scream," and turn around to face the buried emotions of the past. It is generally surprising to find that when those feelings are recognized, encouraged and expressed, they feel as if they are just as raw as when they first happened. That is because where those feelings are stored in the subconscious, there is no time and space. So when they are accessed, those feelings feel just as real as they did the moment they first appeared.

It is very important that a feeling not only be expressed but also validated. Many times people will say, "I have been angry with my mother all my life! Sometimes I even scream at her." The problem is that the anger was always followed by guilt or shame or some other invalidating experience. Even if cognitively this person *knows* she has every right to be angry with her mother, the programming says she is wrong. The programming will furnish guilt feelings and feelings of shame installed by family and the culture at large. Try doing anger work on the topic of "mother" around Mothers' Day and watch the guilt descend like an avalanche. I have had "Honor thy father and thy mother" quoted to me more times than I can count, even when the father and the mother never honored the child. Coming to an understanding of the actions of the parents and an acceptance of them with all their shortcomings can be addressed after healing takes place. M. Scott Peck has said that we cannot forgive until we have pronounced them guilty.

Even if you feel warm, loving and compassionate towards your parents because you know they did the very best they could, it is still possible to champion your inner child. Consider that it is the parental *messages* and the lingering negative programming that is really being condemned. When anger is expressed, it is anger towards the programming, which has affected the quality of your life. Put on your magic glasses and see more than just what the child allowed herself to see. Reassure yourself daily that you can let yourself know whatever you need to know. Encourage yourself by declaring that you are now an adult and strong enough to face whatever needs to be faced. Put your hand over your heart and pledge to your inner child that she is worth the struggle, both internal and external, because only the truth will set her free.

Sadness can be examined in the same light as anger; it needs validation as well. Sometimes people will object to the suggestion of working with feelings, insisting that they have been crying for years and nothing has changed. It is important to know the real reason behind the tears. If reasons are given such as "because I'm a loser" or "because I can't get a date," it is certain that there is something going on at a much deeper level. That underlying feeling will need to be identified and validated before the tears will stop.

In determining the degree with which scare affects your life, consider how you feel in stressful situations. Review the degree of scare or even terror if you have to confront someone, speak to your boss, lodge a complaint or enter a new situation. If one of these situations leaves you feeling frightened to a degree that is out of proportion to the event, consider how old you feel in that circumstance. Generally, it is much younger than your years. This is a certain indication that you have been triggered and old programming has taken over. A frightened inner child, or ego state, is in control of your life at this point. Phobias are an excellent example. We all know that it is exceedingly safer to take a plane trip than to drive an automobile two miles from your home. Nonetheless, few people break into a cold sweat and panic at the thought of entering their cars. Whenever fear is radically out of proportion to the event, it indicates that an internal program is operating

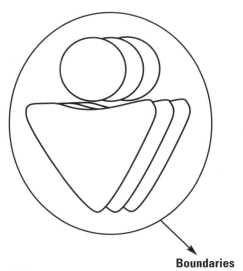

Boundaries

Figure 8-10

that has been accessed by feeling out of control in a situation that is perceived as dangerous in some way. By identifying the internal child, or ego state, that embodies this programming, it is not difficult to work with her and restore control to the rational adult.

In working with any feeling, remember that not only does the feeling need expression, but it also needs to be validated *on a feeling level*. Without validating the feeling, it is almost a re-wounding experience because the guilt and shame surrounding the feeling are reinforced. Trying to do healing work without identifying and validating the feeling is like running a car engine without a drive shaft. There is a lot of racket but no forward movement. And so I encourage what I call the new AA: *A*cknowledge the feeling and *A*ffirm the child/spirit.

When integration has been restored through healing early wounding, reversing the inaccurate conclusions drawn in childhood and affirming the inner child, then there is a sense of unity of body, mind and spirit. When that happens, boundaries are manifested automatically (figure 8-10). *Boundaries* is a term that simply means taking care of yourself, not being co-dependent and refusing to be a victim. Years ago, there was a trend called assertiveness training. Classes were held that taught people how to say "No" and to not be used by others. Assertiveness training is a form of behavior modification. You can be taught to say "No" and you can be taught various phraseology to limit the number of times people take advantage of you. However, assertiveness training does not deal with the feelings of guilt, with the "shoulds" or with the low self-esteem inherent in early programming. So someone finishing assertiveness training may be able to say "No" to heading the cookie drive for the Girl Scouts. Yet, she may still worry that she was being selfish and that no one will like her now. She may feel guilty that she is not doing enough. The behavior may have changed, but no healing has taken place. Once emotional healing has occurred and integration has been restored, there is a sense of being fiercely protective of the Inner Child, the Core Self. The feeling is that, once the spirit has been returned to me, I will never allow anyone to separate me from that integral part of myself again.

INTERPERSONAL IMPLICATIONS

Longing for intimacy and connection is part of being human. It is natural to engage in communication in order to interact and connect with another person. Communication can take place on three levels. The first, the cognitive level, is the most simple (figure 8-11). We can talk about the weather or the price of new homes or the events of the day. It is surface chatter without any lasting or profound effects.

The second level of communication occurs when two Defense Systems engage (figure 8-12). When you are trying to convince your clueless supervisor of something that seems obvious to you and that person is getting on your last nerve, you can bet your Defense

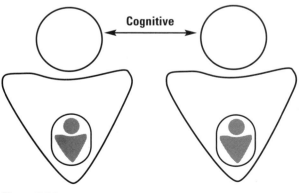

Cognitive

Figure 8-11

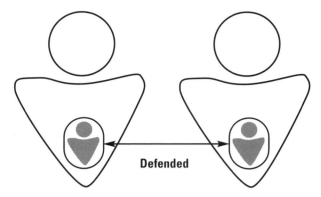

Defended

Figure 8-12

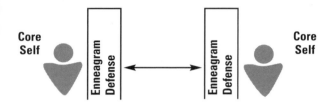

Core Self | Enneagram Defense | Enneagram Defense | Core Self

Figure 8-13

System is involved and so is your boss's. Emotions are always involved, but they are squashed and ignored as best as possible. If you can remember the last time you had a conversation with someone which ended in immense frustration for both of you, you have a good idea of what it feels like when two Defense Systems are engaged. Sometimes, two Defense Systems engage in such a way that does not necessarily feel good but does feel familiar. Sometimes these two Defense Systems are so comfortable with the old, familiar way of relating to each other that they get married and spend the next fifty years living defended and feeling frustrated. Before you laugh, let me assure you that it happens more often than not. They become deeply committed to the dance of "I love you. You are perfect. Now change." The only variable is the length of time the dance continues. Two people trying to relate from a defended position is identical to trying to be intimate while hiding behind a wall (figure 8-13).

The third level of communication happens when the Defense System can relax (figure 8-14) and the interchange can be open and honest between the two Core Selves. This can only happen when each person feels emotionally safe and capable of protecting herself/himself from further wounding. The Defense System is not involved. The old programming is not activated. It feels very open and each person has the sense of being heard, understood, accepted and valued. This type of communication occurs when each person understands, accepts and values herself/himself and is free enough to do the same for the other (figure 8-15).

Sometimes communication is not as clear-cut as these three levels may indicate. Sometimes one person opens up and is willing to share her soul with the other person only to receive a cognitive response. It feels like a lecture and very condescending. It is a quick way to shut down open communication. Other combinations are guaranteed to cause as much frustration. Try to talk cognitive logic to someone's Defense System. Try talking an Enneagram Six out of being scared. Try talking an Enneagram Three out of working overtime. Or try telling an Enneagram Four to lighten up and be happy.

Other times, a person may start to speak openly only to be met by the other person's Defense System. For instance, have you ever shared your innermost feelings with an Enneagram One only to be told you should not feel that way? Or perhaps you have talked earnestly to an Enneagram Nine, only to look over and notice that the Nine is not really present. It is a case of the porch light is on but no one is home. When talking to someone's Enneagram Defense, you feel discounted, not heard and certainly not valued.

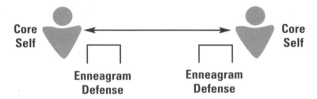

Figure 8-15

COMMUNICATION CYCLE

If we want to be in a relationship with another person, we have to be self-revelatory and the other person has to be willing to be the same. This is one of those things that is very easy to say and yet difficult to do. Most people go through life determined to avoid disclosure at all costs, covering true feelings with a facade, and being tough and/or resentfully compliant.

Each time there is a communication interchange, there is a chance of being misunderstood, of being triggered, of being hurt or of doing these things inadvertently to the other person. In figure 8-16, page 166, the Communication Cycle, the scene is set when there is the initial interchange between two people. Each time there is communication, there is a chance of disagreement. It is at that point that a choice is made, if not consciously then subconsciously, by the Defense System. There can either be an open and honest communication from an undefended position, as detailed on the right side of the cycle, or there can be an emotional shut down with a shift into a very defended and guarded position, as illustrated on the left side of the cycle. Perhaps there is a fear of being hurt again. Or, there can be a sense that "I really don't believe I am adequate and, if I show the other person my true spirit, it will be judged as 'not good enough.'" From feelings of inadequacy such as these, we present a false self to the other person, trying to be who is wanted instead of who we really are. The Core Self is put further and further away. The more healing work is completed, the more the choice to become open becomes conscious. After healing, it is safe to be open and honest, communicating from the Core Self and using the communication style associated with our own particular Myers-Briggs Type Indicator type.

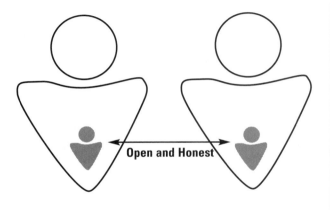

Figure 8-14

Cycle of Communication

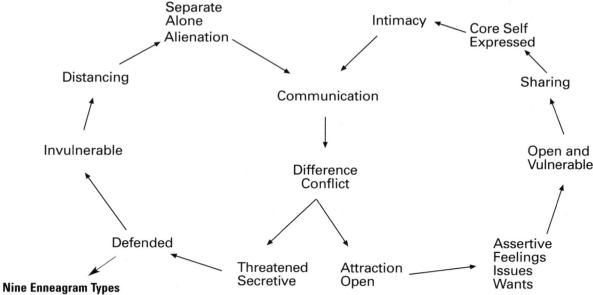

Nine Enneagram Types
1) rage and self-blame
2) care-taking and martyrdom
3) role playing and no authenticity
4) drama and self-absorbed
5) withdraw and observe
6) comply and give in
7) make light and refuse to engage
8) aggression and confrontation
9) leave and passive aggressive

Figure 8-16

When moving to the right side of the Communication Cycle to engage in an open and honest discussion, it is helpful to remember some basic communication tools. The first is to make a conscious decision to momentarily set your own agenda aside and truly listen to the other person. It is always helpful to use some kind of reflective listening to let that person know that he/she has been heard, such as: "So, if I understand you correctly, you are saying that. . . ." When a person feels heard, that person is much less likely to become defensive and much more likely to continue in an open, undefended manner.

When it comes time to state your position, it is essential to use "I" statements to explain your views and feelings. "You" statements have a tendency to shut the other person down and cause that person to shift into a defended position, effectively ending any open and honest exchange. The Communication Model in figure 8-17 provides a loose outline to effectively communicate your thoughts, feelings, concerns and needs. Compare these "You" statements with the "I" statements that follow the Communication Model.

"You" Statements
You make me so mad!
You don't care anything about me!
You are always late.
If you really loved me and our kids, you would come home at a decent hour.
You are out having a jolly time while I am stuck here with screaming, hungry kids.
You are just thoughtless and self-centered, that is what your problem is!

"I" Statements
I see that you are late coming home again.
When you come home late, I find myself imagining you are out having fun while we wait dinner. Whether this is true or not, that is what begins to go through my mind and I just want you to know.
I start to think that you don't really care about or love us.

I feel angry that you didn't call, and I feel that I am not important.

If you are going to be late for dinner, I need you to call by 5:00 p.m. to let me know.

If you are not home by 6:00 p.m., the children and I will have dinner without you, and I will assume that you will get your own dinner when you arrive.

In the first set of statements, the use of the word *you* will immediately put the other person on guard because that person does not know if you are going to say, "You are a jerk!" or "You are wonderful!" So it is always better to be prepared when *you* starts a sentence, and therefore a guarded position takes over. When the statement starts with *I*, the other person is not threatened because you are revealing something about yourself and that is not nearly as scary. Using the Communication Model can be immensely helpful in keeping the conversation open and on track.

The Communication Model is also helpful in allowing you to determine privately which of your buttons are being pushed. The first step is to identify the problem: "I see you are late coming home again." The next two steps reveal what is happening with the wounded inner child. That child often drew inaccurate conclusions because of limited understanding and is continuing to live out of those conclusions. And so we get the child's interpretation of the event: "I imagine you're out having fun." This interpretation is associated with the feelings one would expect: "I feel angry and not important." However, the next two steps show that the wounded child and her Defense System are not in charge. The adult cognition is very much present in taking these two steps in first explaining what is needed and then stating how this woman will be taking care of herself in the future should the situation recur.

Closely and honestly examining our methods of communicating using the Communication Cycle and the Communication Model will shed a great deal of light on relationship problems, but it will also provide useful information on your own programming, your inaccurate childhood conclusions and your thought processes. If studied carefully, it will present patterns in the way you think and the way you respond, showing

Communication Model

	1. Identify the incident:	I see that I hear that
Child	2. Interpretation:	I imagine that I assume that I interpret your actions to mean
	3. Emotional response:	I feel
Adult	4. Intended actions:	In order to take care of myself, I am going to
	5. Requests:	I want I need

Figure 8-17

the same consistently irrational conclusions. This information can be used to work with the wounded inner child to encourage healing.

REFERENCES AND SUGGESTED READING

Arterburn, S. and J. Felton, *Toxic Faith*. Nashville TN: Thomas Nelson Publishing, 1991. This is one of the few books written on the topic of religious addiction. It is presented from a Christian perspective with a twelve-step approach to overcoming the addiction. The authors include a checklist to help identify the addiction, and there is liberal use of examples and much supportive data. The book is stronger in helping identify a religious addiction than in helping to overcome it since the treatment is purely cognitive. Nonetheless, it is a good book for someone raised in a family with a religiously addicted parent, because there is an additional burden of guilt carried by the child who is angry because a parent is too busy with God's work to effectively parent the child.

Bolton, R. *People Skills*. New York: Simon and Schuster, Inc., 1979. Provides some basic communication skills, particularly reflective listening. Many examples and sample dialogues.

Borysenko, J. *Minding the Body, Mending the Mind*. Reading MA: Addison-Wesley Publishing Co., 1987. This is a good discussion of the mind-body connection and how to heighten awareness by learning to observe what is happening in the body. Borysenko describes how to identify feelings by looking objectively at what is happening in the body. She stresses the need to name the feeling, although she does not stress the need to express the feeling in an appropriate and controlled setting. Borysenko recognizes the baggage attached to the word forgiveness and prefers acceptance.

Jung, C. G. *Memories, Dreams and Reflections.* Ed. A. Jaffe and Trans. E. T. Gedanken, New York: Pantheon, revised 1973. Original work published 1963. Jung describes his differences from and split with Freud. He relates the events of his childhood that contributed to his theories and his life's work.

Kasl, C. D. *Women, Sex, and Addiction.* New York: Harper and Row, 1989. An open, nonjudgmental explanation of sexual and relationship addiction in women. Kasl explains how the use of these types of addictions are simply a means of numbing emotional pain and dealing with a sense of powerlessness.

Mellody, P. *Facing Love Addiction.* San Francisco: Harper, 1992. Mellody addresses the confusion between co-dependence and a true love/relationship addiction. She traces addictive behaviors to childhood messages and experiences. A twelve-step approach to recovery is presented. Easy to read with many examples.

Norwood, R. *Women Who Love Too Much.* Los Angeles: Jeremy P. Tarcher, 1985. Norwood traces the roots of relationship addiction to patterns established in childhood. She shows how we find a person with whom to enter a "dance," which will replicate the feelings elicited by an earlier, primary relationship with a parent. It may not be comfortable, but it is familiar. Norwood points out that women who are so addicted endure a great deal of emotional pain in the name of "love." She also addresses how control is an underlying motivation in this type of destructive relationship. Her approach to recovery is twelve-step based and cognitive. Many case studies are presented

and other addictions, which may also be present, are explored.

Palmer, H. *The Enneagram in Love and Work.* San Francisco: Harper, 1995. In this work, Palmer pairs each possible Enneagram combination in both a work and a personal relationship. She describes the dance or game that the pair is likely to engage in and some of the pitfalls to watch for. She also points out how each member of the combination can complement the other. Helen Palmer presents workshops around the world. She is gifted in her ability to work with people in drawing out Enneagram type. Watching her work is like watching an artist and I highly recommend the experience. Contact her at Workshops in the Oral Tradition with Helen Palmer, 1442A Walnut Street PMB377, Berkeley CA 94709; 510.843.7621.

Peck, M. S. *The Different Drum.* New York: Simon and Schuster Inc., 1987. Dr. Peck is devoted to the concept of community building and sees it as the most effective method to attain world peace. His description of the four stages of community building are particularly helpful, whether applied to a large group, a family or two people in relationship. Although he mentions the need for understanding individual differences and the need for lowering defenses before a sense of community can be attained, he does not address how. The sense is that these elements are biproducts of the community-building process.

Pert, C. *Molecules of Emotion.* New York: Scribner, 1997. Pert presents a concept that shocks Western thinking: the body is more than a method of mobility for the brain. As a scientist herself, Pert meets scientific thinking on its own ground, proving through her own research in physiology and biophysics, that each cell of the body has emotions, memory and intelligence. She unequivocally declares that the body and mind are one. A marvelous and extensive list of organizations and resources devoted to body, mind and spirit integration is provided. Candace Pert has explained scientifically what I am trying to explain metaphorically and for that I am grateful.

Satir, V. *The New Peoplemaking.* Mountain View CA: Science and Behavior Books Inc., 1988. A pioneer in family therapy, Virginia Satir outlines the dynamics of the family system and discusses communication.

Springer, S. *Left Brain, Right Brain.* San Francisco: W. A. Freeman, 1981. This book provides a basic understanding of the biology/physiology/neurology of the brain. I feel Jung's theoretical work on archetypes and symbolism is the link between hard-core scientific data, such as that presented in Springer's book, and the type of work done by affective therapists who instinctively rely on symbol and metaphor.

Zukav, G. *Soul Stories.* New York: Simon and Schuster, 2000. Zukav illustrates his concepts of spiritual growth with personal, inspiring stories.

CHAPTER 9

HEALING:
CREATING A SAFE PLACE TO BE YOU

There has been talk heretofore about "emotional healing" and doing healing work. Just what does that mean? How is emotional healing accomplished?

In this chapter, I will be explaining what healing work looks like in a therapy setting. If you prefer working alone, without a therapist, I hope you can take away some helpful hints and exercises that will expedite your healing journey.

SAFE ENVIRONMENT

Carl Rogers, a highly respected and often quoted affective theorist, maintained that the very first step in the healing process was to provide a safe environment.

Without a safe environment, a person will not take the risk of becoming emotionally vulnerable, something that is absolutely necessary for healing work. Therefore, in the therapy setting there is no room for judgment, criticism, condescension or shaming.

One of the tools of cognitive therapy is to confront the client with the intent of forcing an examination of irrational beliefs. In affective work, there is no room for confrontation. Confrontation and a safe environment are mutually exclusive. Whatever the client's worldview may be, the therapist needs to join her there and gently accompany her on her way to wholeness. If a client

> *It is beneficial to create a warm, inviting, comfortable, cozy setting where a client will feel relaxed and safe and sheltered. I prefer not to have an official-looking office with a desk and two chairs that are suitable for a doctor's waiting room, trying instead to reproduce a sitting room with sofa, easy chair and lamps instead of fluorescent lights.*

says, "I am the ugliest (or most stupid) person in the whole world," that is just where that person is for the moment. It is not the job of the therapist to confront or challenge that opinion but to join the client where she is. Obviously, that does not mean a therapist needs to lie and say something like, "Yes, you are certainly the ugliest person I have ever seen!" But the therapist can say something like, "From what I know of your background, I can certainly see how you came to that conclusion. As we go along, we will be closely examining how you arrived at that determination."

Since part of Inner-Healing work is to shift the focus from external authority to Internal Wisdom, it is important that the therapist not lead or become the teacher—yet another external authority figure that has to be pleased. So it is important to trust the process and allow the client to embrace her current worldview until her own Internal Wisdom tells her differently.

It is beneficial to create a warm, inviting, comfortable, cozy setting where a client will feel relaxed and safe and sheltered. I prefer not to have an official-looking office with a desk and two chairs that are suitable for a doctor's waiting room, trying instead to reproduce a sitting room with sofa, easy chair and lamps instead of fluorescent lights. If the client feels the physical setting is unsafe, it is pointless to insist that she is safe. It is better to ask what she needs to feel safe and sometimes it is just a matter of changing chairs or locking the door, simple moves that provide not only a safe environment but also a higher degree of trust in the therapist who is taking her fears seriously. For therapy to be effective, the client must come to feel safer in the therapist's office than anywhere else she has ever been.

The therapist is the key to providing a safe environment. I have conducted therapy in cars, in airports and in various other nontraditional environments. It is not ideal, but it is possible to create a safe enough environment when a certain degree of trust has already been established.

PREPARATION

As you prepare to enter the healing process, keep in mind that everything will change. All relationships will change: some for the better, while others will be lost. Often career changes are made. Many times there are changes in the expression of spirituality. Those who belong to a church may leave and those who have not had a religious affiliation may feel a need for one. Because this work is done on a feeling level and feelings have energy, there is often a huge discharge of energy resulting in exhaustion for a period of time. With all of this, the obvious question is, "Why on earth would anyone want to willingly subject herself to such an experience?" The only answer is that there is a strong, persistent call to come home to the soul that some people just cannot ignore. People who enter this process instinctively know that they *have* to pursue this path. There is an internal drive that will not be silenced.

The NF (Intuitive–Feeling) temperament type is generally associated with a quest or search for self. Although I have found that a greater percentage of NFs enter this type of therapy than is found in the population at large, the same drive is present in all types and temperaments. Once therapy is completed, ISTJs are possibly the most devoted to the process and, although SPs are the least likely to seek it out, they can become equally devoted. So it is not a process designed and embraced by one type or temperament.

Inner-Child Process

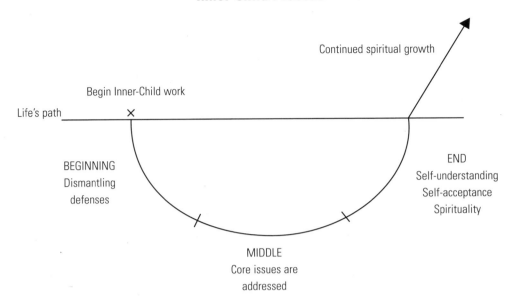

Figure 9-1

PROCESS

As stated before, Inner-Child work is a process with a beginning, a middle and an end (figure 9-1). There are signposts along the way and various ways to ascertain exactly where a person is in the process. Going into this process is entering the dark night of the soul. It can feel like the darkness described by David in Psalm 22, the complete desolation experienced by Job or the sense of unbelievably profound aloneness expressed by Jesus when he cries, "My God, My God, why have you forsaken me?"

So there will be times when it will seem dark, but remember that you can monitor your progress. There are four major transition points within the process. The first point is simply entering the process. This may seem basic enough, however it takes a major internal shift from business as usual to a willingness to change. In order for this to happen, there has to be awareness that something is amiss and a commitment to delve into the unknown. Sometimes that will require making phone calls, seeking support, finding a safe environment and opening up to someone. Just entering into the work takes courage.

The second transition point occurs when the dismantling of defenses begins. There is a certain amount of discomfort in becoming more and more aware of old coping tools and letting them go. In order to negotiate this territory, a safe environment is essential.

Following, and overlapping to some degree, is the next leg of the journey, which is called "core work." Here the negative messages, the programming, the distorted worldview and the clouded perception of self are ruthlessly scrutinized. A strong support system is helpful at this point because there is often a strong pull towards "I don't want to know that."

Finally, as core issues are resolved, there is a movement into self-exploration, acceptance of others and heightened spirituality. This phase is characterized by an unfolding of Internal Wisdom and a persistent hunger for personal growth. Those in this phase are constantly surprised and delighted with the new revelations about themselves and the evidence of a Higher Power in their lives.

There are several methods of monitoring progress throughout this work. First is the degree of control the Enneagram Defense and auxiliary defense tools have over the person's life. As soon as Reilley (chapter 11) entered therapy, she discontinued using alcohol and drugs; as Mary progressed through therapy, her need to rage diminished and all but faded away; and as Paula began to accept and love herself, she no longer needed to keep a perfectly spotless house.

As the defenses decline, there is a commensurate blossoming of the Core Self. The traits of the Myers-Briggs Type Indicator become more visible and are greeted with relish. Mary, an ISTJ, began trusting her abilities to invest her money; Paula, an ENFP, found she was extremely creative and had a gift for the healing arts; and Denise, an ENFP, went back to school to pursue a career as an art therapist. With these discoveries about self, there is excitement, joy and peace.

Imagery and dreams are marvelous monitors of progress. The condition of the child and the adult in imagery, as well as the relationship between the two, will furnish a clear report as to the degree of progress throughout the work. Dream symbolism will not only communicate the progress but also provide a graphic directive of what yet needs attention.

Another amazing monitor of progress is the use of written dialogue with the inner child using the non-dominant hand. When the child shifts from a wounded, isolated, lost waif to a source of wisdom and spiritual guidance, it is plain to see that a transition has been made out of core work and into the phase of personal and spiritual growth. Other indications of progress will become manifested in artwork, increased inner peace and changes in lifestyle and relationships.

IN THE BEGINNING

In the therapy setting, the first order of business after determining personality type is taking a case history or life story. With a new client, I want to know everything from conception and birth to the present and will devote a minimum of two hours to it. The case history provides the big picture which I, as an Intuitive type, need. From this information, I can see patterns and key issues that continually reappear. Besides providing me with a wealth of factual information, I have the opportunity of watching the client's affect while she is telling her story. When the foot starts to jiggle, the arms cross, face flushes or tears appear, I know there is a very deep wound needing attention, and I will be certain to take

note. Another benefit of taking the time for an extensive case history is that there are few times in a person's life when an opportunity presents itself to tell her *whole* story to someone who really wants to hear it. Telling all the unvarnished, gory details is another plus. Often when biographical information has to be given, it is cleaned up for popular consumption. Not too many people want to hear about Dad sleeping off a drunk in the front yard and, conversely, there are not too many people with whom we care to share that information.

At the end of a case history, I ask the client to set goals for therapy, however, I do not phrase it that way. I ask what she would like her life to look like by the time our work together is completed. I encourage each person to go for the moon. Many people are very modest in their goal setting, asking only for inner peace or a better relationship with a specific person. Others take me up on my invitation to set high goals and list things they insist are totally impossible. To date, I have not had anyone finish therapy without attaining all her goals. That is because her Internal Wisdom knows what she needs and, when invited to speak, has shown what life could be like when integration and wholeness are attained. Interestingly, I have never had anyone list winning the lottery or living to be 100. The goals are challenging and meaningful and may appear to be totally out of reach, but they are set by a Higher Wisdom and they are always attainable.

You can do the same thing for yourself by writing your autobiography and reading it over as objectively as you can with the evaluative eye you would bring to reading someone else's bio. Then sit down with paper and pencil to design your life as if you had a blank slate in front of you. Do not let any internal critic or governor throw cold water in your face or insist on your being realistic or practical. If the goal is, "I want out of this marriage" or "I want a totally new career" put those things down, even if you have no clue as to how to attain them. Remember, it is a process. If you were there already, you would have no need to embark on the journey. I would suggest you do not read any further until those goals are set.

Now that you have your goals on paper, I urge you not to stop in your healing process until you have found a way, a mentor, a program, a support group or a therapist to help you make the call of your heart a reality. You have only one task in this life and that is to know who you are and to express yourself to the fullest degree possible. Do not let anything stand in your way.

Does My Inner Child Have a 1-800 number?

After ascertaining personality type, taking a case history and setting goals, it is time to take the first step into the healing process. It is time to make the acquaintance of the inner child. The following exercise will assist you in this process.

Looking at this exercise from a metaphorical perspective, the house represents the body, the child

EXERCISE
MEETING YOUR INNER CHILD

The best way to meet your inner child is through imagery. Here is the imagery I use with every new client. It provides a wealth of information not only with regard to the person's history but also with respect to how she feels about herself and how split she is from her spirit. I invite you to either read over this imagery and go through it by memory, or tape-record it reading very slowly. Then, find a quiet place where you will not be disturbed and replay it. I urge you to actually *do* the exercise rather than figure that you already know the outcome. When you simply *think* it through, you are on the wrong side of your brain. You will not be able to access the information necessary to engage in the process on any level other than the first: the historical. It is essential to shift to the feeling part of the brain, the right side, where additional information is stored.

Close your eyes and take a few moments to focus on your breathing. Following your breath moves you gently into a slightly altered state while drawing your attention inward. Take all the time you need to become totally relaxed and internally focused. Then, enter the imagery by imagining a door; it can be any kind of door that comes to mind. Imagine you are standing in front of the door dressed in clothes you might wear to a meeting or to an important event. Be sure to anchor yourself in your own body, and do not just watch yourself as if in a movie. You can anchor yourself by feeling your feet standing on the floor in front of the door and looking down at the

clothes you are wearing and the shoes on your feet. Look down at your own hands and then look at the door through your eyes.

Take a good look at the door. What style is it? Of what materials is it constructed? What is its color? Size? What condition is it in? Is it old or new? Reach out and touch the door. Run your fingers over the surface. What does it feel like to the touch? Drop your hand to the doorknob or handle. Can you tell the difference in texture? You may even be able to detect a difference in temperature between door and handle. If you begin to open the door, does it make a sound? How would you describe the sound?

Now open the door completely and step through it to find yourself on the street where you lived as a small child. If you lived in many different places, whichever comes to mind is just fine. You cannot do this wrong. Be sure you stay the adult dressed in your power clothes. Be sure you stay in your body. Begin to walk up the street towards the house you lived in as a child. As you are walking, feel the surface under your feet. Feel your legs move. Listen for any sound your footsteps make. Look around you. What time of year is it? What time of day? What colors predominate? If you listen carefully, are there any sounds? Are there any particular smells that you associate with this place?

When you reach the house or building in which you lived as a child, pause for a moment and look at

see next page

MEETING YOUR INNER CHILD *(continued from page 175)*

it. Check out the front yard. Look at the placement of the door and windows. In what condition is the house? What color is it? How big or small is it?

When you are ready, move closer until you are standing at the front door. Take a close look at this door. What color is it? Of what material is it made? Reach out and touch it, feeling the familiar texture, and rest your hand on the doorknob. Take all the time you need to fully experience being there. When you are ready, open the door and step inside.

Take a moment and let your eyes adjust to the change in light. Look around at the layout of the rooms. Reach out and touch something familiar— wallpaper, a picture, a piece of furniture. Take a deep breath and see if there are any smells reminiscent of this house. When you are ready, move slowly through the house, room by room, until you find yourself as a small child. When you find that child, take note of the room in which you found her and what she is doing. Take a good look at the child. How old is she? What is she wearing? How is her hair fixed? Can you see her face?

If possible, move closer to this child and place yourself where you can look in her face and make eye contact. Explain to her that you are from her future and that you have somehow lost contact with her. Tell her that she is important to you and that you have come to re-establish your relationship with her. Let her know you hope to meet with her many times until the two of you will never be separated again. Look deep into that child's eyes and try to see what is hidden there. Look past the face she shows to everyone else. Ask her what is going on with her and what it is like to live there. Let her know that there is no one in the entire world who can understand her the way that you can. If it is comfortable for the two of you, touch her in some way. You might take her hand, touch her hair or her face, or hold her. Tell her anything else you want her to know and tell her whatever you think she needs to hear from you. Feel free to ask her questions, too. Let her answer if she

can. If she does not talk at all, that is OK.

Before you leave, give the child a gift by which she can remember you and your visit. Since it is your imagination, you can give her anything you like. When you are ready to leave, say goodbye in any way that is comfortable to the two of you and move to the doorway of the room. Wave goodbye and tell her you will return. Then move out of the house the same way you came in. When you are at the street, turn in the same direction from which you came. Begin to walk away. Look over your shoulder to see that the farther you walk, the smaller the house becomes until, eventually, you turn a corner or round a bend and it fades from sight. When that happens, allow yourself to become aware of the room in which you are currently sitting by feeling your feet on the floor, feeling the chair that is supporting you and listening for any sounds that are present in this room. Take your time. When you are ready, gently open your eyes and take a moment to write down your experience.

Generally, you will see the house presented as it actually was when you were a child. So even if your parents still live in that house and you just saw it last week, the imagery usually presents it in the same condition and with the same decor as when you were a child. In virtually every case, the child is alone in the house. That is because no matter the size of the family or the age of the child, she felt alone. If the child has her back to you or will not look at you, it is usually because she does not trust anyone, not even you. If she will not talk, it is probably because she was denied a voice and knows better than to speak up. The clothing, the room in which you find her, her age, and all the other details have significance. If you spend some time with those details, you will be able to determine why your subconscious chose the manner in which this child was presented to you. Your subconscious is never flippant about what is presented. Everything has meaning and significance or it would not be there.

represents the Core Self or spirit and the adult represents cognition. The spirit or Core Self is generally presented as emotionally wounded in some way. The spirit feels isolated and alone, abandoned and neglected by those who are supposed to love her. The spirit and the cognitive self are almost strangers. Living in the same body, they have been separated and acting independently forever. There is always a feeling of peace and serenity if a true feeling of connection with the child can be achieved. This provides a taste of what the end result of Inner-Child work is about. The whole purpose of the work is to restore integration of body, mind and spirit, resulting in a sense of homecoming and peace.

In doing this exercise and any other involving the inner child, it is important that you always be completely honest. Never lie to the child because she has been lied to and disappointed all her life. So no matter what words I may have provided, do not use them unless they are absolutely true. Do not say you will return unless you have every intention of doing so. It is better to say you hope to return or you will work at returning than to mislead her, which causes additional wounding of the spirit.

DISMANTLING DEFENSES

It is quite startling to the Defense System to begin toying with issues and feelings that have been locked away so long. An elaborate system was developed very early to avoid just such a thing. Kyla, INFP-3, has a relatively uncomplicated defense strategy, as described in chapter 7. Figures 7-1 and 7-2, page 147, show how Kyla first employs her Enneagram Three defense of looking good, achieving and staying busy. When this fails, she moves into the lethargy of the Enneagram Nine, wanting to sleep, not caring and having no forward movement. In addition, her Core Self will help shore up the defenses by supplying the traits of the NF temperament in being co-dependent. She will also begin looking around for someone to validate her. Experiencing the high of an addiction will temporarily alleviate the painful feelings that are plaguing her. By

the time all this happens, Kyla is in serious trouble and there are no rational abilities available to her.

Darlene, the INFP-5 whose defenses were described with Kyla's, is defended as diagramed in figure 7-3, page 148. Her first line of defense is the Enneagram Five. She withdraws, becomes very quiet, observes and feels absolutely nothing. If the stress continues, she employs some of the tricks of the Enneagram Seven such as a humor defense and minimizing what happened to her. Darlene will always put everyone else ahead of herself. She reports that with every death in her family, even her daughter's, she took care of everyone else's feelings and never attended to her own. When the going becomes rougher than she can endure, she will dissociate, completely leaving the situation so as to numb out and not experience any feelings. When Darlene is in more emotional pain than she can bear, she will console herself with thoughts of suicide so that she knows there is a way out if necessary.

When beginning the Inner-Child process, defenses such as these must be dismantled in order to access the feelings and programming causing the problems. When we manage to pull the plug on the defenses, even for a moment, we can use the feelings that surface to access the programming. It goes without saying that the Defense System is not too fond of this approach and puts up a valiant fight. The Defense System is not the enemy; it just takes its job very seriously. It is charged with preventing emotional pain and will resist all attempts at accessing that pain, no matter what the intent. And so, as we move into the beginning phase of therapy, we are met with a lot of resistance. Kyla will use her Enneagram Three to try to win me over, to act the cooperative client and to tell me whatever she thinks I want to hear. After a session, she most likely will go home and go to sleep. Darlene will use her Enneagram Five to stay in her head, to become numb to feelings and to give forth as little information as possible. When the pressure is applied, she will break into inappropriate laughter. She will proceed to dissociate, leaving me alone in the fight, while she slips silently into despair. Each of these maneuvers is to be expected and must be met with patience and understanding of the personality type involved. Eventually, the Defense System will be circumnavigated and persistence will win out.

During this beginning phase, most people are surprised to find themselves crying unexpectedly. Many report their feelings get hurt more easily. In general, it feels like things are getting worse. With the Defense System thrown off balance, it is perfectly normal although it feels pretty crummy. Many people wonder how being made to feel simply awful once a week is going to improve their lives. It is a necessary step in order to reach the messages stored away in childhood. The only way to access those messages is via a feeling. It is similar to working with a programming glitch on your computer. First you must find and access the program that has the "bug" and then insert the program update or "fix" to correct the problems that came with the early version.

During this beginning stage, core issues that shaped the person's views of self, others and a Higher Power are identified and examined. We take a look at the people who act as triggers and determine what program is being activated. Each time Paula's husband sent a message that she did not do something well, it pushed a button which sent a signal to activate the programming of childhood installed by her father. Paula would become consumed by feelings of guilt and shame with a profound sense of never being good

enough to be loved (figure 9-2). It did not matter that those feelings were irrational and out of proportion to the trigger. The programming is not subject to reason.

It is necessary, then, to identify the triggers, trace them to the original programming and work with it in its original context. In Paula's case, we used imagery to reproduce the messages and the commensurate feelings about herself installed by her father. In imagery, Paula was able to relive an experience with her father, which let her know experientially how she felt as a child. She then entered the imagery as an adult and spoke up to her father on behalf of the child. She expressed the anger that had been stored in every cell of her body since childhood. Paula subsequently sat with her inner child and told her the truth: she is good, smart, talented and of inestimable value. She is deserving of love and should have been recognized for the precious child that she is.

Affirming messages, such as those that Paula gave to her inner child, are only effective if they are expressed with some degree of emotion. Some people will sob uncontrollably while holding and affirming the inner child. Others will have only the slightest change in affect such as a faint flush or a change in breathing. The degree is not important. It is important that there be some emotion so that there has been a shift into the feeling part of the brain where the programming is located.

Having the adult enter the scene provides another

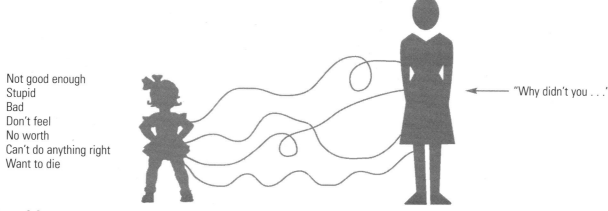

Not good enough
Stupid
Bad
Don't feel
No worth
Can't do anything right
Want to die

"Why didn't you . . ."

Figure 9-2

benefit. The adult can bring cognitive objectivity to the situation that was not possible before. A client who was raped as a preschooler can tell me that it was her own fault because she should have gotten away or should have known he was drunk and dangerous. However, when she enters that situation in imagery and her adult self watches as a man rapes a small child, *her,* the whole thing shifts. She gains access to her feelings of anger, terror and betrayal, and with those feelings as a guide, she changes the conclusions she drew as a child. She replaces the old programming with new information on a feeling, not a logical, level. She discards distorted reality and replaces it with Truth.

Because a small child cannot speak up to a parent, change families or in any other major way affect her situation, she must cope with whatever strategies she can invent. When the adult is brought into the imagery, new coping techniques are also introduced. The adult can do things the child could only dream about, such as taking the child by the hand and walking away from the offending person. A child does not have the power to be so bold. The adult can speak up to the person who is persecuting the child. A child is only safe in such a situation if she is voiceless. The adult has a car, a different house that is safe, money and a voice, just to name a few new coping tools. Together, the adult and the child can examine the child's old coping skills—such as phobias, panic attacks, obsessive-compulsive behaviors, dissociating and multifarious others—and the adult can convince the child that the adult's methods are more effective. The adult can persuade the child that the old ways of coping have become a problem in adulthood and are interfering with living a full and happy life. An outside authority, such as a therapist, spouse or friend, can never convince the child. That is because an outside authority is talking to the adult (cognitive) part who already agrees. It is very difficult for an outsider to access someone else's inner child, which is located outside of cognition.

Finally, by bringing the adult into the imagery, we can create a sense of the rational cognitive part working in cooperation with the irrational feeling part. Each time this occurs, it brings the person closer to integration and wholeness. It establishes a working partnership between mind and spirit that has been missing. (See Perfect Parent exercise, page 180.)

The truth is, each person is waiting to be recognized and acknowledged by the self. No one can do it better. The perfect parent is living within each of us, and it is up to the adult part of the self to mirror back to the soul everything that the soul has been waiting for. It is up to the adult part to acknowledge the inner child.

When this recognition takes place, integration has begun. The process of re-parenting the inner child begins by letting the child know that there is one person in the whole world who will not leave her: *you.* Building a strong adult who is fiercely protective, unconditionally loving and totally devoted to the child is essential to the process. Many people think of re-parenting an inner child as equivalent to carrying a teddy bear and buying toys impulsively. It is nothing like that. It is about making tough decisions that are in the best interest of the child, no matter what the fallout may be. It means having a voice and using it when it is easier and safer to be quiet. It means taking a stand and making changes when others may totally disapprove. It may mean leaving relationships, moving, changing a job/career, and perhaps even breaking ties with certain family members.

Before a strong adult is developed, there may be some temporary transference with the therapist, who at first appears to be the loving parent who has been sought, because ideally, the therapist provides unconditional positive regard and withholds criticism and judgment. When that happens, it is enough to simply be aware of it and think of the therapist as a bridge across troubled waters. The therapist assists in the transition from no self-parenting to complete recognition of and devotion to the inner child. (See Bonding exercise, page 181).

It is immensely helpful to become more conscious of the messages that were sent to you as a child and the programming that resulted from those messages. Half

EXERCISE
PERFECT PARENT

Each of us is looking for the perfect parent. We are waiting to have someone who completely understands us to mirror back that we are simply wonderful. I will often ask a client to draw a picture of the perfect parent. You may want to try this yourself. Around the picture, I ask for words to describe that perfect parent. Invariably, the person has described her True Self, the Core Self as profiled by her MBTI. Take a look at figures 9-3 through 9-6, which show

four different renditions of a "perfect mom." In figure 9-3, Lyla, an ESFP, shows the SP's idea of a fun-loving mom. Sylvia, an ISTJ, gives us a very traditional SJ mom in figure 9-4. Reilley, INTJ, emphasizes the NT's strong desire for guidance, depicted in the NT mom in figure 9-5 and Paula, ENFP, draws a very affectionate NF mom in figure 9-6. The words each person used to describe the "perfect mom" are listed with their appropriate figures.

Lyla, ESFP-7

SP

Play	Patient	Talks with kids
Fun	Understanding	Says "I love you" every day
Interactive	Soccer Mom	Tells me I'm beautiful
Interested	Involved	Friendly to my friends
Attentive	Play	Spends time with me
Good friend		

Figure 9-3

Sylvia, ISTJ-6

SJ

Nonjudgmental
Helpful
Concerned
Happy
Open
Loving
Sensitive

Figure 9-4

Reilley, INTJ-4

NT

Accepting	Guiding
Encouraging	At home
Concerned	Domestic
Interested	Involved
Boundaries	Protective

Figure 9-5

Paula, ENFP-1

NF

Gentle	Carefree
Full of heart	Love
Caring	Sloppy
Compassionate	Flexible
Loving	Kind
Loose	Precious
Fun loving	Mistake maker
Helpful	Tender
Be instead of do	Simple
Humorous	Soft hearted
Concerned	Understanding
Feeling	Patient
Silly	

Figure 9-6

EXERCISE
BONDING

Each time the wounded child is visited in imagery, journaling or any of the other methods of contacting her, there is an opportunity to heal the child's wounds, to build a strong adult and to solidify the union between the two parts. Imagery appears to be the most powerful and effective method to accomplish this. In imagery, the adult can connect with the child in many ways. You can try this yourself. Remember, you cannot just *think* about this exercise. It is without value unless you move into a slightly alerted state where you can access the feeling side of the brain.

Close your eyes and take all the time you need to relax and direct your focus internally. Imagine holding your inner child. Be sure you are anchored in your body, not just watching yourself hold the child. You can touch the child in a manner that feels safe to her such as stroking her hair, touching her cheek or holding her hand and feeling her small fingers. You can hug her and imagine love being sent straight from your heart, like a beam of light, to be received into her heart.

Imagine you have X-ray eyes and can see the healing effects of that beam of love-light. You can imagine rocking her in a rocking chair while you whisper affirming and comforting things in her ear. Remember never to lie or exaggerate. You can breathe on her and let her feel your breath as the breath of life for her. You can let your tears fall on her head, like a baptism, washing away the old hurts.

No one has ever cried for that child the way you can. No one's tears can heal that child the way yours can. If there has been physical or sexual abuse, you can show the child that your touch is safe and appropriate, and that it is all right to relax and enjoy safe touch. You can look into her eyes and send love and affirmation simply through eye contact. You can listen to music such as Shana Noll's *Songs for the Inner Child* or any other meaningful music. Most love songs can be applied to your inner child. You can hug her and feel her small body beneath your touch, giving her a sense of being encircled and protected by your arms. Finally, you can continue your hug until you have pulled her into your heart where you can keep her safe and close to you, even after the imagery is completed.

During the time you connect with your inner child, take the time to ask her how you can best take care of her today. What will give her a sense of being nurtured? What will give her a feeling of being protected? What does she need to hear from you that will be validating and affirming?

It will be up to you to be sure that this child does not go through life thinking herself an ugly duckling. Even if you accept on a head level that you have a lot of gifts and talents, her opinion is much stronger and will always win out. It does not matter that you think of yourself as a swan if she still sees herself as an ugly duckling in a swan's body.

of the job of healing is in making the unconscious conscious. Use the Mirroring exercise on page 182 to assist you in that endeavor. Again, I must stress that it is important that you actually DO the exercise and not just think about it. The exercise must be worked on the right side of your brain. To get the information and the results you need, you actually have to participate in the imagery.

As you become more and more honest about your examination of your childhood, you will see that you need to give up some fantasies about yourself and the family that you invented as a child in order to cope

MIRRORING

Close your eyes and take all the time you need to become inwardly focused by following your breath and releasing tension in the methods described previously. When you feel completely relaxed, imagine that you are walking with your inner child. You have her hand and can feel her tiny fingers in your grasp. Get a sense of her trust in you. Be sure you are anchored in your body and look down at this child. Take a look at how her hair is fixed and what she is wearing. If you cannot clearly see what she is wearing, get down to her level for a moment and touch her clothing, lightly running your fingers over the fabric until it comes into focus. If you have trouble seeing her face or hair, do the same thing.

Continue walking together, feeling your feet touch the ground with every step. Today, you are taking her to an amusement park. As you enter the park, look at all the various rides and attractions, the people, the lights and the many colors. Listen for the myriad of different sounds such as children's laughter, adults talking, sounds of machinery, music and whatever else you can discern in the cacophony of an amusement park.

As you walk through the park, smell the popcorn, hot dogs and other foods being hawked. Keep walking until you reach the Fun House with a Hall of Mirrors where you can see your image distorted in a variety of ways. As you enter the Hall of Mirrors, imagine that the first mirror is cut out in the shape of your mother, or whoever was your primary caregiver, like a silhouette of mirrored glass. Allow your inner child to walk over and stand in front of that mirror. Let her stand there for a minute while you look over her shoulder to see how she is reflected in your Mother Mirror. Has her face changed? Her size? Her clothing? Examine the reflection carefully and take note of how this mirror may distort or change her image.

Next, move to the mirror that is shaped like your father. Let the child move to stand in front of this mirror. Again, look over her shoulder, giving the image a moment to come into focus, and see how this mirror reflects the child. How does this mirror distort or alter her image? Repeat this with every person who had a major impact on you as a child, such as a significant sibling or grandparent. Then repeat it with a mirror in the shape of your spouse or significant other.

Finish the exercise by having the child move to stand in front of a mirror in the shape of *you,* as an adult, and see how she is reflected back to herself when she looks in your mirror. If you find any of these mirrors troubling to the point of evoking anger, that is great. Take a bat, broom handle, wooden spoon or other such instrument, and beat a bed or couch cushion while keeping the image of the offending mirror in front of your eyes. Beat it until, in your mind, the mirror is shattered into bits. Then stand up, holding your inner child's hand, and the two of you grind the shards of glass into the ground with your feet until they are dust.

You can finish the exercise by taking paper and pencil and writing a letter (that you do not mail) to the person whose mirror you destroyed, telling that person what has been done to the mirror and why it had to be destroyed. Finish the imagery by walking away triumphantly from the Fun House, leaving the amusement park the same way you entered. As you walk farther away, you can look back to see it fading from sight. At that time, you may want to find a comfortable place to sit with your inner child, telling her what you both have done today to champion her. Affirm and validate her and assure her that you see her for who she is, and that you think she is a magnificently wondrous swan! When this experience feels complete for both of you, gently reorient yourself to the room in which you are sitting and when you feel ready, open your eyes.

with the events of your childhood. The rule is that we cannot take anything away without having something ready as a replacement. You cannot dismantle a fantasy parent until you are ready to step in to be the true parent to your inner child.

Middle: Beyond This Point Are Dragons

The middle of the Inner-Child process is where you objectively, ruthlessly and honestly examine the core issues that affected your life, the conclusions you drew and the coping techniques you developed with the help of your Defense System. This means getting around denial, repression, excuses and everything else you have employed to mask your own truth. In looking at your

past, never minimize. If anything, "awfulize." Minimizing will only aggravate your inner child who wants you to "get it." She has been carrying the truth around by herself all these years and she wants very much for you to see it and accept it because in accepting the truth, you are accepting her. Defending your past is interfering with living your present life to the fullest. Remember, it is the parental messages you are condemning more than the wounded people who parented you. Take a look at the Changing Faces exercise.

Based on the Mirroring exercise, Kyla drew her perfect mom as someone who was happy and could handle all the duties, stresses and responsibilities of

Exercise
Changing Faces

Earlier in this chapter, I invited you to draw the perfect parent and list some adjectives or descriptive phrases to define what a perfect parent would be like for you. To continue on that course, next choose whether you want to examine your mother or your father more closely (or other primary caregiver). Then draw a picture of that person and list enough adjectives and descriptive phrases to give an accurate verbal picture as well. Do not continue reading until you have completed this part of the exercise. Next, take a moment to close your eyes, relax and release the tension from your body. Give yourself permission to know what you need to know and commit yourself to being open to the truth. Then, imagine an event involving this person that occurred during your childhood, whether you were present as a child or not, but return to that scene as the adult that you are today. Pretend that you are invisible and that you are watching the scene unfold totally unnoticed. Be sure you are anchored in your body and not simply watching yourself be there. Put on magic glasses that allow you to see truth, no matter how painful. If

necessary, revisit several scenes until you feel you have a good, accurate and honest view of this person and how this person operates. Be certain not to dismiss or edit any thoughts or feelings that come to mind. Thank your Internal Wisdom for providing you with the information and gently bring yourself back to the present and orient yourself to the room in which you are sitting.

Next, take up your drawing materials again. This time, do not draw the person as you saw him/her in your visualization. Instead, depict this parent the way you would least like to see him/her. What is the last thing I would want to know about this person? What would disappoint me the most to know about this person? What would I be most afraid to learn about this person? Draw your parent in the least favorable light. Please remember that the thoughts and feelings that might appear do not have to make sense or be supported with substantiating evidence. Just write them down. Later, with more information, you will understand their meaning.

parenting—keeping all her balls in the air (figure 9-7a). Next, she drew the mom she remembered as a woman overwhelmed and almost stunned at the ramifications of having six children (figure 9-7b). Finally, Kyla drew the mom she was most afraid to have as someone who was not really present emotionally, was not capable of handling life and who did not really love her (figure 9-7c). Kyla's middle drawing (figure 9-7b) shows her mother with no legs, implying Kyla knew instinctively that mom was in a situation from which she had no way of removing herself. Her mom was stuck, trapped. In her drawing of the mom she was most afraid to have (figure 9-7c), Kyla does not even give her mother a body, additionally conveying the message that mom was just not there. The *X* over her mother's face and heart emphasizes her absence.

In each case, it is the last drawing, of the parent you would be most afraid to have, that needs to be closely examined. This is the drawing that is closest to your truth. This is the parent that you really perceived you had. The drawing of the perfect parent is a fantasy and is the heart's longing for itself. The second drawing is what we allow ourselves to consciously remember and accept. It is all that a child can handle. In Kyla's case, she did not want to consciously know that her mother was not able to be there for her, did not really want her and possibly did not love her. In the last drawing, we are in touch with the internal messages and programming left over from childhood. This last drawing does not have to make sense. It does not even need to be historically accurate. Here, accuracy is not the issue. The issue is dealing with a child's perceptions and with the child's own reality and truth. This is what was too painful for the child to know consciously; but, in fact, she did know these truths at a deep level, causing her Defense System to be activated and coping techniques to be developed.

Actually, Kyla does know for a fact that her mother was shocked to find herself pregnant for the fifth time with Kyla. She already had more than she could handle. She did not embrace the notion of another baby with joy and cried throughout her pregnancy. But like most women who have an unplanned child, Kyla's mom adjusted as best she could and did love Kyla and the next child who followed to the best of her abilities. It became even more difficult when she found herself a widow when Kyla was eleven years old. As an adult today, Kyla is close to her mother and completely understands *on a cognitive level* the situation her mom was in. However, it is not important what Kyla's rational mind tells her. The very small child (see pages 145–147) who felt unloved and emotionally abandoned

The Perfect Mom   **My Mom**   **My Real Mom**

Figures 9-7a–c

by her mother is the part that is in charge. It is the programming that is associated with this child that plagues Kyla with feeling she is not lovable and can trigger her into relationship addiction. To deal only with what she knows cognitively gets Kyla nowhere. Getting her to understand her mother's situation cognitively will not aid Kyla in the healing process because Kyla is already filled with understanding and sympathy for her mother. This approach will keep Kyla on the wrong side of her brain, away from her inner child, the feelings associated with that child and the programming that is running Kyla's life.

In figure 9-8a, Darlene represented a perfect father, reflecting herself as an INFP for whom love and affection are so important. INFPs have a deep, sage wisdom that is part of their identity, and Darlene referred to that trait. She also referred to the INFP's penchant for being fiercely protective of her children. In her second drawing, figure 9-8b, Darlene drew her father looking much the same physically but she described him the way she has allowed herself to see him all her life. He had flaws but he was basically a good guy. To stop here and work with this version of her father gets her nowhere. In figure 9-8c, her third drawing, her father looks smaller but physically similar to the previous renditions, but the verbal picture has changed a great deal. This is the dad that Darlene's inner child is concerned about. This is the dad that accounts for Darlene's depression, self-loathing and suicidal ideation. And this is the drawing that causes Darlene to remark that she does not want to know these things about her father. There needs to be congruence between what the child knows and believes and what the adult knows and believes. The child's way of knowing is on the right side of the brain; the adult's is on the left. (See Wounded Child exercise, page 186).

In figure 9-9 on page 186, Darlene portrays the child who is in relationship with her father as very small, the earliest of her three main ego states (chapter 7). That small child writes a letter to her dad from her heart:

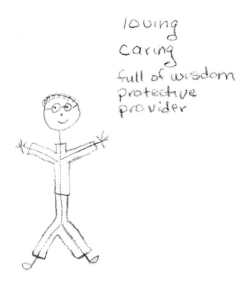

Figure 9-8a

Figure 9-8b

Figure 9-8c

sad
afraid
confused
unsafe
unloved
alone
quiet
unprotected
betrayed
hopeless

Figure 9-9

Daddy,

    *I don't like you. You make me feel guilty
and it is wrong. You are bad not me. It was
not my fault. How could you do it? I don't
understand. Go away.*

                                  D.

You can follow up on your letter from your inner child to your parent with a letter from you as an adult to that parent. (These letters are never intended to be mailed. They are strictly for your personal work.) Acknowledge what happened, explain how it affected you and the price you are still paying. If this were the last or only time you could say something to this person, what would you include? Darlene's first adult letter to her father after acknowledging his sexual abuse is as follows:

Dear Daddy,

    *I love you, but I want to let you know that
I don't like what you have done in the past.
You didn't just screw up the past but now as
well. I'm having to have what you did all
undone. Why did you do it? Do you really
love me? It hurts a lot (actually I'm in a
living hell) over what you did. I don't think
you loved me and that hurts very much.*

                           Love,

                           Darlene

As time went by and Darlene built a stronger adult, her language became a little less tentative and a little more graphic. Three months later, she wrote the following letters to her father from her inner child and her adult:

CHILD:

Daddy,

I hate you. I'm sorry that you already dead because if you were alive I could put you through your on private hell equal to or worse than the one you have put me through. You are worthless. You need to feel physical and emotional pain constantly and be made to see you own blood dripping all over you all the time. You need to be alive so that you can be in a constant state of dying.

ADULT:

Daddy,

Go to hell on a one-way ticket. How could you do what you did to me and make me feel like it was my fault. What a bastard! I hate you. I'm glad your dead, if you weren't I would kill you. IOU scumbag.

D.

Notice the errors in spelling and grammatical structure. This is a sure indication that Darlene is working out of her feeling part and not out of cognition, which would be very conscious of spelling and grammar. In three short months, Darlene found her way around all the defenses that ardently avoided facing what her father did. With this core issue identified and exposed to the light, Darlene can work through the events of her childhood, her feelings, the messages and the programming coming out of those events.

Although your story may be very different from Kyla's and Darlene's, if you have allowed yourself to be open and if you feel safe enough to let the truth come to the surface, you probably have some interesting material by now. Look over what you have drawn and written. If at all possible, read them out loud. Reading your work out loud is much more powerful than reading silently. It literally gives a voice to the child who has been silenced. When you examine what you have produced, ask yourself what your feelings are trying to tell you. It is so very important that you stay focused on what is happening in your body to indicate your feelings rather than analyzing your feelings in your head. If you feel a tightness in your throat, ask that tightness what it is trying to tell you, what it wants you to know. You can let your nondominant hand write an answer from your throat. This type of approach will help you stay in your body and out of your head. That is much better than "The tightness must mean I am sad. I wonder what I'm sad about. Blah, blah, blah." All that analysis will only impede any progress you are making.

Another variation to this approach is to feel the body sensation, such as tightness in your throat, and draw yourself as a child feeling that tightness. Write some words around the drawing to describe the picture. Then, looking at the drawing, imagine what the child is saying to herself. Or, let the child tell you about it by using your nondominant hand. In chapter 10, many other techniques of accessing and working with core issues will be described. Your personal journey can be whatever you want it to be. You can gently stick a toe in the water and decide you are not ready for the plunge as yet. Or, you can dive headlong into the search for self with the attitude that things cannot get much worse.

Moving through this middle part of the Inner-Child process is like going down into the cellar and dusting off some old trunks and boxes to find things that were put away so long ago that you have forgotten about them. You may have forgotten you have your grandmother's Bible, but that does not negate the value and significance of that item. You may have forgotten some of the messages you received about yourself as a child but that does not negate their importance or the impact they have had on your life. This part of Inner-Child work is very much about making the invisible visible and the unconscious conscious.

During this period, an internal struggle ensues between living the same way you have always lived and taking the risk to abandon old operating procedures in favor of new, untried ones. The old way of living defended, with your Core Self locked away, is familiar, and the known always feels safer than the unknown.

Asking the Defense System to chill out while letting your adult cognitive-self take over seems dangerous and chancy. It is like a new foal struggling to her feet for the first time. You want to trust your legs, but it seems safer to stay close to the solid ground. This is a time when you have to let go completely of your old methods of coping and grab onto a new lifestyle. It is like a trapeze artist who has to let go of one bar and hang in empty air before grabbing the other bar. This middle part of Inner-Child work feels very much like that because, for a time, there is a feeling of just hanging over the black hole within you with absolutely nothing to support you.

To encourage yourself to move ahead, you may want to examine what it is like for you to live out of your Enneagram Defense System most of the time, allowing that part to make your decision and guide your life. Read over the MBTI traits of your Core Self and then look at the traits of your Enneagram Defense System. Compare the two parts of yourself. What is the main reason to keep living out of your Defense System? What would you have to give up to move control from your Defense System to your Core Self? What would be the cost in emotional safety to transfer control out of the Defense System? If you are not your defended self, who will you be? Kory (chapters 2, 5, 6 and 7), defended as an Enneagram Eight, came to a frightening moment of truth when she said, "If I am not angry, who am I?" Her Enneagram Eight had been in charge for so long that she had no way of defining herself apart from it. It was frightening for Kory to let go of the trapeze of her anger and hang in dead air while she waited for the bar of her Core Self, the ESFP, to come to her fully. It is literally a leap of faith.

END: THE LIGHT AT THE END OF THE TUNNEL IS NOT A TRAIN

When core issues are brought to the surface and examined thoroughly, and the old programming replaced with new concepts on a feeling level, it feels like a corner has been turned. Hopelessness, depression, emptiness and the sense of being lost are replaced by hope and light when the first taste of integration and wholeness is experienced. Some of the signals that the corner has been turned are increased instances of having a voice, heightened self-esteem, self-care, self-confidence, awareness of feelings, objectivity and a new interest in spirituality. At this point, the internal shift is becoming more visible to the outside world. Others begin complaining because the balance has been changed and boundaries have been set. Co-dependence has lost its appeal. The good news is that, by the time the outside world notices the internal changes, you have grown into a strong adult who is capable of handling the challenges of changing relationships. This adult is no longer willing to be manipulated by guilt and shame.

With a strong adult (cognition) in charge, you become responsible for your actions and behaviors. With awareness comes responsibility. Your foremost responsibility is to love, protect and care for your inner child. When that is the driving force of your life, you have recognized the God part within you. One of the main ways of fulfilling your responsibility to your inner child is to recognize when you are being triggered, to work with the trigger and to choose to respond differently than you have in the past. That means that you will consciously decide to employ the traits of your Core Self to address the triggering event rather than the automatic, outdated response of your Enneagram Defense System.

TRIGGER CYCLE

Much of therapy is about restoring choice. Before choice can be restored, there must be awareness that a choice *exists*. Without this awareness, the Enneagram Defense System takes over decision-making and it becomes business as usual. You continue living in the survival mode governed by your Enneagram designation and are devoid of any conscious choices. By exploring your various triggers, and the feelings around those triggers, it is possible to build in some reaction time during which you can make the choice to take control away from your Defense System. During the reaction time, you are able to objectively examine the situation and deal more rationally and willfully with the trigger.

How you are triggered and the resultant feelings and behaviors can be mapped out with a trigger cycle (figures 9-10 and 9-11). The left side of the trigger cycle depicts the progressive disintegration after a triggering event and is governed by the Enneagram Defense System. The right side of the trigger cycle illustrates what happens with awareness and the ability to deal with the trigger as a cognitive adult with the gifts of the Core Self.

Kyla's story has been told and her Defense System was illustrated (figure 7-2, page 147). Looking at Kyla's trigger cycle provides even more information on how

Kyla operates (figure 9-10). Kyla reports that when she is in danger of "looking bad" or feeling like a "loser," she is sure to be triggered. If Kyla does nothing and lets the triggering situation take its course, the results will be the same as they have been her entire life. She moves into the image-conscious, high performance of the Enneagram Three. She is filled with anxiety at the fear of failing that permeates her life. She becomes extremely busy and increasingly uptight, often taking her distress and anxiety out on her children. She focuses more and more on her image and is aware of the false front she exhibits in order to protect herself. If there is no way to salvage the situation and protect her image of the high achiever, she moves into the additional defense strategies of the Enneagram Nine, at

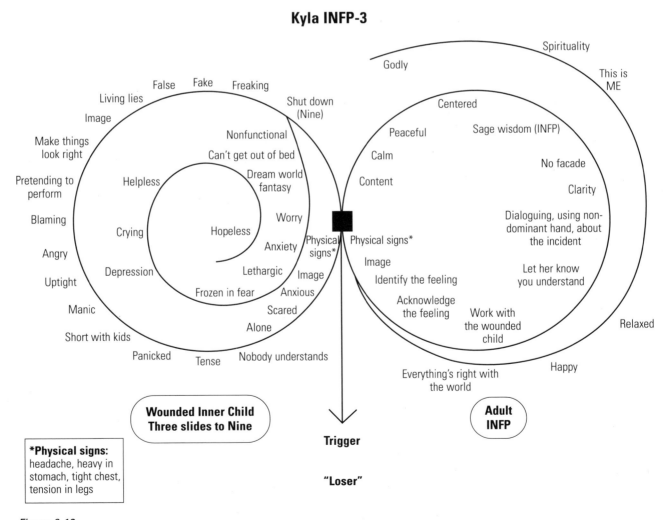

Kyla INFP-3

Figure 9-10

which time she begins to shut down, become lethargic and slide quickly into depression and hopelessness. By the time a person has spiraled down into the center of the left side of the trigger cycle, that person is in a very difficult place emotionally. To reverse the process at this point takes an enormous amount of energy, will and determination. It is very difficult to have those qualities when feeling so completely desolate. Therefore, it is extremely important and beneficial to interrupt the downward spiral as early as possible in the trigger cycle. In order to interrupt the downward progression of her trigger cycle, Kyla must be *aware* that it is even happening.

After a triggering incident, the very first signal that there is trouble is the presence of a feeling or two. Feelings manifest themselves physically, as was noted at the end of the last chapter. Kyla becomes aware she has been triggered by physical signs such as headache, stomach distress, tightness in her chest and tensed muscles throughout her body but especially in her legs. With these symptoms acting as a red flag to alert her to the problem, Kyla notices that she has become more image-conscious, a sure sign that the Enneagram Three is moving into high gear. With this awareness, Kyla now has a choice. She can take the old, easy, familiar way of reacting and just let the Enneagram Three take over. It might not always feel very good, but it often works and, if the Three can turn the situation around to make Kyla look good, there will be an adrenaline rush. Or, Kyla can move to the right side of the trigger cycle where she will address her feelings and work with her wounded inner child with the tools presented in the next chapter to restore an internal sense of peace. Unlike the left side of the cycle, which feels like spiraling down, the right side of the cycle has a feeling of expansiveness of spirit.

Each time a person encounters a triggering situation that allows her to play out the left side of the trigger cycle, that program is reinforced and the Defense System grows in strength. In addition, it becomes more and more likely that there will be a spiraling down into the center of the left side, employing the added coping techniques of the stress Enneagram position, which for Kyla is the Nine.

Each time a person encounters a triggering situation and chooses to take control of her reactions and take care of herself, she will move to the right side of the trigger cycle. The more frequently that choice is made, the more automatic it becomes as the programming changes. When this happens, there is often an incorporation of some of the traits of the Enneagram growth point, which for Kyla is the Six, and a deep sense of peace and serenity. When in such a state of emotional well-being, there is a wonderful feeling of expansiveness and a very strong sense of being a spiritual person who is connected to a Higher Power.

It becomes obvious that if feelings are the primary red flag, warning us that we are in a precarious situation, then it is essential to be very aware of, and alert to, the presence of these feelings. This becomes very difficult in a culture that does everything to discourage a feeling, from the encouragement of addictions such as smoking, alcohol, sex, shopping, and gambling to the rampant prescription of a horde of medications meant to numb out any semblance of emotion. In extreme cases, measures as radical and inhumane as electric shock treatments are used, as was the case with Darlene. I have had clients enter therapy taking more than a dozen prescription drugs a day simply to suppress their feelings. Quick! There's a feeling loose in this room! Do something! Encouraging the awareness and expression of a feeling goes counter to all our cultural messages that demand we feel good whatever the circumstance. But life is not about feeling good; it is about feeling whole. Each time a feeling is numbed out by any means, a part of us is cut off and locked away.

Darlene was never allowed to show a feeling of any type during her childhood. Her Enneagram Five defense was delighted to comply with that directive. Darlene managed to completely numb out all the feelings around her father's sexual abuse and her mother's failure to protect her. She also realized that when there was a death in her family, even her own baby daughter's, she was busy taking care of other people's feelings so as not to focus on her own. When there was a danger she might succumb to a feeling, she solved the problem by automatically dissociating. Darlene's Defense System is diagramed in figure 7-3, page 148, and her trigger cycle is illustrated in figure 9-11.

No one enjoys staying with a difficult emotion and working it through. Kyla certainly does not enjoy feeling like "a loser." Darlene would do just about anything but experience the feelings around her father's incest and her daughter's death. Nonetheless, that is exactly the direction that needs to be taken. Each of us must consciously choose to move into the feeling, experience it and work through it with the tools provided in the next chapter. That is not easy and that is why it is called Inner-Child *work*. In the beginning, I mentioned the

process was more than buying a teddy bear and indulging your inner child's least little impulse. It is hard work and requires a real commitment to living whole.

It is easy to construct your own trigger cycle to help you become aware of your patterns of behavior and to map out your own downward spiral. With this information, you will know exactly where you are at any given time after encountering a triggering event. It will also help you to remember what you have to do to reverse the situation and move to the right side of the cycle towards wholeness.

Working with your trigger cycle (see Trigger Cycle exercise on page 192) will help you recognize sooner when you are in a troubling set of circumstances so that you can move out of the picture where you can be

Darlene INFP-5

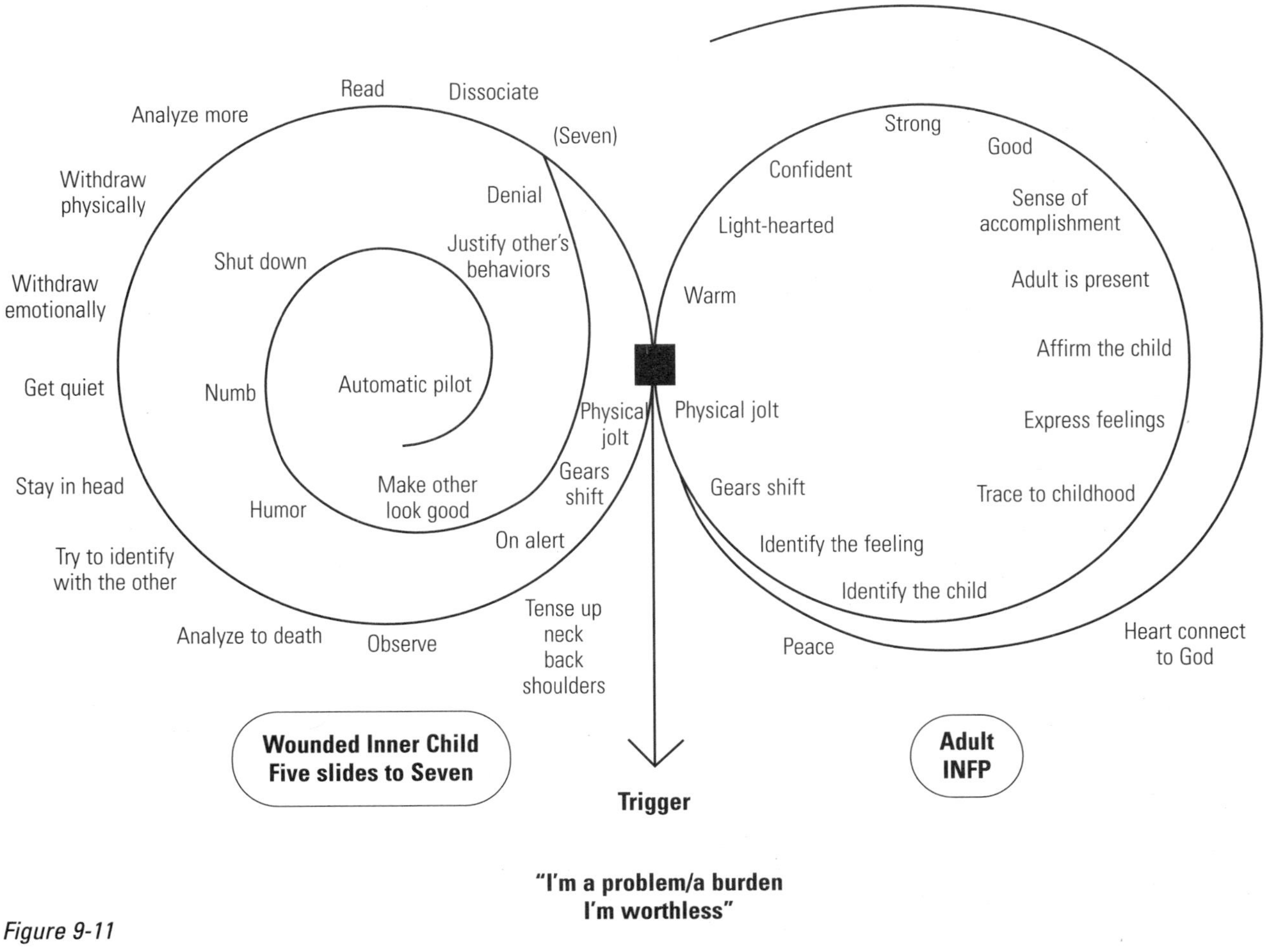

Figure 9-11

more objective. With that awareness, you can make the choice to move to the right side of the cycle by asking questions such as: What just happened here? What button has been pushed? Who is this reminding me of? What am I feeling? How can I best take care of myself? By moving to the right side of the cycle, you can progress into a state of peace and serenity, feel a sense

of expansiveness and being fully human, and have an understanding of being connected to the God Within.

When you recognize your own God Within, you cannot help but recognize and respect the God Within of another as well. That is different from co-dependence because with this type of respect for the other, you are willing to let that person travel his/her own

EXERCISE
TRIGGER CYCLE

Remember a time when you were badly triggered. What is the underlying message implied in the event? Often, the underlying message is that you are defective, a loser, not lovable (or something similar). That is your personal trigger.

Next, take a moment and close your eyes while you think about what happened during that situation and what was said to you. Generally, there is another person involved. If that is the case, watch that person's face and listen to the tone of voice. You will begin to feel your body reacting, indicating the presence of a feeling.

Note the physical signs and then the progression of your feelings. If there is no resolution to the situation and things simply deteriorate, note what you do next. As the situation worsens, your Defense System scrambles to come up with ways to protect you as your feelings escalate. Note all the strategies you automatically employ in the order they appear as well as the progressive escalation of your feelings. Check the Enneagram diagram figure 4-1 page 56, to determine which number the arrow indicates is your point of disintegration.

At some point in your spiral, you will most likely experience some of the traits/coping devices of this Enneagram number. For instance, an Enneagram One will usually react to a trigger with anger that is felt mainly in the abdomen. The One reacts with a sense of being flawed and imperfect and having caused whatever bad thing has happened. This is

often followed by criticism and judgment of self and others, usually accompanied by rage. If the situation simply gets worse, the One will move into an even more defended position and employ some of the techniques of the Enneagram Four: nobody understands me, poor me, all alone and I want to die. Once you have established the left side of your trigger cycle, you will see that the downward spiral is virtually the same whatever the incident.

After constructing the left side of your trigger cycle, see if you can recall a time when you were able to interrupt the downward slide and move into a mode of self-care by expressing your feelings, validating them yourself and basically taking responsibility for your own well-being. You will recognize such a circumstance because you will have had a sense of really feeling good about yourself, feeling like an adult equal to handling the situation. Some people report that they think they have spent their entire lives living on the left side of the trigger cycle. You may identify with that feeling. If so, take it as a wake-up call and resolve to begin your healing journey without delay. If you have instances in which you have successfully worked through your feelings, validated them for yourself and taken charge of your life, you will be able to map out the steps you took to achieve that and the resultant feelings of well-being. Use figure 9-12, a blank trigger cycle, to record what happens to you in a triggering situation.

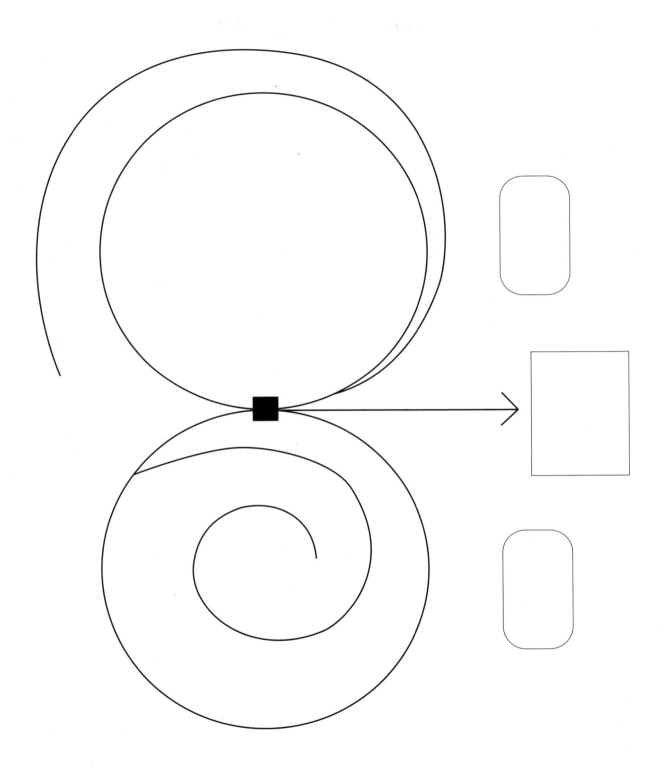

Figure 9-12

journey, make the mistakes necessary, fall down when needed, grow towards independence and anything else that is in the best interest of that person's spiritual growth. During this phase, there is a willingness to give up control of others and of forces outside the self, and replace them with increased faith in a Higher Power.

Before long, there is a sense of wholeness (holiness), feelings of being complete and without emptiness. That is because there is now access to the Core Self, the spirit, the soul. During this stage of Inner-Child work, you will begin to value your Core Self for the magnificent expression of God's creativity that you are. There will be an awe at the beauty of the spirit that is the God part of you. You will begin to celebrate your Inner Child. I have a drawing by artist Corlita Bonnarens of a dancing woman around which she quotes Ntozake Shange, "I found God within myself, and I loved her, I loved her fiercely." I encourage you to love, celebrate and delight in the Child Within yourself. Read over your MBTI traits and find ways to encourage the expression of the gifts and traits. If you read the

qualities of your MBTI type and feel they are not receiving full expression, then you are responsible for making some changes in your life until you feel you are being completely true to yourself and honoring your Inner Child.

REFERENCES AND SUGGESTED READING

Noll, S. *Songs for the Inner Child* [Cassette, CD]. Santa Fe, NM: Singing Heart Productions, 1992. Each song touches the wounded child. Listening to any song on this album while holding your inner child will be a healing experience.

Wyman, P. "Trigger Points." *Enneagram Monthly* 42 (February 1998):1. I first wrote about trigger cycles for the *Enneagram Monthly* using Kory's story to illustrate. For a copy of this article, contact the *Enneagram Monthly,* 748 Wayside Rd., Portola Valley, CA 94028; 877.428.9639.

CHAPTER 10

TRICKS OF THE TRADE:
TECHNIQUES FOR HEALING

The purpose of each of the techniques presented in this chapter is to encourage feelings that will allow access to your early programming and resulting defenses. Once the early programming is accessible, it is not difficult to change it and to replace the old, limited, knee-jerk defenses with more effective coping skills. The purpose of these tools is to assist you along the path back to your spirit. Once you have found that spirit part, you can live authentically out of your True Self—your very nature—so that you can *be*. This is the ultimate goal. Do not get caught up by any of the signposts along the way, thinking you have found *the*

answer. *You* are the only answer.

Before employing any of the techniques described below, please take the time to give yourself permission to go places in your healing journey that you may never have visited before. Assure your inner child of your presence and your willingness to listen to her, know her story and take appropriate measures on her behalf.

Also take the time to create a safe environment for yourself. Be sure you will be comfortable and have all the necessary supplies with you. It is mandatory that you have a place free of distractions and that you have uninterrupted privacy for this work. It would be absolutely wonderful if you had the freedom to make as much noise as you care to make. You may feel a need for gut-wrenching sobs or to loudly express your anger. It is easier to give your inner child a voice and permission to use it if you do not have to be conscious of someone hearing you and possibly becoming troubled by what is heard.

Be sure that your completed work will be safe from prying eyes. Some people keep their journals and artwork locked in the trunk of their cars for safekeeping. You do not want to feel restricted in any way, particularly by worrying about who may gain access to your work.

Although healing can happen in a matter of seconds because it takes place where there is no time and space, it is not possible to know how long it will take to access that part of you. Therefore, allow yourself all the time needed so that you do not feel rushed in any way.

IMAGERY

The language of the subconscious is symbolism. Symbolism is how your subconscious communicates to you in dreams and in imagery. Healing imagery should not be "canned." It should be imagery that is drawn from your life experience. Healing imagery is different from imagery used for relaxation in one very important aspect: the presence of an emotion. An imagery exercise, such as True Colors, that is simply for relaxation or information can be very peaceful and also furnish you with information in the same manner that a dream can.

Exercises such as these are wonderful for the information they can provide. However, without the presence of an emotion, it is doubtful the experience can be healing. Without emotion, it would be difficult to convince a person that the words on the list are really true.

A peaceful exercise that can be tacked onto the end of any other exercise you do is described on page 197. You can also use it to go to sleep at night. Although this exercise can be used on many other levels, for our purposes it is peaceful, restful and allows you to connect with your inner child.

Whenever you finish doing any emotional work, especially something that is particularly disquieting, take your child to her safe house where the two of you can be together to unite and grow in love and mutual trust. I encourage you to write a description of this house and yard in your journal and possibly include a sketch of it.

If you actually participate in the exercise, Relaxation Imagery, on page 197, and not just think it through,

EXERCISE
TRUE COLORS

Barbara Sher gives a delightful imagery that is both relaxing and informative in her terrific book, *Wishcraft*. Barbara suggests you image a color. Let your mind be filled with that color. Answer various questions about the color such as: Solid or gas? Transparent or opaque? What does it feel like to the touch? Any smell? Any sound? Any taste? Get as acquainted with the color as you possibly can. Then take a moment and write down all the words you can think of to describe this color. Do not stop writing until you have 10–20 words or phrases.

Do not continue reading until you have completed the exercise to this point so as not to influence the outcome.

If you were participating in a workshop where the participants were asked to introduce and tell a little about themselves, would you have given your name and read from this color-adjective list? Doubtful. Most likely, the list of color descriptors paints a fairly accurate portrait of your Core Self, but this is the part of yourself you have put so far away from consciousness that it is surprising to accidentally bump into it through an elegant little exercise such as this.

EXERCISE
RELAXATION IMAGERY

Close your eyes and take all the time you need to become relaxed and internally focused. Imagine you are walking with your inner child. Whatever age she is represented to you is just fine. You cannot do an imagery wrong. As you are walking, feel your feet touch the ground and feel the movement of your body with every step. Take note of what time of year it is and what time of day. Keep walking until you come to a perfectly beautiful natural setting. It can be a place you have actually visited or it can be imaginary. Take a good look around the setting with your inner child. Look at the colors, explore the landscape and decide what you like most about the location. What sounds do you hear? What does it smell like in this place? What does it feel like to be here?

As you look about, decide where you might want to put a house for your child. Imagine the house there, just as you would like it. How big or small is it? What style is it? What color? What would the yard be like? Would the yard be large or small? Anything in it? Is there a porch? Place a fence around the property just so the child can see her space defined. It can be any type of fence you like. Put one gate at the front and let the child know you will be the one in charge of the gate and you will decide who is granted entrance and who is not. Since this is your imagination, place an invisible force field, like a dome, over the whole property. You cannot see or feel this force field. Birds can fly through and the breeze can blow gently along. However, no person can get through, so the child knows this house and yard are totally and completely safe. What would it be like inside the house? How would you furnish it? What would the child's bedroom look like? Ask the child what she would like in her house and yard. Price is no object. Finally, find a comfortable place in either the house, porch or yard to sit with your child and connect with her in any of the ways described in chapter 9 that work well for you. Talk with her, touch her, hug her and send her love from your heart to hers. Whenever the experience feels complete for both of you, gently reorient yourself to the room in which you are sitting.

---

you will have finished with a deep sense of peace. Being able to access this peace and serenity lets you know that it does exist within you. The more healing work you do, the more you will be able to really live in that state of peace, contentment and safety.

The imagery you use for healing needs the added ingredient of emotion and that emotion may come from a painful experience in your childhood. For a more in-depth and emotional experience try the exercise, Healing Imagery, on page 198. (Note: If the experience you will use in this exercise was terribly violent and too frightening for you to re-examine, please get professional help. If the feelings are too scary, it is a sure sign that what happened to you is seriously affecting your life. You deserve to live free of the pain left over from childhood. Love yourself enough to find someone to help you work through these feelings, the programming and the resultant defenses, which are limiting your life.)

Another way of using imagery is to employ what I call "body imaging." Recall a physical feeling you had with the experience you used in the Healing Imagery exercise. How did you represent the feeling? Suppose it felt as though there were a rock in your stomach. Close your eyes and look at the rock closely. How big is it? What color is it? Touch it and run your fingers over it. Now imagine being the rock. See what it would feel like to be that rock in the presence of the person who caused that feeling. Act in whatever way you would act if you really were the rock. Express any feelings that demand attention.

continued on page 199

EXERCISE

HEALING IMAGERY

Think back to childhood to a particularly painful experience. Take a moment to close your eyes and concentrate on following your breath to find a quiet space inside yourself where it is safe to re-examine this experience.

Take a good look at the child you were when this happened. What age were you? What were you wearing? In what room did this take place? Where were you in the room? Who was there? Where were the other people positioned in the room? At this point, it is important to anchor yourself in the child's body looking out at the world through her eyes. Look up at the person/people in the room. Look down at your feet. Touch your clothing. Feel what it is like to be standing there in that situation.

When you feel as though you are well anchored in the child's body, replay the scene just as you remember it. Listen for what was said, for voice inflections, tone and the emotions in the voice. Listen not only for what was actually said to you but also for what was implied.

Replay the scene a second or third time, if necessary, until you can feel your body responding. You may feel your jaw tighten, your eyes sting with tears, your breathing change, distress in your stomach or other physical signs indicating that a feeling is present. Try to give form or substance to that physical sensation, perhaps as a knot in your throat, a rock in your stomach or a hand squeezing your heart. Do your best to identify and name the feeling. If you have trouble, begin narrowing it down by deciding in which category it fits: anger, fear or sadness.

What would that child have liked to have said had she been allowed to speak from her heart? If that little person could only say *one* sentence but it came right from her heart, what would that sentence be? Sit with any feelings that may be present for as long as it takes to allow those feelings expression. Do not

shut them down early. Do not minimize what happened; "awfulize" it. Give the feelings permission to literally take over your body for just a moment.

Now, shift your perspective and become your adult self who enters the scene. Have nothing change except that you are now present as an adult who can champion, protect and speak for this child. Stand at the doorway and watch what is happening. If you do not have a feeling reaction, imagine that the child were your daughter, niece or some other child who is important to you. If this same scene were being played out on that child, what would your feeling reaction be? If your feelings intensify, it shows you the degree to which you have had to discount your own feelings and put them away.

Approach the little child and allow her to express any feelings she may have to you. Make her feel safe enough and protected enough to share her feelings.

As an adult, speak up for the child to the person who needs to be addressed. It is much more effective if you can do this out loud. Express any anger you may feel. Give yourself permission to fully express that anger by pounding a pillow. You do not need to imagine pounding on the person in your imagery if that makes you uncomfortable. Instead, you can imagine you are pounding on a table or counter for emphasis as you talk. *Do not stop* until you feel the intensity and depth of your feelings are fully expressed. Then, ask the child if she would like you to say or do anything else. Follow her directions to the letter. When you feel everything has been accomplished that needed attention in this situation, take the child and leave. Always spend a moment expressing your commitment to and love for this child. You may want to ask her how you can best take care of her and what she needs from you. End this exercise when the child feels safe and loved by you and when the experience seems complete for the two of you.

EXERCISE
BODY IMAGING

Body imaging can be used to literally go looking for trouble. Again, to participate in this exercise, you will have to actually DO it instead of just thinking it through, which would be of no earthly assistance.

Close your eyes. Take time to totally relax and draw your attention inward. Imagine that you have a tiny, internal observer who is perched on a glass-enclosed elevator located right in the center of your head. For a moment, become that internal observer and look around the inside of your head. Use your senses to anchor yourself in the experience by noting shapes, colors, size and other qualities or textures around you. Touch the inside of the elevator. Listen for sounds or check for smells.

Take a peek into the left side of your brain. What do you see there? Be very specific in describing it so that you can either draw it or write about it later. Is it anatomically correct or is it represented to you symbolically? How big or small is it? What colors predominate? Does it appear clear or hazy? Is it an open space or broken up? Does there appear to be anything in the space? If so, how would you describe it? Is it light or dark on that side? Is it warm, cozy and inviting or cold, stark and inhospitable? What is your reaction to what you see? Do you like it or not? Is there anything that you see that is troubling, upsetting or in any way a concern to you? If so, just take note of that. If you could change what you see in any way, what would you want to do, if anything?

Next, turn and look into the right side of your brain and repeat the whole procedure. Take all the time you need to make a thorough evaluation of this side of your brain. Take note of anything that is of concern to you. Then compare and contrast the two sides of your brain. Which feels more like home base to you? Which is of greater concern to you? Later, when the exercise is completed, you can enter a dialogue with either side of your brain, or with anything that you have seen in there, by using the nondominant hand procedure (see page 202).

Now, look to see if there is a method for traveling between the two sides of the brain or if there is any obstacle that impedes communication or travel between the two sides. Take note of what you see.

When you are ready, allow the elevator to begin a slow descent through the center of your body. As you reach each important organ, pause the elevator and evaluate that body part from the inside. Begin with your eyes, your ear canals, your jaw, mouth, throat and any other body parts that may elicit your attention. How is each represented to you? Look at each body part carefully, note your reaction to it and note anything that indicates it is not in perfect condition. When you find a part that is troubling to you, take careful note of your reactions and your feelings and be perfectly clear in your mind what is causing you concern. Bring the exercise to a close for now by returning your attention to the world outside your body. Become more aware of the room in which you are sitting and, when you are ready, slowly open your eyes. Later, you can repeat the exercise looking for other parts of your body that need attention or appear in some way to be problematic.

Take the time to write a description or sketch the body part that is of concern. You can work with this material in many ways. You can treat it in imagery in the manner I just described for working with the rock in the stomach or you can use the nondominant hand technique described on page 202. The important thing is to recognize that your subconscious is communicating with you through its own language of symbols. It is up to you to pay attention and work with what is being provided to you. The exercise Body Imaging is another example of using imagery to look for hidden feelings in your body.

Figure 10-1

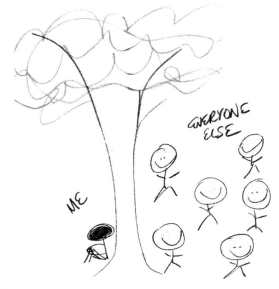

Figure 10-2

Figure 10-3

Many times in doing a body-scan imagery with a client, a problem is discovered in the larynx or voice box. That is because so often the voice was silenced early in life when it came to speaking up for oneself or speaking personal truth. It is always interesting to see what is inside that voice "box." If, in your own body scan, you come across any body part that may have an interior, be sure to take a trip inside and have a look around. Places like the inside of your voice box or your heart are great hiding places for things that were put away very early, including your own Core Self or spirit. Sometimes you will find memories or feelings stored or imprisoned in a body part. Or, you may just find a little child. You may remember Paula found her inner child in her neck, frozen in granite like a fossil. As you work with what you find, be sure to acknowledge any feelings that arise and give them full expression.

Those who are Thinking types will want to analyze and give opinions rather than have feelings. It is the Thinking type's very nature and it goes against their natural methods of coping to identify and express feelings. Fight the strong pull towards analysis. It has been said that "analysis is paralysis" and it is true. Analyzing the imagery will only keep you stuck in it.

Used properly, imagery is a very powerful, very effective tool for healing.

Art Therapy

Using simple creative expression can be extremely helpful in accessing and manifesting feelings. Simply provide yourself with a large tablet of newsprint and a box of crayons and you are on your way. Always keep in mind that the purpose is the process and not the product. It does not matter if you draw like Renoir or simply employ stick figures. No one will see it. It is only for you so it does not matter if it is even recognizable to anyone else. It is especially important for those who possess the Enneagram One or Three defense to be careful to resist focusing on the product. Ones need to do everything perfectly and Threes need to look good. Consciously give yourself permission to just play without any regard to the outcome.

You have seen examples of simple crayon drawings throughout this book. I am including some additional examples to show how the simplest rendering can clearly represent internal programming. In figure 10-1, Sylvia, the ISTJ-6 referred to in chapter 9, depicted how it felt to her as a child to have enormous responsibilities dumped upon her by both parents. Julia, the INFJ-1 in chapter 2, drew how she felt whenever a sense of not belonging overpowered her (figure 10-2). The picture in figure 10-3 shows how Julia felt as a child in relationship to her father. Drawings such as these are meant to evoke feelings that provide access to the programming. After using the drawing to elicit a feeling, we can use any of a number of tools, including imagery, to change the programming. In Sylvia's case, the programming needing change was the deeply ingrained sense that she had to carry all that responsibility in order to earn her parents' love. With Julia, the programming was a firmly held belief that she was innately flawed and defective. Other people *made* mistakes. Julia felt she *was* a mistake and that no matter how hard she tried, she would never be good enough to fit in anywhere with anyone. In both cases, the drawings provided access to those programs and the opportunity to change them.

Another use of art in the healing process is shown in figures 10-4a and 10-4b, first seen in chapter 6. Denise, ENFP-4, shows how her self-concept changed from the beginning of her healing journey to the end. In the very beginning, when I asked Denise to draw herself as a child, she produced the drawing in figure 10-4a. After a lot of hard work facing issues she never wanted to confront, Denise filled her black hole with her own soul as she proceeded along her healing journey. When asked to draw her inner child at this point, she presented the happy child in figure 10-4b. Denise's drawings illustrate how artwork is helpful to monitor progress.

Another use of art is to help make the unconscious conscious. Kyla's drawings of the perfect mom, the mom she had and the mom she was most afraid to have, were presented in figure 9-7, page 184. The same purpose was served in Darlene's drawings of her three

Figure 10-4a

Figure 10-4b

dads shown in figure 9-8, page 185. These drawings helped call attention to issues that needed to be addressed but that these women were not eager to confront.

Drawing is not the only medium used in art healing work. Any creative art project that works for you is wonderful. Collage is a marvelous method of accessing feelings and uncovering information. You can use any topic that comes to mind for a collage:

- My family
- Me and my mom/dad
- My feelings
- Everything that is in my heart
- My first ten years
- My teenage years
- My future (choose this topic after doing healing work)

Collage can be either two- or three-dimensional. You can use poster board or foam core. You can either cover the surface with paper or fabric or leave it plain. You can use found objects such as buttons, twigs, string, yarn, shells, straw, nails, screws, odd pieces from games or anything you find in a junk drawer. You can cut pictures or words from magazines, or shapes from construction paper. Use white glue or spray adhesive to adhere the pieces to the surface. After you have finished, do not just put it away out of sight. Look at your collage daily because each day you will be able to see more information supplied by your subconscious.

Clay is another splendid medium for healing work, because you can work with it to express a feeling. One way of doing this is to create the symbol of your feeling, such as the rock in the stomach suggested previously. Or you can let your hands and the clay express a feeling in any way that feels right. You can put on some music and close your eyes while you work with the clay. See how you feel and see what shapes appear in the clay. Remember, what matters is process not product. You can depict what your heart feels like in clay. You can reproduce your wounded inner child, or you can represent what it feels like when you hold her and she feels safe and loved. The very best suggestion is to ask your inner child what she would like to make with the clay and let her do it. You simply need to get out of the way.

Clay is very good for anger work as well. Throwing the clay against a board or punching a large block of clay can feel very satisfying. Making the face of someone who has hurt you and expressing anger in any way that feels appropriate is a good way to bring that feeling to the surface. Anger is not bad, it is not a sin and it is not a character flaw. It is simply an emotion and should be treated like any other emotion. Its purpose is to gain your attention and help you access your programming.

Oil painting, touch painting, watercolor, finger painting, charcoal, chalk, pastels, colored pencils or any other medium is equally as good. Do not limit yourself. Walk through an art supply store or the arts-and-crafts section of a toy store and let your inner child guide you in your selection.

If you have a trusted person who supports your healing work, share your art with that person, explaining what you have done. Ask that person not to comment on the artistic merit of the work but simply to listen to your explanation and tell you what he/she sees that you may have missed. Ask that person to explain the work as if that person had created it and you may get some other insights. If you do not know why something appears in your work, you can dialogue with that object

using the nondominant hand method and simply ask the object what it is dong in your work. Let your non-dominant hand answer. DO NOT THINK; just write.

Nondominant Hand Dialoguing

Use of your nondominant hand in writing and drawing is a magical and amazing method of working with feelings and subconscious material. It helps to facilitate communication between cognition and spirit. This healing tool can go a long way towards closing the gap between the two sides of the brain. It is a very effective way to restore control to the adult (cognition) after being triggered when the wounded child jumps into control with all her old coping tricks. Nondominant hand dialoguing allows you to re-parent your inner child and is an excellent method of accessing your Higher Wisdom without getting bogged down in "shoulds" and old programming. Lucia Capacchione's works, particularly *The Power of Your Other Hand*, give excellent instruction in this simple yet highly effective technique.

Again, it is not necessary to understand the latest theories in brain research on the topic of "handedness" or to have a working knowledge of anatomy, physiology and neurology. Just pick up a writing utensil in your nondominant hand without trying to comprehend why this method works; simply accept that it does. The nondominant hand will always write for the subconscious part, the feeling part, the hurt part or any part you have trouble accessing. The dominant hand will write for your cognitive part.

When writing with the nondominant hand, use paper large enough so that you do not have to constrict your work but can just let it flow. Use two different colors of pencils, pens or crayons and a pad of newsprint. Put the color representing your cognitive, adult self in your dominant hand and the color representing the part with which you want to dialogue in your nondominant hand. Using this method, you can have a conversation with your inner child, with a feeling, dream symbol, body part, defense trait, disease, physical ailment or any other part not accessible through consciousness. The reason for using the nondominant hand is to keep the left brain occupied with simply constructing the letters, the very act of writing. Furthermore, if you are right-handed, your nondominant hand is controlled by the right side of your brain where feelings and programming are stored.

It is important that you *do not* stop and think before writing with the nondominant hand. That totally defeats the purpose, which is to circumvent the thinking, logical left brain. If the left brain is operational, there is a real danger of knowledge getting in the way of wisdom. Once you begin writing, keep the pen, pencil or crayon moving, even if you have to repeat the same word or words. Then continue writing past the point where you feel like stopping. Force yourself to write another paragraph or page. This is when you have cleared yourself of the reserve of garbage left over from your left brain and have reached a place of emptiness. Into this emptiness will come information and feelings that defy explanation. This work does not happen easily. It takes effort, commitment and dedication. The insights, awarenesses and new perspectives that follow come from a place that is generally ignored but rich in substantial healing material, often accompanied by childlike pure emotion.

You may enhance and augment your work with art. Allow your nondominant hand to draw the part that has just spoken. Around the drawing, list the feelings that are making themselves known during this exercise. Then, you can read your work out loud and listen for the child's voice within yours. Do not be surprised at spelling or grammatical errors. This is only evidence that you are indeed working from the right side of the brain and have accessed the "nonlogical" part. Sometimes you will be forced to look at things you have tried to avoid, such as the "listen up" examples presented in chapter 7. Julia, INFJ-1, presents an example of dialoguing with an addiction. Julia has struggled with a relationship addiction for years and now has it under control. She has assigned the addiction a name, Nikki, and envisions her to represent her late teens. In this example, Julia is simply touching base with her

addictive part, using her nondominant hand to stay on top of things.

JULIA:

Nikki, How are you doing?

NIKKI:

Okay. I'm tired. Lonely too. I want to go on a weekend retreat away from here. I want to do art. I want Chuck to write. I want some excitement in my life.

JULIA:

I know you do, Nikki. I think, however, excitement also equals stress. Don't we have enough stress right now?

NIKKI:

Yeah. I'm just lonely.

JULIA:

I know. Is there anything you need from me?

NIKKI:

I guess just to take it as easy as possible, to maybe call a friend later. To eat healthy and drink lots of water. To rest from 3–4 p.m. Thanks for letting me talk.

JULIA:

You're welcome.

Art and nondominant hand dialoguing give expression to feelings locked in the subconscious. Julia began looking at her own history cautiously. She had some sense there was sexual abuse by her father. She drew a picture that indicated there was considerable shame being carried by her inner child (figure 10-5). Those accusing her are dark and the fingers pointing at her look suspiciously like penises.

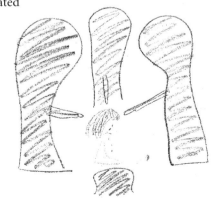

Figure 10-5

Then, Julia drew her inner child (figure 10-6) who was trying to get a message through to her. Expressing the feelings accessed in her healing work, Julia wrote a letter to her father using her nondominant hand:

Figure 10-6

> *Dear Father,*
>
> *You are a liar. You did not take my best interests into account. If you call what you gave me care, I'd hate to see neglect. I am strong. I am good. I'm a lot of positive things. Few of them I inherited from you. Rather, your abuse of me has only strengthened me. You can never hurt me again. Never! You are not my dad. You are my biological father. I make no excuses for my life either. I owe you* NOTHING! *Do not contact me* ANY MORE!

After considerable time and work, particularly with imagery, Julia struggled through her sexual abuse issues. With her nondominant hand, her inner child talked to her:

> *Dear Julia,*
>
> *I love you. Thank you 4 believing me. Thank you 4 hearing me. Please don't 4get about me. I don't want to die.*
>
> > *Love,*
> >
> > *Julia*

Julia is a good example of using a variety of tools to do healing work. Julia effectively combined imagery, art, nondominant hand journaling and another compelling tool, music, which will be explored next. There will be other examples of nondominant hand dialoguing in the next chapter as Reilley's inner child tries to get her to accept her early sexual abuse.

Even after people have completed therapy and the "official" healing part of their journey, many continue to use nondominant hand writing as their method of journaling because it keeps the channel of communication open between the two sides of the brain, between the conscious and subconscious. Whatever is unattended in the subconscious has a great deal of power to run your life. This method of journaling will uncover unrecognized feelings such as those in Darlene's dialogue (chapter 7) regarding her father's grave. You can enter into a dialogue with your inner child easily by placing a drawing or photograph of her before you and asking simple open-ended questions:

How are you today?

What's going on?

What can I do for you today?

Tell me who or what is upsetting you lately?

What do you think about what happened with _____?

How can I better protect you?

What would you like to do today just for fun?

Or my favorite: Whom can I beat up for you?

Throughout the healing journey, we are continually showing the wounded child that there are new, more effective ways of dealing with the hurt and pain she experienced and the feelings that have been trapped within. Using nondominant hand dialoguing helps to expand awareness beyond the child's experience in order to present new ways of handling stressful situations. Many left-brained Myers-Briggs Type Indicator Thinking types, or Enneagram Head-Center types, spend a lot of energy pondering how to figure things out logically when, in fact, using both sides of the brain provides a much broader perspective.

Kyla, the INFP-3 whose story is given in chapter 6, demonstrates another use of this technique. Part of Kyla's healing work revolved around her father's death when she was eleven years old and the guilt she felt at not being able to prevent it. Kyla did the core work around this incident, removing the guilt from her inner child and allowing her and her wounded eleven-year-old inner child to grieve. It then became possible to establish her father as a wisdom figure and source of comfort. This was accomplished using nondominant hand dialoguing:

Dear Dad

    I really need a lot of help. I am making some bad choices and I'm so afraid. Daddy please help! Please! I feel ashamed of myself —Are you there?

Dear Kyla

    I lv U. Please be good to yourself. You are loved. I am not ashamed of you. You have been hurt, that's OK.

Dear Dad

    Will you be here with me to help? I really need for you to be….

Dear Kyla

    I'm here, Honey. I'll always be here.

This initial dialogue began a journaling technique that Kyla has continued to use when she needs advice, comfort and direction. She finds herself calmed and centered by using her father to tap into her own Higher Power and to experience the continuing, now-pure love of her father that sustains her long after his death. Sometimes people will simply write directly to God expressing confusion, anger, sadness or the need for guidance. The nondominant hand can provide access to clear and loving counsel.

MUSIC THERAPY

Music has a powerful and magical way of accessing and affecting emotions; it enters deeply into the human emotional experience. Just listen to a Sousa march, the theme from *Rocky* or the march from *Aida* and you will find you cannot help but respond. Why do the shopping malls start playing Christmas carols right after Halloween? The marketing people know it affects people psychologically and puts them in a mood to buy. Movies have a musical soundtrack to heighten the emotional experience of the movie. Whether we are aware of the effect or not, the music is designed to take us on an emotional journey. Starry-eyed suitors use romantic, intense and/or erotic music to set the tone for a lovers' tryst. Music at weddings, such as *Sunrise, Sunset*, is guaranteed to tap into emotions and elicit tears.

Relaxing music can be used to ease physical and emotional pain, release endorphins, lower blood pressure and heart rate and act as a sedative. Emotionally charged music can access intense feelings and aid in bringing them to the surface. Listening to soul-wrenching blues, Janis Ian singing "At Seventeen," or classical music such as *La Traviata* will lead to sad feelings when these feelings cannot be accessed consciously. Music can circumvent defense barriers that seem to resist all other methods, triggering memories and feelings that heretofore have been locked tightly away. Music bypasses the conscious, cognitive mind causing a response below the conscious level, defying analysis because the response to music resides in the right brain.

Unbeknownst to us, our earliest experiences involve music—the music of womb sounds. The rhythmic beating of a mother's heart, the rushing sound of breath being taken in and released, the sounds of blood moving through the placenta combined with the rhythm of peristalsis and other organ functions provide our first symphony. Listen to a tape of womb sounds such as *Music to Help Baby Sleep*, and you will find yourself relaxing before long to sounds that are recognized and greeted at a very deep level. Soothing sounds of the ocean evoke memories of these early experiences. After birth, we go on to make our very own biological music.

For our purposes, it is not necessary to understand the theories of quantum physics and energy vibrations to explain why music has such a profound effect on us. All that is necessary is to recognize music for the powerful and effective tool that it is and utilize it accordingly.

Just as with imagery, the music you use in your

EXERCISE
MUSIC

Choose a piece of music that feels right for you. Find a comfortable place where you can be undisturbed. Listen to the music once or twice, giving yourself permission to move into the feelings associated with the piece. Once you have accessed the hidden feeling, be aware of how it presents itself in your body. Then, while listening to the music again, gently close your eyes and think of when you felt that way as a child. Get a good sense of that child and look at the circumstances that caused her to feel that way. Allow her to fully express those feelings. As your adult self, encourage the child in the expression of her feelings and join her. After it feels as though the experience is complete and the feeling has been totally released,

move to the second *A* and *affirm* the child. Tell her that you understand why she has those feelings. With heartfelt sincerity, validate her completely. At this point, play a piece of music that symbolizes your love for and commitment to her, such as a selection from Shana Noll's *Songs for the Inner Child* or any song that seems to convey your heart's message to the child. If you prefer instrumentals, much of Stephen Halpern's music, such as *Nurturing Your Inner Child*, will be appropriate. I find many affirming songs in the children's section of a music shop. Lullabies are wonderful. It is very relaxing and healing to go to sleep at night listening to a lullaby while you image holding your inner child.

---

healing journey should be selected for and by you. If you need to access anger, choose music that will help with that task. If you have deep sadness, grief and pain, choose songs that embody and reflect the way you feel. If you feel alone and lost, find songs that touch that aching loneliness. You can find your music from popular songs, classical pieces or music designed for Inner-Child work such as Richard Wagner's *Remember the Child.*

Often people will tell me that they do not care to use music in such a way because they do not want to feel sad, lonely, angry or any other difficult emotion. My response is, "It's too late. You already have that feeling. You simply need to become consciously aware of it." Before you can work with what is happening to you on a subconscious level, you have to become aware of it. The first step of the "new AA" is to *acknowledge* the feeling (see Music exercise).

Another way to employ music is through dance. Instead of sitting and passively listening to a piece of music, try dancing the feeling that it evokes. Put aside embarrassment or feelings of being self-conscious or dance-challenged. This is only for you. It is not a

performance: it is a healing process. If you have a doll or a pet that will oblige you, dance with it as a stand-in for your inner child. Always feel free to sing along with the music, singing from your heart, not as a performance but as an expression of your soul. Change the lyrics, if necessary, to suit you better.

In chapter 9, I suggested that you might have more than one ego state or child. If, like many people, you find you have three major ego states, you might connect with Sinead O'Connor's song, "Three Babies." You may want to choose a theme song for each of the kids or ego states you uncover. That way, you can use the music to quickly access the ego state with which you wish to work.

Music can make a tremendous contribution to the healing process. I encourage you to use it profusely in your healing journey.

COMBINED APPROACHES

When several approaches are combined, the effectiveness of each is enhanced. A multi-faceted strategy increases the chances that you will circumnavigate your Defense System which is capable of developing tactics to block a single approach. The ten-step exercise below is a synthesis of some of the techniques described so far. This combination of several tools can help you work through a difficult or upsetting recent situation. Follow each of the steps through even though some may seem very basic and unimportant. Each step puts you closer to gaining access to your programming and changing it. As always, thinking through the exercise will not be helpful.

EXERCISE

TEN STEPS TO PROCESS A TRIGGERING INCIDENT

1. In your journal, describe a situation in which you were triggered. If you do not know what triggered you but simply felt troubled, go on to the next step.

2. Where in your body did you experience the feelings? Be very specific and thorough.

3. Draw a stick figure showing where you felt this sensation.

4. Acknowledge and name the feelings. Compose an exhaustive list.

5. Close your eyes and imagine a time when you were a child and you felt the same feelings, using your body feelings to guide you. Do not analyze it or think about it. *Stay out of your head.*

6. Draw that child, depicting how she felt. Be as detailed as you can.

7. Together with the child express the feelings: i.e. do anger work or express the sadness and the like for *both* the here-and-now incident and for what happened to the child. Thinking about having the feeling or analyzing why you had the feeling will not help.

8. Using nondominant hand dialoguing, ask the child what she needs from you, what she wants to hear, what she would like you to do, or if she has any other suggestions. Try to dialogue back and forth as long as you possibly can. Try to stay out of your head and *stay in your heart.*

9. Affirm the child. You can write to her telling her positive things; imagine holding her in your arms at your safe house and telling her you understand, you are there, she is good, she deserved more—and anything else you feel is appropriate and applicable. Be sure these things are *true* and *from the heart.* Use the MBTI trait list for your type to give you some ideas of good and affirming things you can tell this child that are true about herself. Reading the chapter that describes your MBTI type as a child in *Nurture By Nature,* by Tieger and Barron-Tieger, will furnish you with a better understanding of this child and with new ways in which to affirm her.

10. Play music that helps you to access your feelings for this child. Use touch to connect with the child: touch her in imagery, touch her photograph or touch a drawing of her. In imagery, feel what her body, face, hair and skin are like to your touch. Send messages to her through touch, with words and by a beam of light from your heart to hers.

This exercise employs imagery, art, music and nondominant hand dialoguing. It is designed to help you process any situation from the loss of a favorite object to the death of a loved one, from anger at the neighbor's dog to anger over violent abuse.

Whenever you feel a sense of disquiet within, it is a signal from your body alerting you to get in touch with your soul. No feeling is too small or insignificant. In this way, you integrate mind, body and spirit, restoring peace and a sense of wholeness.

JOURNALING

Journaling is another tool that can help you turn your focus within, exploring the depths of yourself and avoiding the temptation to look for an external wisdom source. There are many ways of journaling, all of which can be helpful in a healing process. The least effective method is a "Dear Diary" approach simply chronicling your life and achievements because it is a static exercise which keeps you completely on the left side of the brain. Julia Cameron, in her excellent work, *The Artist's Way,* insists on three pages of stream-of-consciousness writing each morning to clear the mind of the myriad details and static that impede us from accessing our creativity and deeper wisdom. That is a good beginning but it is important to fill that cleared space with something substantial that will move you further along your healing path.

Another method of journaling is to choose an emotionally charged topic and begin writing without thinking. The important thing is to not stop when you think you have finished but to push yourself to write more, milking it for all it's worth. Here are some topic suggestions for using this method, but you can certainly substitute anything that strikes a chord with you:

I wish . . .

I sometimes worry about . . .

It hurts when . . .

It is scariest for me when . . .

If only . . .

I can get very sad about . . .

I can feel very safe when . . .

More than anything, I . . .

Whenever I think about . . .

My biggest fear is . . .

I feel loved when . . .

I never felt so rejected as when . . .

The black hole within me looks like . . .

I feel so hopeless when . . .

When I think of my inner child . . .

I feel most alone when . . .

Today, I was most touched when . . .

My heart is filled with . . .

Carrying my secret of _____ is so hard because . . .

Things could be different if . . .

The scar that I am afraid may never heal is . . .

Today, I found my strength in . . .

My greatest delight is when . . .

If I had it to do over again, I would . . .

I learned an important thing about myself when . . .

I see my strongest gift each time . . .

I wish with all my heart that . . .

(Name of person), who saw who I am, saw that . . .

My life would have been different if . . .

My life could still be different if . . .

If you write about any of these topics long enough, you will begin to notice some feelings arising within you. Your body will let you know. Seize the opportunity! Use the ten-step exercise on page 207 to process those feelings and move further along your healing journey. You have been frozen, numbed-out and so disconnected from the wellspring of your being for so long that you owe it to yourself to use every opportunity to reconnect to your own Core Self.

In healing childhood wounds, another journaling method is writing letters to your parents or other primary caregivers. Again, the purpose is to elicit emotions that have been tucked away. When these feelings have been locked away, fragments of the self are stored away with them. When you release these feelings, you reclaim a lost part of yourself. As a child, one woman collected brightly colored pieces of glass in an old coffee can which her mother promptly discarded. The little girl would simply begin her quest again. As an adult, she knows she was searching for the lost pieces of herself. There cannot be a sense of wholeness and integration as long as you feel fragmented, with parts of you locked tightly away. Use every opportunity to follow a feeling, like following the yellow brick road to the Emerald City. It is the only way home.

When writing letters to parents or other primary caregivers, you can write on any topic that feels right to you. If you are at a loss as to how to begin, here are some suggestions:

Dear _____,

I needed . . .

I had to be _____ for you because you . . .

I needed to hear . . .

My assignments from you were . . .

I'm most angry because . . .

You really hurt me when . . .

I'll no longer let you . . .

These are your issues/baggage; I'm giving them back to you by . . .

I remember when . . .

The worst part of my childhood was . . .

You should have . . .

I wish you could have . . .

I only felt safe when . . .

I wanted . . .

As a child, I sometimes thought that . . .

I did not know then, but I know now that . . .

If only you could have . . .

I wonder if I will ever know . . .

I am most angry with you for . . .

I wonder what it would have been like if . . .

The saddest day/time of my childhood was when . . .

The scariest day/time of my childhood was when . . .

When I think about the time you . . .

If I had the chance to tell you just one thing, I would want you to know . . .

I am tired of carrying secrets such as . . .

My biggest regret in our relationship is . . .

To have grown up whole, I needed . . .

I can no longer allow you to . . .

You place me in a position of choosing between you and my inner child when you . . .

Another variety of journaling, developed by Ira Progoff, is called the *Intensive Journal*®. Dr. Progoff's method of journaling takes a Jungian approach and recognizes the need to move beyond cognition to a deeper place where wisdom resides. Using the Progoff method is another way to gain further awareness, access feelings and old programming and examine your own inner processing. This method seeks to establish a continuing relationship or dialogue between the conscious and unconscious, bringing new levels of awareness and insights. It is a very effective tool for self-exploration to use in your healing journey. The best way to learn this method of journaling is by attending a workshop, given nationwide, where you can learn experientially and receive support. If that is not practical, you can work alone with Dr. Progoff's book, *At a Journal Workshop.*

BODY WORK

There has long been an emphasis in our culture to consider healing, both physical and emotional, only from a left-brain perspective. That perspective is embodied in the framework of modern medical technology. Every *dis*-ease is considered pathologically and attacked with pills, surgery or both. It is time for balance. The right-brain perspective takes an approach that considers other methods of healing, such as working with body energy, as all matter and all life is energy. These methods are not always quantifiable, but that does not mean they are not effective and appropriate. Looking at healing simply from within the medical model is *extremely* limiting and, in many cases, no longer serves. A nonlinear, holistic approach which includes body, mind and spirit is the only approach that truly makes sense. The nonphysical, nonvisible, subjective and nonquantifiable must be considered as seriously as the physical, visible, objective and measurable. Gifted and wise people such as authors Jeanne Achterberg and Rachel Naomi Remen, and Capacitar's Pat Cane, are making important contributions in this field.

Much has been written on the topic of the mind, body, spirit connection and interaction. There are many resources available for you to pursue this topic far beyond the scope of this section. Suffice it to say that to ignore the body in pursuing your healing journey keeps you fragmented and ignores a source of much information, direction and wisdom. Moving into the body shifts the focus from your mind, where most of your attention has been directed, and encourages balance. Whether you partake in hands-on modalities such as therapeutic massage or modalities that work with body energy such as Healing Touch, body work is exceedingly beneficial.

Each cell in our bodies, although specialized in some way, holds the entire genetic code necessary to reproduce us. Furthermore, each cell stores memories and emotions. Various types of body work can direct your attention to the places where these are stored and facilitate their release. Many survivors of sexual abuse and other types of violence have places on their bodies that, when touched, will release a sudden flood of emotions—anger, terror, betrayal or whatever feelings were present when the abuse first happened. Working with the body will help locate these somatic triggers so they can be used to work through the original abuse.

Often those who have been most abused are least in touch with their bodies. This is precisely because memories are stored in every cell of our bodies. When awakened, body memories trigger feelings that have been locked away for many years. Sometimes, in order to survive, it is imperative that a child does not feel anything, physically or emotionally. When that survival technique works, it is gratefully carried into adulthood, effectively blocking access to the very feeling work that will aid in healing. When asked to describe what a body sensation feels like, these people give a visual description because they are unable to allow themselves any kinesthetic experiences.

Body awareness, listening to what your body is telling you, keeps you in the present. Most of us have a difficult time staying in the present moment, either projecting into the future or reliving the past. The more you develop body awareness, the more you will be able to truly experience and enjoy every moment of your life. You will be present enough to see all the things you have been missing heretofore.

Connecting with your own body energy helps you to connect to the energy of the Universe. It becomes easier to see your relationship with others, with the earth and with a Higher Power. There are many different modalities of body work. Becoming more consciously aware of what is happening in your body is essential and highly

beneficial, whichever modality is used. Many enjoy a body movement modality such as Tai Chi. Others prefer a hands-on experience such as massage, reflexology, acupressure or acupuncture. Other methods of working with body energy are Reike, Healing Touch, Therapeutic Touch, Polarity, Yoga, as well as many others. It is not important which manner of body work you investigate, it is only important to get in touch with your body and make the mind, body, spirit connection.

BREATH WORK AND MEDITATION

Awareness of breathing furnishes a great deal of information and is helpful in accessing and releasing stored feelings and memories. If you monitor yourself carefully, you will notice that when you are "in danger" of expressing a feeling, you will begin to hold your breath, thereby holding back the feeling. Research is being done to correlate various patterns of breathing and holding the breath with the different Enneagram Defense types. Becoming more and more aware of your breathing can be helpful in providing you with a method of flagging your attention when a feeling is present. If you notice that you are holding your breath, breathing more rapidly or breathing shallowly, you can be assured that a feeling is lurking nearby. When that happens, breathe deliberately into the feeling while you give yourself permission to identify and have the feeling, allowing it to run its natural course.

Breath work, like any technique that will move the center of attention out of the head and into the body, is beneficial. Breath work will unblock energy, memories and feelings. Concentrating on following your breath will also keep you in the present so that you do not spend your energy worrying about what might happen in the future. See Breath Work exercise on page 211.

By concentrating on your breath and making it visible with the use of light, you can inventory your body, taking note of where tension, tightness or pain is located. This information can be used by any of the techniques mentioned in this chapter such as imagery, art or nondominant hand dialoguing to unlock the reasons for the tension and release any emotions stored there. Instead of using light, you can imagine breathing in peace, love, healing, God, a color or any other quality that will bring you comfort and serenity.

If you find breath work to be helpful and would like to do more extensive work through this technique, there are many different modalities of using the breath for inner work. Talk to trained professionals in the field of breath work to determine which type of breath work is best for you, and work with a competent professional you feel comfortable with and you can trust.

There are any number of books and tapes on methods and styles of meditation. The style you choose is not important. What is important is that you use meditation to move out of your head, to get beyond words and images, to a state of mindlessness where you are only conscious of your body and your inner self. The information and awarenesses you gather in such a state of mindlessness can be enormously helpful in your healing work.

EXERCISE

BREATH WORK

Take a moment to experience following your breath. Close your eyes as you direct your attention to your breath. You might imagine that you are breathing in pure white light. With every breath, watch and feel the light as it enters your body and is absorbed into your very being. Breathe into the tight places in your body and imagine the light penetrating the tension and releasing it. With each breath, draw the light deeper and deeper into your body. Watch, feel and totally experience the effect that your breath and the light have as they are drawn into every part of your body.

Let the tension and tightness that is released by your breath flow out of your body through your fingertips and out the bottom of your feet. You might imagine you have little drains on the bottom of your feet and the tension is draining out and "puddling" on the floor. If you feel any pain in any part of your body, send a double dose of light to that area until you can feel the pain diminish. Take your time breathing into every part of your body, one part at a time.

Imagine that you have an internal observer who can see the light move into every area of your body. When you have drawn the light all the way down to your toes, imagine that your internal observer is positioned in your feet and can look up, through the inside of your body, from your toes to your head. Let that internal observer direct the light to any areas that are still in need of attention.

Keep following your breath until you feel it flowing freely throughout your body, permeating every part. Then watch and feel the light as it is absorbed deeply into your muscles, tendons, bones and internal organs. Take all the time you need to watch and feel this happen.

Then, watch and feel as the light you breathe in is absorbed on the cellular level. When you can feel the light in every cell of your body, watch and feel it penetrate through every molecule and atom until even the tiniest places within you are filled with the light you have breathed in.

Allow yourself to remain in this state of relaxation and peace as long as you like. When you redirect your attention to the outside world, bring with you the feelings of peace and relaxation that you experienced as well as any information about various parts of your body that you may have picked up during the exercise. When you are ready to complete the exercise, draw your attention to the feel of the chair you are sitting in, listen for any sounds in the room, touch the fabric of your clothing, take one last cleansing breath and gently open your eyes.

In addition to aiding in body-awareness, meditation and breath work have the added benefit of directing your attention *inward* and away from any external authority or wisdom figure. We are trained to look for answers outside ourselves. All belief in our own Higher Wisdom is programmed out of us at a very early age. The use of meditation and breath work can help reverse the effects of those early messages. I would, however, encourage you not to use meditation and breath work as an end in themselves but as an instrument to aid in your healing work.

FOCUSING

There is a type of meditation called Focusing that I feel is particularly helpful because it incorporates body, mind and spirit. Focusing moves your attention out of your head and into your body, working with the body's own language, and encourages the identification of any feelings you may find there. Analyzing is discouraged and awareness encouraged. The information collected through Focusing is processed noncognitively. Focusing espouses the concept that it is not possible to accept and honor others or the environment until we reconnect with and honor ourselves. It is a gentle process because it allows you to move at your own speed, to choose which issues you wish to address, and does not force or control the outcome. In Focusing, you are encouraged to release and let go of control.

Focusing recognizes that feelings are the entrance to a deeper place of knowing and understanding. Because of that, you are encouraged to go into the feelings and body sensations rather than suppressing them, numbing them or otherwise avoiding them. The Focusing process acknowledges that simply experiencing a feeling is not quite enough. The feeling is only the vehicle by which a more important place can be reached. At the same time, Focusing recognizes the natural resistance that the Defense System offers in avoiding uncomfortable or painful memories and feelings. The process provides methods of dealing with the defense or the fear of addressing the primary feelings.

With Focusing, you are urged to be gentle with yourself and your feelings. Your feelings are not regarded as the enemy but rather as a God-provided part of yourself trying to furnish you with information and teach you. Focusing invites you to find a caring place within yourself to greet and own your feelings. Then you can determine what those feelings are telling you. Focusing affords something more than breath work and meditation because it furnishes a way of working with the feelings once they are uncovered. It recognizes that what needs attention is not located in the outside world but in how the person is interpreting the happenings in the outside world and, then, how those interpretations are being incorporated into the person's concepts of self, others and a Higher Power. Focusing recognizes the need to change the internal programming rather than the people, things or events that triggered that programming.

An added benefit of Focusing is that this technique fosters objectivity; it helps you to take a step back and gain a broader perspective, which will be helpful in working with any wounded inner parts. It is particularly appropriate when you have finished your core work and are looking for a method to help you monitor your feelings and stay on top of things before becoming overwhelmed by triggering agents. For more information, see the references at the end of this chapter.

NEURO LINGUISTIC PROGRAMMING (NLP)

Neuro Linguistic Programming (NLP) is a technique similar to others that have been described in this chapter in terms of examining behaviors and reactions in their original context or frame. To use NLP extensively requires the assistance of someone trained in the method. (However, once you have read this section, you can try the NLP exercise on page 213 as an example of what can be done with this method.)

The premise of NLP is that, in different context, the behaviors would be viewed differently. The idea is to bring a new way of looking at old patterns of reacting. NLP recognizes the need for defenses but also strives to replace outdated responses with more effective coping

NEURO LINGUISTIC PROGRAMMING

Let us suppose that fear of public speaking causes you great anxiety and you need to make a presentation at work next week. Identify how you would like to feel when you stand before your audience. Most likely, you would like to feel calm, in control and perfectly at ease. Now, think of a time when you felt that way. It can be under completely unrelated circumstances such as when you were sunbathing on a beach or floating on a raft.

Close your eyes and imagine being in the peaceful setting. Anchor yourself there using your five senses, staying in your body, until it feels like you are actually there. When you feel that completely, lightly squeeze the tip of your *left index finger* using your right hand. Continue your peaceful experience while lightly squeezing your finger for about a minute. Release your finger and let that scene fade.

Next imagine standing alone in front of a large audience that you are expected to address. Again, be sure to be in your body, where you can feel the fear and tension build. Thoughts of your presentation next week will most likely increase your fear. When you feel the fear, gently squeeze the tip of your *left middle finger* for about a minute.

While holding your middle finger and feeling the fear, let your body guide you to a time when you felt that way before. The circumstances can be different. It may be a time you struck out in little league or when you were late to school. It does not matter. It just has to be a time when you felt the very same way you feel when you have to speak publicly. When you have identified such a time, take note of it, and let your body guide you back to another. Do this a third time. Now you have three instances of these same fearful feelings. Release your middle finger.

Identify the common elements in each of these situations. Perhaps there was public humiliation in each instance or vulnerability, failure or criticism.

Examine each of the three instances and determine the common theme(s).

Next, start with the earliest experience and imagine entering the scene as the adult you are today. How can you make a difference? How can you best protect the younger version of yourself in your imagination? How can you best intervene to show the child that you have other resources and options? What can you specifically do to address the common theme in this particular situation? When you determine how you can best intervene, imagine how that would play out. When you have orchestrated a different and positive ending to this situation, squeeze the left index finger. As you go through each of the three incidents, end by squeezing the index finger when you have successfully intervened for the child.

After examining each of these situations individually, play them over again, one right after the other as if they led right into each other. At the end of each situation, when you have effectively changed the outcome for the better, press both your index and your middle finger for a few moments before releasing them and going on to the next situation.

After replaying all three scenes with new outcomes, release your fingers and take a few minutes to bond with the child. Take her to your safe house and tell the child there is no need for her to attend your presentation next week. She is welcome to stay at the safe house while you handle the public speaking.

Finally, imagine it is next week and you are about to make the presentation. Check to see that the child is comfortably stationed at her safe house. Then imagine addressing your audience while you gently squeeze your left index finger where you have installed a body memory of peace, calm and control. If there is the slightest degree of fear, repeat the entire exercise. When you feel comfortable making the presentation bring the exercise to a close and slowly open your eyes.

tools. The major contribution of NLP is that it brings a greater understanding and awareness of the information furnished by the body to help make the process more effective and efficient. In addition, NLP purposefully stores more appropriate and beneficial information and reactions in the body. These techniques are particularly useful in dealing with phobias and other fears that are out of proportion. Each of us generally has some phobia or fear that is out of proportion and, in some way, limits us. It may be fear of flying, fear of storms or the number one fear of all time: fear of public speaking.

Before beginning the NLP exercise on page 213, identify what your fear might be, then substitute it for the one used to illustrate the method. (Note: The places on your body where you choose to install "buttons" or anchors during this exercise are totally arbitrary. Select any two places that feel right for you.)

When you actually do stand up to make the presentation, you can gently squeeze your left index finger for a burst of peace, calm and control. If something untoward occurs during your talk that triggers the fear, again squeeze your finger while you are speaking and it will restore your calm.

Neuro Linguistic Programming is a fine and effective tool, especially in the hands of someone well trained in the techniques. It is a wonderful quick fix for phobias. It is also a terrific method to prepare yourself for difficult situations you will have to manage in the future.

If you know in advance that you will have to get through an uncomfortable event such as a court appearance, confronting someone or talking with your boss, the adult thing to do is to prepare yourself. Whether you use NLP in this preparation or not, be sure to *acknowledge* the fear-based feelings. Take a good look at the child who is well acquainted with those same feelings. Decide how you can best protect her in the upcoming situation. Talk with her and *affirm* her. Invite her to stay at your safe house while you handle whatever challenges face you. You can use the ten-step exercise outlined on page 207 to do a thorough job.

Adding NLP only increases your sense of well-being and a positive outcome.

DREAM WORK

The topic of dream work can easily be a book in itself. In fact, there are many excellent books available on the topic of working with your dreams. If you decide to explore this topic more in depth, choose books that will guide you in interpreting your own dreams, not interpret them for you.

Your dreams use the language of the subconscious and symbolism to communicate with you. Dreams have been important in every culture throughout the ages. For example, Hebrew scripture refers to dreams on many occasions. Refer to Genesis 41, in which Pharaoh has a dream filled with symbolism. Likewise, Ezekiel 37 presents not only the symbolism of the dream but also the interpretation.

Although dreams can be taken literally, it is generally accepted that they are usually presented on a symbolic level. So, if you have a dream that you ran over your mother-in-law with your car, although you might want to be a little more careful in your driving habits, it is most likely that you are running over what your mother-in-law symbolizes to you. However, should you have a dream regarding a potential health problem, you may want to check with your doctor as well as work with the dream on a symbolic level.

The symbolism presented in your dreams may be terribly disquieting, at times including violence, sex, embarrassing situations, indiscretions, eroticism and the like. Bracket your initial desire to suppress these types of dreams because they are an affront to your values or beliefs. Reassure yourself that what has been provided by your subconscious is to be interpreted symbolically and not necessarily literally.

Working with your dreams allows you to tap into the wealth of information about yourself that is hidden from your conscious knowledge. You have an opportunity to learn about hidden parts of yourself and see yourself from many different perspectives. You can work with each of these parts to get to know them

*Every person, every object, every event and every setting
in your dream is there for a reason. Your subconscious is the perfect
director of your dream and includes exactly what is needed
to elegantly convey the message.*

better, eliciting cooperation from warring parts and encouraging underdeveloped parts. You can receive direction from wisdom parts and information from parts that hold secrets.

Every person, every object, every event and every setting in your dream is there for a reason. Your subconscious is the perfect director of your dream and includes exactly what is needed to elegantly convey the message. Everything contained in your dream has symbolic value. It is up to you to work with what is presented in order to receive the messages.

Just as with Inner-Child work, dreams can be interpreted and worked with on many different levels. You can interpret them literally, symbolically, spiritually or in any other way that seems appropriate to you. You can interpret them as applying to the present moment, as direction for the future or as a clarification of past events. You can interpret them as they apply to you and the many parts of you. You can study them as they apply to your life in general. Or, you can understand them from a more global perspective as you tap into the collective unconscious, seeing your dreams as they may apply to the world at large. Dreams can help you resolve problems, give you direction, reveal potential and possibilities, warn you to change certain behaviors or your lifestyle, explain reactions to various people, eliminate confusion and allow you to better understand yourself and your purpose in life.

I urge you to keep a dream journal by your bedside and write down any dreams you are aware of having. You do not have to work with each and every one of them, but it is good to have them recorded in case you want to refer back to them. Dreams are very elusive. If you are aware that you are dreaming, do not wait until you awaken in the morning to notate the dream. Use a

penlight if there is someone in the room with you and write the dream down with as much detail as you can remember because the chances are excellent you will not remember the dream in the morning. If you wake in the morning after a dream, write it down before leaving your bed. As soon as you move, the dream begins to fade. It is good to keep all the details you possibly can because each one has significance. Be sure to take note of who was in the dream, what was happening, the setting, significant colors, what was said and by whom, the sequence of events and any feelings you had. If you wake with a piece of music in your head, take note of that as well.

Dreams can furnish you with creative solutions to your problems because your subconscious sees much more than your conscious mind. Furthermore, your subconscious is willing to look at distasteful solutions, outrageous solutions and other material your conscious mind has been trying to avoid.

If you are faced with a difficult decision or desire some kind of direction from a Higher Wisdom source, you can incubate, or program, a dream on that topic. You can do that by reviewing the situation thoroughly before you go to bed, including all the options available to you. Then formulate a one-line question on the topic. Concentrate on the question as you go to sleep. When the dream occurs, record it as thoroughly as possible, including as many details and symbols as you can remember. Later, you can work with the information provided.

Working with your dreams enhances and encourages your own creativity. Dreams are illogical and cannot be examined from a left-brained perspective. In your illogical dreams, all things are possible: elephants fly, you are older than your mother, dead people are

A nightmare is a dream that is merely trying to get your attention. The more you try to repress a nightmare because it is troubling, the greater the chances are that it will be repeated or that you will be given another variation.

alive again, you can swim across the ocean, you can drive down the highway without benefit of a car. The process of dream work sends you exploring the right side of your brain where creativity resides. Working with your own symbolism stretches your creativity muscles. Acknowledging and respecting your dreams encourages the subconscious to send you more, and the cycle of nurturing and encouraging your creativity continues.

Keeping a dream journal will help you track dream themes and patterns over a long period of time. You will begin to take note when the same person, setting or entire dream appears repeatedly. It is an obvious sign that your subconscious wants you to "get it." Sometimes, when you have determined the meaning of a symbol, your subconscious is so pleased, it uses it repeatedly after that because it is one concept it knows you comprehend. It is sort of like how Anne Sullivan was able to get the concept and sign for water across to Helen Keller. They then had one symbol to use to communicate with each other. Your conscious mind is as cut off from your subconscious as Helen was from Anne.

Other times, when you have made some necessary changes in your life, an oft-repeated symbol will cease its incessant appearances. When you notice that symbol no longer permeating your dreams, you will be able to see that the changes you have made met with the approval of your subconscious. If a theme is persistent over a long period of time, you should take a very close look at what you are ignoring or resisting in your life.

A nightmare is a dream that is merely trying to get your attention. The more you try to repress a nightmare because it is troubling, the greater the chances are that it will be repeated or that you will be given another

variation. Work with a nightmare the same way you would work with any other dream or imagery. See the information being furnished to you as coming from a friendly, loving Internal Wisdom located in your subconscious. Find out what your subconscious is trying to say to you. What do you need to learn? What feelings are you avoiding?

Archetypes are symbols that seem to be consistent across time and across cultures. Some common archetypes are house, car, adult, child, window. The house usually represents the total self. The car is your life. It is always nice to know if you are in the driver's seat, on the right road or even on the road at all. The adult represents the cognitive part of the self and the child the spiritual part of the self. The symbol of the child, as perfect spirit, abounds throughout mythology and scripture. A window usually represents your outlook on life or how you see your future. There are many other archetypes. Carl Jung wrote extensively about them. Those who work from a Jungian perspective incorporate a generous use of archetypal information and dream work in their approach.

However, as dream meanings are as unique as you are, symbols may hold different meanings for you than the conventional ones. If your personal interpretation of a symbol contradicts the generally accepted understanding of an archetypal symbol, always go with your personal understanding. After all, it is your Higher Wisdom and your subconscious talking. For example, with my avid involvement with the numbers associated with the Enneagram, I am more inclined to interpret a number in my dreams from this perspective rather than through numerology as other people might. Rely on your own wisdom and believe in yourself.

Dreams cannot control your decisions but rather

can reflect the position of your subconscious. Your dreams can give you a general overview of where you are in relation to the healing process and can help you monitor your progress. If, in your dreams, a child is always portrayed as helpless, wounded and alone, it is clear you have not worked through core issues to a degree great enough to heal your soul. If, on the other hand, the child begins to evolve in your dreams, over the course of time, into a bright, happy, wise child, you are receiving validation from your subconscious that you are on the right track and that you now have better access to your Core Self. Or, if you consistently dream of traveling in your car, but someone else is driving, you have an indication that you are not in control of your own life. When, over a period of time, your dreams begin to portray you driving your own car, you can be assured that your subconscious is applauding some of the changes you have made to regain control of your life.

In the next chapter, you will follow Reilley's, INTJ-4, healing journey. Near the end of therapy, Reilley began to dream repeatedly of telling her mother that her mother was in Reilley's house and Reilley wanted her to leave. Her dreams even reflected Reilley forcefully ejecting her mother from her house. Reilley had spent every day of her life controlled by the messages her mother installed within Reilley about herself, the world and a Higher Power. Reilley was finally able to reject all these messages, and her dreams told her she was doing an excellent job.

After the first year of therapy, Paula, ENFP-1, had begun making some changes in her life. One day, she came in reporting a dream: she is teaching at a junior high. She enters her classroom to see a young girl with her head half-shaved. The side that is shaved is not entirely bare. There are strands of blonde hair at intervals, looking somewhat like hair that has been pulled through a cap to be frosted. She asks the girl about her hair and she smiles warmly at her, telling her it is the new style. In working with this dream, Paula immediately determined that the girl represented her inner child. In describing the girl, she used words that apply

to the ENFP part of her personality. She said she was happy, funny, warm, good, caring and that she really liked her. The dream setting is a school, representing therapy, where she has been learning a new style of living. At this point in her therapy, Paula was establishing the locus of control in the ENFP Core Self, rather than in the defense of the Enneagram One, where it had been all her life. The child is telling her that honoring her Core Self is her new style of living. Her subconscious is smiling in approval.

A wide variety of approaches can be used to work with a dream. You can work with your dream in much the same way that you work with imagery, noting all the characters and composing a list of adjectives for each of the people involved to determine who these people really represent. In other words, if you dream about your co-worker, Tina, your dream is probably not about Tina at all. If all the adjectives you use to describe Tina also describe your mother, then your dream is probably using Tina to represent the mother messages within you. Depending on the content of the dream, you can then understand what your subconscious is trying to tell you.

If you need clarification on a dream, you can do what is called "dream re-entry" by which you use the dream much as you would imagery. Replay the dream in your mind but actively direct parts of it by asking questions of the characters, talking up to them or expressing your feelings towards them. To get a wider perspective, you can use dream re-entry to become one of the other people in your dream so that you can get another viewpoint. You can re-enter the dream and be Tina. See the whole situation through her eyes while you think and feel as she does. This will give you new information and a broader understanding of what your dream is conveying.

You can use the nondominant hand dialogue approach to communicate with a figure from your dream or even with an object, color or setting in your dream. You can ask a wide variety of questions such as:

Why are you in my dream?
What do I need to learn from you?

How can you help me?

What do you need from me?

What do you have that I need?

What do you embody that I no longer need?

How can you help me with my decision?

How can I help you?

Do you have anything to give me?

Why are you mad, sad, glad, scared, alone or hopeless?

Why do I need this dream?

I always encourage drawing the part with which you want to work because you cannot draw that part without going there internally, where you can experience that part more fully. That richer experience and deeper connection to the part will help you work with it better. Then, as you dialogue with the part, look frequently at your drawing so that you keep well in touch with that part. You can use the Progoff method of journaling as well as nondominant hand dialoguing to work with dreams.

If there is a song attached to your dream, or if you wake in the morning with a song playing in your head, listen to it carefully. What are the lyrics trying to tell you? Why did your subconscious choose this particular lyric and melody? Enter the song much the way you would enter a dream to try to live it out in your active imagination. What do you need to learn from this music? Try dancing to the song—not a structured, established dance step such as a waltz but a free-flowing, interpretive dance of your own design. Do not allow embarrassment to stop you. Do it privately and see how it feels. You cannot help but receive clarification.

You may take a dream task away from your dream. If your dream portrays you baking bread, you may want to spend some time baking bread and considering the dream as you do this. Later, you can journal about the significance of the task and why it was part of your dream.

In examining a dream, it is always best if you try to see it from as many perspectives as possible. Even if you have a good idea what the dream is trying to convey, ask yourself what else it might possibly mean. See if you can interpret it at a different level. That is, if you have been interpreting it from the perspective of your Inner-Child healing work, try interpreting it on a spiritual level as well.

Always try to get closer to the dream for a while, seeing it from the perspective of each of the dream figures. Then, back away from the dream and look at it objectively. Notice the relationships between various figures or objects. What is the obvious theme? What are the less obvious, underlying themes? What is the sequence of events? If someone or something in your dream is represented very differently from the way you know that person or thing, what is the significance of that representation? In other words, what is your subconscious trying to tell you when Tina, whom you know to be a loud-mouthed, controlling, self-centered witch, is presented in your dream as caring, gentle and considerate? When something is obviously out of place, it is out of place for a reason. Your subconscious is trying to get your attention.

You may wish to involve others in your dream work. If you have a therapist or a spiritual director, particularly someone versed in Jungian psychology, that person can help you process your dreams. You may choose to work with a dream professional to receive guidance in your dream work. If so, be sure it is someone competent and capable who will not interpret your dreams for you, but lead you through your own interpretation. You can take a class on dream work or join a dream group. Another suggestion is to work with a dream partner. This is someone who is on a similar spiritual journey, who respects your healing work and who is, above all, emotionally safe. Sometimes, just in retelling the dream out loud to a dream partner, the meaning and significance become clear. Sometimes your dream partner may make suggestions or give you options. Other times, you can ask your dream partner to tell you how she would interpret the dream if the dream were actually hers. Dream partners can also be good resources for symbols and archetypes. Your dream partner may know more about mythology, numerology, astrology, animal symbols and many other topics than you and can give you some suggestions to read about. Also, a dream partner may remember a dream you had a while back, which you may have forgotten, that coincides with this dream. It could be an important connection in deciphering the dream. Finally, a dream partner may have had the same or a similar dream at some point, and you can work on it together knowing you were brought together on this project for a reason.

There are many ways of working with your dreams, alone or with others; find which method works best for you.

PROSE AND POETRY

A fine method of accessing feelings is through creative writing. Writing an autobiography, children's story, myth, short story, fable or other fictional work will shift your emphasis to the right side of the brain where creativity and feelings are located. Often, people are surprised by the quality of the work they produce. But the product is not important. It is the process that is of ultimate value.

Sarah, ISTJ-9, wrote an autobiography. The portion included here describes what life was like for her in seventh grade:

> Sister Mary Margaret outlines the seven criminal tendencies. I have them all. I already know that I won't amount to any-thing. My mom told me with her tongue, her posture, her sneers. I was at the peak of badness, ugliness and smelliness in this class. One of my zits started to bleed when I was at bat on the playground. Can I just die here??? Dad comes to watch a game. What did I do wrong??? I will try to find out. My science project is a disaster. I could care less. Don't hear a word. Go through the motions of homework. Don't comprehend. Don't hear sermons. Where am I???

A life story such as Sarah's cannot be told without the narrator accessing the emotions associated with these events. The reader can identify and relate to the intensity of the adolescent hell in which Sarah lived. In relating her story, Sarah could then take an objective look at the situation in which she was raised. It helped her to question the conclusions she drew about herself so poignantly described in her narration.

Darlene, INFP-5, in addition to carrying the scars associated with the torments of childhood sexual abuse, also experienced the indescribable anguish of the death of her infant daughter. She writes with the unfathomable sorrow of a grieving mom:

MY DAUGHTER

> When you are asleep you look like an
> angel;
> When you are awake your smile is like
> sunshine.
> Your dark curly hair feels like strands of
> silk thread;
> Your fair skin smells like you.
> Hearing you ba-ba-ba makes me laugh;
> Holding you next to me makes me a mom.
> But, alas, these are just memories.
> Today I woke suddenly to your cry that
> wasn't there.
> My arms ache to hold your fragile body;
> My heart aches with my love for you.
> Tears fill my eyes, but, I have to smile;
> For my daughter is truly an angel.

Darlene tried to continue smiling for the sake of those around her and because she was never allowed to show her feelings. It caused a great deal of depression. Darlene is now allowing herself to feel the emotions underlying her poem and has given herself permission to grieve her daughter.

Led by her inner wisdom, Julia, INFJ-1, made some major changes in her life. She wrote the poem in figure 10-7 on page 220 expressing the grief at her losses, the deep fear she felt living in chaos and the overwhelming

TODAY

The loss
is a huge, bloody, gaping
wound
in my heart.

The dreams
no longer reality.
Were they ever?

Saying goodbye
is the hardest thing
I've ever had to do.

Goodbye dream house.
Goodbye beautiful yard.
Goodbye happy marriage.
Goodbye son or daughter.
Goodbye friends.
Goodbye family.

I am left alone.

I've paid a huge price
for the ultimate freedom.

I answer to no one
but God and my soul.
They speak the truth.

The time has come
to pack my bags
and head west.

What lies ahead?
I do not know.
So many unanswered questions.

The fear slips in
and steals my breath.
It is the enemy.

Figure 10-7

feeling of being out of control of her life. Julia did not realize when she was writing this poem that visually the lines formed two mirror images of a little girl. Just four months later, Julia was settled into her new environment and sent me the poem titled "I AM."

I AM

I am a butterfly,
Sailing high over
Mountains and valleys,
Cool breezes gently flowing
Over my soft, delicate wings.
I am a butterfly.

I am beautiful—
Red, blue, green, black,
Purple, orange, yellow, white.
I am unique, and
I am an integral
Part of the universe
I am beautiful.
I am free,
Floating, soaring, gliding,
Stopping to rest on a moist flower petal,
Sun warming my back,
My wings undulating slowly
Back and forth.
I rest, then continue on my journey.
I am free.

Julia continues to use a variety of techniques such as nondominant dialoguing, journaling, art, poetry and music to work with her feelings and to access and communicate with her inner wisdom.

After using imagery to "look" at the excruciating pain in her neck, Paula, ENFP-1, found her inner child encapsulated in granite. Six months later, after a good deal of hard emotional work, Paula wrote the following poem:

BIRTH OF A CHILD

Forever—an eternity
It has taken for this birth.
Impatience, disbelief, tears,
Regrets, despair, confusion.
It has been a hard pregnancy
For this precious child.
Thoughts of abortion had surfaced
Many times.
Yet this little child would not hear of it.
"Stay with this journey—
Pray, seek, desire,
Ask, read, write,
Believe in
Me"
The little child would demand.
Intense labor pains.
A wail breaks the deafening silence.
A precious child is born.
Rejoice.

Many years before learning of Inner-Child therapy, Carol, ISTJ-4, wrote the poems in figure 10-8 on page 222. Her photo as a small, very wounded child eloquently speaks as clearly as her poems.

Whether prose or poetry, pieces such as these cannot be created without accessing the intense emotions evoked in the writer. This type of writing can help move you into feelings that may otherwise be difficult to reach. If you feel that writing poetry is beyond you, get a set of Magnetic Poetry to jump-start your creativity. The kit contains various colorful words on refrigerator-magnet material. You can play with the words on a cookie sheet or on the refrigerator. As you move the words around, ideas will come to you and with them, the underlying feelings. Your work does not have to be worthy of publishing or ever be shown to another person. It does not have to make sense or be grammatically correct. It does not have to be complete sentences or complete thoughts. It is only to help in your process. Let your creativity free to play and you will be surprised at the results.

IN SUMMARY

These are just some of the techniques that can expedite forward movement on your own journey of personal growth. However, any tool that can help advance you along your path is worth pursuing. Perhaps you can easily identify with characters in movies or novels. Then be pragmatic and use whatever works for you. Read novels such as:

Cold Sassy Tree by O. Burns
The Book of Ruth by J. Hamilton
The Color Purple by A. Walker
Talk Before Sleep by E. Berg
Tuesdays With Morrie by M. Albom (nonfiction)
The Divine Secrets of the YaYa Sisterhood by R. Wells
Ellen Foster by K. Gibbons
Women Who Run With The Wolves by C. Estes
Kitchen Table Wisdom by R. N. Remen (nonfiction)
Cat's Eye by Margaret Atwood
Prince of Tides by P. Conroy
The Horse Whisperer by N. Evans

Or seek out videos such as:

King of the Hill
Terms of Endearment
Mommy Dearest
Beaches
Ordinary People
Big
Forest Gump

Remember, the point is to access your own emotions and then work with them once they have surfaced. If you find yourself responding emotionally to a book, movie or play, and your body will let you know when you do, use that information with a tool such as the ten-step exercise on page 207 to do some healing work. You will have taken a step forward towards yourself and away from being controlled by old programming.

Which techniques you decide to implement in order to advance your healing journey is not important. What is important is that you use everything in your power to propel you towards your own true identity, letting *nothing* and *no one* stand in your way.

TWINS

My parents have twins, but they didn't know it
They just fed and nurtured me
My twin grew independently of love and understanding.

I was the one on the outside going about
She was on the inside, looking out.
I learned to work hard, anxious to please
"It's not good enough," from the inside she'd tease.

Even in accomplishments when I felt proud
Her silent voice I heard shouting out loud.
"Pride's a sin"; her awful din
Would ring inside my head.
"If you're so good, you really should
Do something important instead."

I could never seem to please her
She always reminded me
"You don't belong; you'll do it wrong."
She would not let me be.

If I did melt, each time she felt,
I would have gone insane.
She refused to grow, so I didn't owe
Her space in my domain.

So as the years went by, I did try
To distance her from me.
I got tough and I did stuff her
Deep inside, unseen.

I thought I had succeeded;
I thought her demise well done.
Then I realized Life was passing by
And I hadn't had much fun.

"What has it all been for?" I asked.
This hard work which has achieved
Worldly goods but lost my soul;
I knew not what I believed.

How could God love me; does He exist?
I've worked hard but I don't know why.
Then from down inside of me
Came a quiet, mournful cry.

The little voice I thought was silent;
The urchin I sought to prevent;
This part of me I so denied,
Spoke this soulful lament.

THE LAMENT

You ignored my needs and stifling feelings
As you pursued your worldly deeds.
By not taking time to laugh or cry
You almost starved me but I didn't die.

I may be little but I had power
To subliminally influence you.
How else could I get attention
Though I share this body too?

All those nasty things you say,
I make them up to get my way
All your doubts, distrust, despair
Triple "D's" to make my day!

But all I want and all I need
Is your attention to be, too!
Embrace me now, let me be
A real part of you.

This little girl with straggly hair,
That you so sought to shun
She only wanted love and care
She also wanted fun.

This little girl was created to love
Before I was, before you were
By Him who named her from Above
And in whose palm He did hold her!

This little girl now needs to feel
This little girl, I am quite real
I want to be remembered when you kneel
To thank God for his Blessings on us both
To ask God to bring us very close.

Close to each other and close to Him
Whose Easter gift has not grown dim.
Who asks but that His will be done
Who wants you whole, who wants us One.

Carol E. Clark

Figure 10-8

REFERENCES AND SUGGESTED READING

Asper, K. *The Abandoned Child Within.* Trans. S. E. Rooks. New York: Fromm International Publishing Co., 1987. A highly analytic examination of early emotional wounding from emotional abandonment resulting in narcissistic disorder. Asper uses a Jungian approach and employs metaphor, symbolism, myth and fairy tale to present the archetype of the wounded child and her recovery. Although she insists on the need for repressed feelings to be brought to the surface and expressed, a stronger emphasis on that aspect of recovery with less analysis would have been more beneficial.

Asper, K. *The Inner Child in Dreams.* Trans S. E. Rooks. Boston: Shambhala, 1992. Asper examines the child historically, metaphorically and spiritually. She emphasizes the need to revisit childhood to find the patterns that are still operational. She provides guidance in examining the symbol of the child in dreams. Asper states the need to examine dreams noncognitively, from a deeper place of knowing than the rational mind.

Bandler, R., and J. Grinder. *Frogs Into Princes: Neuro-Linguistic Programming.* Moab UT: Real People Press, 1979.

Bandler, R., and J. Grinder. *Trance-formations: Neuro-Linguistic Programming.* Moab UT: Real People Press, 1981.

Bandler, R., and J. Grinder. *ReFraming: Neuro-Linguistic Programming.* Moab UT: Real People Press, 1982. All three Bandler and Grinder books are transcribed and edited versions of their introductory workshops on neuro-linguistic programming. They are easy to read and understand and provide many examples of application.

Beattie, M. *The Language of Letting Go.* New York: Hazelden, 1990. Daily meditations for dealing with recovery and co-dependency. This book is held in high regard in recovery circles. It is the best book of daily meditations I have seen.

Blakeslee, T. *The Right Brain.* Garden City NY: Anchor Press, 1980. Blakeslee explains how the right brain has a consciousness of its own, and that the two hemispheres of the brain have two different "languages": the left brain is verbal and the right brain nonverbal. The impressions and conclusions formed by each side of the brain may be completely different. For the original breakthrough research on this topic, refer to Roger Sperry's work at the California Institute of Technology in the 1950s.

Bradshaw, J. *Homecoming: Reclaiming and Championing Your Inner Child.* New York: Bantam Books, 1990. An overview of early childhood wounding with exercises for reclaiming your inner child at each age level. Bradshaw repeatedly stresses the need for working with original pain or core issues. He describes the Wonder Child or spirit as the result of Inner-Child work and the impact this work has on spirituality.

Breathnach, S. B. *The Illustrated Discovery Journal.* New York: Warner Books, 1999. A marvelous, hands-on book using collage as a means of creating a "visual autobiography." Very simple to use, this book stimulates and guides your creativity in self-exploration.

Cameron, J. *The Artist's Way.* New York: Jeremy P. Tarcher/Putnam, 1992. Julia Cameron offers a program which challenges limiting beliefs and helps to remove the blocks to creativity that were put in place in childhood by family and culture. She describes the link between creativity and spirituality. Creativity helps tap into our personal Internal Wisdom.

Cameron, J. *The Vein of Gold I: The Kingdom of Story* [Cassette]. Boulder CO: Sounds True, 1996. Addresses the topic of journaling.

Cameron, J. *The Vein of Gold II: The Kingdom of Sound* [Cassette]. Boulder, CO: Sounds True, 1997. Explores sound and body connection. To order either tape, contact: Sounds True, P.O. Box 8010, Boulder CO 80306, 800.333.9185.

Campbell, P., and E. McMahon. *Bio-Spirituality: Focusing as a Way to Grow.* Chicago: Loyola Press, 1985. Focusing is presented from a spiritual and holistic viewpoint. For information on workshops, contact: Institute for Bio-Spiritual Research Focusing, Peter Campbell, Ph.D., Edwin McMahon, Ph.D., P.O. Box 741137, Arvada CO 80006-1137, 303.427.5311.

Capacchione, L. *The Power of Your Other Hand.* North Hollywood CA: Newcastle Publishing Co. Inc., 1988. An excellent guide to using your nondominant hand in healing work and to access your Internal Wisdom. With many examples, illustrations and exercises, the book is written from an inner-child perspective.

Capacchione, L. *The Wisdom of Your Other Hand* [Cassette]. Boulder CO: Sounds True, 1992. Based on her book, *The Power of Your Other Hand,* listed above. To order, contact: Sounds True, P.O. Box 8010, Boulder CO 80306, 800.333.9185.

Diaz, A. *Freeing the Creative Spirit.* San Francisco: Harper, 1992. Presents twenty-five exercises using art, ritual and meditation to free creativity.

Edwards, B. *Drawing on the Right Side of the Brain.* Los Angeles: Jeremy P. Tarcher Inc., 1989. Edwards presents a basic description of the working of the two hemispheres of the brain. She describes methods to move control from one hemisphere to the other primarily to unleash creativity and artistic expression. However, as Edwards points out, with enhanced ability to move freely between both sides of the brain, we have access to the capabilities of both sides of the brain allowing clearer perception and better decision-making.

Finney, L. Speaker. *Clearing Your Past* [Cassette]. Boulder CO: Sounds True, 1997. A discussion of an affective approach to healing with exercises and case studies. To order, contact: Sounds True, P.O. Box 8010, Boulder CO 80306, 800.333.9185.

Ganim, B., and S. Fox. *Visual Journaling.* Wheaton IL: Quest Books, Theosophical Publishing House, 1999. This is a book I frequently and highly recommend. It uses art instead of words to delve into feelings and to work through a triggering incident. This approach helps to keep the analytical left brain out of your work. Frequently, journaling can easily become intellectual and cerebral. Using art as a journaling medium prevents you from falling into that trap.

Gendlin, E. *Focusing.* New York: Everest House, 1978. Gendlin describes his Focusing method to circumvent the analytical left brain in order to gain access to feelings and a deeper level of self. Step-by-step instructions and examples.

Gendlin, E. *Let Your Body Interpret Your Dreams.* Wilmette IL: Chiron Publications, 1986. Presents a method of using Focusing and a felt-body sense to interpret dreams. Provides specific step-by-step instructions and questions to guide you. This method shifts attention from left-brain analysis to a deeper, right-brain approach allowing the body and the subconscious to provide information.

Halpern, S. *Nurturing Your Inner Child* [Cassette]. San Anselmo, CA: Open Channel Sound Co., 1989. Nurturing and relaxing lullabies with subliminal affirmations. Send for a complete catalogue: Open Channel Sound Co., P.O. Box 2644, San Anselmo CA 94979-2644, 800. 909.0707.

Merritt, S. *Mind, Music and Imagery.* Santa Rosa CA: Aslan Publishing, 1996. Provides a variety of activities using five popular classical pieces of music along with imagery for self-discovery and personal growth. Music and imagery guarantee a right-brain approach and can enhance your healing work.

Napier, N. *Recreating Your Self.* New York: W. W. Norton and Co., 1990. This is a splendid book that explores early childhood wounding and describes an affective approach to healing. With complete confidence in the higher wisdom located in the subconscious, Napier presents a variety of exercises to facilitate the healing process through self-hypnosis. She draws on the work of Milton Erickson.

Noll, S. *Songs for the Inner Child* [Cassette, CD]. Santa

Fe, NM: Singing Heart Productions, 1992. Each song touches the wounded child. Listening to any song on this album while holding your inner child will be a healing experience.

Progoff, I. *At a Journal Workshop*. New York: Jeremy P. Tarcher/Putnam, 1975. A comprehensive 400-page description of Dr. Progoff's approach to journaling. Although the material is very helpful, it is a lot to wade through. This method of journaling is probably best explored in a workshop setting. To learn more about Progoff Intensive Journal workshops write: Dialogue House Associates, 80 East 11th Street, Suite 305, New York NY 10003-6008, 212.673.5880 or 800.221.5844.

Savary, L., P. Berne and S. K. Williams. *Dreams and Spiritual Growth*. New York: Paulist Press, 1984. Provides an historical overview of the Judeo-Christian use of dreams for spiritual growth. Explains different types of dreams and presents various techniques and methods of working with dreams.

Sher, B. *Wishcraft*. New York: Ballantine Books, 1979. This is a delightful and creative little book to help you "get out of the box" in figuring out who you are and where you want to go from this point forward. As with the exercises I have provided, do not simply think through the exercises in Sher's book; actually do them in order to benefit from them.

Taylor, C. *The Inner Child Workbook*. New York: Jeremy P. Tarcher/Perigee, 1991. Discusses and explores wounding situations at various age levels and provides a nice variety of exercises to work with unresolved issues. Taylor stresses the need to have feelings, not merely talk about them, and provides direction for re-parenting your inner child.

Tieger, P. D. and B. Barron-Tieger. *Nurture by Nature*. Boston: Little, Brown and Company, 1997. Describes each of the sixteen MBTI personality types from birth through childhood with many examples. This book assists the healing process by allowing you to read about yourself as a child and understand that

your individual needs were probably not met.

Wagner, R., and G. Middleman. Journeys of the Inner Child. *Remember the Child* [Cassette]. Beverly Hills CA: Emerald Forest Entertainment Co., 1991. Featured by John Bradshaw on his TV programs and in his workshops, the compelling lyrics and melody of the title song touch all those who have survived any type of childhood abuse. Distributed by Innerlife Music 818.352.7300.

Wolff, B., and J. Wolff. *Transitions: Soothing Music for Crying Infants* [Cassette, CD]. Atlanta, GA: Placenta Music, Inc., 1990.

Wolff, B., and J. Wolff. *Transitions2: Music to Help Baby Sleep with womb sounds* [Cassette, CD]. Atlanta, GA: Placenta Music, Inc., 1990. Excellent for meditation or simply to relax to while going to sleep. To order, contact: Placenta Music, Inc., 2675 Acorn Ave NE, Atlanta GA 30305, 404.355.4242.

Additional Resources

Capacitar, 23 East Beach Street, Suite 206, Watsonville CA 95076, 831.722.7590. Under the direction of Pat Cane, Capacitar is an organization based on the principle of women empowering women. Capacitar's approach employs some of the techniques described here as well as many others. A multi-cultural approach. Call for information and/or a manual.

The Focusing Institute, 34 East Lane, Spring Valley, NY 10977, 914.362.5222, www.focusing.org.

For information on Focusing combined with the Enneagram, contact: Mary Ann Giordano, P.O. Box 97, Riderwood MD 21139-0097, 410.823.0720. Booklets, spiritual direction and retreats.

Watts, Rosemary. Dream consultant, teacher and facilitator. I am indebted to Rosemary for much of the information on dream work presented in this chapter. To contact her directly or for information on her dream workshops, call 314.432.7909.

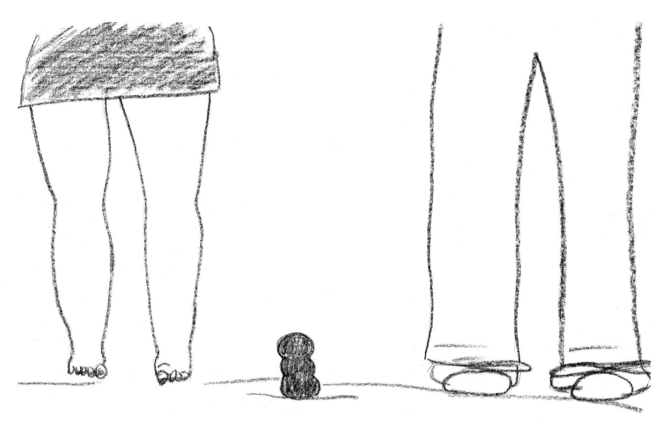

CHAPTER 11

REILLEY: A CASE HISTORY

It was fall when I received the first call from Reilley. Although my practice was full at that time, I decided to squeeze her in somehow because she was referred by a friend. However, I tried to stall her until I could clear my schedule a bit; it takes time and energy to begin working with a new client. She did not stall easily. In a subsequent call, she told me she was a recovering alcoholic and drug addict and recently had experienced a relapse. She was calling me from her car and explained she was "out cruising" to keep her mind off using. There were quiet undertones of urgency in her voice. I sighed in resignation—so much for controlling my tight schedule—and we made arrangements to get together sooner.

As Reilley entered my office for the first time, I could see she was tense, uncomfortable and well defended. She moved to the far corner of the couch, as far away from my chair as she could get. She folded her arms, crossed her legs and looked straight ahead out the window. In the months that followed, she was to become well acquainted with the tree outside my office window.

I have a habit of watching the nervous foot wiggling of clients. Reilley's foot moved constantly and with intensity. She very much did not want to be there. She explained that she had been in therapy before and felt that it had helped, but she knew she was still in trouble. She was very concerned that she would begin using again and did not want that to happen. I had explained the difference between cognitive and affective therapy to her on the phone, and she said she knew instinctively that she would have to do that "f—king feeling therapy" because the cognitive approach had not worked for her. I was to find that Reilley's language would be not only creative and quirky but quite graphic as well. She later confided she fancied herself "a bit of a wordsmith" and I found that to be true, much to my delight.

MYERS-BRIGGS TYPE INDICATOR

I answered her direct and challenging questions, and apparently she felt reassured because she agreed to take the Myers-Briggs Type Indicator. Afterwards, over the next two hours, we discussed the results to verify her MBTI type of INTJ (figure 11-1). During our discussion, she continued to stare out the window with an occasional stolen glance at me. Her arms never

uncrossed and her foot never stopped moving. I whispered a silent "Thanks!" to the friend who referred her. I followed that with a quick prayer as I wondered how I would break through all the defenses I saw before me. To say Reilley brought a new definition to "tough" was an understatement.

We set a time to meet the following week to determine her Enneagram designation. Between sessions, she called under the guise of asking questions about my approach. She was very NT and very intellectual. However, I knew underneath she was struggling and needed to be reassured that I would be able to help her stay sober. In our conversations, I could tell how very bright and articulate she was and knew I would have to stay alert to keep ahead of her. It was clear that if she could ever figure out my game plan, her Defense System would throw every obstacle imaginable in front of us. I also knew from her NT temperament that she would have to respect my abilities if she were going to trust me enough to work the Inner-Child process. To say the least, Reilley was going to be a challenge.

INTJ

Able to confront	Difficulty with bureaucracy, authority	Not easily influenced
Abstract thinker, conceptualizes	Difficulty with being relational; not very	Not outwardly affectionate
Adamant	social	Organized
Appears aloof, arrogant	Dry humor, sarcastic	Perfectionist
Analyzes	Enjoys conceptual discussions	Pragmatic
Anticipates problems	Enjoys debate	Precise
Appears emotionally distant	Enjoys playing with language	Resolute
Attracted to research	Everything needs improvement	Sees reality as arbitrary
Capable, competent, proficient	Fascinated by systems and theories	Self-critical, self-demanding and
Comfortable with change	Fears inadequacy and/or failure	self-doubting
Conscientious, dedicated	Frugal	Serious
Conservative	Good administrator	Straight forward
Consumed by work	High standards, exacting	Terse
Creative, inventive, has ingenuity	Individualist, independent, private,	To speak the thought is redundant
Critical thinking	reserved	Values consistency
Decisive, firm	Inquiring mind	Values intelligence and knowledge
Dedicated to intellectual growth	Logical, rational	Very intuitive
Deep, insightful, introspective	Loves to conceptualize improvement;	Visionary
Determined, disciplined, goal oriented	problem solver	Works at play
Devoted to children	Loyal	

Figure 11-1

THE ENNEAGRAM

She managed to stay sober until our next meeting. I explained the Enneagram to her, and we quickly determined her Enneagram type was a Four (figure 11-2). I knew that Reilley, the addict, worked in marketing for a large brewery. Of course! Who else but a Four would place herself in such an untenable position? I also learned that three years earlier, Reilley had come to terms with a gender identity problem and determined that she was a lesbian. She was quite comfortable with this information but told me the problem was she "freaked out" at the thought of naked women. Another untenable position: Fours do seem to get themselves into these types of predicaments. It assures the push-pull that is so much a part of Four behavior and sets them up for obsessing with longing that can never be filled. As a Four, Reilley had many such examples in her life of pursuing the unattainable. She declared she was the most unique Four of all because she wanted to be "normal!"

The combination of INTJ and Four is not common and not particularly comfortable. Looking at the traits of the INTJ in figure 11-1 and those of the Four in figure 11-2, it is easy to see a conflict. Reilley did not need me to tell her there was a small war raging within her. She was often confused by the conflict between the logic of her NT thinking and the high drama and emotions of the Four. She was most distressed when the Four got out of hand at work where, as an NT, she wanted respect for her competence and intelligence. She did not want a reputation of being out of control of her emotions.

The combination of the unemotional, logical INTJ and the dramatic, intense Four are diagramed in figure 11-3, page 230. Even though, numerically, it appears that there is a balance between compatible and oppositional traits, there is a major internal conflict in this personality combination between the high reliance on cognition by the INTJ and the Four's total submergence in emotions. There is a continual war between head and heart, the intellectual and the romantic. For myself, it was fascinating getting to know this multi-faceted

FOUR

Abhors the ordinary
Appears affected and aloof
Classy, elitist
Competitive
Deep, intense feelings, dramatic, passionate
Desires the unattainable, whatever is missing; longing
Different, unique
Distinctive dress
Drawn to symbolism
Envious
Feelings of not belonging; abandonment
Feelings of deprivation
Feels incomplete
Feels unable to be understood
Heightened sense of loss
Manic-depressive, bi-polar, moody
Melancholic
Needs recognition
Nonspontaneous
Nostalgic
Not a good team player
Not easy to get to know
Perfect love means feeling whole and complete
Personal environment is important
Pessimistic
Preoccupied with death
Prone to self-pity
Push-pull; long for and reject
Regretful
Rejects rather than chance rejection
Romantic
Search for connection
Search for beauty
Search for self-identity
Search for depth, meaning and what is missing
Self-absorbed
Sense of tragedy
Sense of entitlement
Serious
There is never enough

Figure 11-2

MBTI-Enneagram Quality Correlation

INTJ-4

Corresponding Compatible Qualities

INTJ

1. Self-reliant
2. Hypersensitive to rejection
3. Serious, intense
4. Creative
5. Likes symbolism
6. Individualist
7. Not understood
8. Can be eccentric
9. Separate from others
10. Competitive
11. May appear aloof, detached
12. Self-confident yet fearing a mistake
13. Searching for meaning
14. Originality in worldview
15. Sarcastic
16. Uncomfortable with intimacy
17. Complex
18. Aggressive toward competitors
19. Everything can be improved
20. Relationships must be dynamic
21. Intellectualize instead of do
22. Controls personal environment
23. Introspective

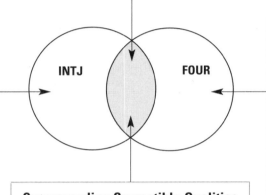

Corresponding Oppositional Qualities

INTJ

A. Decisions are easy
B. Conforms to useful rules
C. Appears unemotional
D. Positive
E. Future oriented
F. Not impulsive
G. Head, intellect oriented
H. Thinks in terms of systems
I. Logical
J. Not interested in wealth
K. No need to possess
L. Accepts change
M. Little need for emotional attachment
N. Search for authentic intellectual moments
O. Intellectual
P. Connection through intellect
Q. Reality is a tool and can be manipulated
R. Intellectually elite
S. Search for meaning in the universe
T. Constantly changing perception of reality
U. Achieves to appear competent
V. Most independent
W. Always asking "why"
X. The other is intellectually aloof
Y. Dedicated to family

Corresponding Compatible Qualities

FOUR

1. Self-absorbed
2. Hates loss
3. Serious, intense
4. Creative
5. Drawn to symbolism
6. Unique
7. Not understood
8. Unique
9. Abandonment, separation
10. Competitive
11. May withdraw from social encounters
12. Sophisticated facade, yet feels deficient
13. Search for meaning
14. Originality in worldview
15. Sarcasm
16. Uncomfortable with intimacy
17. Complex
18. Aggressive toward competitors
19. Drawn to romantic ideal, unattainable
20. Relationships are dynamic
21. Caught in "What if . . .," "If only . . .," dreaming
22. Needs control of environment
23. Introspective

Corresponding Oppositional Qualities

FOUR

A. "If only . . ."
B. Unique, different
C. Emotional extremes
D. Pessimistic
E. Nostalgic
F. Dramatic; drawn to the unattainable
G. Heart, people oriented
H. Thinks in terms of people
I. Emotional
J. Sense of class, needs to acquire
K. Personal environment important
L. Dislikes change
M. Longing for connection
N. Search for authentic connection
O. Romantic, strongly emotional
P. Connection through feelings
Q. Does not live in reality; lives in longing
R. Emotionally elite
S. Search for unconditional love
T. Constantly changing emotionally
U. Achieves to be distinctive
V. Deep need for connection
W. "Who" is more important than "why"
X. The other is not worthy relationally
Y. Self-absorbed

Figure 11-3

young woman. As time went on, I was to find that she had depth, integrity, intelligence, many talents and a remarkable sense of humor. Under all that "tough," there was an interesting, captivating little person who was quite charming.

There are some things that seem to appear with some consistency with an NT-Four combination. First, the mood swings that are a hallmark of the Four seem to be connected more to anger than to the melancholy and sadness usually associated with the Four. Not that NT-Fours are not capable of intense melancholy; they are. However, there seems to be a greater emphasis on anger. The other is that there are often gender identity issues when a T and a Four are combined in a female. The same seems to be true frequently when an F and Four are combined in a male. Both these characteristics were present in Reilley.

CASE HISTORY

The purpose of our third session was to take a case history. I spend two hours, minimum, learning as much as I can about a new client, starting with the earliest memory up to the present. Knowing Reilley's personality type let me know how she interpreted the events of her life and how she incorporated that information into her worldview and self-understanding. Getting the story from beginning to end also gives me the big picture that I need as an INFJ. With a good overview, I can see the major patterns that have been set in place in her life. I think of a client's life as a weaving, the horizontal threads (warp) being the various issues and the vertical threads (woof) being the events that reinforced those issues (figure 11-4). When the family of origin issues are addressed and resolved, the resultant behaviors will collapse. It is like cutting the warp threads and leaving the woof threads no support.

Resultant Behaviors

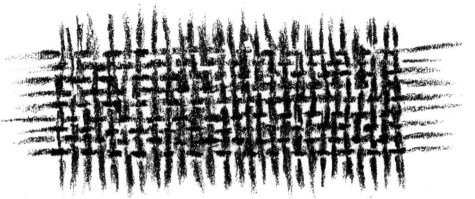

Resultant Behaviors (columns): Poor choice of friends; Grateful for any peer group; Mistrust of her own feelings; Self-loathing; Abusive relationships; Lack of respect for her own body; Addictions; Overachieving; Overresponsible; Obsessing over mother substitutes; Co-dependence; Lack of boundaries; Sexual promiscuity; Fear of emotional intimacy; Tough; anger facade

Family of Origin Issues (rows): Emotional abandonment; Lack of maternal bonding; Sexual abuse; Family role (scapegoat); Parental alcoholism; Lack of parental boundaries; Responsibility for mother's feelings

Figure 11-4

Reilley was thirty-five at the time we began working together. She was born and raised in a large city in Ohio. Her parents separated when she was twelve and divorced shortly thereafter. Her mother eventually remarried but her father never did. She had one sibling, a younger brother Bob, who was their mother's favorite. As the first-born and an INTJ, Reilley was well suited to be the family Hero but that role was given to her brother. At school, Reilley appeared to be the Hero, doing well academically and often becoming teacher's pet. At home, she was on the outside with all the love and approval directed towards "Prince Robert." It took Reilley awhile to adjust to her fate, but as a teenager she eventually settled into the role of Scapegoat.

The normal desire of a child, especially a daughter, to have the love, affection and approval of her mother is heightened to an obsession when that daughter is a Four and the love she desires is withheld. That scenario directly plays into the Four's affinity to melancholy, longing, going after the unattainable, feelings of abandonment and a deep abiding sense of loss.

Reilley gave me a list of descriptors for each of her parents (figure 11-5). Her case history centered around her relationship, or lack thereof, with her mother. The fact that her father was an alcoholic and not present

Figure 11-5

Mom	Dad
Loud	Oblivious
Scary	Argumentative
Erratic	Playful
Emotional (so I won't be)	Drunk
Sleazy	Gone
Uncaring	Work obsessed
Neglectful	Unemotional
F—ked up	Nonthreatening
Illogical	
Oblivious	
Doesn't get it	
Judgmental	
Angry	
Outgoing	
Friendly	
Horny	
Inappropriate	

emotionally for her as a child did not seem to concern her as much as the poor relationship with her mother.

Her father worked long hours. When he was home, he spent a lot of time in the rec room, drinking alone. When he interacted with Reilley, it was with verbal sparring, which he thought was fun. However, he seldom became angry with her and they sometimes watched movies together. When her mother came home each evening, the fighting began. Reilley, alone in her room, silently watched TV and tried to shut it all out. The primary word she used to describe her family was *loud*. She maintained good grades, practiced her music, enjoyed drawing and generally tried to keep a low profile.

Reilley described her mother as loud and scary. She was the disciplinarian, meting out physical and verbal punishment. She made hurtful and cutting comments to Reilley, widening the gap between them. Reilley watched as her mother bonded more and more closely with her brother, and Reilley felt she could do nothing to win her mother's love and acceptance.

One day when she was five, Reilley's parents were arguing in the kitchen. She overheard her mother threaten to kill herself and heard her open the silverware drawer. Reilley went into the room and saw her mother crying. Her mascara made dark trails of tears down her cheeks. That incident had a profound effect on Reilley. She learned that if Mom became too upset, terrible things could happen. She learned to try to keep her mother from becoming upset at all costs.

Five years later, Reilley made the mistake of recounting this incident to a friend. Her mother learned about her "indiscretion" and would not speak to Reilley for a week. "She was COLD." Reilley tried to win Mom back but to no avail. It was a terrible week for her and it made another profound and lasting impression on the ten-year-old child. She knew she had better not upset Mom or she could lose her altogether.

Meanwhile, Reilley continued to do well in school. She was creative, smart and funny. She was, however, not particularly feminine in the traditional sense. She knows now that this factor contributed to her problems

Reilley resented Mom's quick adjustment to the single life and retreated, angry, to her room where she lost herself in melancholy music. At the same time, Reilley's best friend moved away and her little dog died. She was desolate.

with her mother who was very feminine and highly sexual. Reilley made the mistake of sharing some of her gender-identity confusion with her mother and when she saw her mother's distress, she knew that topic was taboo. She received a similar message when she was sent to charm school by her third grade teacher. By the time she was a teenager, she had put all her questioning away, but she knew she never went through the boy-crazy stage her friends experienced.

When Reilley was twelve, her parents separated and divorced. Reilley found herself in the position of taking care of her mother emotionally and feeling ill equipped to do so. The whole tenor of the household changed. The house that had been so loud was now very quiet. Her mother was not home much as she began dating earnestly. Reilley resented Mom's quick adjustment to the single life and retreated, angry, to her room where she lost herself in melancholy music. At the same time, Reilley's best friend moved away and her little dog died. She was desolate.

After the divorce, her mother developed some disturbing behaviors. She would walk around the house without clothes—in front of the children. She compared her breast size to Reilley's. She dated many men, often staying out all night or bringing the man home for the night. Reilley remembers the anger she felt at hearing the sounds coming from her mother's room at night. Sometimes there was nudity on the part of the male visitor in front of Reilley. Her mother did not recognize any of this as inappropriate behavior on her part or on the part of these men towards Reilley. At one point, Reilley asked her mother to change some of her sexual behaviors; Mom paid no attention.

Reilley took care of her brother while her mother was out, became deeply involved in her music and

found alcohol and drugs. High school was about "getting high and being in band." When she became very obvious in her acting out with chemicals, her mother finally had to face it. She "took it very personally," asking Reilley, "How could you do this to me?" Mom sent Reilley to see a counselor. When Reilley explained her mother's sexual activities, the counselor told Reilley her mother was normal and Reilley gave up all hope.

At seventeen, Reilley began dating because "that was what I was supposed to do." It was a way to share a common interest with her mother. She told her mother she was going out of town for a weekend concert with her first boyfriend. Mom asked her about birth control and fixed them a thermos of whiskey sours. "I was wasted all weekend and had sex to be done with it. It was not fun." This was the beginning of many sexual encounters with men she neither liked nor enjoyed.

College was welcomed as an escape, and Reilley did well academically but continued abusing alcohol and drugs as well as escalating her promiscuous behaviors. She also found nurturing women to fill the deep void left by her mother. She was "in search of a new mom" and in four years of college had "five new mommies." She kept finding new moms until age thirty.

By the time she graduated college, she knew she was in trouble and entered treatment for chemical dependency. Over the next thirteen years, Reilley would alternately get sober and relapse until the day she called me.

During Reilley's previous attempts at therapy, she tried to address her mother's sexual issues. She felt the therapy had helped somewhat but that the issue was not resolved. In the course of her last round of therapy, "I figured out I'm gay." She told her mother she was gay and her mother indicated it was "a travesty and not

Reilley
Individualistic
Anti-authoritarian
Sardonic
Wry
Irreverent
Avant garde
Rebellious
Eclectic
Arrogant
Self-willed
Outspoken
Candid
Free spirit
Off-the-cuff
Nonconformist
"Runs with scissors"
Dare to be different
Born to be wild

Figure 11-6

normal." Reilley recalls, "Mom cried and I comforted her." Her mother told her she was hoping never to hear those words. She later told her father who was supportive and acted as if it were a nonissue.

Reilley's description of herself is included in figure 11-6. The choice of words and the picture they paint provide a glimpse into this complex and colorful woman.

At the finish of the case history, I asked Reilley for a list of goals for therapy. What would she want to accomplish during our work together? She gave me the following list to aim for:

- Self-acceptance
- To live in the moment; today is good
- To know how I feel about my mom and to have resolution
- To accept my sadness
- To think it's OK to be a "goof ball"
- To be more accepting of others; to be gentle
- To have compassion for myself and others

And I gave her the only answer a Three could give: "No Problem!" In the course of our work together, we added three more goals:

- To be able to have an emotionally and physically intimate relationship
- To be able to make eye contact
- To be able to dance

The last goal, to be able to dance, reminded me of the doctor and patient discussing the patient's upcoming surgery for carpal tunnel syndrome. The patient asked the doctor, "Will I be able to play the piano after my surgery?" The doctor replied, "Of course!" The patient, looking pleased, said, "Great! I have always wanted to be able to play the piano!" Reilley, however, was not asking me to imbue her with a new talent. She enjoyed music tremendously but was unable to dance because it left her with unexplained feelings of sexual impropriety, making her physically ill.

I found it interesting that the problem that drove Reilley into therapy, her threatened loss of sobriety, did not appear on this list. I believe that was because she instinctively knew that if the other issues were covered, it would no longer be a problem; that has turned out to be true. From our first session and to date, Reilley has not even considered using alcohol or drugs and reports no desire to do so.

Through all of this, Reilley has remained a very spiritual person. She attends a church that is open and accepting of gays and lesbians and is oriented to NT thinking. She feels strongly that God speaks to her through music. She employs the twelve-step program in her own spirituality. She has been sustained throughout therapy by the inner assurance that God is part of her process and is supporting her. She had been very active in the twelve-step program but now finds her need for their support lessening steadily. When we began working together, she was taking Prozac for depression but discontinued that after several months of therapy.

THE WORK BEGINS

With a fairly good map of the territory, we were ready to begin Inner-Child work. The first step was to introduce Reilley to the child within. This exercise was meant to familiarize her with the process, to see how comfortable she was with imagery and to continue to build rapport between us. If there were any as yet undiscovered complications, they were likely to show up during this first session. Reilley was willing to do the imagery and participated fully. I invited her to close her eyes and go back in her mind to the house in which she was raised. I asked her to imagine entering that house as the adult she is today. By asking her to note sights, colors, smells, textures and other sensory data that would compel her to completely enter the imagery, I anchored her in the experience. I suggested that she move through the house until she found herself as a small child. Reilley found her inner child, age five, alone in the house that was devoid of furniture and carpeting. I encouraged her to enter into a dialogue with the child. Although she was willing, she found herself having trouble making eye contact with the child and could not touch her. I suggested she leave the child a gift by which to remember her and as a promise that she would be back. Reilley decided to leave the child "a jam box" for "tuneage" because she knew the child was lonely and liked music. We processed this experience, and I encouraged her to allow any feelings that came during imagery to surface because it is through feelings that we can trace the threads back to their origins and disconnect them.

By now, I was beginning to get an idea of how very well defended Reilley was. I knew the same defenses she used to survive in an unsafe world would instinctively be put up towards me. Of course, the first line of defense is her Enneagram Four. She was easily caught up in the decoy of the Four's intense feelings which pulled her away from her true issues and the legitimate feelings around them. It is rather like the bird that feigns a broken wing to distract the enemy from her nearby nest. Reilley furnished me with an example of this coping. Her mother remarried and Reilley never liked her stepfather. When he died about eight years ago, Reilley was inconsolable. She was sick with grieving. She knew then it was not about her stepfather. It was a way the Four had of releasing feelings without going to the original pain. Interestingly, when her favorite grandmother died, there were no feelings expressed. That event was too real and would have tapped into feelings that were attached to real pain around real loss.

When the Four was insufficient to keep the emotional pain at bay, Reilley employed some of the traits of the INTJ to shore up her defenses. This resulted in her "tough" appearance. She could be formidable and intimidating if she so desired. From the INTJ, her Defense System also borrowed a big need and ability to be in control. This coping skill served her well.

To this, she reinforced her Defense System with some of the traits of the NT temperament. She was quick to utilize the NT's ability to intellectualize. As all NTs do, she could throw us both off track by analyzing everything we did. She wanted the process to be logical and insisted that every move I made should make sense. If I managed to maneuver her too close to a feeling, she was quick to label the feeling "stupid." NTs have great disdain for anything that comes close to being "stupid." If the feeling was stupid, there was no chance she was going near it.

Another line of defense she employed was the Four's penchant to slide to the Two under stress, taking care of other people. Reilley was very concerned with how people responded to her, not wanting anyone to be angry with her. From this, some real co-dependent and boundary issues resulted. Likewise, she borrowed some traits from the One, being self-critical, controlling and quite the perfectionist.

Included in her defense strategy kit was something she learned early in life: to dissociate. Reilley was aware that she left her body on occasion. She reported that she felt "floaty" and heard a rushing sound. When she dissociates, she is unaware of what is happening or being said. Another tool, which she declared to be her favorite, was denial. No matter how compelling the evidence, if she did not like the direction the facts were pointing, Reilley would employ denial.

On top of all this, she threw in humor for good measure. Because she is extremely witty, it was hard not to fall for that tactic. If I pushed her too close to a feeling she was not ready or willing to face, she would throw out a Reilleyism that could throw me off track. She was very adept at sidestepping feelings. Reilley quickly figured out that humor was her best tactic in trying to out-maneuver me. I found her wry humor refreshing, so I knew I had to be careful or we could easily get off track. Sometimes, however, she won a round, such as the evening I was trying to move her closer and closer to a feeling. Suddenly, she threw up her hands and said, "Wait! Wait!"

"What?" I replied.

"I suddenly feel like Yul Brenner," was her response.

So I bit. "Why do you feel like Yul Brenner?"

Then in a perfect King of Siam imitation, she looked at me intently and said, "Mrs. Anna, you are difficult woman!"

It took me ten minutes to get us back on track.

In a subsequent session, Reilley informed me that she was taking me out of "The King and I" and moving me into "Man of LaMancha." When I asked why, she quoted Aldonza:

"See what your gentle insanities do to me—rob me of anger and give me despair. Blows and abuse I can take and give back again. Tenderness I cannot bear."

She said instead of Mrs. Anna I was now Mrs. Quixote. But I eventually won this round because I brought the Aldonza and Dulcinea songs to our next session. I played them for Reilley and pointed out how the "loser" Aldonza really was Dulcinea inside. Don Quixote could see it and he helped her to see it, too. We were able to move into some feeling work with my "counter tactics."

It was when all of these varied defense tools failed her early in life that Reilley employed the additional defense of alcohol and drugs. Fortunately, that was now under control and was not interfering with our work. I showed Reilley a Kachina (stacking) doll I keep in my office and she readily identified with feeling that protected.

Eventually, we employed an imagery to help lower these defenses. Gratefully, Reilley was completely cooperative knowing that, although her defenses were necessary and helpful earlier in life, they were hindering her progress now. That did not make letting them down any easier, however, because they are an automatic

response. When we could convince the Defense System to lighten up, Reilley was often hit with overwhelming terror even though she felt completely safe in my office.

The imagery we used to dismantle some of her defenses for the purpose of our session was simple but effective. Reilley would imagine standing in front of a building we called "The Reilley Building." As she entered the building, she went through a succession of doors, each door representing a defense skill illustrated in figure 11-7, page 237. As she encountered each door, she would do whatever necessary internally to let that coping strategy relax for the time being. When she had successfully executed all the doors, she would be ready to work with any topic on a feeling level. Although it took a while since there were so many doors, it was well worth the time because Reilley visibly relaxed, and I could see her letting go. If I neglected this exercise and moved directly into a topic, Reilley would often stop me saying, "I think I better go through the doors," because she could feel herself resisting. I never ceased being grateful for her cooperation.

HELMETED CHILD—THE BABY

At the beginning of one of our earliest sessions, I suggested we start addressing some of her mother's inappropriate sexual behavior. Reilley folded her arms and her foot shifted into high gear. She was not interested in talking about her mother again. She had talked about her in previous therapies and nothing had changed. However, with a little encouragement, she agreed to draw a picture of her mother (figure 11-8a) complete with descriptors.

Babe
Sleaze
Liar
Oversexed
Exhibitionist
Skin
Boundary-less
Untrustworthy

Figure 11-8a

I then asked her to imagine that she could take all the filters off when she considered her mother. I asked her to draw the mother she was most afraid she would

Reilley, INTJ-4

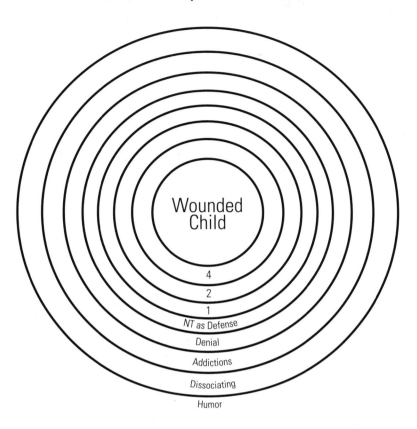

Enneagram Four:
Intense
Suicidal ideation
Depression

Enneagram Two:
Co-dependence

Enneagram One:
Self-loathing
Perfectionism
Control

Use of NT in defense
Tough/anger
Intellectualizing

Humor

Dissociating
Moving into an altered state
Spirit leaves the room
Moving into the subconscious

Denial

Figure 11-7

Gross
Naked
Boundary-less
Embarrassing
Inappropriate
Unnecessary
Ugly
Curvy
Red
Dangerous
Violent

Loud
Insensitive
Promiscuous
Violating
Angry
F—ked up
Irrational
Judging
Boisterous
Outgoing;
    puts out

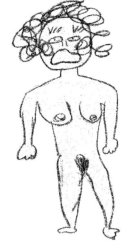

Figure 11-8b

see if those filters were removed. She was surprised at what appeared on the page (figure 11-8b).

The angry letter that followed was an indication that perhaps there was more here than had previously been identified:

> *Get the f—k out of here you f—king ugly*
> *sleazy bitch. I f—king think you are sick —*
> *put some f—king clothes on. Why don't you*
> *grow up and act like a f—king Mom? You*
> *owe me thousands of dollars for therapy. I*
> *want cash.*
>   *Oh, and your son isn't your husband.*
> *F—k you.*

In subsequent sessions, we began to see that each time Reilley discussed her mother's inappropriate sexual behavior, she felt very little. When we tried to use imagery to trace these feelings, there were no pictures or words attached to the feelings. There was just a sense of darkness and silent terror. She felt very, very small; very, very scared; and very sick to her stomach. Each time, she admitted the feelings were around something sexual. As much as she did not want to admit it, there was a connection each time those feelings were associated with her mother. She reported that, for many years, she slept in a tight ball with her arms and legs locked, and wearing socks. When she entered puberty, she slept with a bra under her pajamas as well.

Over the course of the next several months, she drew

Reilley's descriptions of the baby.

Angry	Unheard	Life-changing
Upset	Alarmed	Invaded
Scared–Terror	Hurt	Ignored
Troubled	Betrayed	Powerless
Annoyed	Unsafe	Abused
Disgusted	Shocked	
Confused	Sad	

Figure 11-9

different representations of the child she felt like during these scary experiences and with whom she associated these feelings (figures 11-9 and 11-11a and 11-11b). She called this child "the baby" and "the Helmeted Child" because she often wanted something on the child's head to represent protection (figure 11-9).

Through a felt sense rather than cognitively, Reilley represented her mother in figure 11-10. The descriptors of the baby listed in figures 11-9 make infinite sense when this drawing of Reilley's mother is taken into account. Seeing Reilley's mother through the baby's eyes explains many of the issues Reilley brought into adulthood. Interestingly, Reilley symbolizes her mother by unknowingly using the feminine archetype of the cat. To this day, Reilley is wary of both cats and women.

Figure 11-10

The Helmeted Child was one of five kids or ego states we would eventually define and work with.

Figure 11-11a   *Figure 11-11b*

Encounters with the baby were always accompanied by stomachache and reactions described as "gross" and "disgusting" (figure 11-11a). Reilley identified the major feelings as betrayal and terror, but she also felt there was a great deal of repressed anger associated with this baby (figure 11-11b). She was easily triggered into these feelings by broken trust in any type of relationship. She was also triggered into these feelings physically. If Reilley were to be touched at the back of her neck, at the small of her back and/or her ankles, she would be overcome with feelings of shear terror. When I placed a doll across Reilley's lap with one of Reilley's legs supporting the doll's neck, the small of the doll's back resting on her other leg and then put the baby's feet in her hand, she began to tremble in terror. After months of work encountering this baby, each and every experience left both Reilley and me with the conviction that something terrifying and of a sexual nature happened to her at a very young age and that it involved her mother.

After many sojourns into the world of this baby via the feelings associated with her, Reilley wrote the baby a letter and let the baby respond by using her non-dominant hand:

REILLEY:

I went into your world for not very long but I didn't like it without my "tools." And I wouldn't want to stay there for very long without any protection, like the way you were, I guess.

BABY:

I am there and it is bad and empty here. I can see why you wouldn't like it.

REILLEY:

I can see why you wouldn't like it. I believe that you feel scared and hopeless. And it doesn't feel safe at all. I am sorry that you felt like that a lot.

In the letter, Reilley refers to her defenses, illustrated in figure 11-7, page 237, as her "tools." By this point, Reilley is very aware of them and also very aware that the baby did not have them; nor did the baby have the ability to get herself out of a bad situation.

Being the NT that she is, Reilley could not just accept feelings as evidence. She entered therapy convinced that she was a loser and "f—ked up" and that she needed therapy because she was born defective in some way. Before she would change her mind on this score, she wanted hard evidence. I had her draw a picture of the Helmeted Baby and verbalize as many of the wounding episodes in her early life as she could recall. For each incident, she drew an arrow directed at the baby (figure 11-12). The majority of the arrows represented sexual/mother issues. When she was done, the arrows had obliterated the baby. Reilley, for the first time, began to consider that some of the pain she had been carrying was not her own doing but a result of

Figure 11-12

what happened to her. She allowed the baby to express some of that pain with her nondominant hand:

> Dear Mommy,
>
> You are bad to touch me in places where you aren't supposed to and I don't want you to do that anymore. It hurts me for you to do that and I am scared of you. You are really big and I'm pretty little and I don't know what to do about you. Except go to sleep.
>
> When you touch me bad I feel like I wish I was dead. It feels so wrong and I think it would be best if I wasn't here because it's so scary. I shouldn't be treated like that—like I'm not a person or like I don't matter. I wish you loved me better, Mommy.
>
> Reilley

I led Reilley into imagery that allowed her to take a look at the emotional damage done to this baby in 3-D. She saw the baby wrapped in a blanket. Looking under the blanket, she saw there were so many holes in the baby from those arrows that there was no body. In subsequent sessions, each time she expressed anger and affirmed the child, the baby regained more and more of its body. Reilley and this precious little person were bonding.

Each session concluded with Reilley affirming and protecting the baby. We often used imagery, music, art or letter-writing for this purpose. In the beginning, Reilley had trouble holding and loving the baby in imagery. She was very concerned that it would be misconstrued as sexual. There were no logical reasons why she worried about that because she had never been inappropriate with a child and had no desire to do so. It was reminiscent of her very first imagery, when she met her five-year-old inner child for the first time and was unable to make eye contact or touch the child. It was another indication that her "default setting" was that babies are at high risk for sexual abuse.

As time went on, Reilley became more and more comfortable with the concept of holding and protecting the little Helmeted Baby. She cared a great deal for the baby and was certain she would be able to re-parent the child. Reilley knew she would be a better mom than her mother had been. About this time, friends of hers had a baby and Reilley was able to visit them frequently, holding and comforting the little baby until she became more confident of her own parenting skills. INTJs are loving and devoted parents, and so Reilley's Core Self brought her innate devotion and loyalty to this Helmeted Child, offering support and fierce protection. She became intent on the job of re-parenting this very wounded baby (figure 11-13).

I invited Reilley to bring in a variety of childhood pictures, and we found them to be very helpful. When she looked at herself as a baby and as a small infant, she could see that she was a good child. She could see the INTJ child: serious, intent and curious. Each week, we looked at the pictures until she was convinced that that little baby was not born bad, defective and a "f—ked up loser."

We saw other things in the pictures as well. We saw she was not held with love and affection by her mother or father. In most of the pictures with her mother, the baby had little fists, which were not present in pictures with other people. We also saw how, even as a very small child, she had bonded with her dog, which gave

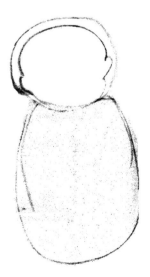

I will never leave you.
You are perfect.
It is OK to be quiet.
You are really cute.
I will take care of you and you don't have to worry about stuff.

It is OK to need things and love.
It is OK to trust some people, when you are ready to.
You are pretty darn lovable.
You don't have to be alone.

I will touch you in a loving way only.
You don't have to perform.

Figure 11-13

her the love, affection, attention and devotion she so desperately sought.

THE FIVE-YEAR-OLD

Eventually, I broached the subject of the argument her mother and father had when she was five, in which her mother threatened to kill herself. Through imagery, Reilley was able to see how frightening that was for a five-year-old child who was ill equipped to discern the degree of seriousness attached to Mom's threat. In her imagery, Reilley looked at the little five-year-old watching the scene and saw she had neither hands nor legs. Her eyes were wide in terror. She was frozen and powerless to do anything to intervene. Reilley could easily understand how the child learned in that incident that she had to do everything possible to keep Mom from getting that upset again. She said that on some level she knew that day that she really did not have a mother. She knew that to keep Mom alive she would have to take care of her and not expect things to be the other way around. Here, the Four's ability to incorporate Enneagram Two caretaker traits came into play. Reilley could see it was true in her life, because she has been very careful of her mother's feelings ever since. She consoled her mother around the divorce and every other major event that involved the two of them. Reilley had to hug and comfort her mother even though her mother's touch made her physically ill. Reilley had no recollections of her mother ever showing concern for her or her feelings. Her mother took

everything about Reilley personally. From Reilley's first period to the information that she was a lesbian, it was always about Mom. Reilley states: "She had a great childhood—mine."

This five-year-old child had to be important in Reilley's self-concept because monitoring her mother's feelings has played such a big role in Reilley's life. Also, in her very first imagery in which she met her inner child, it was this child she encountered. Reilley did some drawings of the child (figures 11-14 and 11-15) and described her:

Shame
Fear of disappointing
Unworthy
Fear of rejection
Fear of her (Mom's) feelings

These poignant drawings make it easy to see how very lost and hurt this little child was. In figure 11-14, the child finds comfort only in the company of her little dog. She gazes out the window towards the green, which she knows is not attainable. On the windowsill, a bottle of alcohol indicates the direction she would take to numb out the emotional pain.

EDITOR CHILD, AGE 10

One evening, Reilley came in complaining about a couple of "loud women" at work whom she found to be very upsetting. It was obvious to both of us that these women were hooking her mother issues. I enlisted her cooperation and she was able to list some

Figure 11-14

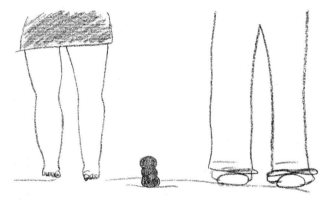

Figure 11-15

Figure 11-16a

Figure 11-16b

of the messages she received from her mother as a child. She drew herself as the child recipient of these messages and listed the feelings associated with that child:

Editor Child
Alone
BAD
Betrayed
Out of control
Unlikable, unlovable
Responsible
Overwhelmed
Troubled
Longing
Never ending
Afraid to make a mistake

She drew a representation of the child she had just described (figure 11-16a). Reilley next drew a picture of her mother through the eyes of that child (figure 11-16b). Then we did some imagery in which she recreated a scene of Mom screaming at the child. In her imagery, she saw the child shrink to the size of a dot. Reilley entered the scene as an adult and expressed anger towards her mother and affirmed the child. The child thought Reilley was cool. Mom left the scene but Reilley noted that there was a "big empty space where she had been."

Imagery is an incredible tool. When utilized in conjunction with emotions, it changes old programming. It also allows the subconscious to communicate with us. I maintain that imagery never lies. In this imagery, Reilley's subconscious supplied us with how this tough, in-charge, brilliant adult really views the power and the importance of her mother. I could spend the next ten years trying to talk her out of this view of her mother as all-powerful and central to her life, but I would be talking to her left brain, her cognitive part. This perception of Mom is in the child, the right side of the brain, and is only accessed through feelings. That part of Reilley is not at all interested or impressed by logic and rational talk. In this imagery, when Mom left the room, she left "a big empty space." This information showed me, if I did not know by now, how central her mother issues were to Reilley's life.

The defining incident for this child happened when, at age ten, Reilley mentioned to a playmate that her mother had threatened suicide when Reilley was five years old. Five years after it happened, that event was still troubling Reilley to the point she would discuss it with her little friend. Unfortunately, her mother became aware of the discussion and, instead of being concerned about the degree of trauma it had visited upon her daughter, became very angry with Reilley. She did not speak to her for a week. Reilley did everything she could to make it be all right again, but her mother would have none of it. Reilley was profoundly affected by this shunning. She felt completely rejected and hopeless that it could ever be reversed. The mother she had been searching for all her short life was slipping even further out of her grasp. When we did some imagery around this incident, Reilley was able to access the feelings she experienced during that week. She wrote the following dialogue with the ten-year-old:

Dear Reilley at 10,
I do remember how that one week was like someone punched you really hard in the stomach and the life was zapped out of you, it felt like.
Your mom was so mean to you to ignore you and act so unforgiving. That was such an unloving thing to do, for days.
So nobody needs that kind of a parent. If you even want to call it a parent. She was a

*mean bitch. I know that I am not anywhere
that mean. I feel bad for telling my employees
what to do. I sure don't ignore them and
treat them like dirt. And they certainly aren't
my kids.*

*So there is no way I would ever treat you
that badly. I would try to encourage you and
be loving for you . . . and your little dog, too!*

THE CHILD RESPONDS (nondominant hand):

*I would like somebody to be interested in
me and protective of me. That would be very
different. And be someone who I'm not afraid
of. I need a nice mom.*

REILLEY ANSWERS:

*I think your mom was really mean to you
and I am sorry that happened because I
know how scared you used to be and how
alone you felt. Certainly not like being a part
of some "family." Now that I know you exist,
I will work on being nice to you, too. And I
can do that if I stop acting so tough. You look
good with me.*

THE CHILD:

*It sure would be nice if you would let me
be around you instead of the mean, scary
mom.*

REILLEY:

*OK, I'll try. You can talk if you want to. I
promise that I will make sure that you know
you are not bad at all. Nothing you could do
would be that bad—You are a good kid.*

*I will be an encouraging, loving helpful
mom and I won't ignore you.*

*I know you are smart, but if you need to
keep hearing it, I will tell you again and
again. But more importantly, you're just a
decent little kid.*

*It is OK to make mistakes. Nothing you
do could really be that bad. You don't need to
protect that other mom. She was supposed to
protect you. So now I will protect you. Then*

*maybe you can relax some. Maybe have some
fun and be more kidlike. And not be afraid to
come home.*

*And it is OK to tell me if you feel scared
or anything else.*

It is important to understand that this was not a
cognitive exercise. Reilley was experiencing some deep
feelings as she dialogued with this child. Because she is
an INTJ, the dialogue does not sound mushy and flowery. To Feeling types, it may sound matter-of-fact and
unemotional, but it was executed on a deep feeling
level. Reilley, as an NT, knows the importance of
affirming the child's smartness and instinctively
includes that in her letter. There is also a touch of her
humor when she goes to the Wizard of Oz for the
quote, ". . . and your little dog, too!" But there was deep
meaning under the humor because Reilley knew how
important that ten-year-old's dog was to her. Her dog
was the only place she could take her feelings and the
only one from whom she received unconditional love.
When the dog died two years after this incident, Reilley
said she knew all hope was lost.

In this exercise, we identified the third of the five
kids or ego states at work in Reilley. Whenever Reilley
was triggered and the resulting feelings were those she
associated with figure 11-16a, she would draw the same
child, the ten-year-old (figures 11-16c, 11-16d, 11-16e).
As we got to know this child better, we learned she had

Figure 11-16c

Figure 11-16d

Figure 11-16e

two major functions. She had to edit everything before it was said for fear it would get her into trouble, and she had to be sure people didn't get angry with her. It was this child and the five-year-old who incorporated the Enneagram Four's slide to the Two, which is the prototype of co-dependent behavior. Everyone else's needs come first.

I was glad to make this child's acquaintance because I had been very familiar with her work. I rely a great deal on the information supplied to me by a client regarding imagery or the feelings evoked during any exercise. With Reilley, it was very clear that before I received any information, it went through an extensive editing process, which rendered it all but useless to me. As much as I begged, prodded, pleaded and reasoned with Reilley, I could not convince her to cease the editing. My efforts were in vain because I was appealing to Reilley's cognitive self, and the one doing the editing was the ten-year-old who was not accessible through reason. I could reach her only through feelings.

Because this child had experienced a week from hell, she was determined not to speak out of turn again. It was of utmost importance not to incur Mom's wrath again. From this, we knew that if Reilley were ever to choose for herself over her mother, this child would very much have to be consulted and be on our team. It would take continual reassuring and reaffirming to keep this child from reverting to her editing role to avoid making Mom or anyone else angry.

The Editor Child was very particular about choice of words. When I suggested that the terms *incest* and/or *abuse* might apply to some of her mother's behaviors, the Editor Child said she would only consider the term "inappropriate behavior." This child knew the trouble in which she found herself was due to talking about Mom threatening suicide. She was certainly not going anywhere near something as potentially explosive as this topic. It was clear we would have to enlist her cooperation before we could communicate more openly.

It is interesting to note that, as a Thinking type, Reilley is very truth-based. As the Scapegoat in her

family, she also has no problem with telling it as it is. The Editor Child's need to package things nicely was at odds with both Reilley's Core Self and her family role.

In working with this child, I employed a number of techniques. One was an imagery in which Reilley visualized an internal rock that impeded the flow of words. When the words were held in, so were the feelings. Reilley often used the common tool of holding her breath in order to hold in her feelings whenever we got too close to them. In the imagery, she and the ten-year-old used a jackhammer to cut a hole in the rock. She invited her inner children to each say something. The teenager, whom we'll meet next, said, "bitch." The ten-year-old said, "hate" and the baby said, "help." Imagery of this nature, when attached to feelings, breaks the old programming and allows new ways of living to be developed by Reilley's cognitive Core Self.

To further illustrate the type of dialogue Reilley had with her inner selves, I am including an exchange that happened when she first began having pictures supplied by her subconscious that indicated sexual abuse. Reilley was well entrenched in denial at the time and did not want to be dragged out. The following is a loving conversation between her cognitive self and the baby:

REILLEY:

What the f—k is wrong with you and these f—king pictures that you think you must send my way, you little bitch.

CHILD:

How can I be a little bitch? I'm too little to be hardly anything. What is your f—king problem?

REILLEY:

I'm just sick of this shit.

CHILD:

I'm sick of being alone with this shit. Why won't you listen to me?

REILLEY:

I don't like talking to you about this junk. I do like nice tunes with you.

CHILD:

> Well f—k you. You just want the stuff that feels good. You are really selfish.

REILLEY:

> I know.

If, as a therapist, I had been unaware of Reilley's personality type, I might be concerned that she was "re-wounding the child," that is, beating up on herself. In actuality, this was a productive and valuable interchange, with each of the two wanting to come together. The baby knew that until Reilley got beyond denial, she, the baby, would be alone. The theme of her letters was "Listen Up!" An INTJ is not going to use the same language or communication style that would be expected of an ENFP whose dialogue would be flowery, loving and filled with metaphors, or an ISFJ who would be concrete, protective and loyal.

DRUGGY GIRL—THE TEENAGER

By the time she was a teenager, Reilley had settled into her role as Scapegoat in the family and was acting out with alcohol and drugs. In college, she added sexual promiscuity. This put her in a difficult position. As an INTJ, she needed to do well in school and be perceived as smart. As Scapegoat and to kill the emotional pain, she had to act out. All the while Reilley was using alcohol and drugs daily, she was making excellent grades in school, studying music and participating in band.

At home, all the Four behaviors were in high gear. She sat in her room alone with unexplained feelings of

longing, listening to melancholy music she termed "Abandonment's Greatest Hits." She felt hopeless. Consequently, we were able to determine that each time a triggering incident resulted in intense Enneagram Four behaviors accompanied by a desire to use alcohol and drugs, yet with a strong sense of responsibility, the teenager was around. Even when Reilley had suicidal thoughts (a Four trait), she laid out her plans in a responsible manner, considering those who would find her body and making arrangements for her dog.

When we were able to define the teenage ego state (figure 11-17a), Reilley immediately felt close to her. She felt she understood her best of all the kids. It was easiest for her to bond with this teenager because she remembered her pain so well and has continued to live in it for most of her life. She brought in a picture of the teenager and wrote the dialogue on the following page. Note the opening lines reflect the same position she takes in the drawing in figure 11-17b, done at a much earlier time.

Teenager	Distrusting
Troubled	Anxious
Intense	Why am I here?
Perfectionist	Unique
Very responsible	Longing
Angry	Lonely
Sad	Overwhelmed
Cute	Death and dying
Baby dyke	Loss
Searching for family	Loner
Druggy	Smart
Gagging	Serious
Guarded	Musical
Suspicious	Serious
Defensive	Dark
Apprehensive	All the Four stuff

Figure 11-17a

Figure 11-17b

This is how the druggy girl felt on the inside. Actually worse than this. This is the coping druggy girl. I don't want to draw the real druggy girl and you can't make me.

THE TEENAGER BEGINS:

I look pretty calm and wholesome in that photo but on the inside I am in total pain and feel so lost and alone and desperate.

REILLEY:

Dear Reilley at 15,

I remember you very clearly, you are hard to forget because it seems like you were in high school, living that nightmare for a long time. Each day felt hopeless and didn't change from one day to another. It was a big empty, endless feeling. And you tried to make yourself have fun and be with friends, but you always knew underneath that the heart of you was still empty.

TEENAGER:

I live here. You should come and get me. If you don't, you are like our real mom who left me places and forgot about me. If you are like her, I am screwed.

REILLEY:

You are definitely more important than that sleazeball woman. I know I can take better care of you than she did. I realize that's not saying a lot because by this age she wasn't doing much of anything for you. But I am a better person for you to be around than she is. So what do you think of that? I'll be the mom.

TEENAGER:

It would have to be an improvement.

REILLEY:

OK. I will be gentle when I think of you and know that you were druggy and "acting out" because you didn't know what else to do. I know that you had a really hard time. I remember your stuff better than the other kids' stuff.

Reilley used music throughout her teen years and up to the present to keep the Four very active. She had a wide collection of recordings by other Fours such as Melissa Etheridge who recorded the theme song for Fours, *Precious Pain*. She languished, longed and lamented with other Fours such as John Denver and kd lang. She listened to them for hours, sinking deeper and deeper into the Four melancholy that had no real defined source. These feelings are intense, but they are not productive unless they can be attached to events that affected early programming and then worked through. She once told me how she longed for the good old days when "the Cardinals were winning and people were dying and I was enjoying life."

Ironically, Reilley felt a high degree of responsibility in many areas. As a teen, she felt a strong degree of responsibility for her brother even though their relationship was strained. Even as an adult, she has felt guilt for "not being a better mother to him" despite the fact that she was just three years older and it was not her job. She was highly responsible at school, going years without an absence. She maintained straight As in college even though she was constantly strung out on alcohol and drugs and was highly sexually promiscuous.

With sexual promiscuity, Reilley found a way to both act out and connect with her mother. It began with the incident she had recounted in her case history. At seventeen, Reilley told her mother she was going away for the weekend with her new boyfriend. Her mother inquired about birth control, fixed them a thermos of whiskey sours and sent them on their way. "I lost all respect for her that day." Reilley reports that she was "wasted" all weekend and it was attributable to coming to a deeper realization that she did not have a mother. That weekend was the beginning of promiscuous behavior that lasted several years. She became filled with shame and remorse yet was unable to stop acting out sexually. In addressing these behaviors in therapy, Reilley had the teenager write a letter to her mother.

Dear Mom

I needed you to tell me I couldn't go f—k Joel and I certainly didn't need you giving me

chemicals to go enjoy my lay with. I think,
and I am young, that you were really f—ked
up to do that. I was your kid.

It was the teenage Reilley who developed the "tough" defense and began using alcohol and drugs. The teenager is the ego state that most personifies the Enneagram Four and carries a lot of Reilley's anger as well. By identifying her, we had a very important tool with which to work on these aspects of Reilley's personality.

THE SMART KID

Reilley and I had been working together for about a year and we were making steady progress. Neither of us was dissatisfied with the work and Reilley was seeing some satisfying changes in her life. Yet, during each session, there was a considerable amount of time spent in intellectualizing and discounting what we had previously covered. We seemed to have to go back time and again to recover ground I thought we had claimed without doubt earlier. Finally, when one session began in this manner, it suddenly occurred to me to wonder, "What is going on here?"

I had suggested that we do some work with the teenager around an incident Reilley had just recounted to me. She responded to my suggestion as if it were a completely unheard of idea. "Why?" she asked. After thirty minutes of intellectualizing as if she had never done anything like this before, I realized this was more than just an NT needing to understand what I was suggesting. She had successfully derailed my approach and kept me occupied in a nonproductive cognitive discussion for half an hour. This was a defense tactic. I began to talk to her about her need to be smart in grammar school. Even though Reilley was the Scapegoat at home, she was able to use her INTJ-ness to fill a more natural Hero role at school where she always led her class academically and managed to be every teacher's pet. In addition to her intellectual abilities, she used her cuteness, her charm, her wit and humor. This combination won her the attention she so

desperately needed from the teachers who were mother-substitutes. Reilley admitted this had been very important to her emotional survival as a child. We found a picture of her at age eight that personified this little intellectual person who took learning very seriously. Figure 11-18 gives a list of descriptors Reilley identified for this child as well as all the "good stuff" she received for this defense tactic.

Reilley acknowledged what an important role this part of her played throughout her life. When I suggested that we work on toning this child down, Reilley was instantly filled with fright. When I asked her to talk about the fear, she said she felt very vulnerable: "You've broken the code." If she no longer had this part of her Defense System, she was afraid I would have free access to her innermost being. She feared losing this defense might mean losing part of her identity as an NT, that is, being recognized for her "smartness." She found that understandably terrifying. Yet she could also see how this intellectual facade kept her from being real. After assuring her she would be no less smart when we were finished, she tentatively agreed to work with this child.

Reilley agreed to image dialoguing with the Smart Child. She complimented the child on her resourcefulness and thanked her for all her hard work. She then told her that, as a child, she was carrying too much responsibility. She should not be in charge of getting attention, self-esteem, value and other such important matters. She encouraged the child to relax a bit and let Reilley as an adult handle the responsibility of getting

THE SMART KID

Description:	**Rewards:**
Intense	Self-worth
Studious	Attention
Alone	Recognition
In her head	Value
Focused	Sense of control
Knowledge hungry	Stand out
Advanced	
On a different plane	
Not very sociable	

Figure 11-18

those needs met. After the imagery, Reilley felt something had shifted and felt a bit uneasy about beginning to dismantle such a major part of her Defense System. The next day, she left me a message saying she felt like "Superman without his cape, Alvin without the Chipmunks, Tony Orlando without Dawn and Cher without Sonny."

In identifying and defining this last ego state, each of the major defense strategies that Reilley has used (delineated in figure 11-7, page 237) were now assigned to a child:

Baby
  Anger
  Dissociating

Five-Year-Old
  Co-dependence
  Slide to Enneagram Two

Smart Child
  Intellectualizing (NT)
  Control (NT)
  Dry humor (NT)

Editor Child
  Denial
  Noncommunication

Teenager
  Enneagram Four
  Anger
  Tough (NT)
  Alcohol, drugs and
    other addictions

This knowledge made it much easier to navigate Reilley's Defense System and gain her unconscious as well as her conscious cooperation. When she is triggered, Reilley's entire Defense System moves into operation (figure 11-7, page 237). The logical INTJ is not accessible, and it is pointless to direct conversation to that part of her brain when it is not engaged. Reilley had a dream that gave her a visual representation of the diagram in figure 11-19b, which shows how she can "switch" back and forth between the rational INTJ and the Defended Child. She was in jail, held in a cell that was on the right side of a two-cell unit. Reilley expressed her dream in the drawing (figure 11-19a) called "Jailhouse Rock." The door of the cell was open but she was too frightened to leave. She had a cellmate who was a happy-go-lucky person oblivious to the seriousness of the situation. The left cell was empty. The two-cell unit was at the top of a set of stairs, indicating metaphorically that it was in her head. The stairs even looked much like neck vertebrae. Reilley's dream confirmed that her own Defense System can hold her captive and that she has the power to leave the cell. It also dramatically illustrated that, when she is under the control of the Defense System, nobody is home on the left side of the brain (figure 11-19b).

ESTABLISHING AN ADULT

By the time we had identified all the kids that were running around unchecked inside of Reilley, she was ready to admit that her rational, cognitive part was not in charge of her life. She had so much wanted to believe

Figure 11-19a

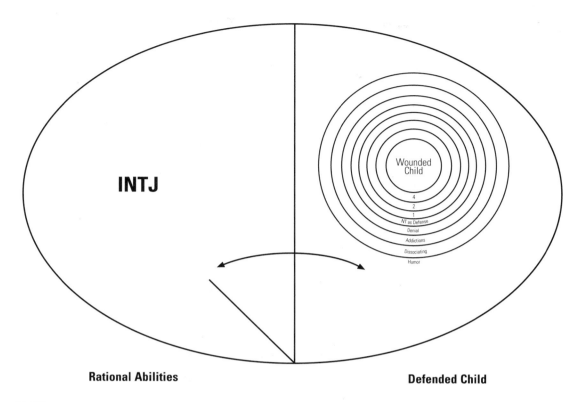

Figure 11-19b

that was not the case. It is very humbling for an extremely cognitive type to accept the idea that something as irrational as emotions may be in control. I have a rule that says, if there is a war between the head and the "programming," the programming wins 100 percent of the time. Each time Reilley was triggered by someone or some incident that was similar in feel to an unconscious childhood memory, one of the kids would take over with her particular set of issues and defense strategies. These kids are not enemies. Their purpose, just like any defense strategy, is to take care of the vulnerable, undefended spirit. I believe the Defense System is activated before birth and grows in strength and versatility throughout childhood. Meanwhile, the child silently grows into an adult, but the Defense System does not take notice and keeps operating, business as usual. It becomes our job, then, to notify the defenses that there are more options available, and that these new adult-style options are more powerful and more effective in taking care of the spirit.

I encouraged Reilley to become completely familiar

with herself as an INTJ. This personality type is strong, competent and in charge (refer back to figure 11-1 on page 228). I kept her consciously aware of that part of her personality by pointing out incidents in her daily life where the INTJ demonstrated its strength. She quickly became familiar with her INTJ traits and found it very easy to distinguish those traits from her defenses, especially the Enneagram Four. She soon realized she had been selling herself rather short in the area of competency. I had her read various authors' descriptions of the INTJ until she readily recognized it was operational in her life. She could then believe and trust in her abilities as an adult, and I could show her how to rely on those abilities to take care of herself instead of letting "the kids" muddle through with all the tricks, tools and coping skills they had developed over the course of her life.

I gave Reilley a pad of newsprint and asked her to list all the traits of a perfect mother. She looked at me, trying to figure out where I was going with this. She headed the page with "To be used to *manipulate* me later." She was on to me; she just didn't know where I was going. She produced the following list:

To be used to *manipulate* me later . . .

> Accepting
> Encouraging
> Concerned
> Interested
> With boundaries
> Guiding
> At home
> Doing domestic things such as cooking and laundry
> Involved
> Protective

Next, I had her draw a picture of what a mom with those qualities would look like (figure 11-20). Finally, I asked her to check off each trait she exhibited in the stellar care she gave to her little dog, Skyler. She checked them all. I asked her to take a look at the drawing of the woman wearing a shirt with "I Love My Kids" on the front and arms outstretched. The rendition of the mom looked suspiciously like Reilley herself. Reilley was beginning to see she had the necessary qualities and the ability to re-parent herself and to break the cycle of pursuing a mom that did not exist. She had projected this perfect mom onto her mother, keeping her longing for the unattainable, the nonexistent.

Figure 11-20

It is important to take a look at the qualities that Reilley indicated were important mom attributes. These are not universal. Each personality type will value certain parenting traits. NTs very much value guidance. The other three temperament types will have their own key traits. INTJs are devoted and supportive parents, fostering independence. Reflected also in

Reilley's list are the qualities she missed because her mother was not around much. These are the attributes that are uniquely important to Reilley, and she knew instinctively that she could do a good job of re-parenting herself using those qualities.

At the end of the session, I sent the drawing home with Reilley and she made a color copy with photos of her "kids" superimposed with this Reilley-mom. She keeps it framed at home as a reminder to take good care of her kids.

The best place to find the adult in any person's life is at work. Reilley knew that at work she was generally very professional, proficient and competent. Through imagery, we could access those feelings and incorporate them into the adult who was then able to interact with the kids. In some of the dialogue reproduced in this chapter, Reilley interacts with an inner child and reassures that part that the adult can handle the situation and be in charge more effectively than the child. The adult has many more resources than the child. The adult has a house, car, paycheck, credit card, telephone, support system, therapist and the ability to take herself out of any situation that is potentially harmful. The child had/has none of these and had to be very creative and inventive to come up with ways of protecting herself. Sometimes, the coping techniques are harmful in the long run—alcohol, drugs, sexual promiscuity, eating disorders, compulsive shopping and other addictions. Yet, I always compliment the kids because they thought of *some* way to kill the pain and survive emotionally.

Application

Once Reilley and I had identified the Smart Child, she seemed more receptive to my suggestions of working with the kids instead of fighting with them and arguing with me. Prior to identifying the Smart Child, no matter how many times I demonstrated the effectiveness of working with the kids, I could not seem to win her total cooperation in applying it to everyday living. As cooperative as Reilley was in session, she still resisted enlisting the kids' help with her day-to-day problems. She would call me with an incident that triggered her and left her feeling out of control with unexplained feelings. When I would ask if she had "talked with the kids," she would groan and argue with me. "How do you know those kids have anything to do with this?!" Once the Smart Child was identified, there was a shift and Reilley began really acting as if she and the kids were on the same team.

Early in our work, I started Reilley working with the ten-step exercise (chapter 10, page 207). She resisted in true Reilley fashion even though she reported success when she used it. I encouraged her to write it all out in her journal, a process she found tedious because she was unable to see its purpose. Eventually, as she trusted the process more and more, we were able to downsize the exercise to two steps done mentally in a matter of a minute or two.

Step 1: Identify the Incident

Each day, we encounter countless triggers that have us operating out of unconscious programming and acting in ways that defy logic and reason. Freud said one of the purposes of therapy is to make the unconscious conscious. Tony DeMello stressed awareness. Before we can deal with a problem, we have to be aware it exists. In this first step, I had Reilley simply write down the triggering incident that caused her to react. One such incident occurred at work and was an ongoing trigger. Reilley was afraid she was going to say or do something inappropriate because it was causing her so much distress. She described a weak, ineffective male supervisor who was a pushover for a loud, manipulative female employee. Their dysfunctional game playing should not have had any impact on Reilley as it did not actually affect her or her job. However, she felt herself responding with anger towards both of them.

Steps 2 and 3:
Identify Feelings Somatically with a Stick Figure

In the second step, Reilley drew a stick figure and indicated where in her body she physically felt herself reacting. She could feel it in her hands, which wanted to be fists, her back, her stomach and her neck and shoulders. The purpose of this step was to make Reilley aware of what was going on in her body so that the body could act as an early warning device for her. For left-brain types like Reilley, the body is often considered nothing more than a delivery system for the head, allowing the head mobility it would not otherwise have. If Reilley could become aware that her body was beginning to react to a situation, she could take steps early to avert a full-fledged triggering situation.

Step 4: Name the Feelings

Next, Reilley listed the feelings her body indicated were present. She identified anger, frustration, fright, disgust and that she was troubled, annoyed, upset and powerless to do anything about it. From this information, we could determine we were working with the Baby. As Reilley worked and cooperated with body messages, she learned that her stomach sent scare messages and her hands and back sent anger messages, and the inability to breathe meant she felt very vulnerable.

Step 5: Trace the Triggering Agent

When there is an over-reaction, it is very helpful to identify the unconscious reaction to the trigger. What is *really* going on here? I asked Reilley to list the adjectives to describe the two people who were causing her to over-react.

Male Supervisor	Female Employee
Wimp	Phony
Funny	Manipulative
Goofy	Loud
Irresponsible	Bossy
Oblivious	Sneaky
Undependable	Irresponsible
Easily manipulated	Unreliable
Scared of confrontation	Drunk
	Liar
	Charming
	Lazy

As Reilley made the two lists, she quickly realized that the woman had the same qualities as Reilley's mother, and the male supervisor, who should have done something about the situation and did not, was very similar to her father.

Step 6: Draw the Child

I asked Reilley to draw herself as a child when she felt the physical sensations she described in Step 3. Her drawing would give form to the ego state reacting to the trigger so that we would have something concrete to work with. When the child is drawn, we know the age and which child, or set of defenses and issues, we are dealing with. In this instance, it was clear it was the Baby who was being triggered.

Step 7: Give the Child a Voice

Since the easiest way to allow the child to speak is by using the nondominant hand to write, Reilley gave the Baby the opportunity to express how she felt. She described how it had been living with those two people and how the two at work made her feel like it was happening all over again. Writing with the nondominant hand occupies the left brain with the mechanics of writing and allows the right brain the opportunity to communicate. It is a very effective tool; many times, the writer is surprised by what appears on the page.

Step 8: Express Feelings

After Reilley allowed the child to write, I asked her to read it out loud. There are two ways to read a letter such as this out loud: one is from the head, the other from the heart. Most people, and especially Reilley, will try to read from the head to avoid any feelings. I asked Reilley to read the letter from a place lower in her body where her feelings were active. By doing this, she could access the feelings, allowing her to physically express her fear and anger.

Anger can be expressed physically in a number of ways. Pillows can be used to beat on with fists or a plastic bat. Some people have punching bags or destroy cardboard boxes with a bat. Sometimes exercise routines such as running up or down stairs or hitting a ball with a racket or bat can be used. It is important, though, to know that you are angry and at whom you are angry both in the present *and* the past. It is also important to allow the feelings full expression and not shut them down prematurely. This is called going all the way through a feeling and not backing out of it.

Backing out of a feeling due to guilt or fear of the intensity of the feeling only leaves the person feeling worse.

Step 9: Affirm and Protect the Child

Reilley could then access the strength and compassion of the adult (INTJ), trusting her to write a letter to the child with her dominant hand. The letter expressed understanding and explained that what was going on at work was not about the child. She assured the Baby that she did not have to handle the situation and was free to leave whenever these two people acted up. Reilley, the adult, would protect the child, speak up when it was appropriate and/or leave the area whenever necessary.

Step 10: Play Music for the Child

Reilley loves music and especially enjoys Shana Noll's *Songs for the Inner Child*. This was one of the few therapeutic tasks she happily embraced.

TRIGGER CYCLE

As Reilley developed more and more confidence in this process, she was able to streamline the whole ten-step exercise down to simply identifying and acknowledging her feelings and protecting and affirming the child. She subscribed to the new AA: Acknowledge and Affirm. She has been able to incorporate this into her operating system so that the exercise that previously took a half hour or more could be handled in a minute or two without benefit of paper and pencil. By working with the kid ego states, Reilley can be sure that they are not directing her professional life, nor are they interfering with interpersonal relationships. Reilley has been able to make some significant changes in how she handles people and situations. Two years after encountering her "parents" at work, Reilley took a new job only to find the exact same personality configuration between her new male boss and a female employee. The difference was that Reilley had changed. She easily detached from the interplay of the two without the high cost of emotional energy and upset in the first situation.

Together, Reilley and I mapped out her personal

Trigger Cycle

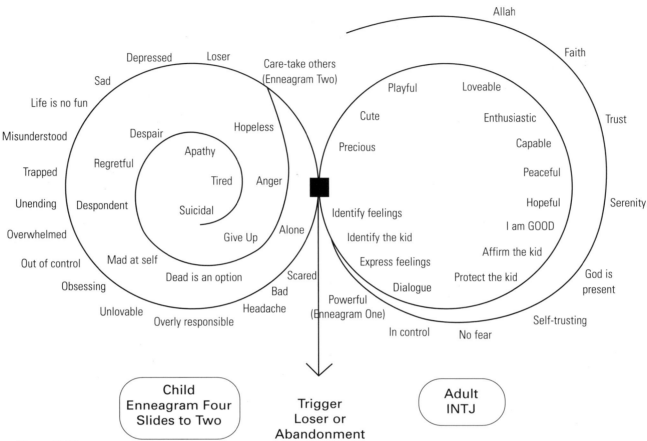

Figure 11-21

trigger cycle (figure 11-21). When she finds she is reacting to a trigger, which is indicated by her body sending her messages, she is in a position to make choices. She can either follow old methods of coping and move to the left side of the trigger cycle where the kids are in control, or she can intervene as an adult and move to the right side and take care of the kids. She can either BE her inner child or PROTECT her. On the left side of the trigger cycle, all the defenses are employed, ending with a spiraling down to suicidal thoughts. On the right side, there is a feeling of personal power, expansiveness and spirituality. At the point of being triggered, Reilley has to move to identify her feelings and work with the kids which will keep her solid, stable and in control. If she does not make use of that opportunity, the further she moves into the left side of the cycle

the more energy and intervention tactics it will take to move out of the downward spiral.

SPIRITUALITY

Reilley is a very spiritual person. She had a need to know that God was part of the healing process from the beginning. Throughout our work together, we often set time aside to address this concern. For the most part, it was a very cognitive approach on Reilley's part. She wanted to document proof that God approved of the approach we were taking and that God was supporting her emotional work. However, near the end of her therapy, she began connecting with God on a noncognitive, intuitive level, which indicated to me that she was on the home stretch. In one such session, I led her in imagery to find the place within her body where the

INTJ - 4

Figure 11-22

God part was centered. She located a place in her abdomen. I invited her to go inside in imagery and take a look at the God part. She described it as an orange-and-yellow ball, with a halolike effect of light. Later, when she drew a picture of it from the front, the halo of light made it look like the Helmeted Child (figure 11-22). From the top, it looked like it had three sections. In discussing the symbolism of these three sections later, we determined they could have a variety of meanings: body, mind and soul; adult, child and spirit; as well as other more specific references in Reilley's life. In the imagery, I encouraged Reilley to enter the orange-and-yellow ball. She was surrounded by light and immediately felt welcomed with warmth and acceptance. Reilley sat peacefully in this inner space and imagined she held her inner child as a baby. She felt very affirmed and very convinced of God's participation in the work she was doing.

On another occasion, I asked Reilley to enter the "Reilley Building" and pass through all the doors of her defenses. When she reached the center of the building and had successfully negotiated all the defense doors, I asked her to take the escalator down flight after flight until she finally reached the bottom. At the very bottom, she found a room filed with white, bright light. In this space, she interacted with the spirit of her loving, affirming grandmother and met with her Future Self. She was very pleased with how she imagined her Future Self whom she saw as cool and very wise. Her Future Self told her she was OK; not that she was going to be OK, but that she *already was OK*. Reilley felt very affirmed and encouraged by the experience.

Again, I believe strongly that imagery does not lie or give inaccurate information. Reilley entered therapy feeling she was a loser and had a considerable degree of dysfunction, most of which she saw as her own doing. Her imagery was telling her otherwise and it was very heartening to see her reach self-acceptance.

At this point in time, Reilley has met nearly all her goals. She has even begun to work on dancing and is entertaining the idea of pursuing a serious relationship. Reilley has shifted from seeing herself as a loser to seeing herself as someone who was trying to cope with the effects of abuse, someone who was struggling to make sense out of a senseless situation. She now surrounds herself with safe and supportive friends. She occasionally attends Twelve-Step meetings including SIA (Survivors of Incest Anonymous). She feels she has a greater ability to live her life as she determines rather than as she has been programmed. Reilley is now able to fully express the person she was designed to be.

> I tuck her in her warm bed,
> a place that she loves and knows she is safe
> a haven of warm flannel.
>
> I kiss her soft eyes and hair
> and place my hand on the top of her head,
> feeling the warmth.
>
> She is small, a child,
> She is me, and I love her.
>
> *Reilley*

This poem was written several years before Reilley entered therapy, which demonstrates that each of us has an innate knowledge of the Child Within.

REFERENCES AND SUGGESTED READING

Bass, E., and L. Davis. *The Courage to Heal.* New York: Harper Perennial, 1988. This is a classic work on the effects of childhood sexual abuse. The authors address the need to have a voice, break the secret, own your feelings and accept that it was not your fault. The personal stories are both compelling and difficult for survivors to read because they will trigger feelings and memories; however, that can be so useful in the healing process. It is the buried memories and feelings that cause unrest, depression and the like. Although this book is excellent, it does not do follow-up interviews with those who shared their stories and it almost exclusively addresses male upon female sexual abuse. Very little attention is directed to female perpetrators or male victims.

Beattie, M. *Codependent No More.* New York: Harper/Hazelden, 1987. This is the first major work devoted to the recovery of the co-dependent. It is a highly acclaimed work and continues to be the handbook for recovering co-dependents. Melody Beattie has written other insightful books on recovery and spirituality. Many of her works are available on tape through any recovery bookstore.

Black, C. *Double Duty.* New York: Ballantine Books, 1990. Although Black is describing the effects of growing up in an alcoholic family, she is also addressing many issues faced by those who come from families that were abusive but without alcoholism. This book emphasizes the problems of children facing other challenges, such as physical disabilities or belonging to an ethnic minority, as well as the problems encountered in a highly dysfunctional family.

Bono, C. *Family Outing.* Boston: Little, Brown and Company, 1998. This book is recommended by both Reilley and Joan for those dealing with issues associated with "coming out" as gay or lesbian because it is presented from a child's firsthand perspective. Chastity Bono relates the immense emotional pain she encountered due to her mother's rejection of her as a lesbian.

Evert, K., and I. Bijkerk. *When You're Ready.* Rockville MD: Launch Press, 1987. Writing under a pseudonym, Bobbie Rosencrans tells her own story of recovery from sexual abuse by her mother.

Forward, S., and C. Buck. *Betrayal of Innocence.* New York: Penguin Books, 1978. Susan Forward delves into one of the last great secrets of our society: incest. She describes a variety of incestuous relationships including mother/daughter incest, which is rare and even more rarely addressed. An incest survivor herself, she presents many personal stories from case histories and describes her methods of working with other survivors.

Mellody, P. *Facing Codependence.* San Francisco: Harper, 1989. A good discussion of co-dependence and the effects of "dysfunction" on a child. Mellody provides a credible description of the various types of abuse. She is a pioneer in the recovery field.

Penley, J., and D. Stephens. *The M.O.M.S. Handbook.* Wilmette IL: Penley and Associates, Inc., 1995. Describes the strengths and struggles of the sixteen MBTI types as mothers. Provides tips to improve parenting skills for each type. To order, contact Penley and Associates Inc., 604 Maple Avenue, Wilmette IL, 60091 or call 847.251.4936.

Rosencrans, B. *The Last Secret.* Brandon, VT: Safer Society Press, 1997. A study and report on the topic of childhood sexual abuse of women by their mothers giving data and case studies of nearly one hundred women.

Tieger, P. D. and B. Barron-Tieger. *Nurture by Nature.* Boston: Little, Brown and Company, 1997. Describes each of the sixteen MBTI personality types from birth through childhood with many examples. This book assists the healing process by allowing you to read about yourself as a child and understand that your individual needs were probably not met. Helpful to parents for gaining insight into their children's behaviors, especially understanding why siblings can be so different. The examples presented in the book appear to portray "perfect," completely savvy parents who at times appear unrealistic.

The Twelve Steps of Alcoholics Anonymous. 1993. Center City MN: Hazelden. A basic book on the twelve-step approach.

Additional Contacts

A. A. World Services Alcoholics Anonymous, 475 Riverside Dr., New York NY 10115, 212.870.3400.

Survivors of Incest Anonymous, World Service Office, P.O. Box 190, Benson MD 21018, 410.893.3322, http://www.siawso.org.

PART IV

Free to Be

CHAPTER 12

VISIBLE RESULTS

Because this type of healing work is a process with a beginning, a middle and an end (see figure 9-1, page 173), it is possible to monitor progress along the way. But, like being in a car traveling through a curving tunnel, the light at the end of the tunnel cannot be seen until the last part of the curve is negotiated. Once core work is completed and that last turn has been made, it can be seen that there has been progress and that very good results are beginning to manifest themselves. This chapter will describe some of the visible results that can be expected. In the next chapter, some invisible results will be addressed.

CONTROL RESTORED TO THE CORE SELF

One of the first things that becomes noticeable is the increased manifestation of the Myers-Briggs Type Indicator traits of the Core Self. Those who are Intuitive begin to trust their intuition and creativity more. Those who are Introverted start respecting that part of themselves and begin providing quiet time for themselves. Each person begins to question whether or not she is living out of her Core Self or if she is simply living the way she has been told to live. People who have always wondered, "Who Am I?" begin to find the answer to that question.

A person who is co-dependent feels without value. She will give away her self, her time and her possessions in order to keep the other person with her because that person could not possibly want to be with her for her merits alone.

Career changes are often made. Denise, ENFP-4, was a hairdresser without a college degree. She went on to get a degree and to begin master's studies in order to become an art therapist. She will be excellent at this because her work will be an expression of her True Self and will manifest her giftedness.

Mary and Sarah, both ISTJs, never trusted their financial abilities because they had been programmed to believe they were not competent. ISTJs are extremely astute investors. I encouraged both of them to trust in themselves and begin investing money; they both started very slowly, not completely believing me or in themselves. Both have done well and are enjoying their financial ventures tremendously. I gave the same advice to Sylvia, an ISTJ-6, telling her that because she had the financial prowess of the ISTJ combined with the conservative traits of the Enneagram Six, she could not help but do well. She had never even entertained the idea that she could succeed in the area of investments. Sylvia bought several books on investments and found she had trouble putting them down. To her, reading them was as compelling as reading a mystery book to most other people.

Anita, ENTP-1, developed a long-range plan that would enable her to retire while still in her forties and work full-time on her art and other creative interests. Without working as determinedly on her personal healing, Anita would have devoted herself to climbing the corporate ladder and to accumulating more and more material possessions as proof that she was "OK."

Judy, INTP-6, left her office job to attend school full-time in order to pursue scientific research, a career to which she is much more suited but never believed in herself enough to try before doing healing work.

And finally, Jeanne, an ENFP-4, who was mentioned in the Introduction and who came to see me completely unable to work due to depression, has completed studies and is working as a hospital chaplain. She brings an understanding and gentle presence to those she assists because she has walked through her own dark night of the soul and come out into the light.

BOUNDARIES

Boundaries are a visible sign that there has been considerable emotional healing. What are boundaries? What does it mean to "set boundaries?" Before pursuing how to set them, the place to start to understand boundaries is by understanding how they are lost. When the soul is put away, a huge black hole opens up (as described in chapter 8). Because there is a basic instinct to fill this void with the Core Self, there is an insistent and persistent demand by the black hole to be filled. When we do not recognize the need for self, there is always an attempt to fill the black hole with other things and other people. This never works but can provide a temporary fix. When things are thrown into the black hole to appease it, addictions are often the result (chapter 8). When people are thrown into the black hole, it can result in sex or relationship addictions and in co-dependence.

Co-dependence is when you are compelled to take care of the other person at your own expense because, in truth, you are hiding from yourself. You are hiding in relationships, focusing on another so that you do not have to look at yourself or deal with your pain and problems. Regardless of what your wants, needs or desires are, they are subordinated to those of the other person. In focusing on the other person, you can blame your circumstances on someone else and feel assured that you can only be happy when that person does something (or stops doing something). You completely give up responsibility for yourself because you do not feel you have personal worth or personal power. How could you have worth? You do not have a soul!

When you feel you have no value, then you try to earn people's regard by serving them, by taking care of their feelings and by not burdening them with your feelings or your wants. You feel you are not entitled to opinions that differ from the other person's. You have a deep sense of questioning your own worth that arises from that wounded child within you: How could someone so defective have anything valuable to contribute? The other person must be right. Women, who make up three-fourths of the MBTI Feeling types, are more prone to monitoring other people's feelings and "reading" them than men, who constitute more than half of the Thinking types. Intuitive Feeling (NF) types cannot avoid being intensely aware of other people's feelings. When an NF is without boundaries, she becomes extremely co-dependent.

In the realm of the Enneagram Defense types—Ones in their need to be perfect, Twos in their need for identity through serving, Threes through their need to win the other person's approval, Sixes in their need to be obedient to authority, and Nines in their need to avoid conflict and merge—all are exceedingly prone to trying to fill the black hole with co-dependent behaviors.

A person who is co-dependent feels without value. She will give away her self, her time and her possessions in order to keep the other person with her because that person could not possibly want to be with her for her merits alone. It becomes next to impossible to say "No" to anyone, even someone she dislikes, because everyone has more value than the co-dependent. It becomes her job to fix everyone's problems no matter what the personal cost.

If the Core Self has been put away and there is no sense of self, it is very easy to be defined by someone else. Without access to the soul, there are no boundaries. The co-dependent is subject to familial and cultural dictates as to role, appearance, values, beliefs and even thoughts about herself, others and a Higher Power.

When asked for personal information, the co-dependent person feels compelled to furnish it no matter how uncomfortable it feels because, having no sense of self, she feels she has no right to say "No." Saying "No" risks the other person's disapproval and the black hole would feel even bigger and emptier.

A co-dependent in an abusive relationship continually tries to figure out what she is doing wrong or what she is doing to cause the abuse so that she can change and get the abuse to stop. A co-dependent is unable to leave the relationship because, not having any sense of self, she feels that this type of treatment is justified. There is an underlying fear that no one else will ever want to be with her. The wounded child wonders: Who would want to be with someone who is so defective? Within a relationship, the co-dependent feels compelled to relinquish dominion over her own body to the other person, feeling she cannot afford to reject any unwanted sexual advances and that she does not have the right to say "No."

Along with the insistence of the black hole to be filled by anything and anyone, there is the commensurate programming from outside sources such as culture, family and religion which leave the recipient believing she has no right to boundaries, no right to a voice and certainly no right to say "No."

Clients and workshop attendees often tell me that to confront all of this and put oneself first is selfish. I am not opposed to serving, giving to and doing for another person, but it needs to be a gift freely given, without resentment, without anger, without expectations and with a sense of free choice and joy. When giving is done out of co-dependence due to having no boundaries, it is not the selfless act people purport it to be. Giving for the purpose of filling the black hole is done for the person doing the giving, not for the recipient. That is a truly selfish act. When the Core Self is restored, then any giving that is done comes out of a place of genuine love for self and others and not to assuage the cravings of the black hole.

When our culture does not allow women to have anger, it lays the groundwork for boundary-less women. When family and culture raise young girls to have no sense of self, as Mary Pipher so aptly points out in *Reviving Ophelia,* then another generation of co-dependent women who have no sense of boundaries is inevitable. When women spend more time and energy worrying about being nice and unselfish than they spend on taking care of their own souls, then our culture becomes seriously out of balance and it becomes imperative to address this.

It is crucial to have boundaries. Without them, it becomes impossible to determine if someone else's behaviors are appropriate or not. With a co-dependent being completely focused on the other person's needs, wants, and desires, it would be impossible to know if and when her boundaries are being invaded. How would someone without a sense of self know the difference between having sex with someone out of love, out of duty or being assaulted? A game or dance develops between the co-dependent person and the other person who needs to control and dominate.

A parent without boundaries cannot teach boundaries to her children. And so, the legacy continues. The child and the parent become emotionally enmeshed, and the child grows up to find someone to partner with in order to carry on the dance.

There was a trend a few years ago to try to teach the art of having boundaries. It was called assertiveness training. Co-dependent people flocked to classes to learn how to say "No." It worked as well as a diet works when food is being used to kill pain. After telling the black hole that it may not have a donut to kill the pain, then what? Likewise a co-dependent person can be taught to say "No" the next time the PTA asks for a volunteer, but then what? How are the insistent demands of the black hole going to be addressed? What happens to the guilt held when the person feels too unworthy to have said "No?" How can a person be taught that she has the right to say "No" when she is convinced she does not?

Having boundaries is about knowing where you end and someone else begins. It means having a good, solid sense of self and a working understanding of the personality of the other person, all the while knowing that the other person has full responsibility for self-care. This can only happen when there has been enough healing work to restore the Core Self to its rightful place of authority. Once your Core Self is restored to you, you will treasure it beyond belief. It becomes so precious to you that you will not let anyone or anything take it from you again. You will not allow anyone to stand between you and your Core Self. You cannot help but protect, nurture and generally are for the Core of your being. To paraphrase Scarlett O'Hara: "As God is my witness, I will never hunger for my soul again!"

And so, one of the visible indications that the corner has been turned in healing work is the appearance of boundaries. Many people have told me they are shocked to hear their own voices speaking up at work or in a family or social setting where they would never have stood up for themselves before. After healing, it becomes impossible to stay silent when someone threatens your emotional safety or says something offensive about who you truly are. Therese, ISTJ-9, reported that she heard someone speaking up to her boss at a staff meeting, something that is rarely done, only to realize that the voice was her own! Many people list in their goals for therapy that they want to be able to stand up to a controlling parent. When I tell them that it is quite do-able, they always remark that it would be a miracle. When therapy draws to a close and boundaries are in place, it is impossible *not* to stand up to that person.

Boundaries do not require much work, they just automatically appear. However, a little attention to communication skills may be needed to maintain the boundaries but at the same time not turn people away. That is why I refer to boundaries as being semi-permeable membranes. They need to keep out anything harmful, but not close down communication altogether.

In the imagery of the safe house, I asked you to

Having boundaries is about knowing where you end and someone else begins. It means having a good, solid sense of self and a working understanding of the personality of the other person, all the while knowing that the other person has full responsibility for self-care.

install a fence around your property and a gate in the fence with the instruction that your adult self would determine who may come in and who may not. If you take the imagery to another level, you can consider that the house represents your body, the Child represents your spirit or Core Self, the adult represents your cognitive abilities and the fence represents your boundaries. The gate in the fence, which the adult controls, keeps the boundaries from becoming walls which barricade other people out and barricade you inside.

Once core healing work is complete, the adult is always careful to monitor her boundaries, keep invaders out and realize immediately when her boundaries are threatened.

RELATIONSHIPS

Every relationship, no matter how superficial or how important, is affected by doing deep emotional healing work. A person's whole operating system is changed. Instead of operating out of a position of defense (figures 8-12 and 8-13, page 164), she begins operating out of her Core Self. Instead of being in relationships to appease the black hole, she is in a relationship to mutually share in a spiritual journey. When such profound shifts occur within, it affects a person's attitudes and behaviors towards other people, who tend to notice.

Of course, boundaries are a major factor affecting relationships but there are other factors as well. One major factor is expectations. With each relationship, we all have a tendency to project onto a perfectly unsuspecting person someone we want that person to be. If you interview for a job and your potential boss seems pleasant enough, you begin to project onto your boss the person you expect her to be. When your boss goes about being who she really is, it often bumps up against your expectations. Wait a minute! Your boss was not

supposed to be short-tempered or take credit for something you did. You *expected* something different. You expected the boss you had designed for yourself. Generally, you expect your boss to have viewpoints similar to yours. The most common expectation in a relationship is that the other person sees things the way you do. However, as common as the expectation is, that is never the case.

Suppose you are an INFP who is working for an ESTJ boss. You have wonderful, exciting, visionary ideas as to how the company can grow and a myriad of creative approaches to change the old ways things have been handled. When your boss is less than enthusiastic, you are offended. When your boss asks for documentation, you feel she does not trust your competency. When your boss is skeptical about the outcome of your ideas, you feel defeated and not valued. You have projected an NF personality onto your unsuspecting ESTJ boss. Before healing work, there is a need to project a version of the self onto the other person. The attitude is that if the other person thinks as I do or sees the world I see, then I am validated. It is a matter of looking for that original parental mirroring which has been discussed throughout this work. After healing work, you are the mirror for your own soul, validating yourself. The other person does not have to be just like you in order for you to be OK. You *know*, without a shadow of a doubt, that you are already OK. It has been said that if two people are exactly alike, one of them is expendable. When you feel confident in your own identity, you feel very comfortable allowing the other person to have his/her own identity as well.

And so, after emotional healing work, as the INFP above, you would still present your ideas but you would not take your boss's reaction as a personal affront. You would be more willing to meet your boss's needs as an ESTJ, whose only goal is to keep the company running on a smooth and steady course. You would be more willing to accept that it is your boss's company and, as such, your boss is entitled to run it in a manner that is consistent with an ESTJ's views and values, not yours.

The same is true of personal relationships. If romance is introduced into the mix, it becomes even more complicated. If you are attracted to someone romantically, it is usually someone who is reminiscent of a parent or primary caregiver. You will immediately begin to find things in that person that seem validating, thereby proving to your parental unit that you really are OK. You have finally won over Mom or Dad by winning the approval of a look-alike. You begin to project upon this person the perfect parent and perfect spouse. It is only a matter of time before your expectations are dashed. When that happens, there is additional anger because the residual anger left from your parent is added to the pot.

When the core issues in healing work have been addressed, it is easier to see the other person for who that person is. That is both good news and bad news. Sometimes you do not like what you see. Most often, it is possible to see all the baggage the other person is carrying along with who that person really is. Sometimes, you are so tired of having carried your own parental baggage for so long that you are unwilling to help shoulder the other person's baggage.

After healing work, one thing is universally true. The balance in every relationship is changed because half of the people involved in that relationship are changed— you. The other person is often confused, frustrated and rather dazed by the whole procedure. That person feels like the rules have been changed in the middle of the game. If you are in a relationship with someone who is controlling and demanding and you have been the co-dependent server all this time, you can understand your partner's confusion when you are not willing to play that way any longer. When you began healing work, your partner may have been encouraging, wanting simply a happier version of the suffering servant.

Your partner did not expect someone who no longer wants to be the Co-dependent Poster Child of the Year.

With access to your Core Self restored and boundaries in place, it will become very important to you to have open, honest relationships without any game playing involved. A semi-permeable membrane replaces the walls, and you are ready to connect with the other person on a level that feels real and authentic. If that person is still living defended with walls and defenses very much intact, there are bound to be problems. When the problems begin to mount, there are three options. First, the other person escalates old behaviors in an effort to restore balance to the relationship. In the example of the controlling/co-dependent relationship, the controlling person will become even more controlling hoping to pull you back into your co-dependent position. If this fails, the other person may take a long, hard look at himself/herself and decide it is time to face his/her own issues. Of course, this is the most desirable option because the whole relationship would then have an opportunity to reach a greater level of honesty, openness and intimacy. If neither of these options succeeds, the relationship generally ends. It is seldom that the balance in a relationship can be thrown off so profoundly and yet remain solid and unchanged. Clearly a very visible outcome of healing work is the renegotiating of relationships. You will insist on only open, honest and real interactions whether on a professional level, social level or very intimate level.

Once there is a willingness to understand the other person in the relationship and to forego projecting a fantasy upon that person, it will take effort to really understand that person. Even after you have reached an understanding of the person and how he/she is wired up, it will still take work to resist the attitude that your partner ought to change. No one's basic personality needs to be changed for you any more than you should change yours for another person. I am not talking about annoying habits such as leaving the cap off the toothpaste. I am referring to basic traits of personality that are inherent in either the Core Self or in the Defense System. Those traits are genetic and cannot

EXERCISE

EXPECTATIONS

Suppose you have made arrangements with another person to take a trip. You have talked about what you would both like to do and you feel your plans are nicely in place. Unexpectedly, the other person suggests a totally different itinerary, changing the itinerary or perhaps withdrawing from the trip altogether. You react with anger, frustration and a myriad of other emotions. Besides using the ten-step exercise in chapter 10, page 207, to process these feelings, you can approach the experience as an opportunity to grow in understanding and acceptance.

First, if you know the person's MBTI Core Self and Enneagram Defense System, read about those. If not, proceed with an open mind. You might prop up a picture of the other person in front of you while you work.

1. Using the nondominant hand method, begin an imaginary dialogue with this person. Your nondominant hand will represent the other person, and you will be represented by your dominant hand. Talk back and forth just as if you were having a conversation, all the while remembering with whom you are talking; this is not a mirror image of you. Do not stop the dialogue until you have reached some resolution between the two voices.

This exercise, used with the ten-step exercise in chapter 10, will clear the air of your anger and allow you to have a nonemotional, nondefended conversation with the other person to work through what happened and come to some consensus.

2. A variation of this exercise is to write a letter to yourself from the other person explaining to you why that person took the actions in question. Again, keep writing. Do not stop until you have reached some resolution. Using your nondominant hand would be more effective than using the dominant hand.

change nor should they be *expected* to change. The challenge, then, becomes one of dropping expectations, gaining understanding, coming to acceptance, and then loving the other person fiercely for exactly who that person was designed to be.

In order to proceed in that direction, participate in the two exercises above to help you gain a better perspective on interacting with another person.

Sometimes simply reading about the personality type of the other person, both MBTI and Enneagram, will help you to see why the person acted in the manner you are questioning. If you do not understand the motivation behind that person's actions, you are very likely to assume those actions have the same meaning as if you were to take them. That is a completely false premise. I guarantee that the other person does not process information and make decisions exactly as you do. If the person is a Perceiving type and you are a Judging type, it is possible the person is simply exploring other options. If the other person is an Extravert and you are an Introvert, it is possible the other person is simply thinking out loud while you are listening; you are not expected to take the external processing as the final answer. Or an Enneagram Six may have become frightened or overwhelmed by the trip and pulled out due to panic. An Enneagram One might change the plans for the trip because they were not quite right and needed some fine-tuning. So, there may be an underlying motivation, of which you are completely unaware, for the behaviors you witness. If you arbitrarily assign meaning to these behaviors based on your own personality type and your own history, you are only adding fuel to the fire.

One very surprising and welcome visible result of doing healing work is improved relationships with parents. It is surprising because so often Inner-Child work is labeled and condemned as "parent bashing." However, the point of Inner-Child work is not to have people hate their parents, but rather to bring feelings that already exist into consciousness where they can be addressed, worked through and dispatched. When that happens, the old anger and resentment fades and you can see your parents with new eyes. When boundaries are in place, when expectations of the perfect parent are dropped and when you can be the mirror for your own soul, it is possible to have a relationship with your parent under conditions that you define. This can happen whether your parents are alive or deceased.

Please bear in mind that I am talking about the normal, garden-variety dysfunctional family. If a parent sexually abused you or was violent in other ways, you may have no desire to enter into any kind of relationship with that parent. That is perfectly all right and I urge you to resist pressures by culture, religion and greeting card companies to "forgive and forget." Listen to your own heart and decide how you can best protect and provide for your inner child. Then follow those directions to the letter no matter what anyone else says or implies.

But suppose your family was of the standard dysfunctional variety with, for instance, a workaholic, nonpresent dad and a co-dependent, controlling mom. After you have completed all your work around these two as suggested in Part III, you may be ready to work on understanding your parents and accepting them for who they are instead of who you wanted and needed them to be.

To begin with, uncovering their personality types and reading about them will help enormously. If you are able to do that, read about them in *Nurture by Nature*, by Tieger and Barron-Tieger, which describes the MBTI types as children. If you read about your mom's MBTI type as a child, you will be reading about the child she was trying to raise when she was really raising you. What she was doing was providing you with everything that she had wanted as a child, without realizing that you needed something entirely different. You can also use the exercises on page 265 using the

nondominant hand to enter into a dialogue with your parent.

Finally, there is a little imagery exercise on page 267 that may bring a wider perspective and additional understanding to your relationship with your parent. As with any imagery exercise, if you just *think* it through, you will be on the wrong side of your brain to receive any valuable help. You must fully experience the imagery in the manner described.

You may wish to journal about this experience. The information you receive does not need to be accurate or factual. Your subconscious will furnish you with whatever you need.

The purpose of this exercise is not to produce a historical document or prepare a brief for a court case; it is merely to gain greater understanding and acceptance of a person who is significant in your life.

There are three major factors that help enormously in understanding and accepting another person. First, knowing and understanding the Core Self or MBTI type. Second, knowing and understanding the Enneagram Defense System of that person. Third, constructing a general idea of the baggage that person is carrying which activates the Defense System and restricts the Core Self. The more you understand these three keys, the more you can accept the person for who that person was designed to be, drop your expectations that the person will be anything other than that and, finally, love that person without conditions or expectations. Then you can get on with *be*-ing yourself and allowing the other person to *be* as well.

COMMUNICATION

As noted previously, when boundaries are established, a voice appears to enforce them. What you will notice, however, is that the voice generally has a good communication style. You will find that you speak without hidden anger, sarcasm or manipulative tactics. You will not feel defensive or need to be on the attack. You will become more and more comfortable with giving "I messages" (chapter 8) rather than accusations, criticisms and judgment. The change in communication style reflects the fact that you are now operating out of your Core Self and not out of your Defense System.

You will find as well that you can discuss any topic without becoming defensive as long as you work through the issue using the techniques in chapter 10 before having your discussion. If you need to have a difficult talk with someone important to you such as your boss, spouse or friend, take the time to visit with

EXERCISE

MEETING YOUR PARENTS

Find a comfortable place where you will be undisturbed. Close your eyes and take as much time as you need to focus on your breathing in order to draw your attention within. Find a safe and quiet place inside to examine whatever is provided to you during this exercise. Decide which parent or primary caregiver relationship you wish to review. When you are ready, ask your inner child to be present with you in imagery. Whatever age she is represented as will be fine. Be with her as the loving, protective adult just as you have in other exercises. Be sure you are grounded in your adult body, not just watching yourself, by feeling your feet on the ground, feeling the child's hand in yours, looking down at the child and at what you are wearing. Begin walking with the child, all the while letting her know that you are there to take care of and protect her. Eventually, imagine that you come to a house or building, which you may or may not recognize, but it is the childhood home of your parent. Stop and take a good look at this house. Take note of size, condition, color, style and the like. When you are ready, move to the front door. Reach out and touch the door, letting your fingers examine the texture of the door. Drop your hand to the doorknob and let yourself and the child inside. While you hold firmly to your child's hand, explore the house until you find your parent as a small child. When you find that child, take note of the room, what the child is doing, the child's age and what the child is wearing. Try to get a close look at the child's face and to look deeply into the child's eyes in order to see what is behind the face presented to the outside world. Ask this child

some questions such as:

"What is it like to live in this family, in this house?"

"What is hardest for you right now?"

"What do you hope for in your future?"

"What makes you sad, scared, angry?"

"What do you like to do most?"

(Notice the absence of "why" questions. "Why" questions will move you to the left side of your brain. Try to avoid them.)

Then ask your inner child if she would like to talk to this little person or ask any questions. When their interaction feels complete, perhaps you and your inner child would like to leave a small gift for this little child. Whenever you are ready to leave, bring your visit to a close in any manner that feels comfortable to all concerned. Then take your child by the hand and leave that house the same way you came in. Out on the street, turn and begin walking in the same direction from which you came. As you are walking, you can discuss your visit with your child and process any new information or feelings you may have experienced. Look back to see the house getting smaller and, eventually, round a bend or turn a corner, causing the house to completely fade from view. When that happens, take your inner child to her safe house where you can spend as much time bonding with her as you wish. When the experience feels complete for you, begin to draw your attention back to the room in which you are sitting by feeling the chair supporting you, feeling your feet on the floor, recognizing any familiar sounds and, when you are ready, open your eyes.

your inner child, whether in writing or in imagery, and make arrangements with her regarding the upcoming conversation. Suggest she stay at the safe house and let you, the cognitive adult, handle the interchange. If you are taken by surprise and drawn into a testy or unpleasant situation without time to prepare yourself, you do not need to have that conversation on the other person's timetable. This is a very important point, especially for Introverts. You can stop the conversation and make arrangements to meet again later, giving you time to prepare. If that is not possible, you can say you were just on your way to the restroom and will be right back. This will give you a few minutes to prepare. In these kinds of situations when you are not able to journal or take time for imagery, you can imagine putting your inner child behind you or tucked away safely in your heart (or whatever works for you) in order to give her a sense of being protected and to let her know that the adult is going to handle the situation. When the situation is over, do not simply put it behind you. Take the time to journal or dialogue with the child and use the ten-step exercise in chapter 10, page 207, to process your feelings.

Remember that the best way to diffuse a difficult situation is to present the other person with someone unwilling to enter the dance. As long as the other person is not abusive, try to let that person know that you are not only listening but also hearing. Then present your side using the communication model in chapter 8 (figure 8-17 on page 167), with *I* statements. You will find that the tension between you will diminish and your child will not only feel protected but also realize that you have a voice to use on her behalf.

When your healing work is well underway, you will find this type of communication becoming very natural. It is a very visible sign that you have turned the corner and have moved into the home stretch.

REFERENCES AND SUGGESTED READING

Beattie, M. *Codependent No More.* New York: Harper/Hazelden, 1987. This is the first major work devoted to the recovery of the co-dependent. It is a highly acclaimed work and continues to be the handbook for recovering co-dependents. Melody Beattie has written other insightful books on recovery and spirituality. Many of her works are available on tape through any recovery bookstore.

Bolton, R. *People Skills.* New York: Simon & Schuster, Inc., 1979. Provides some basic communication skills, particularly reflective listening. Many examples and sample dialogues.

Mellody, P. *Facing Codependence.* San Francisco: Harper, 1989. A good discussion of co-dependence and the effects of "dysfunction" on a child. Mellody provides a credible description of the various types of abuse. She is a pioneer in the recovery field.

Pipher, M. *Reviving Ophelia.* New York: Ballantine Books, 1994. An excellent discussion of the effects of culture on young girls. Mary Pipher throws a light on many previously unexamined sources of wounding to little girls. She presents a compelling case for a thorough scrutiny of the culture from a feminist perspective. She gives little attention, however, to the primary source of wounding to young children: the family.

Tieger, P. D. and B. Barron-Tieger. *Nurture by Nature.* Boston: Little, Brown and Company, 1997. Describes each of the sixteen MBTI personality types from birth through childhood with many examples. This book assists the healing process by allowing you to read about yourself as a child and understand that your individual needs were probably not met. Helpful to parents for gaining insight into their children's behaviors, especially understanding why siblings can be so different. The examples presented in the book appear to portray "perfect," completely savvy parents who at times appear unrealistic.

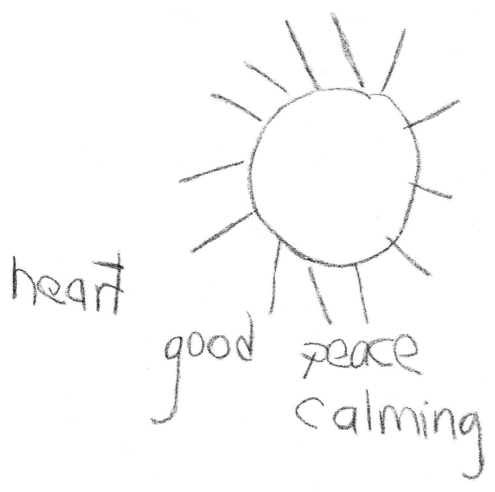

CHAPTER 13

INVISIBLE RESULTS: SPIRITUALITY

"And a child shall lead the way." (Is 11:6)

What is Spirituality?

Generally, at the end of healing work, an increased interest in spirituality begins to emerge. Spirituality is an ongoing process, as figure 9-1, page 173, indicates. Like defining God, it is easier to say what spirituality is not than what it is. It is not religion, although religion can be used to express spirituality or to hide from it. It is not discerning right from wrong and living morally. It is not living a good life and earning entrance into heaven. Spirituality has more to do with how we define ourselves and the resulting relationship with a Higher Power and with other people. If we define ourselves as

bodies with souls, we will see ourselves differently than if we think of ourselves as souls with bodies. If we reach true spirituality, we see ourselves more as spiritual beings than as corporal beings. With such a view, it is easy to conceive of tapping into the collective unconscious. Each person can be thought of as a spring originating from a great underground source of water. Following the spring to its source puts us in touch with the collective unconscious, with a Higher Power and with other people on a purely spiritual level.

Spirituality is highly individualized. Each Myers-Briggs Type Indicator personality type will have a different approach to, and understanding of, spirituality. (For a review of MBTI theory please see chapter 3.) We have encountered problems throughout history due to the fact that we have tried to come up with a one-size-fits-all approach. Just as we are often attracted to a mate or friend with a different personality type or temperament, we are often drawn to investigate a means of spirituality different from our native style. We find the difference at once interesting and compelling, yet frustrating in that the match is not completely comfortable. That is when we try to change the person, or the religion, to be more like us. Therefore, when an NF religious figure, such as Jesus, Gandhi or Martin Luther King, Jr., speaks in metaphor, as any NF will do, it has appeal to those attracted to an approach that is different from their own; it is intriguing. However, it is not long before the culture, basically SJ, will try to change the approach to fit the SJ worldview. Soon, every metaphor will be interpreted literally. Judeo-Christian tradition and scripture illustrate this perfectly. Starting in Genesis with Adam and Eve, biblical writings are taken literally to the point that people spend entire careers searching for the place that was the Garden of Eden or for the wreckage of Noah's ark. When Jesus taught, he spoke as an NF, in metaphor and generalities. The SJ culture codified and solidified the concepts into rules and regulations. As time passed, the very words that Jesus brought to liberate were reframed and used to establish and sanctify a form of spirituality comfortable for only one segment of humanity.

The same is true in Hebrew scripture, so rich with metaphor and stories used to illustrate concepts. Long before being recorded, these stories were passed on orally and understood in that context. Eventually, various collections were assembled and written down. As time passed, scholars, scientists and theologians filled volumes trying to explain how Jonah stayed alive inside the belly of a whale—and other such metaphors. There are many different interpretations of the New Testament passage stating that it is easier for a camel to pass through the eye of a needle than for a rich man to

gain heaven. Seldom does an explanation point out that it is simply metaphor and not meant to be taken literally.

Sensing types predominate in the population and are concrete and literal in their thinking. As noted previously, the culture is SJ and, therefore, directs the forms of spirituality found in most organized religions. Of course, there is nothing wrong with the SJ form of spirituality; however, as SJs comprise only 47 percent of the population, SJ spirituality does not feel comfortable to the rest of the population. This creates a situation in which 53 percent of people cannot completely relate to the religious concepts of their heritage. Consequently, many people blame themselves for not fitting in. Therefore, I am fond of the saying "God has no grandchildren," which encourages us to examine the belief system handed to us by our parents; it points out the need for each of us to come to terms with our Higher Power in our own way and through our own personality temperament.

Religion works the same as any communication situation; when one personality speaks, another listens. What is spoken is most often not what is heard. When sitting in a traditional church or synagogue listening to an ESTJ minister, priest or rabbi speak, what is heard is only that which conforms to the worldview of the listener's type. For instance, an NF can only interpret what an SJ says through an NF temperament. It is not right or wrong to interpret in such a way; it just is. Similarly, when an NF speaks, the SJ listener can only take that information in through an SJ worldview. When the NF speaks in metaphor and generalities, the SJ hears facts, rules for living, and specific directions. Problems arise when these unintended interpretations are taken to the extreme—when families are divided, church schisms occur and religious wars and unspeakable horrors such as the Inquisition and the Holocaust result.

An understanding of the different temperaments' approaches to spirituality would lead to greater acceptance of our own personal path to a Higher Power. In accepting our own personal spirituality, we would be

An understanding of the different temperaments'
approaches to spirituality would lead to greater acceptance
of our own personal path to a Higher Power.
In accepting our own personal spirituality, we would be more likely
to allow others the freedom to follow their Internal Wisdom.

more likely to allow others the freedom to follow their Internal Wisdom.

Accessing the Internal Wisdom, the God Within, is the most effective method of exploring a personal spirituality. It develops a spirituality with personal integrity, following the directive that the kingdom of heaven is within. It honors the uniqueness of the individual and respects different personality types. However, accessing this Internal Wisdom is not as easy as some purport it to be.

To follow the metaphor found in Hebrew scripture, because of early wounding, we left our souls, represented by the Garden of Eden. The gates closed and we were on the outside, saddened, lonely and longing to go back home. We took up residence on the outside, in our defenses, and went about making the best of things. Yet always, we are drawn towards the Light, instinctively knowing where we are is not where we want to be. An attempt to reach an altered state through addictions is an indication of the heart's search to get back home. However, as many can attest, it can be a long trek through the desert before reaching the River Jordan.

EXPECTATIONS

When the Core Self is put away because of early wounding, access to the spiritual self is limited. But the longing is always there. Authors Charles Whitfield, Lucia Capacchione and John Bradshaw, just to name a few, indicate that spirituality is the end product of healing. Before healing, we are impeded in our attempts at true-to-self spirituality by many things, one of which is expectations. Expectations are the property of the wounded self and are at the root of emotional pain.

Instead of living with *who we are* and *what is,* we live with who we *could/should be* and *if only.* Instead of accepting another person for who that person is, we expect behaviors and thinking more in line with our own. Instead of relaxing in the care of a Higher Power, we try to control our own lives and the lives of those around us.

Expectations prevent us from seeing Truth. Truth lives at the very core of our existence. Truth is the hallmark of our Higher Wisdom. With Truth, we know we are in harmony with a Higher Power. With expectations, we do not see reality; we see the world through a distorted lens. Spirituality requires that we live in reality to the best of our abilities, always seeking the Truth. Expectations, by their very nature, preclude that from happening. Before expectations can be eradicated, we must be aware of their existence. That is why all great spiritual leaders stress "awareness, awareness, awareness." It is the first step in the healing process (chapter 2). Psychologist Sam Keen, like many concerned with spiritual growth, encourages us to live the question. M. Scott Peck in *The Road Less Traveled* urges us to question everything. This is especially true of our beliefs, assumptions and certainties.

EXPECTATIONS OF SELF

Anita entered my office for the first time one bright summer day and filled the room with her energy. She was obviously very bright, very competent, very accomplished and very wounded. We talked for a bit about what brought her into therapy, and she volunteered that she was looking for someone to tell her how she "should be" and what was "normal" so that she could just get about doing it. She was forty years old, a middle-management executive, and felt she was missing something. She wanted me to tell her what that "something" was and how to get it. She was confident she could put "it" into effect in her life.

How do you explain to someone that she is missing and longing for her own soul?

Anita was certain that fulfillment was about doing something she had not done before, something she had overlooked. I was not surprised to find Anita was an Enneagram One and an ENTP. In taking her case history, I learned that her mother was also an Enneagram One, but probably an ESTJ. Her mother had some very strong, strict and narrow religious and family rules. Anita's mother ran the household during Anita's childhood; her dad was very passive.

Anita's Enneagram One Defense accepted that the only way she could gain Mom's approval was by embracing all Mom's "shoulds." Since Mom was herself an Enneagram One, the "shoulds" were in abundance. Anita certainly brought some of her own self-imposed "shoulds" to the arrangement, which, all in all, turned her life into continuous striving for the unattainable— perfection. Anita now wanted me to help her figure out what she needed to accomplish in order to reach her goal of perfection. She was hoping that it would bring the happiness and peace that had eluded her until now.

Anita was surprised and a little confused when I suggested that therapy would not quite go along in those directions. She elected to stay with it anyway and we embarked on an adventure that took two years. The emotional pain Anita lived with every minute of every day was incredible. For the most part, it came from her Enneagram One trying to live up to her mom's impossible standards. The expectations she put upon herself were inhuman and unreal. She readily acknowledged she would not put those expectations on anyone else in the world, but, for some reason unknown to her, felt that she *should* be able to live up to them.

Anita was certain happiness came from doing— doing more, doing better. Every time I said to her, "It's not about doing, it's about being," she looked at me with the confusion of a puppy trying to understand the loving chatter of its owner. Most of our sessions dealt with the expectations she put upon herself to be perfect, which were easily traced back to the child trying to be perfect to achieve Mom's acceptance and love. In imagery, Anita saw her inner child with perfectly braided hair, in a perfectly starched and ironed dress, wearing perfectly white anklets and shiny patent leather dress shoes. She was always looking to Mom to see if she was good enough.

In the beginning of therapy, Anita was looking for information on how to improve the little girl to make her finally acceptable. She equated her mother's approval with love. She was surprised and intrigued to find that her happiness did not become attainable until she was able to put the child in overalls, loosen her hair and let her go barefooted to get dirty. She was able to relinquish the need for her mother's approval only when it was replaced with her own love for her inner child. Each time Anita came into the office in emotional pain, her imagery went to the little girl in the braids and starched dress. When we had resolved the issue at hand, her imagery automatically turned the child loose in the back yard, dressed for fun. When we had restored the "dirty girl" to being loved and cherished by Anita, Anita could feel peace, contentment and serenity within.

Certainly Anita was wounded from the expectations her mom had inadvertently put on her. Yet Anita herself bought into those expectations. As children, we have no defense against the externally imposed standards by which we are evaluated. However, as adults, we can make the decision to re-evaluate these standards and do the emotional healing work that would change the expectations we have of ourselves.

Does this mean we should have no expectations of ourselves? Of course not, but those expectations have to be closely examined before they are embraced. If we do whatever is necessary to know, accept and love ourselves, then we can be expected to live out of that knowledge and be true to the person we were designed to be.

Anita illustrates another point on expectations as well. Anita could never be her mother's clone nor could

> *So, we expect that we should be able to do what*
> *we can do and what others can do as well.*
> *These misplaced expectations are built*
> *on the expectations that our early caregivers had of us.*

she be an ESTJ to please her mother. We expect that we can do the things we are designed to do naturally. We also expect that we should be able to do the things others do, and as well. Anita, an ENTP, is creative, imaginative, and inventive and was filled with dreams and ideas. Her mother, an ESTJ, is practical, detailed and realistic. Anita could not see her own abilities. She could only see that it was very hard to be like her mother. She was aware that she was able to be creative yet she took that very much for granted, focusing on what she was not: practical, detailed and realistic.

Because we live with our own personal gifts and talents from birth, we assume everyone can do those things. We are amazed at the abilities of others. We think, "How do they do that?" In grade school, I remember being amazed at children who could memorize all the multiplication tables. That was an unbelievable feat to me. I never saw the things I could do that they could not do. I just knew something was wrong with me because I could not keep all those tables in my head.

So, we expect that we should be able to do what we can do and what others can do as well. These misplaced expectations are built on the expectations that our early caregivers had of us. We simply accepted the programming and the resulting wounding, and now we continue to live our lives around the misperceptions we internalized. When we are in this state of self-alienation, we have limited access to our Internal Wisdom and to our own spirituality. Therefore, we question everything about ourselves and certainly do not believe in ourselves. Henry Ford said, "Whether you think you can or can't, you're right."

When Anita completed therapy, she was firmly grounded in a relationship with a Higher Power that was very separate from the religious beliefs of her mother. She developed her own, personal relationship with God and began living her life out of that orientation. She communicated with God in her own language and in a method that felt natural and comfortable to her. She found a church that supports her style of spirituality. She now sees herself for the extraordinarily gifted person that she is and is shaping her life in order to live out of her giftedness. Anita now fully understands the concept of "being." She is exploring "Paradise Regained." It is certainly new territory but she finds it very exciting, rewarding and the source of the peace she sought.

People who experience Inner-Child healing and begin to free their Core Selves risk the danger of being called "weird" or "different" because they are allowing their nonstandard inner beauty to shine. If you are called "weird" you can choose to hear that in any number of ways. I urge you to not hear it as saying something is wrong with you. Instead, choose to hear it as saying someone noticed that you are different from the cultural norm. Celebrate being weird! Be grateful that it is so strong that it shows! And do not forget to say "thank you."

EXPECTATIONS OF OTHERS

The first universal expectation we make of another is that the other person is like us. Each person assumes everyone sees the world the way she does, or, if not, they should. Each new parent expects that the baby is a little replica of herself. A new parent wants to give this beloved child everything she did not receive, whether the child needs it or not. Many religions embrace the concept of original sin. In fact, this expectation—to be like me—is part of the wounding messages parents send to a child and is the real definition of original sin because it causes the child to "turn away" from his/her own soul and consequently from God. It is the atrocity passed down from one generation to the next, without exception, "visiting the sins of the fathers on the children to the third and the fourth generations" (Numbers 14:18; Exodus 34:7). How can a new parent celebrate the baby's uniqueness, her separate and individual spirit, when the new parent is focused on making the baby just like herself? The same is true with other relationships. If we expect each person we encounter to be a replica of ourselves to some extent, we will never be able to acknowledge, accept and celebrate that person's uniqueness.

When we are intent on placing expectations on another person, it can be very frustrating for both involved. Someone once said that wanting another person to meet your expectations is like teaching a pig to sing; it is frustrating for you and it annoys the hell out of the pig. Besides inflicting emotional damage on the other person, our expectations take us out of our Core Self and anchor us squarely in the Enneagram Defense. We can start to think that if the other person is not like us, then perhaps there is something wrong with us. We begin to think that the other person may be right and we are wrong, or that somehow it has become our job to make the other person over and we have failed in the mission.

Another reason we have expectations of others is because we have an innate need to be heard. If the other person can see the world as we do, we feel heard and understood. We feel a sense of "I Am-ness." We feel we have been recognized and that we exist; it is validation for our very being. When we search for that external validation, the search continues to keep us looking for unconditional love from sources not equipped to provide that kind of love. With emotional healing, we can look to the God Within (*Yahweh*, "I Am;" Ex 3:14) for validation and for the standards against which we measure ourselves.

When we can completely accept ourselves for the miraculous creatures we were designed to be, we can drop our expectations of others as well. Just as in the story of the ugly duckling, we can stop expecting to interact with a duckling and honor the creature for whomever or whatever it really is. Not expecting either a duckling *or* a swan, we can enjoy and appreciate the miracle as it unfolds before our very eyes. Suppose I plant some petunia seeds only to find that the plants come up as daisies. I can either curse the daisies and miss their beauty entirely or be delighted in my surprise, letting go of my expectation to have petunias. We need to greet each person we encounter in the same way, just as the Hindus do using *Namaste* ("I honor God within you"), dropping expectations and acknowledging the uniqueness of, and the God Within, that person. We can never change the other person to meet our expectations; therefore, it is imperative we learn to change ourselves by discarding the lens that is distorting our perception of the other.

EXPECTATIONS OF A HIGHER POWER

We all have expectations of God. Some of us expect God to be a Santa Claus figure. As children, we pray for a bicycle or a baby brother. We learn to say our prayers like a shopping list of wants and blessing requests, rather than to connect or interact with a Higher Power. When we turn to God with a list of specifics, we generally have the desired outcome in mind and are disappointed when God does not see what is best for us the same way we do. We are praying for the mountain to be moved instead of equipment and strength to climb. We forget that God is not so much interested in our surface happiness as in our wholeness (holiness).

Others of us expect God to be like a punitive parent. With this attitude, we see God as a vindictive judge-in-the-sky. Because of our expectations of God, we learn to follow rules and anticipate what might please or displease God. We interpret troubling events in our lives to be some sort of punishment from an angry deity.

Then there are those of us who expect God to be humanlike, believing that God would think, behave and feel in the same manner as humans. When we expect God to respond in a manner commensurate with human behavior, we expect human behavior that is in agreement with our own personality type. In addition, we will then usually attach a gender to God and expect God to act according to that gender assignment. Here, God is either a loving or a strict father figure, embodying all the masculine traits associated with the stereotypical male. Fewer people see God as a nurturing mother. This viewpoint is more often associated with indigenous cultures such as the Native American rather than with traditional western culture.

Most people expect God to be wholly other, to exist outside and apart from themselves. Feeling so separate from God makes it very difficult to enter into a personal relationship with a Higher Power.

The expectations a person places upon God tell us more about that person than about God. Most of us acknowledge a Higher Power, but the expectations placed on that Higher Power do not define God. Rather, those expectations tell us about the needs of the person holding the expectations. Each person sees God through her own lens of personality type, personal history and programming. The need to define God and set expectations on a Higher Power speaks volumes about the need to control and our discomfort with mystery. The deepest mystery we can encounter is the mystery within ourselves. It is the most difficult journey, the most challenging search, the most frightening quest and, at the same time, the most rewarding adventure imaginable. One of the biggest barriers to accessing our Higher Power is our concept and expectations of God; the other is our concept and expectations of ourselves.

Hebrew scripture tells us God is *Yahweh,* the great "I Am" (Ex 3:14). Christian scripture quotes Jesus as asking, "Who do you say *I am?*" (Mt 16:15). When we are separated from our own identity, from our Self, we are separated from our own "I Am-ness." In Christian scripture, Jesus directs us repeatedly to look for the kingdom within ourselves, not externally (i.e., Lk 17:21). Over many centuries, we have molded the word *sin* to mean some kind of moral failure, when in actuality it means turning away or being separated from God. This happens not by actions, but by being alienated

from the very center of our being, our Core Self. The only real sin is the loss of Self. Accordingly, the only purpose in life is to know and embrace the Self. Consequently, spirituality is found in *be-*ing, never in doing or in knowing.

Therefore, rather than following spiritual leaders, searching in books or looking to institutions, we must come to know instead that what we are searching for is something we already possess. "Be still and know that I am God." Access to a Higher Power needs merely to be uncovered, recognized and released. If we can do that, and then get out of the way, God will lead us to amazing places.

> *I laugh when I hear that the fish in the water*
> *is thirsty.*
> *You don't grasp the fact that what is most*
> *alive of all is inside your own house;*
> *and so you walk from one holy city to the*
> *next with a confused look!*
> *Kabir will tell you the truth: go wherever you*
> *like, to Calcutta or Tibet;*
> *If you can't find where your soul is hidden,*
> *for you the world will never be real!*
>
> The Kabir Book
> Versions by Robert Bly

JUDGMENT, SIN AND FREE WILL

Right along with expectations comes judgment. Judgment can only bring separation and divisiveness. The story in Genesis describes in metaphor how humans became judgmental. Adam and Eve ate of the Tree of the Knowledge of Good and Evil, which caused them to think they knew the difference, resulting in judgment. The judgment of others, and the judgment felt from others, caused separation from each other and from their very souls, the Garden of Eden. It is this "knowledge" of good and evil, right and wrong that causes expectations and judgment.

When a client asks me what is the right thing to do in any given situation, my answer is always, "Right

Our concept of sin, then, needs to be re-examined.
We can reject the relatively recent definition of sin
as moral failure and return to the original meaning:
"turning away from" or "separated from."

according to whom?" If we line up ten people and ask each what is right or wrong in any situation, we will receive ten different answers. Even if some of the answers are similar, the reasons for arriving at those conclusions will be different. The only true source of what is right or wrong is our own Internal Wisdom, the God Within. The only access to the God Within is via our own souls. When we rely on someone else's values and truths we discount and devalue ourselves. It tells us and God that we do not believe we were created "good enough" to figure out our own truths, values and spirituality. This turns our focus to an external wisdom source; all the while the kingdom of God is residing right inside of us. Author Stephen Wolinsky has said, "People are smarter than God. People know the rules; God just is." If we can drop our expectations and look to our Internal Wisdom, we will see there is no absolute right or wrong.

Our concept of sin, then, needs to be re-examined. We can reject the relatively recent definition of sin as moral failure and return to the original meaning: "turning away from" or "separated from." If we continue to accept the cultural meaning, a transgression, we have to accept that there was choice, or free will. Certainly there are behaviors that are vile, reprehensible and injurious to others. To call them sins brings judgment and we, as mere mortals with limited knowledge and understanding of any situation, have no business entering the judging game. If we are addressing these behaviors in others, we cannot possibly know the motivation behind what we see. If we are addressing these behaviors in ourselves, then we are called to determine what is happening to cause us to act in such a manner.

When we act in a "sinful" manner, we are operating out of some type of coping device. We are not operating out of our Core Self or Spirit but out of an elaborately constructed Defense System, which *will do anything* to protect us emotionally. If you will remember, the Defense System does not have a brain. Its only job is to defend. Ted Bundy, the Florida mass murderer, in the last interview before he was put to death, stated that each time he killed, he vowed he would never do it again, only to find himself compelled to repeat his horrendous acts. People in prominent positions, from politicians to clergy, find themselves risking their careers, families and futures by acting out sexually. These people do not make these decisions out of the rational part of their brains but out of their Defense Systems, which have no rational abilities. The same is true for each of us on a perhaps less conspicuous or blatant level. Why did Mary (ISTJ-1) continue to rage when she hated herself for doing it? Why did Denise (ENFP-4) continue with an eating disorder that could be life-threatening? Why did Paula (ENFP-1) allow her obsessive-compulsive behaviors to rule her life? Why did Darlene (INFP-5) consider suicide when she wanted to be a part of her children's lives for a long time to come? Why did Kyla (INFP-3), Peggy (ENTJ-1) and Julia (INFJ-1) allow their relationship addictions to threaten their futures? Why did Kory (ESFP-8) permit her anger, and Reilley (INTJ-4) permit her chemical addiction, to jeopardize their careers? Why do so many women enter relationships with or marry unsuitable men when every fiber of their bodies screams out against it? Why are so many women consumed with guilt over abortions they never wanted to have? Add to this list your own list of unwanted behaviors. In each of these instances, there was no choice, no free will and no "sin." Each person acted out of a defended position.

The only true sin is the separation from the Core

Self, from the God Within. Undesirable behaviors are simply symptoms of the alienation from Self. This separation prevents access to our Wisdom and the ability to make good cognitive decisions for ourselves. With healing work, access to the Core Self is restored and, with that, responsibility increases. We then become responsible for staying integrated in body, mind and spirit and, thereby, in touch with the Core Self. If we willingly allow separation to take place again, we *do* sin, and it feels as if we are living in hell because we no longer have access to the Kingdom Within.

After healing, the coping devices of the Defense System are no longer needed. That is why the women listed above feel they are now in control of the behaviors that used to control them. That is why Reilley could address her twelve-step meeting, explaining that she could now ask God to remove her "character defects" because she no longer needed them to cope with the pain of childhood sexual abuse. She could now see them as part of her defense strategies.

FORGIVENESS AND ACCEPTANCE

Forgiveness is a word I try studiously to avoid because it carries a lot of religious baggage, and every person will hear "forgiveness" in her own way. In addition, forgiveness implies there has been a transgression. Since I do not believe in transgressions, or sins, there is no need for forgiveness. I prefer the word *acceptance.* Acceptance means that we see the other person for who that person is, drop our expectations and honor that person without judgment. This cannot be done merely on a cognitive level. It must be done on a feeling level as well or it will result in residual feelings of guilt. For instance, it is unlikely that, the day after being fired, a person can say honestly, "I 'forgive' or 'accept' my former boss." If religious tradition encourages such proclamations, it may leave that person with feelings of guilt at hidden anger. Failure to attain such a lofty ideal leaves the person feeling flawed. However, if feelings of anger, sadness, fear and the like are acknowledged (remember, the new AA—Acknowledge and Affirm) and then expressed privately in any of the many ways

outlined in earlier chapters, eventually acceptance is attained. This does not mean that the situation is pleasing, but the hurt can be released and an understanding and acceptance of the boss's actions can be attained. This can only be done if Affirmation follows the expression of the feelings where the person sees her own innocence in so far as she did the very best she could. When that happens, we have achieved a higher degree of healing and now we have the new AAA: Acknowledge the feelings, Affirm the inner child and Accept oneself and others.

Accepting ourselves is the most difficult task and should be addressed first in the healing process. There is no need to ask forgiveness of a Higher Power because God, who resides within us, already accepts and understands our behaviors for exactly what they are. God is love. God can only look upon us, God's creations, with love, never with judgment, anger or blame. We can do the same for ourselves if we overcome the separation and alienation from our Core Self.

Accepting others is the next step. The less impact someone has on our life, the easier it is to accept that person and his/her behaviors. It is not as difficult to accept the grocery clerk's error, as it is to accept an extremely abusive parent. Although it is possible to come to acceptance of an abusive parent, it does not follow that we need to be in an active relationship with that person. Some people feel that the damage was so great, so lasting and with so many ramifications that they cannot interact with a parent who refuses to own, or in any way acknowledge, that parent's own actions. Most people, though, find that they can come to acceptance and have limited interactions with abusive parents as long as the emotional work is done to keep the inner child protected and the adult (cognition) in charge.

When you feel ready to work on accepting a parent without expectations or judgment, use the exercise, Meeting Your Parents, in chapter 12 on page 267 to visit that parent as a child. The exercise can be repeated, if you feel it would be helpful to do so, as many times as you like. It will provide you with a greater degree of acceptance and understanding of that parent by making you more aware of the coping techniques and defense strategies your parent brought forward into adulthood and which caused your woundedness.

In order to come to such a level of acceptance, there can be no shortcuts. There must be an open and honest examination of the parent; no stone can remain unturned. There must be the release of stored feelings around the abuse and there must be validation of the child who experienced the abuse. The innocence of the child must be affirmed. If we do not enter into this process thoroughly, we are putting the parent before the Inner Child, before our Core Self, before our God Within. This is blasphemy in the truest sense of the word. It is having a false god because we have made another person, or the approval of another person, more important than our connection to God. Christian scripture states in Luke 14:26: "If anyone comes to Me, and does not hate his own father and mother and wife and children and brothers and sisters, yes, and even his own life, he cannot be My disciple." The only thing that stops us from looking honestly at our parents is fear, fear of being alone and fear of death. Healing requires courage to overcome our greatest fears and lets nothing stand between us and our soul, which leads us ultimately to God. Courage is not the absence of fear but the act of facing our fears and moving ahead in spite of them. So the basic spiritual challenge throughout healing work is the struggle between the inherent and instinctive desire for Truth and the inherent and instinctive avoidance of pain, suffering and dying.

DEATH AND LIFE
A basic paradox of the spiritual path is that choosing death results in *life*. We must be willing to die to our need for control and simply fall into nothingness. We need to die to our "false self," that is, our Defense System and the person we have been defined as by others. We need to die to our addictions and compulsions because they protect us from feeling pain. We need to die to ours fears and to any desire for

emotional security. In other words, we need to die to anything that stands between us and being totally empty and ready to receive our Core Self. It is only in doing so that we can truly live. Without such dying, we are only surviving. When we consider truly dying to all of these things, it can be so frightening as to literally take our breath away. There is an old saying that goes, "Everybody wants to get to heaven, but nobody wants to die." Instead, we may want to consider taking the attitude that we will all have to die eventually and so you really have nothing to lose.

Whenever I get on the subject of dying, I am reminded of a joke I heard years ago about a ninety-eight-year-old man who was marrying a twenty-year-old woman. His friend was alarmed and said, "Harry, having sex with her could be fatal!" Harry replied with a shrug, "If she dies, she dies!" We need to take that kind of attitude for ourselves. Our lives without our souls are without depth, meaning or true happiness. Why not take the risk and step off the edge and into the black hole. If you die, you die. (No one ever does.)

THE BLACK HOLE
The subject of the black hole was discussed in chapter 8 with reference to addictions and in chapter 12 with reference to co-dependence. From a spiritual perspective, the black hole represents the absence of the Core Self, which leaves an incredible spiritual void. The Core Self or spirit is often equated with light. The black hole is always dark, deep, seemingly endless and terribly frightening. It can easily be equated with the representations of hell. When the black hole is visited in imagery, it can be incredibly terrifying. For instance, when Darlene, INFP-5, entered her internal black hole in imagery, she eventually reached the bottom where she saw waves of fire and the distorted faces of crying, wailing, whimpering children, representing all the ages at which she was sexually abused by her father. Her imagery was telling her that she was literally living in hell with the pain of his betrayal and the alienation from her Core Self that his betrayal caused. When Mary, ISTJ-1, looked into her internal black hole

(figure 8-7, page 159), she declared that entering that space was the scariest thing she has ever done. Julia, INFJ-1, upon entering her black hole in imagery, felt like a five-year-old child. She began to cry as the walls became narrower and narrower and said, "I don't want to die." She labeled her drawing of her black hole "hell."

The darkness and the vastness of the black hole shows us the degree of emptiness felt due to alienation from the Core Self. With healing, the Core Self is restored to fill the space and bring Light into every crevice of the black hole. In Hebrew scripture, Genesis opens with the darkness being replaced by Light. Jewish tradition celebrates the Festival of Lights. Like any metaphor or image, these references can be taken on many levels. One approach is to understand the Light as replacing the emptiness of the black hole once healing work has been accomplished. Healing work cannot take place, however, by skirting the black hole. It must be faced and conquered or it will forever have the power to keep us alienated from our Core Self.

FEAR

We have explored how alienation from our Core Self takes place. Reversing the process raises many fears. It requires a willingness to give up control, to die to the defended way we have lived, to be willing to move into unfamiliar and uncharted territory on faith. Giving up that much control causes us to become exceedingly vulnerable, which can be terribly frightening. Who wants to walk up to the edge of the known universe and take a step off into darkness?

Fear is the major impediment to embracing the God Within, self-actualization and spirituality. As a therapist, I have seen people stay for an inordinate length of time in the pain of self-loathing, despair and hopelessness rather than move beyond their fears into the unknown territory of self-love. If self-acceptance and self-love are so desirable and if so many wise and highly spiritual people throughout all ages and cultures have espoused it as the road to serenity and bliss, why do so few people take it? The basic answer is Fear. We are afraid of the unknown, afraid of losing control,

afraid of losing our known identity, afraid of our strength, afraid of our innocence, afraid of our wisdom, afraid of our feelings, afraid of knowing too much, afraid we are not enough, afraid of change, afraid of reality, afraid of being alone and, ultimately, afraid of dying. We fear that we literally may not survive the process.

Of course, the most compelling fear of all is the fear of death. It is that fear that causes us to put away our spirits in the first place. We are so afraid that we cannot survive without the perfect love of our parent(s) that we opt not to see their imperfections. We close ourselves away from reality because we are not yet old enough and strong enough to deal with it. By the time we are old enough and strong enough to meet reality head-on, we are so entrenched in the programming, and our spirits have been put so far away, that it is easier and less frightening to simply keep on keeping on. We have found a way to emotionally survive. Why mess with success? If it ain't broke, don't fix it. Yet surviving and living are two very different things. Author and psychotherapist Rachel Naomi Remen quotes a client with cancer as saying there are two kinds of people in this world: those who are alive and those who are afraid. Both Hebrew scripture, starting with Genesis, and Christian scripture, repeatedly encourage us with phrases such as "Fear not" and "Do not be afraid." We cannot live afraid and still live free. If we are imprisoned and held hostage by our fears we will never take the risks necessary to let go of the known and move into the unknown. Spiritual growth can never occur under these conditions.

SUFFERING

One of the major fears impeding healing work and spiritual growth is the fear of emotional pain and suffering. Well-known author M. Scott Peck begins his classic book, *The Road Less Traveled,* with the phrase, "Life is difficult." Looking honestly at our history is painful. Often accepting our goodness and innocence is extremely painful because it means that the people that we wanted and needed so badly were, in reality, not the people we thought they were. It is painful to give up our illusions, to look at reality and to face Truth. To do so is an acquired taste. To use a computer analogy, it is as if the default setting on our computer is set to avoid pain. That programming must be changed. We need to consciously choose to embrace Truth and to live free, without restriction of our Core Self.

The avoidance of pain is at the heart of all mental illness. As Jung said, "Neurosis is always a substitute for legitimate suffering." The avoidance of suffering is what keeps us alienated from our souls, perpetuates the black hole and condemns us to a living hell. Hebrew scripture describes how the Israelites spent forty years in the desert before reaching the Promise Land. The Book of Job describes the need to enter suffering and the necessity to be willing to lose everything to gain the Self. Christian scripture, especially the gospel of Mark, extols the need for suffering, describing Jesus's willingness to suffer and die, even to descend into hell. There could not be an Easter Sunday without Good Friday. The Native American tribe of the Minquass put it poetically: "The soul would have no rainbow if the eyes had no tears." Even athletes have the slogan, "no pain, no gain," indicating the need to suffer to realize benefits. John Bradshaw, in all his various works on Inner-Child healing, stresses the need to do original pain work; author Jack Kornfield says, "True maturation on the spiritual path requires that we discover the depth of our wounds."

Trying to avoid suffering may make life more tolerable or even pleasant on the surface, but only suffering the pain will lead us to Truth and foster spiritual growth. Moving into pain and suffering takes courage and an act of the will. It goes against our every instinct. Our Defense System screams, "Are you crazy?!" when, in fact, by moving into the pain we are trying to avoid going crazy. Our entire culture is geared to the avoidance of every type of pain, especially emotional pain. The mental health profession will often do anything to numb the legitimate suffering of a patient, from prescribing countless medications to electric shock treatments. However, anyone who has faced her greatest

fears or moved into the pain and felt her feelings will report the relief and the peace that follows. There is a phrase in affective therapy, "when we're feeling, we're healing," that can be encouraging through some of the most difficult of feelings. Legitimate emotional pain and suffering can be life-changing and transforming, as long as we understand what the pain is about. Legitimate suffering always leads to spiritual growth. Proust said it succinctly: "We are healed of a suffering only by experiencing it to the full."

ALONENESS

Closely linked to the fear of death is the fear of being alone. To a baby or young child those two fears are virtually one and the same. It takes a good deal of emotional work as an adult to separate the two fears. The fear of accepting the fact that we are each alone keeps many people from spiritual growth. Yet there is no more profound aloneness than being alone in the midst of people who are supposed to love you. In order to grow spiritually, we must come to terms with a paradox. We must each come to accept the fact that we are ultimately alone in this world. There is absolutely no one who can be there for us 100 percent, no matter how seemingly devoted. In accepting this ultimate truth, we can direct our focus away from finding an external answer to the emptiness we feel, and turn our attention inward. It is in the recognizing and embracing of the Self that we are brought in contact with our Higher Power where we come to know we can never be alone. And so the paradox: We are alone and never alone. As Jung said, "Bidden or not bidden, God is present."

LOVE

Romantic love extols the premise that, if we find the right partner, we will never be alone—that somehow the other person will complete us. Nothing can be further from the truth. If we give that much power to another human being, we put ourselves at great emotional risk. It is only a matter of time before that person disappoints us. M. Scott Peck's often-quoted definition of love is "the will to extend one's self for the purpose of nurturing one's own or another's spiritual growth." Spiritual growth cannot be accomplished by denying our aloneness, by being dependent on another emotionally or by a sense of needing to be completed by another.

And so we need to understand that love is not a chemical or hormonal reaction to another. It is not born out of neediness or dependency. True love, as M. Scott Peck defines it, cannot occur unless there is first self-love. Without self-love, we are continually searching for the perfect, unconditional mirroring we expected and never received as children. With self-love, we can be wholly present to the beloved, fully allowing that person to express completely the unique being God created the beloved to be, without being saddled with the burden of our unmet childhood emotional needs. It is our responsibility to see that we meet those needs ourselves. When that task is accomplished, we can enter into a real loving relationship in which love is seen as a free choice, an act of the will.

When love is a conscious, cognitive act of the will, it involves commitment. This differs from romantic love that is born of neediness. Romantic love is based on chemistry, programming and fantasy. It is rampant with unrealistic expectations. True love is lasting, even when the beloved cannot meet our emotional needs at the moment. We do not see that as the beloved's responsibility. With romantic love, we will be disappointed sooner or later, leading us to believe that love has died and the relationship is over.

True love allows for separateness on the part of both people. Each person in the couple-ship feels complete and accepts the partner as complete. This can only happen with total self-acceptance and self-love. In such a case, it is natural to then honor the uniqueness of the beloved and not expect that this person will be other than who he/she was designed to be.

CHAOS

Eventually, all relationships will lead to chaos. There will be conflict, misunderstandings and some break-down in communication in the very best of partnerships. The fear-based response is to avoid the conflict and resort to the Defense System's coping skills and the childhood programming. Doing so will not foster spiritual growth on the part of either person and will not result in the growth of the relationship. Avoiding the conflict may even result in the eventual breakdown of the relationship, the very thing that was being so studiously avoided.

The courageous approach is to walk willingly and deliberately into the chaos, using good communication skills (chapter 8), and know that both parties are committed to the growth of the relationship. With this approach, there will come a point of emptying during which each partner can bracket his/her own issues, agenda and/or hurts and be open to the other person. This is true intimacy in which there is mutual vulnerability and mutual empowerment. The health of the relationship is not determined by the number or intensity of the crises that arise, but rather by how these crises are met and resolved.

LISTENING

Real listening can only come about if we feel no need for perfect mirroring, expecting the other person to be the same as we are and to hold an identical worldview. Real listening can only take place when we do not expect complete and total understanding from the other because we are already complete in ourselves. If we can truly be open and listen to the other without judgment, we bring an extraordinarily loving gift to the beloved. Listening means we understand that the other person has a different personality type, a different worldview and different coping skills than we do. We understand the other has a different method of processing information and different life experiences that have been brought to each situation. True listening allows us to put aside our own needs in an attempt to understand the perspective of the other person. When a person feels truly heard, it is the closest thing to the unrealistic ideal of perfect mirroring that this person can receive. There is a sense of being deeply loved,

loved enough that the other is willing to bracket everything out of care and respect for the beloved.

When each partner in the couple-ship has felt completely heard, the relationship is much stronger than it was before the conflict. Therefore, what started out as troublesome has turned into an opportunity for growth on the part of both persons and has brought about growth and strengthening of the relationship. What each has found through the experience is that it is safe within this relationship to put down the Enneagram Defense in order to show the Core Self to the beloved. The beloved has become safe enough to share her most precious possession, her Inner Child. Fear has been overcome, a risk has been taken and growth has occurred.

Wounded Child; Wisdom Child

As noted, in the beginning of the healing process, the inner child is seen in imagery, art and dreams as very wounded, frightened, alone and hopeless. As the healing journey continues, the inner child becomes magically transformed into a beautiful, captivating and incredibly wise Child. This transformation takes place because the image of the Child is metaphor for the soul. Before healing work, the soul is represented as the wounded, abandoned and unloved Child. As healing work progresses, the Child can be seen metamorphosing until her radiance and wisdom are resplendent and awe-inspiring. When imagery presents the Inner Child this way, it is clear that healing has occurred and the Core Self has been restored to its rightful place. Integration has transpired. In his book, *Homecoming: Reclaiming and Championing Your Inner Child*, Bradshaw quotes C. G. Jung about this transformation:

> "The child is all that is abandoned and exposed and at the same time divinely powerful—the insignificantly dubious beginning, and the triumphal end. The "eternal child" in man is an indescribable experience, an incongruity, a handicap, and a divine prerogative, and an imponderable that determines the ultimate worth or worthlessness of a personality."

Alice Miller recognizes the Wisdom Child saying,

"Only when I make room for the voice of the child within me do I feel myself to be genuine and creative."

In looking at the Wisdom Child, we see the fullness of who we were designed to be. She is the promise fulfilled. She is the manifestation of our potential. From that point forward, we are responsible for maintaining integration and keeping full and open access to our Core Self. Every minute of every day, we must make the choice to let our Inner Child lead or to reject her again. The more we choose for our Inner Child, the easier the future choices become and the more difficult it is to ignore her ever again.

While Darlene, INFP-5, (chapters 6, 7 and 9) still felt hopeless and with little desire to live, she had done enough healing work to transform the wounded inner child into her Wisdom Child whom she calls Molly.

Darlene

> *How's it going with you? Do you feel like you're in the hammock?*

Molly

> *Yes. I'm in the hammock. It's fun! I feel like I'm being held. I think it's God.*

Darlene

> *I'm glad that you are having fun. What makes you think that God is holding you?*

Molly

> *I don't see God with my eyes, I see him with my heart. I can tell with my heart that he is holding us all.*

Darlene

> *Is he watching me, too?*

Molly

> *Yes, he is holding you, too.*

Darlene

> *Where has God been lately? Where was he when we were being sexually abused?*

Molly

> *He has always been with us. When we were being sexually abused, he was with us.*

He couldn't stop it because that was our dad's choice but he held us and cried the tears that we couldn't cry. He is still crying tears until we can do it ourselves. Then he will cry with us.

DARLENE

I'm glad you can answer my questions about God. I love you very much.

MOLLY

I'm not really answering your questions about God, he is. I love you very much, too, and God loves us, too. He wants us to hang in there because he needs us.

INTEGRATION

The ultimate goal of healing work is integration of body, mind and spirit. This is an especially challenging goal for left-brain types in a left-brain culture who read the phrase as body, MIND, spirit. Nonetheless, the goal is to put all three members of this trinity into open and continuous communication with each other. The body has many memories and can serve as an early warning system to alert us that there is a problem. The body can act as well; it can remove us from hurtful situations and can vocalize when necessary. The body is more than a mobility system for the head.

It is essential to heal the wounded inner child, thereby transforming and freeing that child to be an incredible source of wisdom. Without access to the spirit, or Wisdom Child, we are nothing more than robots, living out of an outdated Defense System. Freeing the spirit provides access to our deepest wisdom, our feelings, our spirituality and our Higher Power. We become regenerated, reborn.

The mind needs to be trained to honor the body and spirit and treat them as equal partners in the union of body, mind and spirit. The mind has the power to lead us to untold heights by accepting and not discounting the wisdom provided by the body and spirit. To be fully integrated is to be fully alive and fully human.

Therefore, I urge you to remember your ABCs:

Affective
Feel your feelings to get in touch with your spirit

Behavioral
Act with your body

Cognitive
Think with your mind, using it to coordinate the team

In chapter 10, an exercise was presented that asked you to design an internal safe house for your inner child. You were invited to tour the house in your mind, to draw it and to journal about it. You might want to take a moment and revisit that place now to see if it looks the same or if it has changed in any way:

Notice any changes and make note of them. Then review this house from a spiritual perspective. If you understand that the house represents you, what kind of shape is it in? What kind of shape does it tell you that you are in? Is the fence, representing your boundaries, in good shape? Is the back yard and back of the house as nice as the front? Is there an attic? If so, does this represent a high spiritual place to you or does it represent your mind? Is there a basement? What does it look like? That will most likely represent your subconscious and contain issues you have buried. Look in every room. What is the kitchen like? How well do you nourish yourself? Is there a bathroom? What does it look like? What about the most personal room, the bedroom? What does it tell you about yourself? Your Inner Child represents your spirit. Is she happy and comfortable in her space? Does she have everything she needs? How are you represented as an adult in that place? The adult is your cognitive abilities. How does the adult interact with the child? Is the adult strong, protective and effective? Is the child able to be free, spontaneous, creative and wise? Look at each symbol in this imagery and interpret it from a spiritual perspective reflecting your degree of integration.

As you do more healing work, you can use this imagery and the symbols contained in it to take your own spiritual inventory and monitor your progress because the house will evolve as you do. Trust your imagery. It cannot lie.

I have stated many times that you have everything you need for peace, serenity and Wisdom within yourself. It is simply a matter of uncovering and releasing it. It is helpful to be able to embody your Internal Wisdom by the use of imagery. There are many ways to accomplish this and the specific imagery you use is not important. I have indicated that the wounded inner child, once healed, becomes a Wisdom Figure. The Future Self exercise offers you another method of embodying your Internal Wisdom in order to more easily access and interact with it. No matter what

imagery you employ, your subconscious will give you what you need. You can create an imagery in which you meet and talk with an ancestor; a monk or other such religious figure; an animal talisman; a person with whom you felt close and who has died, such as a grandparent; a person from scripture; or an imaginary friend. Regardless of which you choose, or if you come up with one of your own, you will arrive at the desired destination. Your subconscious will use the vehicle you present to provide you with the information you need.

This exercise allows you to access and conceptualize your own Internal Wisdom. It establishes a Wisdom Figure. Just as the image of a Child can embody or act

---

EXERCISE

FUTURE SELF

Close your eyes and take a few moments to focus on your breathing. Following your breath moves you gently into a slightly altered state while drawing your attention inward. Take all the time you need to become totally relaxed and internally focused.

Imagine that you are walking in a beautiful natural setting. As you walk along, feel the surface under your feet. Feel your legs and body moving. Listen for any sound your footsteps make. Look around you. What time of year is it? What time of day? What colors predominate? If you listen carefully, are there any sounds? Are there any particular smells that come along?

Pause on this path which represents your life journey and turn around to see where you have been. How is your past represented to you? Take note of what you have come through and survived.

When you are ready, turn forward again and notice that there is an older woman ahead of you. This is your Future Self. For a few minutes, catch up to her so that you can have a chat. When you get close to her, take a good look at her. How old is she? What is she wearing? How is her hair fixed? What do you see in her face? Then begin to ask her some questions such as:

Are you happy? Should I stay on the same path that I'm now on? If not, what should I do differently? What advice do you have for me? And any other questions that are important to you. After each question, give her ample time to answer you, and be sure to listen well. Stay anchored firmly in your present-age adult body. Take all the time you need to interact with your Future Self, receiving all the information and guidance necessary for your higher good. You may want to invite your Inner Child to be present as well and ask your Future Self how you can best protect and nurture this Child. When your discussion seems complete, bring your meeting to a close, knowing you can return to talk with this woman whenever you wish. You may feel comfortable ending with a group hug. When you are ready, leave that place and return to your place on the path. When you arrive there, begin to draw your attention back to the outer world by feeling the chair that is supporting you, listening for any sounds in the room and touching an object close to you. Take time to reorient yourself to your surroundings and gently open your eyes.

(Adapted from an exercise by Nancy Napier as described in Gloria Steinem's book, *Revolution from Within: A Book of Self-Esteem.*)

---

as metaphor for the soul, a Wisdom Figure can do the same for that part of your soul that supplies you with insight, depth, discernment and guidance. Most people find it helpful to draw their Future Self or find a picture that closely resembles their concept of the Future Self. Keep that picture in your journal where you can refer to it, revisit her in imagery or use the nondominant hand method to dialogue with her any time you need counsel and guidance.

The Hopi Indian tribe has a proverb that says, "Teaching should come from within instead of without." Going to a source outside yourself for advice, counsel and guidance discounts your very own Wisdom and does not honor your connection to the God Within. Other people can tell you what may be good or right for them; no one but you can tell you what is good or right for you.

INCARNATION

Gary Zukav, *The Seat of the Soul,* suggests that each incarnation is a part of a larger soul, which he refers to as the "mothership." Perhaps we are in relationship with, or put in the presence of, people who share a part of our larger soul. Perhaps I personally embody the INFJ part of a soul, and the people with whom I struggle, because their personalities are so different from mine, are actually, incarnations of other aspects of the same soul. Perhaps we are called to not only understand ourselves in our known incarnation but to understand others, not because it is the noble thing to do, but because they are aspects of our very soul. Wiser people than I have said that the whole purpose of being alive is to know ourselves. Perhaps it is not just the immediate self that we need to know but a larger soul-self. Perhaps we need to reincarnate in order to be in some kind of relationship, again, with an incarnated part of our greater soul that we have not come to accept in earlier incarnations. Perhaps we would greet and treat people differently if we looked at them literally as soul mates. Perhaps some parts of this "mothership" or greater soul are not currently incarnated and act as guides to those of us who are.

This way of looking at things may be valid or it may not be. It may make sense to some personality types and sound like utter nonsense to others. Do not accept my viewpoint or my spirituality—or that of your family or culture—but use it as a jumping off point to ask your own questions and come up with your own "perhaps."

Author and family therapist Virginia Satir acknowledged that we are composed of various psychological parts when she developed the concept of a "Parts Party." You can use the exercise on page 286 to understand how you work. It helps to make you aware of some unconscious forces directing your life; with this awareness will come the ability to make any desirable changes.

Therese, ISTJ-9, (chapter 6) participated in this imagery. She represented her strong, businesslike ISTJ as Hillary Clinton, who remained solid and unchanging throughout the imagery. Her Enneagram Defense of the Nine was represented as a beanbag chair; it had no spine and conformed to whoever sat in it. She recognized that there also were positive traits associated with the Nine. She imaged the Nine as a frog when those positive traits supported her Core Self instead of dominating her life. Therese likes frogs because she says they get to sit on a lily pad in the sun all day. As she worked with the parts, the beanbag chair began to grow a small head and arms. She thanked it for protecting her as a child by helping her to be "invisible" and keep a low profile. The chair then turned into a baby in a pumpkin seat—her Inner Child. The entire team bonded around the baby.

As an ISTJ, Therese's imagery is clean, clear and concise. Her counterpart, an ENFP, would have a meeting that was busy, intricate and elaborate. Again, the effects of personality type are quite clear.

The exercise, Parts Party, and others like it will foster continued spiritual growth because their purpose is to heighten awareness and foster integration. Without awareness, there can be no growth. You cannot arrange for your release until you are aware you are imprisoned; without awareness of the parts that are operating

PARTS PARTY

Make a list of the parts of your personality that you would like to know better and with which you would like to develop a better working relationship. Start your list with your Inner Child, your Defense System and your Future Self. To that list, choose two to four other aspects of yourself from the list below, or come up with some of your own:

- Your creativity
- Your strongest talent
- Your major trait
- Your dominant feeling (anger, sadness, scare, aloneness and the like)
- Your shadow self
- Your sexuality
- Your guilt
- A debilitating or chronic illness
- Your addiction
- Your co-dependence
- Your neediness
- Your spirituality

After you have chosen the parts you would like to work with, take them one at a time and use your imagination to decide what each would look like if it were embodied as either animal, vegetable, mineral or human. Then either draw each part or find a picture that accurately represents the part for you. For instance, if you decide to work with your workaholic nature, you can draw yourself with your brief case, calendar, cell phone and laptop in your business suit. Or, you can find a picture in a magazine of the achievement-oriented, success-driven person that embodies the concept of your workaholic nature.

When you have each part defined to your satisfaction, move into imagery using the following guidelines:

Close your eyes and take a moment to draw your attention inward. Follow your breath for a few moments, being aware of the intake of air, when the air turns around and, finally, the release. Focus on each muscle that moves in facilitating your breath-ing. Take a moment to check your entire body for tension. Breathe into the tension, vaporizing it, and then imagine that you can exhale the vaporized tension. When you feel sufficiently relaxed and internally focused, image a comfortable room where your various parts can get together and interact. It may be a room you have actually seen or one that you simply construct in your imagination. Imagine being in that room in your adult body. Anchor yourself in your body in that room by touching things around you, feeling the temperature of the room, being aware of the light source, listening for sounds and noticing any smells. Move around the room, inspecting the various furnishings in the room. When you feel you are at home in that room, fully anchored in your body there, you are ready to begin your meeting.

As your adult self, welcome each part into your meeting space, one at a time, and invite it to have a seat. Take note of where each part chooses to sit and which parts sit next to each other. Thank each part for the contribution it has made to your life. Even those parts that you may have judged undesirable have been active for a purpose. If you do not understand the purpose, ask the part to explain its purpose to you. If it is an addiction or other behavior that you would prefer was not so actively present, find out what purpose that part has had in your life. How does it think it is helping you? Ask the part if there is another or better way to accomplish the same goal. Or you may suggest to the part that you are now strong enough, old enough and capable enough to take care of yourself and you have another way of getting that particular need met. You may ask the part if it would consider a new job assignment. For instance, perhaps your workaholic self would be willing to be in charge of outdoor activities or an exercise program.

PARTS PARTY CONTINUED

If you are trying to work with a feeling part, thank the part for getting your attention. Ask the part to show you how you can be more aware of its presence by a physical signal. For instance, you may ask your fear to show you which part of your body it would like to use as a signaling agent to let you know that fear is present. Ask the feeling how you can best honor it, express it and take care of your Inner Child.

Continue in a like manner with each part, including your Future Self and your Defense System. Thank each part for its contribution, ask any questions, receive any information and make any requests you feel appropriate. Try to resolve any conflicts between parts by allowing dialogue and suggesting workable compromises.

Finally, bring your Inner Child into the room and place her in the center of the group. Realize that the ultimate role of all these parts is to take care of this Child in the very best possible manner available to each part. You may like to have each part touch the Child, bless the Child or present the Child with a token gift. In closing, have the parts join in a circle where you, as leader of the group, can conduct a closing ritual. When the experience feels complete, begin to reorient yourself to the room in which you are sitting and, slowly and gently, bring yourself back to present time and space.

If you have any issues that feel unresolved or any parts that seem troubled, you can work with them individually in imagery or using nondominant hand dialoguing. You can also reconvene the meeting whenever you feel it appropriate in order to resolve internal conflict. You may want to invite additional parts to any subsequent meetings.

---

in the subconscious, those parts will control your life. Knowledge that they exist is not sufficient. Knowledge is only on the head level. There needs to be a full understanding and awareness of these parts. That kind of knowledge can only be acquired when those parts are brought into full consciousness where you can watch them operating in your life. Then you are free and able to interact with them in order to bring about any desired changes.

People often enter therapy saying they want to change. They rarely really want to change. They want others around them to change and they want to be free of pain. Spouses often give their blessings to their partners entering therapy, indicating they are in favor of changes being made. That is also rarely true. They generally do not want any changes in behavior; they want a happier version of the spouse who will then be less complaining and more fun. If healing work is entered seriously, change is inevitable; count on it.

As each client finishes our formal work together, I love to gift her with a beautiful imagery that I learned from Maria Beesing, coauthor of *The Enneagram*. I call this imagery The Sculpture (page 288). As we close our work together, I would like to offer it to you. It is an exercise that is best employed after some healing work has been done. It is not generally appropriate for someone suffering from depression to any great degree.

I hope you could see the beauty and the miracle of who you are through meeting, accepting and loving your Inner Child. We were each conceived perfectly and have lost sight of the magnificence of the creation that we are. But with healing work, we embark on a journey of self-exploration, self-knowledge, self-acceptance and finally self-love. As author T. S. Eliot's oft quoted wisdom from *Little Gidding* states:

> We shall not cease from exploration
> And the end of all our exploring
> Will be to arrive where we started
> And know the place for the first time.

The late U.N. Secretary General, Dag Hammersjkold

THE SCULPTURE

Close your eyes and draw your attention to a quiet space within where you feel comfortable and safe enough to completely relax. Focus on your breathing while you move into a state of deeper relaxation. Imagine that you are completely surrounded by, and bathed in, a beautiful and radiant light. Experience what it is like to breathe that light in, pulling it deeper and deeper within yourself, until you can feel the benefits of the light throughout your body. Take a moment to fully experience how it feels to have this light fully permeating your entire being.

When you are ready, imagine that you are dressed in business or dress clothes, standing at the end of a long hallway. Imagine you have commissioned a world-famous master artist to create a sculpture of you. At this time, you are about to walk to the room at the end of the hall where the draped sculpture is waiting for your first viewing. Begin to walk down the hallway taking note of any doors you pass along the way. These rooms can be visited at another time. Be aware of the size of the hallway and any colors that come to your attention. When you arrive at the room at the end of the hall, pause for a moment and see if there is a door to the room or if it is open to the hall. If there is a door, investigate the door for a moment, taking note of style, color, construction and the like. When you are ready, open the door and step into the room.

As you move into the room, become aware of the placement of the draped sculpture. Take note of any other furnishings in the room. Notice the dimensions of the room and how high the ceiling is. What is the light source? Are there windows? If so, what do they look like? What do you see out those windows?

Now turn your attention to the draped sculpture. How large is it? What color is the fabric draping it? Move closer and reach out to touch the fabric, feeling its texture. When you are ready, give the drape a gentle tug and let it fall softly to the floor. Take your time to look at the sculpture. Of what type of material is it constructed? What is its color? Is it realistic or abstract? Reach out and touch it, exploring it with your fingers. If possible, move around to see it from all sides. What is your reaction to seeing the artist's rendition of you? What feelings are you experiencing?

Now become aware of the artist's presence in the room and turn your attention in that direction. What does the artist look like? Do you recognize the artist? Express your feelings about the sculpture to the artist. Ask any questions of the artist that you may wish. See if the artist has anything to say to you.

When you are ready, express your thanks to the artist and prepare to leave the room through the doorway you entered. Remember that you can return to this room to visit the sculpture or to examine it further at any time. Walk back down the hallway, in the same direction from which you came. While walking, gently draw your attention back to the room in which you are sitting, becoming aware of the chair supporting you and of any sounds in the room. Begin to slowly move your extremities and, when the experience feels complete, open your eyes.

You may enjoy sketching the sculpture and might want to keep the sketch in your journal. Once you know the identity of the artist, you may want to interact with that person as a Wisdom Figure or spiritual guide. You can return to talk with the artist in imagery any time you like or you may want to do a nondominant hand dialogue with the artist. What does the light source in the room tell you about your spirituality? What does the size of the room tell you? If the windows represent your outlook on life, what did you see outside? Finally, would you have rendered yourself the way the artist portrayed your likeness? Do you consider yourself a work of art?

said, "The longest journey is the journey inward, for he/she who has chosen his/her destiny has started upon his/her quest for the source of his/her being." We are all called home, to the Higher Power which is within each of us. Some of us will cave in to our fears and others will conquer those fears and move into the process of self-discovery, but we are all called to spiritual growth. I hope you will answer the call and use the three keys to healing—the MBTI, the Enneagram and Inner-Child work—to facilitate your journey. I urge you to let nothing and no one stand between you and your miraculous Inner Child. She is calling you.

REFERENCES AND SUGGESTED READING

Anderson, J. *A Year by the Sea.* New York: Doubleday, 1999. In a short autobiographic work, Anderson describes how she took the risk, got out of the box and redesigned herself.

Beesing, M., R. Nogosek and P. O'Leary. *The Enneagram.* Denville NJ: Dimension Books, Inc., 1984. This is one of the first books written on the Enneagram. It contains some interesting and thought-provoking information written from a Catholic/Christian perspective with a chapter purporting that Jesus embodied all nine Enneagram types.

Bly, R. *The Kabir Book: Forty-Four of the Ecstatic Poems of Kabir.* Boston: Beacon Press, 1971, 1977. The wisdom within the poetry of Kabir illustrates that the theme of a God Within has been present throughout all ages and cultures.

Borysenko, J. *A Woman's Journey to God.* New York: Riverhead Books, 1999. Borysenko presents a feminist approach to spirituality, seeking to restore respect to feminine wisdom and methods of relating to a Higher Power. She links spiritual growth with psychological growth, stressing the importance of emotions.

Bradshaw, J. *Creating Love.* New York: Bantam Books, 1992. Bradshaw treats love as an act of the will and looks at how we relate in love to a Higher Power, others, ourselves and how we see our world. He examines the cultural rules and beliefs of patriarchy on the topic of love. As an Inner-Child therapist, he brings a deep understanding of the effects of childhood wounding on the ability to truly love.

Bradshaw, J. *Homecoming: Reclaiming and Championing Your Inner Child.* New York: Bantam Books, 1990. An overview of early childhood wounding with exercises for reclaiming your inner child at each age level. Bradshaw repeatedly stresses the need for working with original pain or core issues. He describes the Wonder Child or spirit as the result of Inner-Child work and the impact this work has on spirituality.

Capacchione, L. *The Power of Your Other Hand.* North Hollywood CA: Newcastle Publishing Co., Inc., 1988. In the last chapter of her book, Capacchione presents techniques for using the nondominant hand to access the God Within and a Higher Wisdom source.

A Course in Miracles. 1975. New York: Foundation for Inner Peace. For maximum benefit, this program is best undertaken after doing some healing work, otherwise it may be too cognitive. The *Course in Miracles* helps us to become more objective, to recognize the effects of culture and programming and to own and value the spirit within us.

De Mello, A. *Sadhana.* New York: Doubleday, 1984. A Christian book of meditations and imagery from an Eastern approach. Very helpful for getting out of the mind and into the body.

Hirsh, S. K. and J. A. G. Kise. *SoulTypes.* New York: Hyperion, 1998. This book will help to explain the different approaches to spirituality as defined by psychological type using the MBTI as framework.

Huebsch, B. *Spirituality of Wholeness.* Mystic CT: Twenty-Third Publications, 1992. Christian; Catholic; an NF and feminist approach to Catholicism, advocating the concept of the God Within using Jesus as model.

Keen, S. *Living the Questions* [Cassette]. Boulder, CO: Sounds True Recordings, 1992. Scott Peck suggests we question everything. Keen picks up that theme, challenging the listener with a variety of thought-provoking questions that will help define personal beliefs as well as identify those beliefs that have been accepted without question. To order, contact: Sounds True Recordings, 735 Walnut Street, Boulder CO 80302, 800.333.9185

Kidd, S. M. *Dance of the Dissident Daughter.* San Francisco: Harper, 1992. A popular Christian writer tells her personal story of spiritual healing which lead her from conventional religion to the Sacred Feminine. Her approach has strong appeal to NF women because it is rich with non-traditional, feminine ritual.

Napier, N. *Getting Through the Day.* New York: W. W. Norton and Co., 1993. Nancy Napier gives a thorough discussion of the benefits of dialoguing with your Future Self.

Napier, N. *Recreating Yourself* [7 Cassettes]. Boulder CO: Sounds True, 1991. This series presents these seven different topics along with guided meditations to facilitate healing: *The Multiple Self, The Child Within, Envisioning Your Future, Bonding With the Infant, Improving Your Self-Image, Creating Your Optimal Life, The Power of Shame.*

Pagels, E. *The Gnostic Gospels.* New York: Vintage Books, 1979. An analysis of the writings that were not included in the New Testament collection. Pagels compares and contrasts the texts included in the New Testament with the Gnostic gospels. In describing Orthodox vs. the Gnostic approach, Pagels delineates the difference between the SJ culture and an NF and NT approach to spirituality without naming it as such. The Gnostic gospels encourage a more feminist approach and direct attention to the God Within.

Pearson, C. L. *Mother Wove the Morning* [Video]. Walnut Creek CA: Pearson, 1992. Dramatically brings to light wounding due to the repression of the Feminine Divine in our patriarchal culture. To order, contact: Carol Lynn Pearson, 1384 Cornwall Ct., Walnut Creek CA 94596, 510.906.8835.

Peck, M. S. *The Road Less Traveled.* New York: Simon and Schuster, 1978. A classic that links psychology and spiritual growth. The title alone speaks volumes about deep healing work.

Peck, M. S. *Further Along the Road Less Traveled.* New York: Simon and Schuster, 1993. Further suggestions for spiritual growth from a psychological perspective; some Christian references.

Raub, J. J. *Who Told You That You Were Naked?* New York: Crossroad, 1998. Christian; this is a beautiful book emphasizing the release of guilt and shame and encouraging self-acceptance and self-love.

Remen, R. N. *Kitchen Table Wisdom.* New York: Riverhead Books, 1996.

Remen, R. N. *My Grandfather's Blessings.* New York: Riverhead Books, 2000.

Remen, R. N. *Final Wisdom* [Cassette]. Boulder CO: Sounds True, 1998. In each of these selections, Rachel Naomi Remen brings stories of her personal history of dealing with a serious medical condition and of her professional work with those facing cancer and other life-threatening diseases. She brings an incredible wisdom and understanding of the healing process. Remen provides a rich description of her Jewish heritage. She writes and speaks simply, from her heart, and conveys uncommon depth, sagacity and spirituality. To order the tape, *Final Wisdom,* contact: Sounds True, Boulder CO 80302, 800.333.9185.

Sanford, J. A. *The Kingdom Within.* San Francisco: Harper, 1970. Christian; I highly recommend this excellent book that ties psychological type and psychology together with spirituality by emphasizing integration, search for self-understanding and acknowledgment of the God Within. Sanford includes a discussion of personality type based on the Jungian theory behind the MBTI.

Steinmen, G. *Revolution from Within: A Book of Self-Esteem.* Boston: Little, Brown and Company, 1992. This book clearly shows that, before we can change the world, we need to address our own issues and make our own personal changes. Steinmen explores the early effects of family and culture on self-esteem with her personal story and those of other women. In the course of her journey, Steinmen does some personal work with Nancy Napier and recounts the Future Self imagery that Napier used with her.

Viorst, J. *Necessary Losses.* New York: Simon and Schuster, 1986. Viorst writes from a Freudian psychoanalytical background and perspective. She maintains growth is only attained through loss, through letting go of illusions, expectations and ideals as well as loss due to separation and death. She notes that our responses to losses shape and control our lives. There is recognition given to the losses caused by cultural stereotyping. She calls attention to the different agendas in the conscious and unconscious minds. I take exception to her treatment of guilt, which implies there is more ability to make free and conscious choices than I see in reality.

Whitfield, C. *Healing the Child Within.* Deerfield Beach FL: Health Communications, Inc., 1987. This classic book on Inner-Child work contains a final chapter on spirituality that is insightful and thought provoking. Dr. Whitfield graphically illustrates the Inner-Child process on page 120 showing how spirituality enters near the end of healing work and continues to grow.

Zona, G. A. *The Soul Would Have No Rainbow if the Eyes Had No Tears.* New York: Simon and Schuster, 1994. A collection of Native American wisdom and spirituality.

Zukav, G. *The Seat of the Soul.* New York: Simon and Schuster, 1989. A "big-picture" approach to spiritual growth with an underlying eastern theology. Thought provoking, it challenges the reader to stretch and expand perceptions and examine previously held beliefs and worldviews. Unlike Viorst, Zukav believes we grow through relationships.

Zukav, G. *Soul Stories.* New York: Simon and Schuster, 2000. Zukav illustrates his concepts of spiritual growth with personal, inspiring stories.

PART V

Therapy

CHAPTER 14

PROFILE OF A THERAPIST

It is my profound hope that the information, suggestions and exercises in this book have assisted you on your healing journey. Healing comes only with considerable work. It does not happen by talking about it or reading about it. It does not happen just with the passage of time. It has been documented that nursing home residents suffering from depression can access the emotional wounding of childhood in a nanosecond. With healing work, these nursing home residents perked up and their depression lifted. It will take more than just the passage of time to reverse the effects of early wounding. It will require a conscious decision on your part to move into the healing process. If you have read this far, you have made that decision. Do not stop here. Do not let anything at all interfere with your quest for your Core Self.

You may find that your healing work is not a do-it-yourself project. That is often the case, especially if the early wounding has been extreme and extensive. You may find you need to seek out someone to facilitate your work and companion you on your journey. This is a wise decision, although sometimes a scary one. You will be moving into uncharted territory and it is always frightening to move from the known, no matter how unpleasant, to the unknown. But it is good to have your feelings validated and to have accepting eyes to mirror your Core Self back to you. Even if you feel that your childhood was not particularly traumatizing, you may want to consider working with someone who can encourage, assist and support you in your work. After all, you cannot take yourself where you have not yet been because you have been afraid of what you might find. You will bring the lens of the child to your examination of your past, your issues, your behaviors, your programming and your coping skills. It is helpful to have someone who will ask the difficult questions, who will poke, prod and spur you on when necessary yet comfort, console and reassure you when you need a cheering section. When you begin to drop all your defense tools and begin living authentically, it is wonderful if someone is there to clap!

If you decide to seek a therapist to guide and facilitate your work, here are some guidelines to help you choose that person.

Do not just take the word of your physician, neighbor or Employee Assistance Program (EAP) person. If your work goes well, your therapist will know you better than anyone in your life, no matter how close. The choice of a therapist is too important to leave to chance or to someone else's judgment. Many people only enter the counseling field to figure themselves out but then decide to make a living with the degree they have earned. I personally would not be as concerned with credentials, licensing and the like as I would be with the innate abilities of the person and the amount of personal healing work of his/her own that person has done.

Do not be afraid to ask questions, even personal questions. If the therapist is reluctant to answer, or if the answers do not meet your needs, move on to someone else. You are not insulting potential therapists by asking them if they have been in therapy or if they have a therapist currently. The answer to both these questions should be a resounding "Yes!" If your therapist has not worked through a certain issue, subconsciously you will know not to go near that issue during your

own work. For instance, if your therapist has unresolved sexual abuse issues and you suspect you may have been sexually abused, you instinctively will not bring up the topic nor will the therapist. Your subconscious is in the business of protecting you. It will not allow you to be vulnerable to someone who is unsafe on such a sensitive subject. Someone who has not addressed the issue at hand cannot possibly help you address it.

Because with healing work the Defense System relaxes and the gifts and talents of the person emerge, you will want a therapist who has done, and continues to do, personal healing work. You do not want someone working with you who is operating out of a well-developed Defense System. You want a therapist who has access to all the therapeutic talents in the art of facilitating healing which reside in the therapist's Core Self. Such a person feels that the therapist is an instrument, a tool, in the healing process, and will not take anything that happens in the course of therapy personally. A therapist who has done personal healing work is able to be fully present to you.

In addition, you may be interested to know if the person uses the term *counselor* or *therapist*. A counselor is one who counsels or gives advice. You do not need advice; all you need is guidance. Having someone who counsels and advises you establishes yet another authority figure, another source of external wisdom, which takes away from your search for your own. *Therapist* implies healing by a facilitator. A therapist should guide you in finding your own Internal Wisdom source.

In working with a therapist, you should never feel a need to take care of that person's feelings, to build up that person's self-esteem or in any other way take the focus off your healing to meet the needs of the therapist. There must be clear boundaries at all times. There should be no clouding of roles. I am in favor of a therapist sharing personal information with a client if the therapist is comfortable doing so, if the situation warrants it and if the purpose is to help the client, not the therapist.

Your therapist has to be someone who is comfortable
with the expression of all feelings, no matter how intense.
You must feel completely safe and free to express feelings
such as anger, sadness or grief, as needed.

Another reason to extensively interview and question a potential therapist is the need for a one hundred percent safe environment for any healing to take place. You may have extensive trust issues, meaning that you do not feel you can trust anyone. You may even expect any therapist to eventually betray you as everyone else has. That is not an unusual attitude. Even if you feel this way, try to ascertain if the lack of trust is on your part, or if the potential therapist is giving you cause to doubt or mistrust. For the best results in therapy, you must eventually trust this person with the most vulnerable part of yourself. It would be unfortunate to begin work with someone around whom you have reservations because rapport will not build and you will never feel completely safe. You need someone who is totally nonjudgmental, completely accepting, not confrontational and very affirming. Your therapist should be able to support you by believing in you when you do not believe in yourself. This person should respect you *for who you are,* celebrate your progress and be happy when you are independent and autonomous enough to no longer need therapy. Just like a good parent, a good therapist should continually be working to be out of a job by encouraging your strength and independence.

One of the first questions to ask the therapist is whether the approach that will be used in therapy is affective or cognitive. The answer to this question should be an unqualified, "affective." Some therapists will say they take an eclectic approach, meaning they use whichever style seems to suit the client. You should not settle for this answer. It is very tempting and much easier to fall into a more cognitive method. Affective therapy is very hard work and takes a high degree of concentration on the part of the therapist. If the therapist is going to get paid the same amount of money to

talk about your feelings as to help facilitate you *having* your feelings, it would be a continuous temptation to list to the former.

Your therapist has to be someone who is comfortable with the expression of all feelings, no matter how intense. You must feel completely safe and free to express feelings such as anger, sadness or grief, as needed. The rules around the expression of anger should be minimal. The only rule I insist on is "You cannot harm yourself." Some therapists add "or the therapist," but I have never had anyone turn her anger on me personally so I have never felt a need to state that. Your therapist's office should be conducive to doing feeling work. It should feel warm and welcoming. It should not be sterile with a desk and two chairs. Look around for appropriate equipment for anger work, whether you ever use it or not. Having pillows and other equipment for anger work is an indication your therapist is not afraid of the expression of anger. You definitely do not want a therapist whose goal is to help you contain your anger. It is not unusual for a client to be afraid to move into a feeling for fear of getting stuck in it. The therapist should be able to reassure you that you will be kept safe and that you will leave the office functioning. I have never had anyone become suicidal or need hospitalization because of doing feeling work. In fact, just the opposite occurs; it is the suppression of feelings that causes despair.

You do not want a therapist who needs to diagnose you with some form of mental illness, phobia, neurosis or the like unless it is necessary for insurance purposes. The best person to help you is someone who understands that any unhealthy or distressing behaviors you may be harboring are due to wounding, not mental illness. As you are interviewing a potential therapist, if you hear a lot of mental health jargon indicating intent to find a diagnostic box to fit you into, keep looking.

It would be an asset if your therapist would be comfortable with occasionally talking in spiritual, not religious, terms. It is difficult to discuss inner healing without referring to what is being healed.

Another bonus would be a therapist who understands the Myers-Briggs Type Indicator and the Enneagram. However, practically speaking, there are not many therapists who work affectively *and* use the MBTI *and* the Enneagram. If your therapist is willing to look at any material you have accumulated on your personality type and discuss it with you, then that is an indication of openness and a willingness to work with you as a team.

There are many marvelous drugs on the market today that have helped innumerable people live more productive lives. However, if you are on medication, it is preferable to have a therapist whose goal is to have you off as quickly as possible by working hard to find the underlying need for the medication. (The exception would be someone who has been on medication for so many years that her body cannot make the adjustment to living without it.) If your potential therapist sees pharmaceuticals as a viable part of therapy on a long-term or permanent basis, you may wish to consider someone else.

If you have any issues, situations or matters that may be culturally controversial, please discuss these with a potential therapist to see if that person has any reservations or personal biases around working with you. For instance, if you are gay or lesbian, have had an abortion or intend to have one, are engaged in an extramarital affair, have acted out sexually, or have been a perpetrator of any kind, ask your potential therapist if the topic would pose a problem in your relationship. If there is any hesitation or any other indication that the potential therapist would be uncomfortable, look for someone else. There should be no shame brought to a

therapeutic relationship by the therapist. If your potential therapist has a problem working with issues such as these, it tells you more about that person than it says about you.

Most importantly, in choosing a therapist, listen to your own instincts. If you have reservations, respect your Inner Child who is speaking to you. If you feel more comfortable interviewing a potential therapist in person, ask if there is a charge for an initial interview. If there is, you may decide it is worth the cost to feel confident you have made the right decision. If you feel a need to work with someone of the same gender, honor that preference. Remember, you will need to feel totally comfortable and completely safe with this person.

Your therapist is someone you will have to lean on for a while but who will encourage you to take responsibility for your own work. The person you choose should act as a bridge, assisting your movement across a great chasm from where you are now to a safe and rewarding promise land. A good therapist will temporarily help re-parent your Inner Child until you are strong enough to do it on your own. This person must honestly believe in you when you doubt everything about yourself. So if you find that you feel uncomfortable because you seem dependent on your therapist at some point, rest assured that it is temporary and simply a transition phase. You first need to learn to trust another person, something you probably did not learn in childhood. Then you will lean on that person until you feel strong enough to stand alone. Your therapist should feel comfortable with this process.

After meeting with your potential therapist for the first time, go home and use the nondominant hand method of talking with your Inner Child to ask for her recommendations.

EPILOGUE

I have asked some of the women whose stories you have heard to let you know how they are doing today. I am gratified that everyone I asked to share the intimate details of her life, her struggles, her pain and her healing readily and enthusiastically agreed without reservation. I am deeply grateful for their openness and their willingness to share the details of their journeys. In the comments that follow, I am awed by the depth of spirituality of these brave, amazing and wonderful women. I am delighted at every opportunity to applaud them.

Anita (ENTP-1)

I am doing much better than I was several years ago. I was wound really tight when I first came in for therapy. I would say that those binds have loosened significantly . . . although not completely gone. I have become much more forgiving of myself and able to see the "gray" in life, not just the black or white. All of my work with personality typing and inner child helped me to appreciate that I am different from others and why I am different, as well as begin to embrace those differences. I still struggle with seeing my unique gifts and abilities, and seeing myself as others do, but growth takes time . . . oh yeah, I have also learned about patience.

My life is better. My financial and physical circumstances still remain tenuous, but my emotional, mental, spiritual life is better than it has ever been. I feel more grounded. Little by little, I feel more in charge of my life.

—*Danielle*

My understanding of personality typing has also given me greater sensitivity to others, in my relationships and my work . . . as to what makes them do and see things the way that they do.

Doing this work also opened me to explore my spirituality, which has been a tremendous gift. Understanding myself and developing my spiritual relationships has given me the peace and courage to reach my current level of professional success, to take risks in new interests/career options and to navigate the delicate and sometimes painful world of personal relationships.

Overall, I would say that I have "softened" up and now experience more true joy and happiness in my life.

Bernadette (ESFJ-6)

I am doing well. I still work at the same place, but moved to a different department. I like it. I stand up for myself and speak up if need be. Not too much has changed with my relationship with my mom. The only time we talk is if I call her. She does sound happy to hear from me. I don't feel as if I really have a mother, just someone whom I talk to about how my children are. I feel so blessed to be close to my own children. I guess the part of missing a mom I give to my own children. We've had a few trials this past year but seem to be handling them well. My husband was let go from his job after twenty-two years. I'm a little surprised at myself at how calm I've been. I think with the Inner-Child work I did, I have become a stronger woman who has learned to judge myself a bit softer. Even though childhood years seemed so awful and *so long*, I know my experiences have helped me become a more loving, understanding person.

Danielle (ENTJ-7)

I have renewed hope for my future. Prior to doing this therapy, I had suffered from bouts of depression. They were severe by the age of ten. I endured the bouts and entertained the idea of suicide. Later, I just learned to live and endure the depression until it passed. During the second year of therapy, I realized that I wasn't experiencing these dreaded episodes or waiting for them to descend. Now I may have periods of sadness, but I recognize them as caused by real situations. I have the tools to address the feelings gained from both twelve-step work and therapy. If I had gained nothing more than the release from depression as a result of this approach, the journey would have been worthwhile, but I also have gained "myself" too.

My life is better. My financial and physical circumstances still remain tenuous, but my emotional, mental, spiritual life is better than it has ever been. I feel more grounded. Little by little, I feel more in charge of my life. Finally, I'm getting to know myself. When someone questions my actions and decisions, I don't assume there is something wrong with me. I like myself more and I'm daily gaining confidence that I'm heading in a healthy direction. I'm more at peace with my circumstances and myself. I can trust myself to make healthier life decisions. Even when my Seven and NTJ are vying for control, I'm not so frustrated or confused. I simply ask, "Who is driving whom?" I have more energy to pursue normal everyday activities and even take some risks like pursuing more creative activities and career options. I feel more *free*.

Because I understand my personality type, I feel that I can address the ways I was wounded and separated from myself. I have been able to re-parent myself in healthier ways. Additionally, I'm now able to negotiate the internal wars that frequently flared up between my ENTJ and Seven combo. I'm learning to mediate and give each aspect time to be appropriately expressed. I sense the warning signs before there is an all-out war. A Seven on the rampage causes major problems for an ENTJ. My credibility and work suffer. An NTJ on the warpath can be relentless, angry and scary. Now I plan for blow-off-steam and play times.

I respond to people differently, especially when I experience conflicts. I ask myself, "What are their M-B and Enneagram types?" If there is a conflict, I don't want it to be a result of miscommunication. I'm starting to be more realistic about my expectations. I'm also more sensitive to how wounded people are and how these wounds prevent them from being all they were meant to be.

My spiritual life has been part of me, even when I couldn't voice it. I long ago recognized the difference between religion and faith. Until I discovered who I was, I didn't have a sense of direction even as a spiritual being. I just need to be a healthy, happy, functional and compassionate ENTJ-7. If it is good enough for the Universe, then it is good enough for me.

I found some of the Inner-Child work strange at best. I would have liked to have checked out, but I was desperate: traditional therapy hadn't worked. This model of therapy was very interactive and incorporated verbal, visual and kinetic exercises. I started to soak it in and I sensed subtle changes despite myself. For me, it was critical that I be an active part of the recovery. I'd do it again if I had to. I feel very lucky and grateful to have stumbled onto this model.

(Danielle's Inner Child included a note through the use of Danielle's nondominant hand)

You're both nice people. I like Pat a lot. But you're wackos. Pat always made me do wacky things and Danielle you insisted on us doing them so that makes you wacky too. You were both nice. Sometimes Danielle you could of been nicer, but you were going thro

some tough times so I'll give slack. The therapy worked cause I'm happier than I use to be, but I sure don't want to repeat it. I worked hard so I wouldn't.

Darlene (INFP-5)

When I'm asked how I'm doing, I have usually given an automatic answer of "Fine." In the past year, I've changed it to "All right" because I realized that I wasn't "fine." Lately, I've been answering that question with "Good!" and I'm happy to say that is how I really think I am.

Since starting therapy a year ago, my life has changed a great deal. I had been in a living hell and didn't really want to live. The hell didn't go away immediately. If anything, it became more intense. I found out that my childhood wasn't what I thought it was, my parents didn't love me and my father sexually abused me for many years. I've been trying to work through my past so that I can have a future. I'm still not where I want to be but I do want to live now. I don't want my parents, especially my dad, to take any more of my days away from me. I'm becoming my own person. I haven't known who I was for forty-five years and it's fun and scary to find out who I am. I am standing up for myself more often. I'm getting a voice. I am finding out what I want from my life instead of being totally influenced by those around me.

I don't guess it was ever fun to be totally zoned out, but it is even less so now because I realize the adult Darlene is not in charge and that is scary. I am more aware of my feelings and try to express them instead of hiding them. I'm glad to be alive. The changes take a lot of effort to keep in place but the new me keeps pushing and tugging to keep at it. I like the new me (or the one that was hidden) and I'm looking forward to seeing how I continue to change.

I think that the info that I have on the Myers-Briggs

Type Indicator and the Enneagram is fascinating and it helps me understand how I tick. It also helps my therapist understand me and work with me. I know that as a Five, my defense is to go farther back in my cave. I'm learning to recognize when I'm doing this and to do what I need to do to come out of my cave.

Because of my personality type, I have found cognitive therapy isn't very helpful. I still was hospitalized twice, had shock treatment once (they wanted to do it again) and I was on many medications. I really didn't care if I lived or not. I was not dealing with the cause of my depression or even finding out the true cause. Instead, I was masking it.

Understanding personality type helps me realize people act according to their type. I've learned to be more tolerant of people when they do things that irritate me. It helps with my family because it helps to understand that they all process things differently and I can give them info in such a way that they can get the most out of it.

I am finding out what my spirituality really is. Before, my spirituality, like everything else, was formed and influenced by others. I'm getting to know God as the real me and I'm responding as the real me. This part of the healing work is probably the least threatening because I don't have to worry that what I'm becoming will be a problem with God. I can also be angry with God and not worry that I will be left by him/her. God's love for me is the only constant that I can count on.

My relationships have been affected big time by my healing work. I'm becoming the real me which is not the same person that my husband married or that my children have known. I'm getting a voice and standing up for myself. I see things in them that before didn't bother me or I ignored. It is putting a strain on my marriage from the standpoint that I'm changing and my husband doesn't know what to do with the changes. This is causing him to realize that now it's his problem, too, and he is going to have to do some healing work of his own or we won't make it.

I see myself improving most of the time but I still

have times when I doubt myself, when I still think that I am bad and I want to hurt myself, but those times have slowly decreased. So this approach has worked for me. I tried "talk therapy" and I probably went farther back in my cave because of it. Without this approach to therapy, I wouldn't be alive today and I'm thrilled I'm off drugs and have not been hospitalized. This approach takes a lot of hard work on the part of the client and the therapist.

Denise (ENFP-4)

After reading the short summary of my life, I again felt that sickness in my stomach. And the word "prostitution" was really quite hard for  me to swallow. However, I thought about it for a while, and I realized that I used my body for a place to stay, and never even received any money for it. But the most important thing is that those things will never happen again because I would never allow them to. This is quite a loud statement as to the effect of Inner-Child work. I know of no other way for someone to realize that she has just as much right to be happy in this world as anyone else, no matter what she did or how she has been treated.

How am I doing? Well, I have taken control of my own life. No longer are circumstances controlling me. I am about to move to a different location to work instead of remaining in a dead-end situation, and I am continuing my search for the correct path that I was created for. My relationships are continually improving and my search for freedom is always a sunset closer than the day before. I truly believe that I could not have achieved any sense of self but through Inner-Child therapy, and the MBTI and the Enneagram information about my personality has helped me to not be so hard on myself and others.

Dorothy (ENFP-1)

I remember worrying that I would be too old to enjoy life by the time I finished working through my issues and being told that life was just starting. It is so true. I made it, the whole way! I feel alive, whole and incredibly "blonde" (read ditzy, crazy at times).

I am off on a European vacation with my best friend-lover-adventurer, my husband. I'm working at a job I love with people I love, and I am president of the board at the place that has become my "spiritual home" these past years.

This is the eleventh year after I confronted my dad. I have been officially cut off from communication with them for over a year—an event that proved I *did really* do the grief work. No energy goes to them—not in sadness, anger, hatred—not in any form. The empty holes I had in me are full. I talked with each of my kids about this. My daughter, seventeen, asked why my parents would be doing this. I told her I was raped by my father from age nine to sixteen and that when I recovered the memories and said it aloud to them, they did not want to continue the relationship in any form. She cried and cried and spent the whole evening with me. I've recovered in myself the response of a full-functioning feminine *feeling* that can put value and meaning to life. And it was looking back at me from across the table in the eyes and tear-stained cheeks of my daughter!

I made it all the way to "me."

Jeanne (ENFP-4)

I am doing very well. Work is very good. I feel a deepening confidence and competence. I plan to apply for certification soon. I feel I am respected and valued by staff and colleagues as a team member. My feeling of not belonging, not being wanted or liked, comes rarely. I feel I am living most often out of my Core Self. I feel blessed to still have very close friends. Several of my closest friends consider me to be an inspiration and a guide to their own spirituality. My relationship with my spiritual director is very nourishing and strengthens my spirituality.

There is one thing I do strongly feel helps me stay on an even keel and that is medication. I do feel there is a chemical problem and I take something for depression and anxiety.

I feel my ministry, dealing with the sacredness of life and death, is very healing. I experience a sense of awe with those I meet every day.

Joan (ENFP-1)

Things have changed for me. I thought that I had accepted finding out that I was gay. I had come to terms rather rapidly about my being a lesbian, and I thought that I was home free. Recently, I found myself coming to terms at a deeper level with what being gay means to me. I made a retreat for lesbians and came to accept myself even more. I realize that I am a pearl, and that God has created me the way that I am. I realize now that I am wonderful, and that there is nothing wrong with me. I have come out to several people that I thought I would never be able to tell. They have been extremely supportive and this was important for me to have them accept me as I am. I knew that God would support me and love me, even if these people abandoned me. I was blessed, as these people have been so understanding and accepting. I realize that my being a lesbian is only one part of who I am, and it does not make me any less of a person. I am coming to terms with the fact that how God made me is wonderful.

Julia (INFJ-1)

While my life looks nothing like I envisioned for myself, I have achieved a happiness and a peace I've never before known. I am living in the Southwest, 1200 miles from where I was raised,

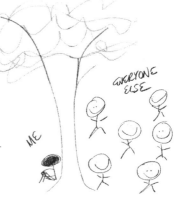

and for the first time, I feel like I am home. I left behind my dream house, and I am now living in a studio apartment and enjoying the simplicity of my surroundings. I have had the courage to leave a career that was draining me of my passion, and I am working in an entirely new field. Although I am not earning the kind of money I was before, I lack nothing material or otherwise. At thirty-three, I am single, without children, and without a significant other. And I am content.

My spirituality has become the central focus of my life, and faith is the foundation upon which I rest, knowing that God is guiding me gently on my path. I have a sense of my True Self, and I try, in all my activities, to honor Her.

My feelings of being defective have greatly diminished. While I still occasionally find myself compulsively cleaning, I am no longer giving in daily to such impulses. I am free of feeling like my worth as a person comes from my outward appearance, and I no longer spend long periods of time putting on makeup or doing my hair.

I am learning to accept others as they are and to look for the Divine in each of them. Greatly aiding me in this process is a spiritual path to which I am dedicated, *A Course in Miracles*. I am finding great healing for myself in my study and practice of this course, and I have been able to move toward repairing a very damaged relationship with my sister as a result. I hope ultimately to be able to do the same in my relationship with my father. I have more friends now than I have ever had, and in working to be authentic and loving in these relationships, I am confident that I am making amends to all those with whom, in the past, I failed.

I know that the healing work I did in Inner-Child therapy was paramount to being where I am now. I am forever grateful and forever changed.

Kory (ESFP-8)

I continue to grow daily, since my beginning journey, through my Inner Child. My life has changed so much. My relationship with my body has changed. I am exercising three to four times a week and I am only consuming healthy foods. My husband and I are on a similar spiritual path and are able to enjoy each other now more than ever.

Occasionally, I am still the Enneagram Eight that tries to motivate or move my husband, the Enneagram Nine, but he quickly puts me in my place. I don't mind telling you I like it.

I have learned how to be responsible with my money. I am working on healing my relationship with my older sister. The Child in me has been protected from her. The adult Kory has taken over and is loving it. My sister, too, has begun to look at her child and is recognizing the pain.

The Inner-Child work I have done has made all the difference in the world to me. I am still a therapist and incorporate the Inner-Child approach and the Enneagram in my work today.

Kyla (INFP-3)

I'm really pretty okay, happier and more "calm" and accepting of myself through this new understanding than ever before. And because of that, I am now open to new experiences of a metaphysical nature that interest and thrill my Core-Soul-Self. Feels *good!*

Heightened comprehension of my True Self, the Defense System, and triggers have allowed me to virtually reconstruct my life to the place it is intended to be. By listening more closely to that quiet little God-voice within, I am living more closely to my inner "real me" (although not as much as I'd really like to be at this present time!). The reality of it is that without this type of therapy I would not even have a clue as to what that Core Self is even about! This is truly God's work working within me! I am happy!

I am better equipped to self-analyze why I process life and its events the way I do. The ability now to step back, disengage for the moment in times of crisis or "trigger" and shift over to the nondefended place where the ego cannot control is a wonderful gift. I still have my moments of inability to do that, but those times are becoming less frequent. (Thank Goodness!!) My coping skills have subsequently improved. My life-altering decisions, especially my decision to leave an unhealthy marriage, have been supported and based upon my discoveries and revelations in this mode of therapy.

Knowing what it means to live as an Enneagram Three where image and the look and activities of success are everything, versus my INFP "porch mom" self where introversion, introspection and intuition are the name of the real Kyla's game, helps me live an authentic life. My two young sons benefit from my heightened abilities to not only analyze the way I process me, but also the way I can now help them process themselves. I am a better mother to them—and to the cherished Little Kyla within—than I could have been without this knowledge. I can apply this knowledge to my birth family and the role I have previously played—and why—versus the healthier, truer place for me.

I have recognized my original interest in areas, such as reincarnation, as having a valid place in my life. I've learned to trust my intuition that I hear inside me and have embraced those ideas despite my "traditional" upbringing. I have been blessed to have found "like minds" and have broadened my "spiritual family" in ways that make my Little Girl sing and sing and smile and smile!

Another blessing has come from the sharing of this therapy with my oldest sister with whom I struggled in secret competition all those years. It has brought our sisterhood to a glorious new height. Also being given the opportunity to overcome the guilt and inability to grieve my father's death has freed me to have a close relationship in ways I could not have perceived years ago.

I like who I am—and all of what I'm about—because now I understand me! This is obviously a unique approach, this triple integration of MBTI, Enneagram and Inner-Child work, as is evidenced by the fact that women fly across the country to partake in its benefits! Its effectiveness is immeasurable in that it changes lives so much for the better. We can understand the motivations of why we do what we do; can

better identify, and even *predict,* the triggers that can trip us up; and can now possess tools to guide us through the minefields of what our lives have been, are now, and *can be* in the future. This re-engineered my life and self-concept! Life altering in ways that I truly believe are *God*-driven, to say the least.

Mary (ISTJ-1)

"You don't go there as often, you don't stay there as long" was just a phrase. I can now say that it applies to me. Healing is, for me, such a slow process that I wonder, at times, if I'm progressing at all. Only when I look behind me and see where I've been do I fully acknowledge that I am healing! Now I can see where I "live," what I've learned, and I understand that I'm "catching on."

It was described to me early on that once you start the process of Inner-Child therapy, you can never go back. Sometimes the pain of what I know I have to walk through has been so intense, I wanted to unlearn what I knew and go back to where I had been. However, knowing what is authentic for me, and understanding what it takes for me to get there, is a piece of the puzzle that I wouldn't trade for the world. Knowing the truth inside my heart and knowing who I am and what I need has brought about wonderful changes in my life and also presented some devastating life-changing decisions for me, as well. But living life less than what I know it to be at present is not an option.

I have connected and have an understanding of God/spirit/soul on a deeper, more loving level. I feel supported by a part of the universe that previously I didn't know existed.

Understanding MBTI and Enneagram has helped me to be a more loving, nurturing and understanding mother to my children. I can now let them "be" and support them and encourage them to be themselves.

I can communicate more easily with people when I

*I do not blame the people who have brought
about these drastic changes in my life.
I believe that I would not be alive right now if these people
had not done the things that changed my path.*

—*Paula*

understand who they are, what they need, and how they speak/listen. When I have difficulty connecting with people, I understand it's a lot about "them" and not always so much about me.

I can now see "angels" and "teachers" in places where I've never thought to look for them. Now, I'm remembering to look!

Paula (ENFP-1)

It has now been a little over three years since I began therapy. There have been many changes in my life since the first day I dragged myself in for help. I am growing stronger with the passing months. Things do not always improve as fast as I would like them to, but I am realizing that it is the Enneagram One Defense System that wants perfection and wants it yesterday. I am more patient with not expecting as much of myself and others. I realize that this growth is a process and that I am better physically, emotionally and mentally when I stop trying to control all the outcomes. My Enneagram One has always been so stubborn and demanding that everything turn out right. That was a laugh because I lived a miserable life and nothing was really right about how my body felt.

My life has been turned around a complete 180 degrees. I am now divorced from my husband of twenty-three years. I moved away from the toxic neighborhood where I would never have healed. I have lost many people from my life that I thought were dear friends, but I now know were never really there for me. I realize that it has to do with their wounded-ness and that it really has nothing to do with me. I am no longer a practicing Catholic. I have made peace with my parents, who are deceased, because I know they were

only working out of their wounded parts and doing the best that they could.

I do not blame the people who have brought about these drastic changes in my life. I believe that I would not be alive right now if these people had not done the things that changed my path.

I am happy with the changes in my life and I am very grateful for the opportunity to find out that I do have a life ahead of me. I was miserable for most of my life and had sought help in many different types of therapy and with prescribed medications. None of them had been successful until I did Inner-Child work. It has not been easy work, but I am grateful for the changes in my life and the healing that I am seeing.

I believe that I have never really felt the pain that constituted most of my life. I used my Defense System Enneagram One to block my feelings. The greater the pain, the faster I would run to avoid the pain. When I finally stopped running and looked at my wounded parts, it was not pretty. I had been a victim all my life. I never realized that I had a right to life, and that I was fine just the way God created me. I always thought that I was garbage, and that I was so flawed and had made mistakes that God could never forgive. I am not "perfect" in controlling the Enneagram One Defense when it goes berserk, but I do recognize when it happens a lot faster than I used to. This sure is a lot easier on my body—physically, emotionally and spiritually.

A big thing I have found is that my Enneagram One Defense System and my ENFP are at odds a lot of the time. So many times I get upset because the One kicks in and does not allow the ENFP to play. The ENFP is learning what toys are and how to play. When the One runs things, my body tells me with pain.

The greatest thing my healing work has done for me is to help me see why people act the way they do. The more I read about the different MBTI personalities and Enneagram Defense Systems, the more I can heal because I can see that it says more about the other person than about me when the other person reacts or does things that I used to think were directed at me personally. I have been able to back off in judgment of other people, and realize that they are wounded and cannot help acting the way that they do.

My whole concept of God has changed. From being a strict Catholic and a nun, I have become a person who thinks about my relationship with my God. I know that when I am taking care of my soul, I am growing more in love with my God. My gentle, caring, loving, nurturing God is so awesome and I am beginning to see just how awesome I am, too. This concept, that I am awesome, is so new to me. Just this week, I heard myself saying out loud that "I am awesome." This nearly floored me as I was a person who did not just hate myself, I really loathed. I no longer feel that I have to go to church to find God, and I can find God in myself and others.

Another big thing in my growth has been getting a handle on the concept of BEING instead of DOING. It has taken a loooooong time to understand it. I can see how it has helped my healing process.

I know that the cognitive therapy I tried did not work for me. After Inner-Child work, I have a better sense of who I am now and how I defend myself and what my personality is. I can grow into the awesome person that God created me to be.

Peggy (ENTJ-1)

My life has greatly improved since entering therapy. I can now recognize when I'm in my "One" Defense mode and take care of and protect myself. When I become anxious or angry because life is not happening "perfectly" I'm usually able to stop, talk to my inner kid about what is making me/her feel this way. Then I can comfort myself

or express my anger without it becoming rage. I can feel joy without the guilt of being "bad" and not deserving any happiness.

I'm also able to live as myself now and not as my Defense System. I used to deny many parts of my ENTJ but can usually be my true self now. I'm much more independent or I realize the strength I've always had. I have more confidence in all areas of my life. It's OK to be a strong intelligent woman! I even can call myself a feminist, a title I used to fear and loathe. I try to surround myself with friends who are also NTs. It helps me to feel more understood and not alone. I'm now beginning to explore new career options that complement my ENTJ so that I can do what I am. I like being an ENTJ!

Having now dealt with unresolved childhood issues, much of my negative self-talk, "I'm bad, I'm not enough, I don't deserve to be loved," has quieted. I'm able to counteract this talk with positive statements or see it for what it is, my mother's voice not mine. I also have an adult relationship with my parents. I ask for what I need and confront what I don't. For example, I've asked my parents to tell me they love me more and now I hear "I love you" in every conversation. I can tell my mother not to "fix" me when she disapproves of my appearance. I can be honest with my parents and not fear they will think I'm not perfect. I'm not perfect and don't have to be.

I've felt safe enough to explore my spirituality. This began through Twelve-Step groups and has progressed to attending a metaphysical church, yoga and meditation. I no longer view God as a condemner but as a loving force within all of us. I also still journal, especially with my nondominant hand. I strive to do this daily but realistically journal less. I can notice a difference in my behavior when I don't journal for several weeks. I begin to be triggered by my "addict" part and feel insecure. These feelings subside when I begin to journal regularly again. Before therapy, I lived only in my head, never allowing myself to feel much or reach out to God.

I also can usually accept my physical self now. I have

begun making changes in my body for me and not for a man or parent. Since I'm making these changes just for me, it hasn't been difficult to lose weight or change my appearance. I've lost twenty-two pounds, I've colored my hair and I got contacts. I feel good about my body whether I'm in formal wear or in gym shorts, with my hair in a ponytail and my glasses on. I don't think I ever would have had the courage to make the physical changes I wanted without this type of therapy. I also know I don't have to be pretty and perfect. I'm who I want to be.

I still fear being alone and remain in a marriage that doesn't meet my needs any longer. I continue to work towards being able to be alone without a man for the first time in fifteen years. I see myself being able to do this soon. I never would have even considered being alone before therapy. It is my greatest fear and therefore my greatest challenge.

I like myself now and am proud of the changes I've made through therapy. Knowing I'm an ENTJ-1 helps me to understand myself and know why I feel/act/think the way I do. It also helps me to be less judging of others. When I can see their "type," I know it's just how they are and not a personal reaction to me. I still have problems and issues in my life, but therapy has taught me how to take care of myself and see my options. I could never go back to the way I was before therapy. My self-esteem will not allow it.

This type of therapy forced me to feel and look at things I would have never volunteered to look at on my own. Once I felt the hurt through, I could feel the joy. I truly believe it saved my life and without it, I would have continued to remain in my own personal hell.

Reilley (INTJ-4)

The Post-therapy Life of Reilley:

I feel grateful to have learned about my personality type and Enneagram because I really didn't have a very good feel for who I was and what my strengths were until they were explained to me. I knew about my Four-ness because I had lived in the longing,

abandonment, self-absorbed mind-set for a long time. As I have learned more about my true nature and have dealt with family emotional issues that were perfect for a Four to have, I have felt the melancholy, mood swings, anger and longing diminish. I can now tell the difference between a real, present-day feeling and a feeling that is left over from childhood. And, if it is a childhood feeling, I talk to "the kids" to acknowledge what we are feeling and where it came from. I can tell them that the experience was real but it is over now and I am here for them. (It took a few years to accept that this is a reasonable solution to a feeling.) I also don't have to protect myself by acting tough any more because I accept my gentleness as well as my strengths. So I don't need to overcompensate with an inner and outer facade.

I haven't used alcohol or drugs since I first entered this type of therapy. It was in therapy that I really understood the need to abuse myself and to cope in such a self-destructive way. Once I could see that I had a lot of emotions and memories that I was hiding with chemicals, I decided that using chemicals was just another way to damage what was already damaged by other people. I didn't want to do that to myself anymore.

The Inner-Child part of therapy was very annoying to me for a long time because I have never seen myself as a parenting kind of person, so I figured my inner child was screwed if it (they, actually) were going to have me as a parent. I could feel "the kids" and understand why they were upset, but it took a long time to accept that I have warmth, compassion, etc. required by a kid from a parent because I felt so intellectual, not warm and fuzzy. But in time, with lots of self-observation, I could see that I have caring, nurturing traits, too, but they don't look like Barney the Dinosaur. (As a Four, I could not succumb to the typical June Cleaver comparison.)

Understanding my personality type is one of the most important things I learned in therapy. Knowing that I was not built to be Miss Sociable Touchy-Feely was a great thing to learn because I had compared myself to other women, my mother especially, and saw how different I was, which I deduced as being "wrong." I still feel challenged a lot in the world of Extraverts because that is what most people want me to be. I am doing better, daily, at accepting that my need is more for quiet than parties. I do have a social life, but it usually does not involve large gatherings of people.

Through therapy, I have accepted that my mom and I never bonded and never really had a loving relationship. I have accepted the ample physical and emotional evidence that she molested me. As I grew into young adulthood, I shared my friends with her and we partied together. But as I have matured, I can see that there is nothing there, except some common genes. Being the gay daughter of the Queen of the Most Feminine Heterosexuals hasn't helped our situation. We are extreme opposites in personality type and sexuality and just do not connect. I can handle that now with no longing attached.

I have also learned to appreciate my brain and what a little analyzer, questioner I am. I was not really aware of this until therapy, and now I am constantly amused by what goes on up there. I know that toddlers like to ask "why," and I am right there with them when I see people conforming "because it's always been done that way," or when I see dysfunctional work systems or rigid societal norms that do not take diversity into account. I am grateful that I am not a person who performs without thinking. Even as a kid, I questioned inconsistencies like, "Why do girls have to wear stupid swim caps and boys don't?" We both have hair, don't we?

I had over ten years of therapy and Twelve-Step programs before I got into this Inner-Child, look-at-your-numbers-and-letters therapy. All of that was helpful, I suppose, but none of it helped me go as deeply into my Real Being as this type of therapy did. I know myself better than I ever have, and unfortunately my family dynamics better than I ever have. Actually I guess knowing my family story is a good thing, but the truth is still painful and difficult sometimes. But now I know ways of coping that involve actually dealing with emotions, instead of denying them.

I feel I have more ways to grow—I would like a more satisfying career—but I know myself better than I ever have and I am the most emotionally healthy I have ever been. *And,* I now own *two* tuxedos.

Rhonda (ENFJ-7)

The biggest change is in my career. The year after I began Inner-Child work was the most phenomenal year of change in my career. It started with a project that pushed all my triggers and ended with a project that was a wonderful experience in which I felt I did "shine," utilizing my talents and doing it all for me and *not* for other people. I felt like I had made great progress. I had shifted into doing what I want to do, instead of trying to please others.

Another big change came in understanding my husband's Defense System and how mine works very differently from his. It has greatly improved our relationship and communication, even when we are both stressed and/or upset with each other. Also, because of my own inner changes, he has dived into his own healing work. So, as a couple and as a family, we can continue to grow and improve.

It has also improved my family of origin relationships, which keep getting better.

Things are still in progress:

My Enneagram Seven still gets me into patterns of overcommitting, becoming overly tired, and of running myself ragged. I am still struggling with being too available and wanting to please others.

I feel like now I want to focus this same energy on improving other aspects of my life's work, moving into a place of inner confidence to realize my dreams in the same way that progress was made in my career.

I want to come into better in-the-moment awareness, behavior patterns, and communication with my daughter, so that my Enneagram Seven does not feed her Enneagram Three and we end up overwhelmed.

I feel this combination of MBTI, Enneagram and

Inner-Child work is the most helpful form of therapy in which I have ever participated. I have seen more practical, tangible, positive results from this inner work (in conjunction with my own personal spiritual work, which goes hand in hand) than anything else I've tried. I have many tools that I access and utilize on a regular basis. It is something I continue to use and that I recommend to many others.

Sarah (ISTJ-9)

I am doing great. I now see blue skies and white clouds. I have become a good listener. I can taste food. I love to hug 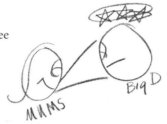 now. My senses have been sharpened. I use all my senses now. I did not realize that I could appreciate so much. Before Inner-Child work, my senses were gray.

My life has changed exponentially!!!! I now see problems as challenges. I can now be grateful in all that I have and do. My children have benefited greatly because of my healing work. I see them as gifts and as individuals. I can embrace each day now instead of waiting under the covers for the sky to fall.

Yes, I am happy with the changes. I now live life instead of avoiding it!!!

Healing work has helped me in so many ways:

Spiritually—I now believe in a Higher Power that I can converse with and ask for guidance.

Mentally—I used to believe everything people said about me. I used to teach people how to treat me poorly. Now I no longer care what others think of me. I am because I am. This is profoundly empowering for me!!!

Emotionally—Before Inner-Child work, details ran my life. I was a chronic worrier. Now I know I have the power to handle any crisis that comes my way. I am no longer a victim stuck in her tracks unable to go forward.

Physically—I now enjoy being a wife and spouse. I am grateful for a healthy body. I can do the visualizations and feel clean and vibrant. I can now look in a mirror and smile and actually like what I see!!!! Before Inner-Child work, I would not look in a mirror. I still struggle with weight issues.

Understanding the ISTJ and the Enneagram Nine has helped me tremendously. I now know when I am in my defense mechanism. I am no longer at war with myself. When I am in the Nine, I try to ask myself what I am feeling. I try to journal and would like to hone this skill. Once I get to those feelings, I can usually toggle to my full productive self, the ISTJ.

Understanding myself as an ISTJ has helped me. I used to beat myself up because I would have to have everything organized before I could proceed. I now know that organization skills are my gift. I have actually had friends who do not have these skills. I now celebrate the differences in people instead of judging them.

Healing work has helped me tremendously with my relationships. As a spouse, I now see that we each have unique gifts. I am much more accepting and grateful towards my husband. As a parent, I am no longer continuing the cycle of abuse. I try to listen to the feelings of my children. I see them as unique. I see their gifts. As a friend, I now listen to others and hear their pain and joy. Before healing work, I was too focused on my own pain and refused to share in anyone's joy!!!

The effectiveness of this approach to therapy is quantifiable for me. I had tried six different approaches to therapy and spent thousands of dollars trying to figure out why I was so bad!!!

I have concrete visualizations that I work through every day. I have something to always go back to. The Enneagram Nine mode forces me to address what I am feeling. The ISTJ lets me be a productive, happy member of society. I am!!!!

Therese (ISTJ-9)

Overall, I am doing well. I go through periods where I like to fall back into my old patterns. When I realize where I am, that place doesn't do anything for me. It's not safe like it used to be. I am happy about the changes most of the time. I still

do not like feeling emotions. It makes me feel vulnerable—human. It was so easy to be a robot and not deal with problems that existed. I used to put off confrontations. After time passed, when I was ready to deal with a situation, too much time passed and the situation seemed irrelevant. Understanding my personality makes things much easier for me. I am able to see why I do the things I do. It is fun to figure out other people's personalities, too. It is amazing how many people around have excess baggage. I look at them and think "Wow, that was me; how sad for them that they do not realize they need help." Then, I am very thankful that I'm not like that anymore.

Going through this program has helped my relationship with my husband in many ways. There are times when I am hesitant to bring up a subject that I know my husband will not like. I now have several ways to approach a subject instead of letting a situation brew inside of me until I explode. It is much harder to stuff my problem into my pocket and keep it there.

I look back to the whole process and still cannot see the steps/levels that I achieved. It all seems to have blurred together. I was a very skeptical person and had to put blind faith into this program. After I was able to get past that point and put one hundred percent of my faith and trust into one person, I knew that I would be able to complete the program. It is a hard, scary and very emotional process, but I recommend it to people that I feel need it the most. A friend of mine who had finished the program kept dropping hints to me until I was finally ready to seek the help that I needed. I learned that trick from her and I have used it, but the people that I speak with are not ready to accept they have issues to deal with. It takes time, but I am a persistent person.

To all of the above, I can only add: AMEN!

INDEX

D

E

F